The Ghost Hunter's Favorite Cases

Hans Holzer

BARNES
&NOBLE
BOOKS
NEW YORK

Table of Contents

Introduction

When the Ghost Hunter Meets a Ghost

The time comes in every researcher's life when he wants to experience personally something with which he has hitherto been involved only through other persons. Mind you, I became convinced that so-called Ghosts are very real many years ago simply by the weight of evidence obtained from what I, and others, consider reliable sources. After all, very few people doubt that Australia exists even if they have never been there themselves; others have and have reported this fact.

In science the quality of observation and of the observer are just as important as the observed facts themselves. I get tired of being asked, "Do you believe in ghosts?" Belief has nothing to do with it.

I deal in facts. Opinion is a detriment when observing, an advantage *only after* the facts are in.

As time went on, my own keen but rather detached and critical interest in the Uncanny, the so-called Supernatural, yielded much fascinating material. I learned to sift the false from what seemed to me probably true material, and then went into the corroboration of this material with the same approach I use when I do purely historical research. Sometimes I tell a librarian that that is all I'm doing, for checking the veracity of ghostly statements is not always apt to bring too much co-operation from a stuffy librarian!

I started to become interested in psychic matters simply by virtue of picking up a technical book on the subject; I have talked to a great many people who have had Sixth Sense experiences and I have learned to evaluate their testimony.

When I made my initial survey for the Parapsychology Foundation, I used a specially designed questionnaire which helped me determine the nature of my witnesses, their moods and motivations and other pertinent facts about the cases.

I still use this "interview in depth" technique in all my investigations, and simple story telling won't do the trick.

When I report someone's experiences, you can be sure I have looked into the person's background and checked other details before accepting the story.

By the same token, one must not discount a person's testimony simply because it sounds odd, or does not fit into the accepted scheme of things. This is a common mistake orthodox scientists make when dealing with parapsychological material. Unless one has "been there" when an event happened, or has available some strong facts that would tend to lessen a person's value as a witness presumably telling the truth, one has no scientific basis for being a "doubting Thomas." If mere doubting were by itself science, the world would not have radio, television, space flight, and practically every other unusual sign of progress we now possess, for all of these accomplishments of mankind were at one time doubted and assailed as impossible by the more orthodox element among the men of science and learning.

The point I wish to make is that secondhand information can be just as exact and valid as firsthand experiences and in many branches of accepted science it is the only way one obtains information and knowledge. Historical researchers rely entirely on other people's reports, even other people's opinions; there is hardly a modern doctrine or branch of learning where the testimony and word of accepted authorities is not an important and integral part of the current structure of belief, conviction, view—whatever the "now" of scientific thinking may be called at any given time.

In psychic research, our main body of information is people's observations. This forms the cushion upon which the basic theories are built. Added to this are two types of scientific participation: laboratory experiments and spontaneous phenomena.

Laboratory experiments have for many years been conducted by Dr. Joseph Rhine of Duke University and have certainly proved the existence of a nonphysical world which Dr. Rhine calls the "World of the Mind." He has amply proven the actuality of "psi" factors in determining the "guessing" of sequences in card tests, and the falling of experimental dice has shown that the mind can influence their courses. But the greater human experiences of precognition, premonitions, apparitions, physical manifestations ranging from footsteps to actual materializations of human forms—these cannot successfully be produced at will within the confines of a laboratory simply because they require the presence of an actual, true emergency—an emotional factor not present in a laboratory. It is this point that some orthodox scientists fail to appreciate.

Of course not every valid scientific fact need be capable of duplication at will. Some of the fireworks in the heavens, stars colliding or otherwise behaving in a unique fashion, may not be reproduced in the laboratory; they are nevertheless valid scientific facts of great importance.

The second class of observable phenomena is called spontaneous because they are unplanned and one cannot always know when and where they will occur, or even why they do. Sitting in a haunted house all night long will seldom produce anything more than a stiff back, unless one uses a trance medium the way I have done and am doing.

Yet one may walk into a house with psychic connotations and unexpectedly something does occur that is extraordinary.

As Ghost Hunter I always consider such experiences a bonus, not expecting them, but happy if they do come my way. For years, I had to be content with other people's testimonies, but as time went on, I discovered a subtle change taking place within me. Evidently by associating with psychics so much I had also developed my own latent powers to a point where I might have firsthand experiences in the psychic realms. Mind you, just because I do on occasion hear or see "something" uncanny, I haven't stopped taking others' testimonies seriously. I am not a medium. But I am convinced that within all of us there is a budding psychic sense, born into us completely naturally, which can be developed as time goes on. Some have more of it than others, but to me it seems a lost or suppressed faculty worthy of attention.

As I have told my radio audiences time and again, there is really nothing supernatural in the world—there are only some facets of human personality not yet fully understood that should be explored further.

From time to time I have seen whitish outlines in darkened rooms where a medium has assured me she saw a figure. How much of this was mere suggestion and how much of it objective truth is hard to tell.

My first experience with an apparition in good light came when I was quite alone in the room.

My father and I were living in a two-room penthouse apartment on the nineteenth floor of a building on New York's Riverside Drive. The door between the two rooms was shut, and the entrance door, as well as the door to the terrace, was always kept locked at night. Nobody could come into my room by natural means.

Because I suffer at times from low blood pressure and migraine headaches, I sleep with my head on several pillows. One night, in my sleep my head slid off the pillow and dangled down from the bed. Had I remained in this position for more than a few moments, I would have had an attack of severe migraine and been an invalid for a week.

Suddenly I awoke to find a gentle hand pushing my head back onto the pillow. The room was fairly bright because of the light of the moon pouring through the many windows—practically an entire wall was made of windows. Looking up, I saw next to my bed the white-gowned figure of my late mother, who had passed on in 1954. It took some moments to rally my senses, and by the time I had fully come to, she had vanished into thin air. But I am sure of what I saw. It was not a dream. Dreams don't cast shadows, and my mother did just that! Evidently she had come to me when there was an emotional need for her to do so.

My first physical contact with a ghost happened when my wife and I went ghost hunting in Connecticut.

I received more than I bargained for when I accompanied my good friend, psychic Ethel Johnson Meyers, to a 1,700-foot-high mountaintop in deepest Connecticut.

Not only did I investigate a haunted house, but I was touched by "Grandma Thurston," who passed in the eighteenth century, but is still very much in evidence in the 1754 house atop Mount Riga.

In an almost inaccessible part of New England, this wooden structure was once owned by the Wentworth family, but now belongs to the Sawtelles. They take their ghostly guest in their stride.

Time and again steps are heard when there is nobody visible, the door opens of its own volition, the dog is nervous for no reason, and once, when one of the men went to fetch some drinks on a tray, they were all spilled for no accountable reason. Perhaps Grandma Thurston, puritan that she was, didn't approve of drinks.

At any rate, we arrived at this picturesque, candle-and-kerosene-lighted house (no electricity or telephone up here!) around 10 PM. The "loom room," the oldest part of the house, is now a guest room. A woman staying there has clearly heard at night the sound of a loom going—even though there is nobody around.

As I walked into the main room of the little house, and stood before the fireplace, I suddenly felt someone tug at my elbow. It was unmistakable, a strong, yet gentle tug. I turned around. Nobody was behind me or near me. I talked to the owner about it.

5

He nodded. Oh, yes, they all had been tugged at the elbow at various times in that spot. Seems as if Grandma Thurston wants attention after all these years!

At midnight we drove still farther into the wilderness, to an Indian rock deep in the backwoods. In the still of the mountain night, I could clearly hear the whispering of voices. Eventually I made out a whitish shape above the rock.

Ethel Meyers made contact with the spirit of the Indian, executed, they say, by white settlers, when he tried to regain his lost homestead, back in the eighteenth century when there were still Indians in that part of the country. After a short seance, the white form dissolved, and the voices trailed off, until they were indistinguishable from the faint croaking of a frog in the underbrush.

Ethel Meyers had a glow on her face. The restless one was free, thanks to her good services.

North East

The Haunted Trailer

Sometimes, one would think, the work of a Psychic Investigator must be downright drab. Little old ladies having nightmares, imaginative teenagers letting off steam over frustrations in directions as yet unexplored, neurotics of uncertain sex fantasizing about their special roles and talents. All this is grist for the investigator's mill, poor chap, and he has to listen and nod politely, for that's how he gets information. (As when Peter Lorre whispered across the screen, "Where is the information?" this question is the beacon onto which the psychic sleuth must be drawn.)

And in fact it is perfectly possible for such people to have genuine ESP experiences. Anybody can play this game. All he's got to be is alive and kicking. ESP comes to just about everyone, and there's nothing one can do about it one way or the other.

It is therefore necessary to have a completely open mind as to the kind of individual who might have a psychic experience of validity. I can attest to this need to my regret. Several years ago, people approached me who had witnessed the amazing Ted Serios demonstrate his thought photography and who wanted me to work with the fellow. But my quasi-middle-class sense of propriety shied away from the midwestern bellhop when I realized that he drank and was not altogether of drawing-room class. How wrong I was! A little later, Professor Jule Eisenbud of the University of Colorado showed better sense and less prejudice as to a person's private habits, and his work with Serios is not only a scientific breakthrough of the first order, but was turned into a successful book for Eisenbud as well.

Of course I don't expect my subjects to be proprietors of New England mansions about to collapse, or Southern plantation owners drinking mint juleps on their lawns, but I have yet to hear from a truck driver who has seen a ghost, or a State Department man with premonitions. Hindsight maybe, but not precognition.

So it was with more than casual interest that I received a communication (via the U.S. mail) from a comely young lady named Rita Atlanta. That she was indeed comely I found out later from her Christmas cards. Christmas cards don't hardly come any comelier. Hers show all of Rita in a champagne glass (a very large champagne glass without champagne in it—only Rita) underneath a Christmas tree, which is very thoughtful of her since she could have been placed into a Christmas stocking and what a shame that would have been, at least in part.

Her initial letter, however, had no such goodies in it, but merely requested that I help her get rid of her ghost. Such requests are of course not unusual, but this one was—and I am not referring to the lady's occupation, which was that of an exotic dancer in sundry nightclubs around the more or less civilized world.

What made her case unusual was the fact that "her" ghost appeared in a thirty-year-old trailer near Boston.

"When I told my husband that we had a ghost," she wrote, "he laughed and said, 'Why should a respectable ghost move into a trailer? We have hardly room in it ourselves with three kids.'"

It seemed the whole business had started in the summer, when the specter made its first, sudden appearance. Although her husband could not see what she saw, Miss Atlanta's pet skunk evidently didn't like it and moved into another room. Three months later, her husband passed away, and Miss Atlanta was kept busy hopping the Atlantic (hence her stage name) in quest of nightclub work.

Ever since her first encounter with the figure of a man in her Massachusetts trailer, the dancer had kept the lights burning all night long. As someone once put it, "I don't believe in ghosts, but I'm scared of them."

Despite the lights, Miss Atlanta always felt a presence at the same time her initial experience had taken place—between three and three-thirty in the morning. It would awaken her with such a regularity that at last she decided to seek help.

At the time she contacted me she was appearing nightly at the Imperial in Frankfurt, taking a bath onstage in an oversize champagne glass with under-quality champagne. The discriminating clientele that frequents the Imperial of course loved the French touch, and Rita Atlanta was and is a wow.

I discovered that her late husband was Colonel Frank Bane, an Air Force ace, who had originally encouraged the Vienna-born girl to change from ballet dancer to belly dancer and eventually to what is termed "exotic" dancing, but which is better described as stripping.

(Not that there is anything wrong with it *per se*, although the Air Force never felt cool under the collar about the whole thing. But the Colonel was a good officer and the boys thought the Colonel's Missus was a good sport—so nobody did anything about it.)

I decided to talk to the "Champagne Bubble Girl" on my next over-seas trip. She was working at that time in Stuttgart, but she came over to meet us at our Frankfurt Hotel, and my wife was immediately taken with her pleasant charm, her lack of "show business" phonyness. Then it was discovered that Rita was a Libra, like Catherine, and we repaired for lunch to the terrace of a nearby restaurant to discuss the ups and downs of a hectic life in a champagne glass, not forgetting three kids in a house trailer.

I asked Rita to go through an oriental dance for my camera (minus champagne glass, but not minus anything else) and then we sat down to discuss the ghostly business in earnest. In September of the previous year she and her family had moved into a brand-new trailer in Peabody, Massachusetts. After her encounter with the ghost, Rita made some inquiries about the nice, grassy spot she had chosen to set down the trailer as her home. Nothing had ever stood on the spot before. No ghost stories. Nothing. Just one little thing.

One of the neighbors in the trailer camp, which is at the outskirts of greater Boston, came to see her one evening. By this time Rita's heart was already filled with fear, fear of the unknown that had suddenly come into her life here. She freely confided in her neighbor, a girl by the name of Birdie Gleason.

To her amazement, the neighbor nodded with understanding. She, too, had felt "something," an unseen presence, in her house trailer next to Rita's.

"Sometimes I feel someone is touching me," she added.

"What exactly did *you* see?" I interjected, while outside the street noises of Frankfurt belied the terrifying subject we were discussing.

"I saw a big man, almost seven foot tall, about three hundred to three hundred fifty pounds, and he wore a long coat and a big hat."

But the ghost didn't just stand there glaring at her. Sometimes he made himself comfortable on her kitchen counter. With his ghostly legs dangling down from it. He was as solid as a man of flesh and blood, except that she could not see his face clearly since it was in the darkness of early morning.

Later, when I visited the house trailer with my highly sensitive camera, I took some pictures in the areas indicated by Miss Atlanta—the bedroom, the door to it, and the kitchen counter. In all three areas, strange phenomena manifested on my film. Some mirrorlike transparencies developed in normally opaque areas, which could not and cannot be explained by ordinary facts.

When it happened the first time, she raced for the light, turned the switch, her heart beating in her mouth. The yellowish light of the electric lamp bathed the bedroom in a nightmarish twilight. But the spook had vanished. There was no possible way a real intruder could have come and gone so fast. No way out, no way in. Because this was during the time Boston was being terrorized by the infamous Boston Strangler, Rita had taken special care to double-lock the doors and secure all windows. Nobody could have entered the trailer without making a great deal of noise. I have examined the locks and the windows—not even Houdini could have done it.

The ghost, having once established himself in Rita's bedroom, returned for additional visits—always in the early morning hours. Sometimes three times a week, sometimes even more often.

"He was staring in my direction all the time," Rita said with a slight Viennese accent, and one could see that the terror had never really left her eyes. Even three thousand miles away, the spectral stranger had a hold on the girl.

Was he perhaps looking for something? No, he didn't seem to be. In the kitchen, he either stood by the table or sat down on the counter. Ghosts don't need food—so why the kitchen?

"Did he ever take his hat off?" I wondered.

"No, never," she said and smiled. Imagine a ghost doffing his hat to the lady of the trailer!

What was particularly horrifying was the noiselessness of the apparition. She never heard any footfalls. No rustling of his clothes as he silently passed by. No clearing of the throat as if he wanted to speak. Nothing. Just silent stares. When the visitations grew more frequent, Rita decided to leave the lights on all night. After that, she did not *see* him any more. But he was still there, at the usual hour, standing behind the bed, staring at her. She knew he was. She could almost feel the sting of his gaze.

One night she decided she had been paying heavy light bills long enough. She hopped out of bed, turned the light switch to the off position, and as the room was plunged back into semidarkness, she lay down in bed again. Within a few moments, her eyes had gotten accustomed to the dark. Her senses were on the alert, for she was not at all sure what she might see. Finally, she forced herself to turn her head in the direction of the door. Was her mind playing tricks on her? There, in the doorway, stood the ghost. As big and brooding as ever.

With a scream, she dove under the covers. When she came up, eternities later, the shadow was gone from the door.

The next evening, the lights were burning again in the trailer, and every night thereafter, until it was time for her to fly to Germany for her season's nightclub work. Then she closed up the trailer, sent her children to stay with friends, and left, with the faint hope that on her return in the winter the trailer might be free of its ghost. But she wasn't at all sure.

It was getting dark outside now, and I knew Miss Atlanta had to fly back to Stuttgart for her evening's work soon. It was obvious to me that this exotic dancer was a medium, as only the psychic can "see" apparitions.

I queried her about the past, and reluctantly she talked of her earlier years in Austria.

When she was a school girl of eight, she suddenly felt herself impelled to draw a picture of a funeral. Her father was puzzled by the choice of the so somber a subject by a little girl. But as she pointed out who the figures in her drawing were, ranging from her father to the more distant relatives, her father listened with lips tightly drawn. When the enumeration was over he inquired in a voice of incredulity mixed with fear, "But who is being buried?"

"Mother," the little girl replied, without a moment's hesitation, and no more was said about it.

Three weeks to the day later, her mother was dead.

The war years were hard on the family. Her father, a postal employee, had a gift for playing the numbers, allegedly upon advice from his deceased spouse. But the invasion by Germany ended all that and eventually Rita found herself in the United States and married to an Air Force Colonel.

She had forgotten her psychic experiences of the past, when the ghost in the trailer brought them all back only too vividly. She was frankly scared, knowing her abilities to receive messages from beyond the veil. But who was this man?

I decided to visit Peabody with a medium and see what we could learn, but it wasn't until the winter of the same year that I met Rita and she showed me around her trailer. It was a cold and moist afternoon.

Her oldest son greeted us at the door. He had seen nothing and neither believed nor disbelieved his mother. But he was willing to do some legwork for me, to find out who the shadowy visitor might be.

It was thus that we learned that a man had been run over by a car very close by, a few years ago. Had the dead man, confused about his status, sought refuge in the trailer—the nearest "house" in his path?

Was he trying to make contact with what he could sense was a medium, able to receive his anxious pleas?

It was at this time that I took the unusual photographs in Rita's presence of the areas indicated by her as being haunted. Several of these pictures show unusual mirrorlike areas, areas in which "something" must have been present in the atmosphere. But the ghost did not appear for me, or, for that matter, for Rita.

Perhaps our discovery of his "problem" and our long and passionate discussion of this had reached his spectral consciousness and he knew that he was out of his element in a trailer belonging to people not connected with his world.

Was this his way of finally, belatedly, doffing his hat to the lady of the house trailer with an apology for his intrusions?

I haven't had any further word from Rita Atlanta, but the newspapers carry oversize ads now and then telling this or that city of the sensational performance of the girl in the champagne glass.

It is safe to assume that she can take her bath in the glass completely alone, something she could not be sure of in the privacy of her Massachusetts trailer. For the eyes of a couple hundred visiting firemen in a Frankfurt nightclub are far less bothersome than one solitary pair of eyes staring at you from another world.

A New Hampshire Artist and Her Ghosts

Elizabeth Nealon Weistrop is a renowned sculptress who lives far away from the mainstream of city life in rural New Hampshire. I talked to her the other day when I had occasion to admire a particularly striking bronze medallion she had created for the Society of Medallists. It was a squirrel such as abound in her New England woods.

Mrs. Weistrop's experiences have given her a sense of living with the uncanny, far from being afraid of it or worried.

"What were the most striking examples of your brush with the uncanny—that is of yourself or your family?" I queried her.

"There are many," Mrs. Weistrop replied, "but I'll try to give you the most evidential incidents. For example, when our Debby was six years old, the doctor decided she should be taken out of the first grade and remain at home to recover from nervousness that resulted from a serious infection she had recently recovered from. She missed going to school with her sister Betsy, two years older, but played every day with five-year-old Donna Esdale, a neighbor's little girl.

"Our family, my husband, our two girls, and I, were living in a cottage in West Dennis on Cape Cod at the time and located a better place in Yarmouthport—a warmer house with a studio I could use for sculpture. Donna's father owned a truck, so we paid him to move us to the new house.

"Three weeks later (we had seen no one from West Dennis), Betsy, Debby, and I were eating breakfast and Debby said, 'What happened to Donna?' I said, 'What do you mean?' Debby said, 'Why was Donna's face all covered with blood?' Then Betsy and I explained to Debby that she had just had a bad dream and that Donna was all right, but Debby insisted with questions. 'Did a truck hit her?' 'Did someone hit her in the face?' 'Why was her face all covered with blood?' And no matter how Betsy and I explained about dreams, Debby refused to understand and asked the same questions.

"Finally, the school bus came. Betsy went to school and Debby looked after her wistfully, wanting to go to school too.

"During the day Debby played with her new black puppy, and I was busy working at sculpture, and the breakfast session left my mind.

"About nine o'clock that evening, Donna's father, Ralph, came to the studio and asked how everyone was. I said we were all fine and automatically asked {after} his family. He said, 'All right, except that last night my wife and I were up all night. Donna had nose bleeds all night and her face was just covered with blood!'

"Debby was asleep but Betsy was standing near me, and we turned and stared at each other in wonder.

"While living on Cape Cod in 1956, we rented a house from a Mrs. Ridley in West Hyannisport. The house she rented to us had belonged to her mother, a woman in her eighties who had recently died. Mrs. Ridley lived next door with her husband and a daughter, Rodella. I found them pleasant people, proud of their American Indian ancestry and sadly missing the grandmother fondly referred to as 'Gunny.' They spoke of her so often and of her constant activity making repairs on the home she loved that I almost felt I knew her. When they told me of their own supernatural experiences, they did not find a skeptic in me, as my own mother whom I had loved dearly had been gifted with ESP. My mother had been the old child born with a caul {veil} in an Irish family of eleven children, and as I grew up I became very familiar with my mother's amazing and correct predictions. My own experiences with the unknown had been limited to a strong feeling of a force or power leading and directing me in my work as a sculptor.

"One sunny fall afternoon, I was alone concentrating on a sculpture of St. Francis. My husband, Harry, was away for the day and our two girls were in school, when I heard a loud thump from the bedroom which our girls shared. This room had been the large sunny bedroom of 'Gunny' and within easy view of where I was working. I stopped work to investigate, expecting to see that a large piece of furniture had collapsed or been overturned. As I searched the room and looked out of the window, I could discover nothing that could have made such a sound. Still puzzled, I walked into the next room, the kitchen, and noted that our highly nervous dog was sleeping soundly—a dog who was always on her feet barking at the slightest sound. The clock in the kitchen said 2:30 and that would give me one half hour more to concentrate on St. Francis, so I went back to work, still wondering.

"That evening after the girls were asleep I walked outside in back of the house, and Mrs. Ridley, who was sitting on her back porch, invited me into her house to have coffee with her, her daughter, and her daughter's fiance.

"While we chatted around the table, Mrs. Ridley told of sitting by her kitchen window that afternoon and having *seen her mother*, 'Gunny,' *just as clear as day, walk up the path from the woods* to our house and go over and knock on her own bedroom window at our house.

"I asked, 'What time was that?' and Mrs. Ridley answered, 'At 2:30.'"

John, up in Vermont

This isn't exactly a ghost story, if ghosts are troubled individuals unaware of their passing and status, with some sort of compulsion unresolved. But then again, it is, if you consider the afterlife full of fine distinctions as to who is a ghost and who is simply a troubled spirit.

Not far from Stowe, Vermont, in what I have long thought of as the most beautiful part of New England, there is a country house that once belonged to the late lyricist John LaTouche. He and a friend, who shall remain nameless, co-owned the place, I believe, and for all I know, the friend still does. But John hasn't really left entirely either. He is buried up there in Vermont in a flower bed, amid his favorite trees and hills. That is, his body is. As for the rest, well now, that is another matter entirely.

I first met John LaTouche through the late medium and psychic investigator Eileen Garrett over lunch at the Hotel St. Regis in New York. She thought, and rightly so, that we would become friends since we had in common not only our professional pursuits—I, too, am a lyricist, among other professional aspects—but also our intense involvement with the paranormal. Soon after this initial meeting, John invited me to a private dinner party at his home on East 55th Street, right across from an ancient firehouse, where he occupied the magnificent penthouse—at the time he was doing well financially (which was not always the case) because his "Ballad for Americans" and the musical *The Legend of Baby Doe* were paying him handsomely.

With the party was also my late friend and medium Ethel Johnson Meyers and the actress Future Fulton, who was very psychic, and the four of us held a seance after dinner.

Picture my surprise when it was John who went under first, showing he had trance abilities also. Regrettably, I do not have an exact transcript of what came through him at that time, but it seemed that a distant ancestor of his, a Breton lady, wanted to manifest and reassure him in his work and quest for success. No sooner had he returned to his normal state, than Ethel described in great detail what the spirit looked like, and considering that Ethel would not have known the details of an eighteenth century Breton woman's costume, this seemed rather interesting to me at the time.

Sometimes, when people with psychic gifts link up, the mediumship goes back and forth as the case may require. Several months after this initial get-together, I was in rehearsal with a musical revue, my first theatrical involvement, in which Future Fulton had a singing role. I had made an appointment with John to see him the Friday of that week. "Are you fry Freeday?" I asked, "I mean, are you free Friday?" We set a meeting for three o'clock. Unfortunately, it slipped my mind in the heat of rehearsals until about 2 on Friday. It became impossible for me to break away from the goings-on and get to a phone, and I had visions of John never wanting to speak to me again for having stood him up. When Future noticed my distress, she inquired as to its cause, and when I told her, she said, "Oh well, that's nothing. I will get through to John."

With that she sat down on a bench, leaned back, closed her eyes for a moment, and then said cheerfully, "It is done. Don't worry about it."

Being forever the scientific investigator, I was not really relieved. As soon as I could, at around seven o'clock. I rushed to the nearest telephone and called John. Before he could say a word, I began to apologize profusely for the missed appointment, and my inability to notify him.

"What are you babbling about?" John interjected, when I caught my breath for a moment. "Of course you called me."

21

"I did not."

"No? Then why is there a message on my tape machine from you telling me you could not make it?"

"There is?"

"Yes . . . must have been around two or so because I got back in time for our meeting a little after that, and it was on the tape."

I did not know what to say. Later, I told John, who just shook his head and smiled.

Time went on, and we met now and again, usually at his house. On one occasion, we were invited for a run-through of a new work he and his friend with whom he shared the house in Vermont had written. John seemed in the best of health and creative activity.

It was in August of 1956, and I had just come home from the opening night of my play *Hotel Excelsior*, a less than brilliant piece of mine at the Provincetown Theatre in Greenwich Village, and I checked my answering service as was my custom.

"Only one message," the operator said laconically. "John LaTouche has died."

I was in a state of shock. But as I found out, John had gone to his Vermont retreat that weekend and nothing had been wrong. Now John was overweight, and he liked to eat well. Apparently too well, for after a heavy meal he had had a heart attack and died. Or rather, his body gave out.

For it was not the end of our friendship by a long shot. I did not attend the funeral up in Vermont, which was for close family only. His mother Effy did, and Effy and I were friendly for a while after, until she too passed into the Great Beyond.

Maybe three or four months passed.

Ethel Meyers and I were doing a routine investigation of a haunted house somewhere in Connecticut. Picture my surprise when she suddenly went into trance, and the next voice I heard was not some obscure ghostly person stuck in that particular house for whatever personal reasons, but my old friend John LaTouche!

"Greetings, Hans," he said in almost his usual voice, and then went on to explain how touched he was by his funeral amid the flowers up in Vermont. But he was not there. Not John.

Since that time, John has communicated with me now and again, telling me that he has adjusted to his sudden departure from the physical world—he was only 39 at the time of his death—and that he was still creating works of art for the stage, Over There.

Then, too, he became sort of an adviser to me, especially in matters theatrical, and he began to use not only Ethel Meyers as his channel, but also others.

I don't know when the celestial Board of Directors will want to send John back to earth in his next incarnation, but for the moment at least, he seems to be a free spirit doing his thing, communicating hither and yon, apparently able to drop in, so to speak, at seances and investigations, at will. The only place I am sure he is not at, is up in Vermont under the flowers.

Ghosts Around Boston

Sometime back, I often went to Boston to appear on radio or television, and as a result people kept telling me of their own psychic adventures—and problems. I tried to follow up on as many of these cases as I could, but there are limits even to my enthusiasm.

Since having a ghostly experience is not necessarily what people like to advertise—especially to the neighbors—some of these stories, which are all true, contain only the initials of the people involved. I, of course, know them but have promised not to divulge their full names, or heaven forbid, exact addresses.

*   *   *

Mrs. Geraldine W. is a graduate of Boston City Hospital and works as a registered nurse; her husband is a teacher, and they have four children. Neither Mr. nor Mrs. W. ever had the slightest interest in the occult; in fact, Mrs. W. remembers hearing some chilling stories about ghosts as a child and considering them just so many fairy tales.

One July, the W.'s decided to acquire a house about twenty miles from Boston, as the conditions in the city seemed inappropriate for bringing up their four children. They chose a Victorian home sitting on a large rock overlooking a golf course in a small town.

Actually, there are two houses built next door to each other by two brothers. The one to the left had originally been used as a winter residence, while the other, their choice, was used as a summer home. It was a remarkable sight, high above the other houses in the area. The house so impressed the W.'s that they immediately expressed their interest in buying it. They were told that it had once formed part of the H. estate, and had remained in the same family until nine years prior to their visit. Originally built by a certain Ephraim Hamblin, it had been sold to the H. family and remained a family property until it passed into the hands of the P. family. It remained in the P.'s possession until the W.'s acquired it that spring.

Prior to obtaining possession of the house, Mrs. W. had a strange dream in which she saw herself standing in the driveway, looking up at the house. In the dream she had a terrible feeling of foreboding, as if something dreadful had happened in the house. On awakening the next morning, however, she thought no more about it and later put it out of her mind.

Shortly after they moved in on July 15, Mrs. W. awoke in the middle of the night for some reason. She looked up to the ceiling and saw what looked to her like a sparkler. It swirled about in a circular movement, then disappeared. On checking, Mrs. W. found that all the shades were drawn in the room, so it perplexed her how such a light could have appeared on the ceiling. But the matter quickly slipped from her mind.

Several days later, she happened to be sitting in the living room one evening with the television on very low since her husband was asleep on the couch. Everything was very quiet. On the arm of a wide-armed couch there were three packages of cigarettes side by side. As she looked at them, the middle package suddenly flipped over by itself and fell to the floor. Since Mrs. W. had no interest in psychic phenomena, she dismissed this as probably due to some natural cause. A short time thereafter, she happened to be sleeping in her daughter's room, facing directly alongside the front hall staircase. The large hall light was burning since the lamp near the children's rooms had burned out. As she lay in the room, she became aware of heavy, slow, plodding footsteps coming across the hallway.

Terrified, she kept her eyes closed tight because she thought there was a prowler in the house. Since everyone was accounted for, only a stranger could have made the noises. She started to pray over and over in order to calm herself, but the footsteps continued on the stairs, progressing down the staircase and around into the living room where they faded away. Mrs. W. was thankful that her prayers had been answered and that the prowler had left.

Just as she started to doze off again the footsteps returned. Although she was still scared, she decided to brave the intruder, whoever he might be. As she got up and approached the area where she heard the steps, they resounded directly in front of her—yet she could see absolutely no one. The next morning she checked all the doors and windows and found them securely locked, just as she had left them the night before. She mentioned the matter to her husband, who ascribed it to nerves. A few nights later, Mrs. W. was again awakened in the middle of the night, this time in her own bedroom. As she woke and sat up in bed, she heard a woman's voice from somewhere in the room. It tried to form words, but Mrs. W. could not make them out. The voice was hollow and sounded like something from an echo chamber. It seemed to her that the voice had come from an area near the ceiling over her husband's bureau. The incident did not prevent her from going back to sleep, perplexing though it was.

By now Mrs. W. was convinced that they had a ghost in the house. She was standing in her kitchen, contemplating where she could find a priest to have the house exorcised, when all of a sudden a trash bag, which had been resting quietly on the floor, burst open, spilling its contents all over the floor. The disturbances had become so frequent that Mrs. W. took every opportunity possible to leave the house early in the morning with her children, and not go home until she had to. She did not bring in a priest to exorcise the house, but managed to obtain a bottle of blessed water from Lourdes. She went through each room, sprinkling it and praying for the soul of whoever was haunting the house.

One evening, Mr. W. came home from work around six o'clock and went upstairs to change his clothes while Mrs. W. was busy setting the table for dinner. Suddenly Mr. W. called his wife and asked her to open and close the door to the back hall stairs. Puzzled by his request, she did so five times, each time more strenuously. Finally she asked her husband the purpose of this exercise. He admitted that he wanted to test the effect of the door being opened and closed in this manner because he had just observed the back gate to the stairs opening and closing by itself!

This was as good a time as any to have a discussion of what was going on in the house, so Mrs. W. went upstairs to join Mr. W. in the bedroom where he was standing. As she did so, her eye caught a dim, circular light that seemed to skip across the ceiling in two strokes; at the same time, the shade at the other end of the room suddenly snapped up, flipping over vigorously a number of times. Both Mr. and Mrs. W. started to run from the room; then, catching themselves, they returned to the bedroom.

On looking over these strange incidents, Mrs. W. admitted that there had been some occurrences that could not be explained by natural means. Shortly after they had moved to the house, Mr. W. had started to paint the interior, at the same time thinking about making some structural changes in the house because there were certain things in it he did not like. As he did so, two cans of paint were knocked out of his hands, flipping over and covering a good portion of the living room and hall floors.

Then there was that Saturday afternoon when Mr. W. had helped his wife vacuum the hall stairs. Again he started to talk about the bad shape the house was in, in his opinion, and as he condemned the house, the vacuum cleaner suddenly left the upper landing and traveled over the staircase all by itself, finally hitting him on the head with a solid thud!

But their discussion did not solve the matter; they had to brace themselves against further incidents, even though they did not know why they were happening or who caused them.

One evening Mrs. W. was feeding her baby in the living room near the fireplace, when she heard footsteps overhead and the dragging of something very heavy across the floor. This was followed by a crashing sound on the staircase, as if something very heavy had fallen against the railing. Her husband was asleep, but Mrs. W. woke him up and together they investigated, only to find the children asleep and no stranger in the house.

It was now virtually impossible to spend a quiet evening in the living room without hearing some uncanny noise. There was scratching along the tops of the doors inside the house, a rubbing sound along the door tops, and once in a while the front doorknob would turn by itself, as if an unseen hand were twisting it. No one could have done this physically because the enclosed porch leading to the door was locked and the locks were intact when Mrs. W. examined them.

The ghost, whoever he or she was, roamed the entire house. One night Mrs. W. was reading in her bedroom at around midnight when she heard a knocking sound halfway up the wall of her room. It seemed to move along the wall and then stop dead beside her night table. Needless to say, it did not contribute to a peaceful night. By now the older children were also aware of the disturbances. They, too, heard knocking on doors with no one outside, and twice Mrs. W.'s little girl, then seven years old, was awakened in the middle of the night because she heard someone walking about the house. Both her parents were fast asleep.

That year, coming home on Christmas night to an empty house, or what they presumed to be an empty house, the W.'s noticed that a

Christmas light was on in the bedroom window. Under the circumstances, the family stayed outside while Mr. W. went upstairs to check the house. He found everything locked and no one inside. The rest of the family then moved into the lower hall, waiting for Mr. W. to come down from upstairs. As he reached the bottom of the stairs, coming from what he assured his family was an empty upper story, they all heard footsteps overhead from the area he had just examined.

On the eve of St. Valentine's Day, Mrs. W. was readying the house for a party the next evening. She had waxed the floors and spruced up the entire house, and it had gotten late. Just before going to bed, she decided to sit down for a while in her rocking chair. Suddenly she perceived a moaning and groaning sound coming across the living room from left to right. It lasted perhaps ten to fifteen seconds, then ended as abruptly as it had begun.

During the party the next evening, the conversation drifted to ghosts, and somehow Mrs. W. confided in her sister-in-law about what they had been through since moving to the house. It was only then that Mrs. W. found out from her sister-in-law that her husband's mother had had an experience in the house while staying over one night during the summer. She, too, had heard loud footsteps coming up the hall stairs; she had heard voices, and a crackling sound as if there had been a fire someplace. On investigating these strange noises, she had found nothing that could have caused them. However, she had decided not to tell Mrs. W. about it, in order not to frighten her.

Because of her background and position, and since her husband was a respected teacher, Mrs. W. was reluctant to discuss their experiences with anyone who might construe them as imaginary, or think the family silly. Eventually, however, a sympathetic neighbor gave her one of my books, and Mrs. W. contacted me for advice. She realized, of course, that her letter would not be read immediately, and that in any event, I might not be able to do anything about it for some time. Frightening though the experiences had been, she was reconciled to living with them, hoping only that her children would not be hurt or frightened.

On March 3, she had put her three young boys to bed for a nap and decided to check if they were properly covered. As she went up the stairway, she thought she saw movement out of the corner of her eye. Her first thought was that her little boy, then four years old, had gotten up instead of taking his nap. But, on checking, she found him fast asleep.

Exactly one week later, Mrs. W. was in bed trying to go to sleep when she heard a progressively louder tapping on the wooden mantle at the foot of the bed. She turned over to see where the noise was coming from or what was causing it when it immediately stopped. She turned back to the side, trying to go back to sleep, when suddenly she felt something or someone shake her foot as though trying to get her attention. She looked down at her foot and saw absolutely nothing.

Finally, on March 26, she received my letter explaining some of the phenomena to her and advising her what to do. As she was reading my letter, she heard the sound of someone moving about upstairs, directly over her head. Since she knew that the children were sleeping soundly, Mrs. W. realized that her unseen visitor was not in the least bit put off by the advice dispensed her by the ghost hunter. Even a dog the W.'s had acquired around Christmas had its difficulty with the unseen forces loose in the house.

At first, he had slept upstairs on the rug beside Mrs. W.'s bed. But a short time after, he began to growl and bark at night, especially in the direction of the stairs. Eventually he took to sleeping on the enclosed porch and refused to enter the house, no matter how one would try to entice him. Mrs. W. decided to make some inquiries in the neighborhood, in order to find out who the ghost might be or what he might want.

She discovered that a paper-hanger who had come to do some work in the house just before they had purchased it had encountered considerable difficulties. He had been hired to do some paper hanging in the house, changing the decor from what it had been. He had papered a room in the house as he had been told to, but on returning the next day found that some of his papers were on upside down, as if moved around by unseen hands. He, too, heard strange noises and would have nothing further to do with the house. Mrs. W. then called upon the people who had preceded them in the house, the P. family, but the daughter of the late owner said that during their stay in the house they had not experienced anything unusual. Perhaps she did not care to discuss such matters. At any rate, Mrs. W. discovered that the former owner, Mr. P., had actually died in the house three years prior to their acquisition of it. Apparently, he had been working on the house, which he loved very much, and had sustained a fracture. He recovered from it, but sustained another fracture in the same area of his leg. During the recovery, he died of a heart attack in the living room.

It is conceivable that Mr. P. did not like the rearrangements made by the new owners and resented the need for repapering or repainting, having done so much of that himself while in the flesh. But if it is he who is walking up and down the stairs at night, turning doorknobs, and appearing as luminous balls of light—who, then, is the woman whose voice has also been heard?

So it appears that the house overlooking the golf course for the past hundred and twenty-two years has more than one spectral inhabitant in it. Perhaps Mr. P. is only a johnny-come-lately, joining the earlier shades staying on in what used to be their home. As far as the W.'s are concerned, the house is big enough for all of them, so long as they know their place!

*   *   *

Peter Q. comes from a devout Catholic family, part Scottish, part Irish. One June, Peter Q. was married, and his brother Tom, with whom he had always maintained a close and cordial relationship, came to the wedding. That was the last time the two brothers were happy together.

Two weeks later Tom and a friend spent a weekend on Cape Cod. During that weekend, Tom lost his prize possession, his collection of record albums worth several hundred dollars. Being somewhat superstitious, he feared that his luck had turned against him and, sure enough, his car was struck by a hit-and-run driver shortly afterwards.

Then in August of the same year, Tom and his father caught a very big fish on a fishing trip and won a prize consisting of a free trip during the season. As he was cleaning the fish to present it to the jury, the line broke and Tom lost the prize fish. But his streak of bad luck was to take on ominous proportions soon after. Two weeks later, Tom Q. died instantly, his friend David died the next day.

Even before the bad news was brought home to Peter Q. and the family, an extraordinary thing happened at their house. The clock in the bedroom stopped suddenly. When Peter checked it and wound it again, he found nothing wrong with it. By then, word of Tom's death had come, and on checking the time, Peter found that the clock had stopped at the very instant of his brother's death.

During the following days, drawers in what used to be their bedroom would open by themselves when there was no one about. This continued for about four weeks, then it stopped again. On the anniversary of Tom's death, Peter, who was then a junior at the university, was doing some studying and using a fountain pen to highlight certain parts in the books. Just then, his mother called him and asked him to help his father with his car. Peter placed the pen inside the book to mark the page and went to help his father. On returning an hour later, he discovered that a picture of his late brother and their family had been placed where Peter had left the pen, and the pen was lying outside the book next to it. No one had been in the house at the time since Peter's wife was out working.

Under the influence of Tom's untimely death and the phenomena taking place at his house, Peter Q. became very interested in life after death and read almost everything he could, talking with many of his friends about the subject, and becoming more and more convinced that man does in some mysterious way survive death. His wife disagreed with him and did not wish to discuss the matter.

One night, while her husband was away from the house, Peter's wife received a telepathic impression concerning continuance of life, and as she did so, a glowing object about the size of a softball appeared next to her in her bed. It was not a dream, for she could see the headlights from passing cars shining on the wall of the room, yet the shining object was still there next to her pillow, stationary and glowing. It eventually disappeared.

Many times since, Peter Q. has felt the presence of his brother, a warm, wonderful feeling; yet it gives him goose bumps all over. As for the real big send-off Tom had wanted from this life, he truly received it. The morning after his accident, a number of friends called the house without realizing that anything had happened to Tom. They had felt a strong urge to call, as if someone had communicated with them telepathically to do so.

Tom Q. was a collector of phonograph records and owned many, even though a large part of his collection had been stolen. The night before his fatal accident, he had played some of these records.

When Peter later checked the record player, he discovered that the last song his brother had played was entitled, "Just One More Day." Of the many Otis Redding recordings his brother owned, why had he chosen that one?

*   *   *

Mr. Harold B. is a professional horse trainer who travels a good deal of the time. When he does stay at home, he lives in an old house in a small town in Massachusetts. Prior to moving to New England, he and his wife lived in Ohio, but he was attracted by the Old World atmosphere of New England and decided to settle down in the East. They found a house that was more than two hundred years old, but unfortunately it was in dire need of repair. There was neither electricity nor central heating, and all the rooms were dirty, neglected, and badly in need of renovating. Nevertheless, they liked the general feeling of the house and decided to take it.

The house was in a sad state, mostly because it had been lived in for fifty-five years by a somewhat eccentric couple who had shut themselves off from the world. They would hardly admit anyone to their home, and it was known in town that three of their dogs had died of starvation. Mr. and Mrs. B. moved into the house on Walnut Road in October. Shortly after their arrival, Mrs. B. fractured a leg, which kept her housebound for a considerable amount of time. This was unfortunate since the house needed so much work. Nevertheless, they managed. With professional help, they did the house over from top to bottom, putting in a considerable amount of work and money to make it livable, until it became a truly beautiful house.

Although Mrs. B. is not particularly interested in the occult, she has had a number of psychic experiences in the past, especially of a precognitive nature, and has accepted her psychic powers as a matter of course. Shortly after the couple had moved into the house on Walnut Road, they noticed that there was something peculiar about their home.

One night, Mrs. B. was sleeping alone in a downstairs front room off the center entrance hall. Suddenly she was awakened by the sensation of a presence in the room, and as she looked up she saw the figure of a small woman before her bed, looking right at her. She could make out all the details of the woman's face and stature, and noticed that she was wearing a veil, as widows sometimes did in the past. When the apparition became aware of Mrs. B.'s attention, she lifted the veil and spoke to her, assuring her that she was not there to harm her but that she came as a friend. Mrs. B. was too overcome by it all to reply, and before she could gather her wits, the apparition drifted away.

Immediately, Mrs. B. made inquiries in town, and since she was able to give a detailed description of the apparition, it was not long until she knew who the ghost was. The description fit the former owner of the house, Mrs. C., to a tee. Mrs. C. died at age eighty-six, shortly before the B.'s moved into what was her former home. Armed with this information, Mrs. B. braced herself for the presence of an unwanted inhabitant in the house. A short time afterwards, she saw the shadowy outline of what appeared to be a heavy-set person moving along the hall from her bedroom. At first she thought it was her husband so she called out to him, but she soon discovered that her husband was actually upstairs. She then examined her room and discovered that the shades were drawn, so there was no possibility that light from traffic on the road outside could have cast a shadow into the adjoining hall. The shadowy figure she had seen did not, however, look like the outline of the ghost she had earlier encountered in the front bedroom.

While she was wondering about this, she heard the sound of a dog running across the floor. Yet there was no dog to be seen. Evidently her own dog also heard or sensed the ghostly dog's doings because he reacted with visible terror.

Mrs. B. was still wondering about the second apparition when her small grandson came and stayed overnight. He had never been to the house before and had not been told of the stories connected with it. As he was preparing to go to sleep, but still fully conscious, he saw a heavy-set man wearing a red shirt standing before him in his bedroom. This upset him greatly, especially when the man suddenly disappeared without benefit of a door. He described the apparition to his grandparents, who reassured him by telling him a white lie: namely, that he had been dreaming. To this the boy indignantly replied that he had not been dreaming, but, in fact, he had been fully awake. The description given by the boy not only fitted the shadowy outline of the figure Mrs. B. had seen along the corridor, but was a faithful description of the late Mr. C., the former owner of the house.

Although the ghost of Mrs. C. had originally assured the B's that she meant no harm and that she had come as a friend, Mrs. B. had her doubts. A number of small items of no particular value disappeared from time to time and were never found again. This was at times when intruders were completely out of the question.

Then Mrs. B. heard the pages of a wallpaper sampler lying on the dining room table being turned one day. Thinking her husband was doing it, she called out to him, only to find that the room was empty. When she located him in another part of the house, he reported having heard the pages being turned also, and this reassured Mrs. B. since she now had her husband's support in the matter of ghosts. It was clear to her that the late owners did not appreciate the many changes they had made in the house. But Mrs. B. also decided that she was not about to be put out of her home by a ghost. The changes had been made for the better, she decided, and the C.'s, even in their present ghostly state, should be grateful for what they had done for the house and not resent them. Perhaps these thoughts somehow reached the two ghosts telepathically; at any rate, the atmosphere in the house became quiet after that.

*　　*　　*

Barbara is a young woman with a good background who saw me on a Boston television program and volunteered her own experiences as a result. The following week, she wrote to me.

My family home, in Duxbury, Massachusetts, which is near Plymouth and the home of such notables as Myles Standish and John

Alden, is one of the oldest houses in town although we do not know just how old it is.

Last February my brother Edward and his wife Doris and their family moved into the house. Before this my brother Carl and my father were there alone after my mother's death nearly a year ago.

The first occasion of odd happenings was on March 17, St. Patrick's Day. We are a very small part Irish—the name is about all that is left, O'Neil. A friend of mine and I went up to the farm to visit. Shortly after we arrived we heard a noise, which to me sounded like a baby whimpering as it awoke and to my sister-in-law as a woman moaning. I spoke to Doris, something about her baby being awake. She said no and let it pass until later when she told us that she had heard the same noise earlier in the morning and had gone upstairs to check on the baby. As she stood beside the crib, the baby sleeping soundly, she heard the noise again. She then called to the barn to see if all the dogs were accounted for—which they were.

Since this first noticed phenomenon the following things have occurred.

My sister-in-law is keeping a log—I may have omissions.

1. The upstairs door opened and closed (the latch type door) and a shadow filed the whole staircase. It was a calm, cloudy day, and the possibility of a draft is somewhat unlikely. Witnessed by Doris.

2. My brother Carl heard a voice saying, "Bring it back." This went on for several minutes but it was clear for the full time.

3. Footsteps upstairs heard by Doris.

4. Doris went into the front room to see the overstuffed rocker rocking as though someone was in it. After she entered the chair began to stop as though someone got up.

5. July 4, Doris went upstairs and saw the outline of a man which just seemed to disappear.

Before Edward and Doris moved in, Carl and my father were living there alone (all are in the house now). There was no one in the house most of the time since my mother died nearly a year ago. During this time the girl who rents the other house on the farm twice saw the outline of a man over there—once sitting in a chair and another time she woke my brothers about this. She is very jittery about it and as a result does not know about the other things.

I suppose I could go on a bit about the family history. My grandmother traces her ancestry back to Myles Standish and John Alden; my grandfather from Nova Scotia of Scotch-Irish ancestry. I don't know who it was, but someone who lived in the house hanged himself in the barn.

Carl is a sensible, hard-working dairyman who graduated from the University of Massachusetts. Edward is a scoffer since he has observed nothing, recently discharged from the Navy as a lieutenant and is a graduate of Tufts University.

Doris is a very intelligent, levelheaded girl who, before these events, would have called herself a scoffer or disbeliever.

I graduated from Bridgewater Teachers College and at first tried to say that there was a logical explanation to these things but there have just been too many things.

My friend is an intelligent, clear thinking person.

I give you this background on the witnesses, not as a bragger or being vain, but to give you an idea of the type of witnesses. We are not the hysterical, imagining type.

The house has thirteen rooms (not all original) and the ghost seems to roam around at will.

It has been said that the people of Boston—proper Bostonians—are a breed all their own, polite, erudite, and very determined to have things their own way. I have found that these proper Bostonian ghosts are no different in the afterlife. Some of them may not be exactly erudite, but neither are they insolent or, heaven forbid, dumb.

Banshees and Ominous Warnings

I've been all over Ireland three times and have written a book called *The Lively Ghosts of Ireland*, but I've never met anyone in the Emerald Isle who had a banshee. Now there are things a Psychic Investigator considers legitimate and well-supported phenomena in the realm of the Uncanny, such as ghosts, haunted houses, and precognitive experiences.

Then, too, there are borderline cases involving phenom-ena of a more offbeat kind, such as the legendary stories about the Irish lep-rechauns and "little people," the fairies and brownies of Britain, and the dwarfs of Central Europe. To reject out of hand all such material as fantasy is of course no more scientific than to admit all spiritualist phe-nomena as genuine on the face of it without individual search and eval-uation. What little we Know of nature and our universe should have made us realize how much more there may be that is as yet unrevealed. A little humility can be most use-ful in modem science, but unfortu-nately the average physical scientist is filled with his own self-impor-tance and has little patience with the bizarre.

The banshee is a Celtic spirit specializing in death warnings and they say it runs only in "old" Irish families. But I've heard of similar cases in other Celtic traditions and even outside of Britain. The ban-shee is usually described by those who actually have seen it as the fig-ure of an ugly old woman, seated on the doorstep of the family about to be bereaved, and crying or screaming loudly. Banshees announce the forthcoming death of a member of the family without, however, telling the family who and when. That's part of the banshee game. Naturally the family is scared stiff when the banshee wails and everybody wonders who is next to go.

Died-in-the-wool Irish traditionalists will swear that banshees only run in the very good, ancient families and having one may be frightening, but it is also flattering: sort of a pedigree of death.

Now I have always been doubtful about the nature, though not the existence, of such strange creatures as ele-mentals and banshees, considering them indeed part and parcel of ghostly manifestations, and thus human.

I've also learned that you can take the Irishman out of Ireland, but you can't take Ireland out of the Irishman. Even generations after, an Irish family transplanted into the New World may have the family banshee on their necks. Such is the case with the Shea family who live a pretty prosaic life in northern Massachusetts. Joanne Shea's grandmother, and even her mother, came from Ireland, as the song goes, and with them came accounts of strange goings-on whenever death was near for a member of the family.

The grandmother's particular banshee was mild in com-parison to that of others: a strange creaking noise on the stairs, which she always tried to tell herself was natural, knowing full well, however, what it meant.

One day the grandmother was visiting Mrs. Shea and her sister and, upon leaving, startled the two girls by telling them it was her last visit. She would never see them again!

The family joked about this. Then two weeks later their grandmother fell and fractured her hip, and was hospital-ized with the injury.

A few days afterwards, Mrs. Shea's sister, who is a nun, was standing by a window in her chapel. Suddenly she heard a terrible scream which she later described as sound-ing like the scream of a wildcat.

Terrified, she looked out the window, but could see nothing. Later, the two girls compared notes. At the exact moment when the nun had heard the scream, Grandmother had died.

A year went by. One evening, as Joanne lay in bed, she heard her brother's footsteps come up the stairs outside her room. Just then the clock chimed 11 P.M. To her surprise, Joanne clearly heard the footsteps of two people coming up the stairs, and wondered who the friend was her brother was bringing home at so late an hour. At the top of the stairs, the two pairs of footsteps separated, and one person went into the brother's room. The other footsteps came into Joanne's, and she suddenly felt petrified with fear.

Then all of a sudden, there, in front of her bed, stood her late grandmother.

Looking at the girl, the apparition turned her head a little, smiled—and then was gone like a puff of smoke.

When Joanne reported the matter to her mother the following morning, her mother brushed it aside as "probably a dream."

But then she stopped herself. What was the day's date? It was November 3—the anniversary of Grandmother's passing. Mother had forgotten to put Grandmother's name on the list of those for whom a prayer was to be said in church, as had been the custom in this Catholic family. The matter was immediately attended to, and when Joanne's brother came in that day, she questioned him about the other footsteps she had heard the night before.

He insisted that he had come in quite alone. He had not heard the ghostly steps either. Only Joanne had, and she never saw her late grandmother again after that.

Joanne's older sister, who was later to become a nun, evidently had also inherited the psychic talents so strong on the female side of the family tree.

One evening only the women were home, while the men—Joanne's father and her two brothers—were away at a ball game. Mother was downstairs, and the two girls were in bed in their room upstairs. Joanne was already beginning to doze off, when her sister suddenly jumped out of bed and ran downstairs to her mother's room.

"Did you hear the terrible scream?" the twenty-year-old girl asked her mother, who could only nod a silent yes. But Joanne had not heard it. It was a scream not unlike the cry of the wildcat, coming in from over the hill in back of the house. There was nothing outside in the yard to account for it.

For several days the women of the family were in a dither, waiting for fate to drop the other shoe. Everybody was told to be extremely careful and to avoid accidents. One could never know whom the banshee meant. On the eighth day after the unearthly scream had been heard, the waiting game was over. Joanne's uncle, her mother's brother, was hit by an automobile and died a few days later.

*   *   *

Just as the Germans have a peculiar name for the noisy ghost phenomena associated with disturbances of a physical nature which they call a Poltergeist, so they have a special term for the terrifying experience of a warning of impend-ing death. These announcements of disaster or doom are called Gaenger in Central Europe, a word meaning, literally, "he who will go" (off stage), the stage being our physical world.

In a memorable but now very rare book called *Gaenger, Geister und Geslchter* (*Death Announcements, Ghosts and Visions*), Friedrich von Gaggern reported some of these occurrences that were peculiarly tied in with the Gennanic mood and landscape.

I was thinking of the Gaggern work when I first heard about Jane Marquardt of Rhode Island. Not so much because of her Germanic name—after all it is her husband's—but because of the nature of the incidents that both enlivened and beclouded her life.

The most terrifying of these incidents took place when she was

eighteen, at the time of World War II.

Her boy friend was a bombardier overseas, while she lived with her family in Chicago. One night she awoke from deep sleep with the sudden realization that someone was pounding on her bedroom door. There was no rational explanation for the loud knocks. She got up and checked the time. It was just 3 A.M. With a vague feeling of uneasiness, she return to bed. Somehow she connected the uncanny knocks with her boy friend. He was due to return home soon, and they would be married.

Was it fear or the natural worry about a boy overseas in the war, or was it something more?

For two days Jane lived in a state of suspended animation. Then a telegram arrived with the tragic news that her boy friend had been killed. He and his buddies had safely completed their seventy-fourth mission and were returning home to their quarters in a bus. The bus went out of control and plunged over a cliff, killing the entire crew. Everyone on that bus was due for a furlough and return to the United States. The time of the accident was exactly 3 A.M., allowing for the difference in time zones.

The years went by and her shock wore off. She married another man, also in the military, and the family moved to New Jersey, where her husband was stationed. Jane was now twenty-five years old and the mother of a little girl. One evening they were coming back from a drive-in movie, and were within a few miles of their home, when she clearly saw a human face approaching the car on her side. As it drew near, she recognized her mother. Now she knew perfectly well that her mather was at that time in Chicago. Yet, there was her mother's face, smiling up at her and speaking to her in a clear and rather happy voice: "Jane, I'm going to die!"

With that, the vision faded quickly. Jane let out a scream. "No, dear God, no!"

Her husband, who had seen nothing, naturally assumed she was ill. Rather than alarm him, she kept her counsel. What was the point of telling him? she reasoned. Might it not make it happen in some unknown way? Also, she could tell by the way he cast sidelong glances at her, that he wondered about his wife's sanity.

Jane and her mother had always been very close and had kept in frequent contact over the miles. The vision occurred on a Tuesday at midnight. On Saturday Jane received an ominous telegram advising her of her mother's sudden death. The news hit her strongly and she took it badly. But later she realized that this had been her mother's way of softening the coming blow, by forewarning her of impending death. Had her own mother done this through subconscious channels? Had an agency out there created this vision for her benefit?

Jane was soon to learn more about her uncanny ability to tune in on distant dangers.

In 1952 she and her husband had to leave for Japan where he would hence be stationed. This was a heavy blow for her widowed father.

She was all he had left, for he, too, had taken his wife's passing badly. His tears of farewell seemed to stay in Jane's memory as she left for Japan.

She had not been in her new home more than three weeks when a strange thing happened. Her husband was downstairs, reading, while she was upstairs doing her nails. Their little girl was already asleep. Suddenly she heard clearly, so clearly it could have come from the next room, a voice calling her by name.

"Jane!" it said and at once she recognized her father's voice. She shook her head in bewilderment, wondering if she had imagined it due too her longing for her father. But again the voice called out to her. Now she dashed downstairs and questioned her husband about it. No, he had not called her. At this point she told him of her experience but he laughed it off.

A cable brought fearful news two days later. Her father had been taken ill and might not survive. But this time death did not exact the usual toll. After a long illness, Jane's father got well again. She checked the time of her experience with him and found that he had just had his first attack then. In desperation, he had actually called out to her, wishing she could be near him in this difficult hour. Somehow, his voice had traveled across the Pacific in a fraction of a second and reached his favorite daughter's ears—and only hers!

*   *   *

Mrs. V. works as a law secretary for a prominent attorney in the State of New Jersey. She never had any interest in the occult, but her innate psychic sense broke through eventually whether she wanted it or not. At first, there were just trifling things. Like handing her cleaner a pair of gloves and instantly knowing he would lose them. He did. Or looking for the gravestone of a friend in a cemetery she had never been to and finding it "blindly." Then, the night her mother died, she and her sister saw the lights in the living room go on by themselves. Since these were lights that had to be turned on individually, this was indeed unusual.

Soon, Mrs. V. was to have the shock of her life. It started as an ordinary working day. Her boss was dictating to her at her desk, which was located in a long hallway leading to his private offices. During a pause in the dictation, she looked up idly and saw, to her left, through a glass separation, a woman standing in the hall. The woman looked at her, and then moved quickly behind the elevator wall and out of her line of vision.

The woman was about twelve feet away and Mrs. V. saw her clearly through the glass. Her boss was part-owner of the building and often interviewed prospective tenants, so she assumed this was someone looking for office space and called his attention to the woman.

"Woman? What woman?" he demanded to know. "I don't see any-one."

"She has stepped behind the elevator wall," the secretary explained, somewhat sheepishly. The elevator is one of those older, noisy installations which one can hear approach quite clearly. Neither of them had heard the elevator coming up to the fourth floor, where they were, so they naturally felt the woman had still to be on the landing. But there was nobody there. Had she decided to walk down four flights—most unlikely in view of the elevator's presence—she could not have gotten far as yet. Also, in order to reach the stairwell, the woman would have had to brush past her employer.

Mrs. V. insisted there had been a visitor. The lawyer pressed the elevator button. The cab stopped at the fourth floor. It was empty. Evidently nobody had been riding it during the time of the incident, since the noise of the ele-vator's coming up could not have escaped them.

"You must have seen your own reflection in the glass partition," he reasoned. Some lawyers will reason peculiarly. Mrs. V. shook her head. She knew what she had seen was not her own image. To prove her point, she re-enacted the whole thing. From the spot she had seen the woman stand, no reflection could be gleaned from inside the office. The lawyer shrugged and went back to his work. Mrs. V. sat down quietly and tried to collect her thoughts. What had she seen? A woman of about sixty-five years of age, a little stocky in build, wearing a close-fitting hat and a brown, tweedy coat. Moreover, something about the woman's appearance seemed to be vaguely familiar. Then all at once it hit her who the woman was!

It was none other than her late mother, Mrs. T., who had been dead for thirteen years. She had owned a coat similar to the one Mrs. V. had seen and always favored close-fitting hats. Why had her mother's ghost appeared to her at this moment? she wondered.

Was it because her father was in ill health? Was this an omen, a warning of his impending death?

Grimly preparing for the unwanted, Mrs. V. went through her work rather mechanically for the next few days.

The following week, she received a phone call from one of her sisters. Her mother's favorite sister, their aunt, had suffered a stroke. One week to the day of her mother's appearance, Mrs. V.'s aunt was dead.

Mid-Atlantic

The "Spy House" Ghosts of New Jersey

In June, 1696, one Daniel Seabrook, aged 26 and a planter by profession, took his inheritance of 80 pounds sterling and bought 202 acres of property from his stepfather, Thomas Whitlock. For 250 years this plantation was in the hands of the Seabrook family who worked the land and sailed their ships from the harbor. The "Spy House" is probably one of the finest pieces of Colonial architecture available for inspection in the eastern United States, having been restored meticulously over the years.

The house is built in the old manner, held together with wooden pegs. There are handmade bricks, filled with clay mortar. The house has two stories and is painted white. Every room has its own fireplace as that was the only way in which Colonial houses could be heated.

Today, the house, which is located near Middletown, New Jersey, can easily be reached from New York City. It is being kept by a group headed by curator Gertrude Neidlinger, helped by her historian-brother, Travis Neidlinger, and as a museum it displays not only the furniture of the Colonial period but some of the implements of the whalers who were active in the area well into the nineteenth century. As an historical attraction, it is something that should not be missed by anyone, apart from any ghostly connections.

One of the rooms in the house is dedicated to the period of the Battle of Monmouth. This room, called the spy room by the British for good reasons, as we shall see, has copies of the documents kept among General Washington's private papers in the Library of Congress in

Washington, D.C.

In 1778, the English were marching through Middletown, pillaging and burning the village. Along the shoreline the Monmouth militia and the men who were working the whale boats, got together to try to cut down the English shipping. General Washington asked for a patriot from Shoal Harbor, which was the name of the estate where the spy house is located, to help the American side fight the British. The volunteer was a certain Corporal John Stillwell, who was given a telescope and instructions to spy on the British from a hill called Garrett's Hill, not far away, the highest point in the immediate area.

The lines between British and Americans were intertwined and frequently intercut each other, and it was difficult for individuals to avoid crossing them at times. The assignment given Corporal Stillwell was not an easy one, especially as some of his own relatives favored the other side of the war. Still, he was able to send specific messages to the militia who were able to turn these messages into attacks on the British fleet.

At that point, Stillwell observed there were 1,037 vessels in the fleet lying off the New Jersey coastline, at a time when the American forces had no navy at all. But the fishermen and their helpers on shore did well in this phase of the Revolutionary War. John Stillwell's son, Obadiah Stillwell, seventeen years old, served as message carrier from his father's observation point to the patriots.

Twenty-three naval battles were fought in the harbor after the battle of Monmouth. The success of the whaleboat operation was a stunning blow to the British fleet and a great embarrassment. Even daylight raids became so bold and successful that in one day two pilot boats were captured upsetting the harbor shipping.

Finally, the British gave the order to find the spy and end the rebel operation. The searching party declared the Seabrook homestead as a spy house, since they knew its owner, Major Seabrook, was a patriot.

They did not realize that the real spy was John Stillwell, operating from Garrett's Hill. Nevertheless, they burned the spy house. It was, of course, later restored. Today, descendants of John Stillwell are among the society of friends of the museum, supporting it.

Gertrude Neidlinger turned to me for help with the several ghosts she felt in the house. Considering the history of the house, it is not surprising that there should be ghosts there. Miss Neidlinger, herself, has felt someone in the entrance room whenever she has been alone in the house, especially at night. There is also a lady in white who comes down from the attic, walks along the hall and goes into what is called the blue and white room, and there tucks in the covers of a crib or bed. Then she turns and goes out of sight. Miss Neidlinger was not sure who she was, but thought she might have been the spirit of Mrs. Seabrook, who lived through the Revolutionary War in a particularly dangerous position, having relatives on both sides of the political fence.

I brought Ingrid Beckman, my psychic friend, to the spy house, which is technically located in Keansburg, New Jersey, near Middletown. The number on the house is 119, but of course everyone in the area calls it the Spy House. As Ingrid walked about the place, she immediately pointed out its ancient usage as an outpost. While we were investigating the house, we both clearly heard footsteps overhead where there was no one walking. Evidently, the ghosts knew of our arrival.

Without knowing anything about the history of the house, Ingrid commented, "Down here around the fireplace I feel there are people planning strategy, worried about British ships." Then she continued, "This was to mobilize something like the minutemen, farming men who were to fight. This was a strategic point because it was the entry into New York."

I then asked Ingrid to tell me whether she felt any ghosts, any residues of the past still in the house.

When we went upstairs, Ingrid tuned into the past with a bang.

"There's a woman here. She ties in with this house and something about spying, some kind of spying went on here." Then she added, "Somebody spied behind the American lines and brought back information."

Upstairs near the window on the first floor landing, Ingrid felt a man watching, waiting for someone to come his way. Ingrid felt there was a man present who had committed an act of treason, a man who gave information back to the British. His name was Samuels. She felt that this man was hanged publicly. The people call him an ex-patriot. This is the entity, Ingrid said, who cannot leave this house out of remorse.

Ingrid also asserted that the house was formerly used as a public house, an inn, when meetings took place here. The curator, Miss Neidlinger, later confirmed this. Also, Ingrid felt that among the families living in the area, most of the members served in the patriot militia, but that there were occasional traitors, such as George Taylor. Colonel George Taylor might have been the man to whom Ingrid was referring. As for the man who was hanged, it would have been Captain Huddy, and he was hanged for having caused the death of a certain Philip White. Captain Joshua Huddy had been unjustly accused of having caused the death of the patriot Philip White and despite his innocence, was lynched by the patriots. Again, Ingrid had touched on something very real from history.

But ghostly lady and the man who was hanged and the man who stared out the window onto the bay are not the only ghosts at the spy house. On the Fourth of July, 1975, a group of local boys were in the house in the blue and white room upstairs. Suddenly, the sewing machine door opened by itself and the pedals worked themselves without benefit of human feet. One of the boys looked up, and in the mirror in the bureau across the room, he could see a face with a long beard. Another boy looked down the hall and there he saw a figure with a tall black hat and a long beard and sort of very full trousers as they were worn in an earlier age. That was enough for them and they ran from the house and never went back again.

One of the ladies who assists the curator, Agnes Lyons, refuses to do any typing in the upstairs room because the papers simply will not stand still. A draft seems to go by all the time and blow the papers to the floor even though the windows are closed. A Mrs. Lillian Boyer also saw the man with the beard standing at the top of the stairs, wearing a black hat and dressed in the period of the later 1700s. He had very large eyes, and seemed to be a man in his forties. He just stood there looking at her and she of course wouldn't pass him. Then he seemed to flash some sort of light back and forth, a brilliant light like a flashlight. And there were footsteps all over the house at the same time. She could even hear the man breathe, yet he was a ghost!

If you want to visit the spy house, address yourself to Gertrude Neidlinger, Curator, at the Spy House, postal address, Port Monmouth, New Jersey 07758. She's a gracious lady and I'm sure will make you welcome.

The Metuchen Ghost

One day last spring, while the snow was still on the ground and the chill in the air, my good friend Bernard Axelrod, with whom I have shared many a ghostly experience, called to say that he knew of a haunted house in New Jersey, and was I still interested.

I was, and Bernard disclosed that in the little town of Metuchen, there were a number of structures dating back to Colonial days. A few streets down from where from where he and his family live in a modern, up-to-date brick building, there stands one wooden house in particular which has the reputation of being haunted, Bernard explained. No particulars were known to him beyond that. Ever since the Rockland Country Ghost in the late Danton Walker's colonial house had acquainted me with specters from George Washington's days, I have been eager to enlarge this knowledge. So it was with great anticipation that I gathered a group of helpers to pay a visit to whoever might be haunting the house in Metuchen. Bernard, who is a very persuasive fellow, managed to get permission from the owner of the house, Mr. Kane, an advertising executive. My group included Mrs. Meyers, as medium, and two associates of hers who would operate the tape recorder and take notes, Rosemarie de Simone and Pearl Winder. Miss de Simone is a teacher and Mrs. Winder is the wife of a dentist.

It was a midafternoon in March when we rolled into the sleepy town of Metuchen. Bernard Axelrod was expecting us, and took us across town to the colonial house we were to inspect.

Any mention of the history or background of the house was studiously avoided en route. The owners, Mr. and Mrs. Kane, had a guest, a Mr. David, and the eight of us sat down in a circle in the downstairs living room of the beautifully preserved old house. It is a jewel of a colonial country house, with an upper story, a staircase and very few structural changes. No doubt about it, the Kanes had good taste, and their house reflected it. The furniture was all in the style of the period, which I took to be about the turn of the eighteenth century, perhaps earlier. There were several cats smoothly moving about, which helped me greatly to relax, for I have always felt that no house is wholly bad where there are cats, and conversely, where there are several cats, a house is bound to be wonderfully charming. For the occasion, however, the entire feline menagerie was put out of reach into the kitchen, and the tape recorder turned on as we took our seats in a semi-circle around the fireplace. The light was the subdued light of a late winter afternoon, and the quiet was that of a country house far away from the bustling city. It was a perfect setting for a ghost to have his say.

As Mrs. Meyers eased herself into her comfortable chair, she remarked that certain clairvoyant impressions had come to her almost the instant she set foot into the house.

"I met a woman upstairs—in spirit, that is—with a long face, thick cheeks, perhaps forty years old or more, with ash-brown hair that may once have been blond. Somehow I get the name Mathilda. She wears a dress of striped material down to her knees, then wide plain material to her ankles. She puts out a hand, and I see a heavy wedding band on her finger, *but it has a cut in it*, and she insists on calling my attention to the cut. Then there is a man, with a prominent nose, tan coat and black trousers, standing in the back of the room looking as if he were sorry about something . . . he has very piercing eyes . . . I think she'd like to find something she has lost, and he blames her for it."

We were listening attentively. No one spoke, for that would perhaps give Mrs. Meyers an unconscious lead, something a good researcher will avoid.

"That sounds very interesting," I heard Bernard say, in his usual noncommittal way. "Do you see anything else?"

"Oh, yes," Mrs. Meyers nodded, "quite a bit—for one thing, there are *other* people here who don't belong to *them* at all . . . they come with the place, but in a different period . . . funny, halfway between upstairs and downstairs, I see one or two people *hanging*."

At this remark, the Kanes exchanged quick glances. Evidently my medium had hit pay dirt. Later, Mr. Kane told us a man committed suicide in the house around 1850 or 1860. He confirmed also that there was once a floor in between the two floors, but that this later addition had since been removed, when the house was restored to its original colonial condition.

Built in 1740, the house had replaced an earlier structure, for objects inscribed "1738" have been unearthed here.

"Legend has always had it that a revolutionary soldier haunts the house," Mr. Kane explained after the seance. "The previous owners told us they did hear *peculiar noises* from time to time, and that they had been told of such goings-on also by the owner who preceded *them*. Perhaps this story has been handed down from owner to owner, but we have never spoken to anyone in our generation who has heard or seen anything unusual about the place."

"What about you and your wife?" I inquired.

"Oh, we were a bit luckier—or unluckier—depending on how you look at it. One day, the front door knocker banged away very loudly. My wife, who was all alone in the house at the time, went to see who it was. There was nobody there. It was winter, and deep snow surrounded the house. *There were no tracks in the snow*."

"How interesting," Bernard said. All this was new to him, too, despite his friendship with the family.

Mr. Kane slowly lit a pipe, blew the smoke toward the low ceiling of the room, and continued.

"The previous owners had a dog. Big, strapping fellow. Just the same, now and again he would hear some strange noises and absolutely panic. In the middle of the night he would jump into bed with them, crazed with fear. But it wasn't just the dog who heard things. They, too, heard the walking—steps of someone walking around the second floor, and in their bedroom, on the south side of the house—at times of the day when they *knew* for sure there was nobody there."

"And after you moved in, did you actually *see* anything?" I asked. Did they have any idea what the ghost looked like?

"Well, yes," Mr. Kane said. "About a year ago, Mrs. Kane was sleeping in the Green Room upstairs. *Three nights in a row, she was awakened in the middle of the night, at the same time, by the feeling of a presence.* Looking up, she noticed a white form standing beside her bed. Thinking it was me, at first, she was not frightened. But when she spoke to it, it just disappeared into air. She is sure it was a man."

Although nothing unusual had occurred since, the uncanny feeling persisted, and when Bernard Axelrod mentioned his interest in ghosts, and offered to have me come to the house with a qualified medium, the offer was gladly accepted. So there we were, with Mrs. Meyers slowly gliding into trance. Gradually, her description of what she saw or heard blended into the personalities themselves, as her own personality vanished temporarily. It was a very gradual transition, and well controlled.

"She is being blamed by him," Mrs. Meyers mumbled. "Now I see a table, she took four mugs, four large mugs, and one small one. Does she mean to say, four older people and a small one? I get a name, Jake, John, no, *Jonathan!* Then there are four Indians, and they want to make peace. *They've done something they should not have,* and they want to make peace." Her visions continued.

"Now instead of the four mugs on the table, there's a whole line of them, fifteen altogether, but I don't see the small mug now. There are many individuals standing around the table, with their backs toward me—then someone is calling and screaming, and someone says 'Off above the knees.'"

I later established through research that during the Revolutionary War the house was right in the middle of many small skirmishes; the injured may well have been brought here for treatment.

Mrs. Meyers continued her narrative with increasing excitement in her voice.

"Now there are other men, all standing there with long-tailed coats, white stockings, and talking. Someone says 'Dan Dayridge' or 'Bainbridge,' I can't make it out clearly; he's someone with one of these three-cornered hats, a white wig, tied black hair, a very thin man with a high, small nose, not particularly young, with a fluffy collar and large eyes. Something took place here in which he was a participant. He is one of the men standing there with those fifteen mugs. It is night, and there are two candles on either side of the table, food on the table—*smells like chicken*—and then there is a paper with red seals and gold ribbon. But something goes wrong with this, and now there are only four mugs on the table . . . I think it means, only four men return. *Not the small one.* This man is one of the four, and somehow the little mug is pushed aside, I see it put away on the shelf. I see now a small boy, he has disappeared, he is gone . . . but always trying to *come back.* The name *Allen* . . . he followed the man, but the Indians got him and he never came back. They're looking for him, trying to find him. . . ."

Mrs. Meyers now seemed totally entranced. Her features assumed the face of a woman in great mental anguish, and her voice quivered; the words came haltingly and with much prodding from me. For all practical purposes, the medium had now been taken over by a troubled spirit. We listened quietly, as the story unfolded.

"*Allen's* coming back one day . . . call him back . . . my son, do you hear him? They put those Indians in the tree, do you hear them as they moan?"

"Who took your boy?" I asked gently.

"They did . . . he went with them, with the men. With his father, *Jon*."

"What Indians took him?"

"Look there in the tree. They didn't do it. I know they didn't do it."

"Where did they go?"

"To the *river*. My boy, did you hear him?"

Mrs. Meyers could not have possibly known that there was a river not far from the house. I wanted to fix the period of our story, as I always do in such cases, so I interrupted the narrative and asked what day this was. There was a brief pause, as if she were collecting her thoughts. Then the faltering voice was heard again.

"December One . . . ."

December One! The old-fashioned way of saying December First.

"What year is this?" I continued.

This time the voice seemed puzzled as to why I would ask such an obvious thing, but she obliged.

"Seventeen . . . seventy . . . six."

"What does your husband do ?"

"Jonathan . . . ?"

"Does he own property?"

"The field. . . . ."

But then the memory of her son returned. "Allen, my son Allen. He is calling me . . . ."

"Where was he born?"

"Here."

"What is the name of this town?"

"Bayridge."

Subsequently, I found that the section of Metuchen we were in had been known in colonial times as *Woodbridge*, although it is not inconceivable that there also was a Bayridge.

The woman wanted to pour her heart out now. "Oh, look," she continued, "they didn't do it, they're in the tree . . . those Indians, dead ones. They didn't do it, I can see their souls and they were innocent of this . . . in the cherry tree."

Suddenly she interrupted herself and said—"Where am I? Why am I so sad?" It isn't uncommon for a newly liberated or newly contacted "ghost" to be confused about his or her own status. Only an emotionally disturbed personality becomes an earthbound "ghost."

I continued the questioning.

Between sobs and cries for her son, Allen, she let the name "Mary Dugan" slip from her lips, or rather the lips of the entranced medium, who now was fully under the unhappy one's control.

"Who is Mary Dugan?" I immediately interrupted.

"He married her, Jonathan."

"Second wife?"

"Yes . . . I am under the tree."

"Where were you born? What was your maiden name?"

"Bayridge . . . Swift . . . my heart is so hurt, so cold, so cold."

"Do you have any other children?"

"Allen . . . Mary Anne . . . Georgia. They're calling me, do you hear them? Allen, he knows I am alone waiting here. He thought he was a *man*!"

"How old was your boy at the time?" I said. The disappearance of her son was the one thing foremost in her mind.

"My boy . . . eleven . . . December One, 1776, is his birthday. That was his birthday all right."

I asked her if Allen had another name, and she said, Peter. Her own maiden name? She could not remember.

"Why don't I know? They threw me out . . . it was Mary took the house."

"What did your husband do?"

"He was a *potter.* He also was paid for harness. His shop . . . the road to the south. Bayridge. In the tree orchard we took from two neighbors."

The neighborhood is known for its clay deposits and potters, but this was as unknown to the medium as it was to me until *after* the seance, when Bernard told us about it.

In *Boyhood Days in Old Metuchen,* a rare work, Dr. David Marshall says: "Just south of Metuchen there are extensive clay banks."

But our visitor had enough of the questioning. Her sorrow returned and suddenly she burst into tears, the medium's tears, to be sure, crying—"I want Allen! Why is it I look for him? I hear him calling me, I hear his step . . . I know he is here . . . why am I searching for him?"

I then explained that Allen was on "her side of the veil," too, that she would be reunited with her boy by merely "standing still" and letting him find her; it was her frantic activity that made it impossible for them to be reunited, but if she were to becalm herself, all would be well.

After a quiet moment of reflection, her sobs became weaker and her voice firmer.

"Can you see your son now?"

"Yes, I see him." And with that, she slipped away quietly.

A moment later, the medium returned to her own body, as it were, and rubbed her sleepy eyes. Fully awakened a moment later, she remembered nothing of the trance. Now *for the first time* did we talk about the house, and its ghostly visitors.

"How much of this can be proved?" I asked impatiently.

Mr. Kane lit another pipe, and then answered me slowly.

"Well, there is quite a lot," he finally said. "For one thing, this house used to be a tavern during revolutionary days, known as the Allen House!"

Bernard Axelrod, a few weeks later, discovered an 1870 history of the town of Metuchen. In it, there was a remark anent the house, which an early map showed at its present site in 1799:

"In the house . . . lived a Mrs. Allen, and on it was a sign 'Allentown Cake and Beer Sold Here.' Between the long Prayer Meetings which according to New England custom were held mornings and afternoons, with half hour or an hour intermission, it was not unusual for the young men to get ginger cake and a glass of beer at this famous restaurant. . . ."

"What about all those Indians she mentioned?" I asked Mr. Kane.

"There were Indians in this region all right," he confirmed.

"Indian arrowheads have been found right here, near the pond in back of the house. Many Indian battles were fought around here, and incidentally, during the War for Independence, both sides came to this house and had their ale in the evening. This was a kind of no-man's land between the Americans and the British. During the day, they would kill each other, but at night, *they ignored each other over a beer at Mrs. Allen's tavern!*"

"How did you get this information?" I asked Mr. Kane.

"There was a local historian, a Mr. Welsh, who owned this house for some thirty years. He also talked of a revolutionary soldier whose ghost was seen plainly 'walking' through the house about a foot off the ground."

Many times have I heard a ghostly apparition described in just such terms. The motion of walking is really unnecessary, it seems, for the spirit form *glides* about a place.

There are interesting accounts in the rare old books about the town of Metuchen in the local library. These stories spoke of battles between the British and Americans, and of "carts loaded with dead bodies, after a battle between British soldiers and Continentals, up around Oak Tree on June 26th, 1777."

No doubt, the Allen House saw many of them brought in along with the wounded and dying.

I was particularly interested in finding proof of Jonathan Allen's existence, and details of his life.

So far I had only ascertained that Mrs. Allen existed. Her husband was my next goal.

After much work, going through old wills and land documents, I discovered a number of Allens in the area. I found the will of his father, Henry, leaving his "son, Jonathan, the land where he lives" on April 4th, 1783.

A 1799 map shows a substantial amount of land marked "Land of Allen," and Jonathan Allen's name occurs in many a document of the period as a witness or seller of land.

The Jonathan Allen I wanted had to be from Middlesex County, in which Metuchen was located. I recalled that he was an able-bodied man, and consequently must have seen some service. Sure enough, in the *Official Register of the Officers and Men of New Jersey in the Revolutionary War*, I found my man—"Allen, Jonathan—Middlesex."

It is good to know that the troubled spirit of Mrs. Allen can now rest close to her son's; and perhaps the other restless one, her husband, will be accused of negligence in the boy's death no more.

The Strange Case of the Colonial Soldier

Somerton, Pennsylvania, is now a suburb of Philadelphia, albeit a pretty outlying one. It takes you all of an hour by car from downtown Philadelphia, but when you get there, it's worth it, especially Byberry Road. How the builders of modern chunks of concrete managed to overlook this delightful country lane in the backyard of the big city is beyond my knowledge, but the fact is that we have here a winding, bumpy road, good enough for one car at a time, that goes for several miles without a single high-rise building. Instead, old homes line it in respectable intervals, allowing even a bit of green and open spaces between the dwellings.

One of the most unusual sights along this winding road is a pretty, wooden Colonial house built in 1732, and untouched except for minor alterations, mainly inside the house. That in itself is a rarity, of course, but the owners who lived here since the Revolutionary period evidently were house-proud people who *cared.*

The current tenants are David and Dolores Robinson, whose greatest pleasure is being in that house. They don't advertise the fact they've got an authentic pre-Revolutionary home, but they're not exactly shy about it either; to them, it is a thrill to live as our ancestors did, without the constant urge to "improve" things with shiny new gadgets that frequently don't work, or to tear down some portion of their home just because it looks old or has been used for a long time.

The Robinsons are house-proud, and they have a keen sense of the antiquarian without any formal education in that area. Mr. Robinson works for the telephone company and his wife works for her brother, a photographer, as a retouch artist. Both are in early middle age and they have three children in the pre-teenage group.

Theirs is a happy family without problems or frustrations: They'd like to make a little more money, advance a little faster, get a better car—but that is the normal average American's dream. With the Robinsons lives Mr. Robinson Senior, an elderly gentleman whose main occupation seemed to be watching TV.

I first heard of the Robinsons and their homestead when I appeared on a local radio show in the area, and I was fascinated by the prospect of an apparently untouched house with many layers of history clinging to it that a psychic might be able to sense. I put the house on my mental list of places to visit for possible psychometry experiments.

Finally, several years ago, that opportunity arose and a friend of ours, Tom Davis, drove us out to Byberry Road. There is something strange about Philadelphia distances; they grow on you somehow, especially at night. So it was with considerable delay that we finally showed up at the house, but we were made welcome just the same by the owners.

The house could not be missed even in the dark of night. It is the only one of its kind in the area, and sits back a bit from the road. With its graceful white pillars that support the roof of the porch, it is totally different from anything built nowadays or even in Victorian times. From the outside it looks smaller than it really is. There are three stories, and a storage room beneath the rear part of the house, the oldest* portion. We entered through the front door and found ourselves in a delightfully appointed living room leading off to the left into the older portion of the house. The house had a mixture of Colonial and Victorian furniture in it, somehow not out of context with the over-all mood of the place, which was one of remoteness from the modern world. Across the narrow hall from the downstairs living room, a staircase led to the next floor, which contained bedrooms and one of the largest bathrooms I ever saw. Considering the Colonial reluctance to bathe to excess, it struck me as incongruous, until I realized later that the house had had some quasi-public usage at one period.

A few steps led from the living room to the rear section, which was the original portion of the house. A large fireplace dominates it. Next to it is a rear staircase also leading to the upper stories, and the low ceiling shows the original wooden beams just as they were in pre-Revolutionary days.

The Robinsons weren't particularly addicted to the psychic even though they're both Irish, but Mrs. Robinson admits to having had ESP experiences all her life. Whether this is her Irishness (with a well-developed sense of imagination, as she puts it) or just a natural ability, it's there for better or worse. When she was fourteen, she was reading in bed one night, and it was very, very late. This was against the rules, so she had made sure the door to her bedroom was shut. Suddenly, the door opened and her brother Paul stood there looking at her reproachfully. He had been dead for eight years. Dolores screamed and went under the covers. Her mother rushed upstairs to see what was the matter. When she arrived, the door was still wide open! Since that time, Mrs. Robinson has often known things before they really happened—such as who would be at the door before she answered it, or just before the telephone rang, who would be calling. Today, this is just a game to her, and neither her husband nor she takes it too seriously. Both of them are high school graduates, Dolores has had some college training, and her husband has electro-engineering skills which he uses professionally; nevertheless they don't scoff at the possibility that an old house might contain some elements from its violent past.

When they first moved into the house in 1960, Mrs. Robinson felt right at home in it, as if she had always lived there. From the very first, she found it easy to move up and down the stairs even in the dark without the slightest accident or need to orient herself. It was almost as if the house, or someone in it, were guiding her steps.

But soon the Robinsons became acutely aware that the house was *alive:* There were strange noises and creaking boards, which they promptly ascribed to the settling of an old building. But there were also human footsteps that both husband and wife heard, and there were those doors. The doors, in particular, puzzled them. The first time Mrs. Robinson noticed anything unusual about the doors in their house was when she was working late over some photography assignments she had brought home with her. Her husband was out for the evening and the three children were fast asleep upstairs. The children have their bedrooms on the third floor, while the Robinsons sleep on the second floor. Suddenly Mrs. Robinson heard footsteps on the ceiling above her bedroom. Then the door of the stairwell opened, steps reverberated on the stairs, then the door to the second floor opened, and a blast of cold air hit her. Without taking her eyes from her work, Mrs. Robinson said, "Go back to bed!" assuming it was one of her children who had gotten up for some reason. There was no answer.

She looked up, and there was no one there. Annoyed, she rose and walked up the stairs to check her children's rooms. They were indeed fast asleep. Not satisfied and thinking that one of them must be playing tricks on her, she woke them one by one and questioned them. But they had trouble waking up, and it was evident to Mrs. Robinson that she was on a fool's errand; her children had not been down those stairs.

That was the beginning of a long succession of incidents involving the doors in the house. Occasionally, she would watch with fascination when a door opened quite by itself, without any logical cause, such as wind or draft; or to see a door open for her just as she was about to reach for the doorknob. At least, whatever presence there was in the old house, was polite: It opened the door to a lady! But reassuring it was not, for to live with the unseen can be infuriating, too. Many times she would close a door, only to see it stand wide open again a moment later when she knew very well it could not do that *by itself.*

She began to wonder whether there wasn't perhaps a hidden tunnel beneath their back living room. Frequently they would hear a booming sound below the floor, coming from the direction of the cold storage room below. The doors would continually open for her now, even when she was alone in the house and the children could not very well be blamed for playing pranks on her. During the summer of 1966, there were nights when the activities in the house rose to frenzy comparable only with the coming and going of large crowds. On one occasion her daughter Leigh came down the stairs at night wondering who was in the living room. She could hear the noises up to the top floor! That night Mrs. Robinson was awakened six times by footsteps and closing doors.

Around that time also, her father-in-law reported a strange experience in his room on the second floor. He was watching television when his door opened late one night, and a woman came in. He was so startled by this unexpected visitor, and she disappeared again so quickly, he did not observe her too closely, but he thought she had either long black hair or a black veil. There was of course no one of that description in the house at the time.

Then there were those moments when an invisible rocking chair in the living room would rock by itself as if someone were in it.

Just prior to our visit, Mrs. Robinson's patience was being sorely tried. It was the week of April 4, and we had already announced our coming about a week or so afterward. Mrs. Robinson was on the cellar stairs when she heard a clicking sound and looked up. A rotisserie rack was sailing down toward her! Because she had looked up, she was able to duck, and the missile landed on the stairs instead of on her head. But she thought this just too much. Opening doors, well, all right, but rotisserie racks? It was high time we came down to see her.

I carefully went all over the house, examining the walls, floors, and especially the doors. They were for the most part heavy hinged doors, the kind that do not slide easily but require a healthy push before they will move. We looked into the back room and admired the beams, and I must confess I felt very uneasy in that part of the house. Both Catherine and I had an oppressive feeling, as if we were in the presence of something tragic, though unseen, and we could not get out of there fast enough.

I promised the Robinsons to return with a good psychometrist and perhaps have a go at trance, too, if I could get Mrs. Leek to come down with me on her next visit east. The prospect of finding out what it was that made their house so lively, and perhaps even learn more about its colorful past, made the mysterious noises more bearable for the Robinsons, and they promised to be patient and bear with me until I could make the required arrangements.

Finally Mrs. Leek and I were planning to appear on Murray Burnett's radio program together, and when I mentioned what else we intended doing in the area, Murray's eyes lit up and he offered to include himself in the expedition and drive us to and fro.

The offer was gladly accepted, and after a dinner at one of Murray's favorite places—during which not a word was exchanged about the Robinson house—we were off in search of adventure in his car. "It it's one thing I do well," he intoned, as we shot out onto the expressway, "it's driving an automobile." He did indeed. He drove with verve and so fast we missed the proper exit, and before long we found ourselves at a place called King of Prussia, where even a Prussian would have been lost.

We shrugged our combined shoulders and turned around, trying to retrace our steps. Murray assured me he knew the way and would have us at the Robinson house in no time at all. There was a time problem, for we all had to be back in the studio by eleven so that we could do the radio program that night. But the evening was still young and the Pennsylvania countryside lovely.

It was just as well that it was, for we got to see a good deal of it that evening. There was some confusion between Roosevelt Boulevard and Roosevelt Avenue, and the directions I had faithfully written down were being interpreted by us now the way two of Rommel's Afrika Korps officers must have studied the caravan routes.

"We should have turned off where we didn't," I finally remarked, and Murray nodded grimly. The time was about an hour after our appointed hour. No doubt the Robinsons must be thinking we're lost, I thought. At least I hoped that that's what they would think, not that we had abandoned *the project*.

The neighborhood seemed vaguely familiar now; no doubt it was. We had been through it several times already that same evening. Were the "forces" that kept opening and closing doors at the Robinson homestead preventing our coming so that they could continue to enjoy their anonymity?

When you're lost in Pennsylvania, you're really lost. But now Murray came to a decision. He turned north and we entered an entirely different part of town. It bore no similarity to the direction in which we wanted to go, but at least it was a well-lit section of town. I began to understand Murray's strategy: He was hoping we would run across someone—no, that's an unhappy word—*find* someone who just might know which way Somerton was. We met several motorists who didn't and several others who thought they did but really didn't, as we found out when we tried to follow their directions.

Ultimately, Murray did the smart thing: He hailed the first cop he saw and identified himself, not without pride. Everybody in Philadelphia knew his radio show.

"We're lost, officer," he announced, and explained our predicament.

"It's Mercury retrograding," Sybil mumbled from the back seat. All during our wild ghost chase she had insisted that astrologically speaking it was not at all surprising that we had gotten lost.

"Beg your pardon?" the officer said, and looked inside.

"Never mind Mercury," Murray said impatiently, "will you please show us the way?"

"I'll do better than that, sir," the policeman beamed back, "I'll personally escort you."

And so it came to pass that we followed a siren-tooting patrol car through the thick and thin of suburban Philadelphia.

Suddenly, the car in front of us halted. Murray proved how skillful a driver he really was. He did not hit anyone when he pulled up short. He merely jumbled *us*.

"Anything wrong, officer?" Murray asked, a bit nervously. It was half past nine now.

"My boundary," the officer explained. "I've already telephoned for my colleague to take you on further."

We sat and waited another ten minutes, then another police car came up and whisked us in practically no time to our destination. When the Robinsons saw the police car escort us to their house, they began to wonder what on earth we had been up to. But they were glad to see us, and quickly we entered the house. Sybil was hysterical with laughter by now, and if we had had something to drink en route, the whole odyssey might have been a jolly good party. But now her face froze as she entered the downstairs portion of the house. I watched her change expression, but before I had a chance to question her, she went to the lady's room. On emerging from it she reported that the first word that had impressed itself upon her was a name—"Ross."

She explained that she felt the strongest influence of this person to the right of the fireplace in the oldest part of the house, so I decided we should go to that area and see what else she might pick up.

Although the house itself was started in 1732, the particular section we were in had definitely been dated to 1755 by local historians, all of whom admired the Robinson house as a showcase and example of early American houses.

"Seventeen forty-six is what I get," Sybil commented.

"Sybil's underbidding you," I remarked to Mrs. Robinson.

"This is some kind of a meeting place," Sybil continued her appraisal of the room, "many people come here . . . 1744 . . . and the name Ross. The whole house has an atmosphere which is not unpleasant, but rather *alive*."

Just as Mrs. Robinson had felt on first contact with the house, I thought. As for the meeting place, I later found out that the house was used as a Quaker meeting house in the 1740s and later, and even today the "Byberry Friends" meet down the road! John Worthington, the first owner of the house, was an overseer for the meeting house in 1752.

"There are many impressions here," Sybil explained as she psychometrized the room more closely, "many people meeting here, but this is superimposed on one dominant male person, this Ross."

After a moment of further walking about, she added, "The date 1774 seems to be very important."

She pointed at a "closet" to the right of the ancient fireplace, and explained that this personality seemed to be strongest there.

"It's a staircase," Mrs. Robinson volunteered, and opened the door of the "closet." Behind it a narrow, winding wooden staircase led to the upper floors.

I motioned to Sybil to sit down in a comfortable chair near the fireplace, and we grouped ourselves around her. We had perhaps thirty minutes left before we were to return to Philadelphia, but for the moment I did not worry about that. My main concern was the house: What would it tell us about its history? What tragedies took place here and what human emotions were spent in its old walls?

Soon we might know. Sybil was in deep trance within a matter of minutes.

"Ross," the voice speaking through Sybil said faintly now, "I'm Ross. John Ross. . . . Virtue in peace. . . ."

"Is this your house?"

"No."

"Then what are you doing here?"

"Praying. Hope for peace. Too much blood. People must pray for peace."

"Is there a war going on?"

"I say there's war . . . the enemies are gone. . . ."

"Are you a soldier?"

"Captain—John—Ross," the voice said, stressing each word as if it were painful to pronounce it.

"What regiment?" I shot back, knowing full well that regimental lists exist and can be checked out for names.

"Twenty-first."

"Cavalry or Infantry?"

"I—am—for—peace."

"But what branch of the Army were you in?"

"Twenty-first of Horse."

This is an old English expression for cavalry.

"Who is your superior officer?" I asked.

"Colonel Moss is bad . . . he must pray. . . ."

"Who commands?"

"Albright."

"Where did you serve?"

"Battle . . . here. . . ."

He claimed to be thirty-eight years old, having been born in 1726. This would make him thirty-eight in the year 1764. His place of birth was a little place named Verruck, in Holstein, and when he said this I detected a very faint trace of a foreign accent in the entranced voice of the medium.

"Are you German then?" I asked.

"German?" he asked, not comprehending.

"Are you American?"

"American—is good," he said, with appreciation in his voice. Evidently we had before us a mercenary of the British Army.

"Are you British?" I tried.

"Never!" he hissed back.

"Whom do you serve?"

"The thirteen . . . pray. . . ."

Was he referring to the thirteen colonies, the name by which the young republic was indeed known during the revolutionary war?

"This Albrecht. . . . What is his first name?"

"Dee-an-no . . . I don't like him. . . . Peace for this country!!! It was meant for peace."

I could not make out what he meant by Dee-an-no, or what sounded like it. I then questioned the personality whether he was hurt.

"I wait for them to fetch me," he explained, haltingly, "sickness, make way for me!"

"Why are you in this house—what is there here?"

"Meeting place to pray."

"What religion are you?"

"Religion of peace and silence."

Suddenly, the medium broke into almost uncontrollable sighs and cries of pain. Tears flowed freely from Sybil's closed eyes. The memory of something dreadful must have returned to the communicator.

"I'm dying . . . hands hurt. . . . Where is my hand?"

You could almost see the severed hand, and the broken tone of voice realizing the loss made it the more immediate and dramatic.

"I—am—for peace. . . ."

"What sort of people come here?"

"Silent people. To meditate."

What better way to describe a Quaker meeting house?

"Don't stop praying," he beseeched us.

We promised to pray for him. But would he describe his activities in this house?

"Send for the Friend . . . dying."

He wanted spiritual guidance, now that he was at death's door. The term Friend is the official name for what we now call a Quaker.

Was there someone he wanted us to send for?

"William Proser . . . my brother . . . in England."

"Were you born in England?"

"No. William."

"He is your brother?"

"All—men—are—brothers."

He seemed to have trouble speaking. I started to explain what our mission was and that we wanted to help him find the elusive peace he so longed for.

"Name some of your fellow officers in the regiment," I then requested.

"Erich Gerhardt," the voice said. "Lieutenant Gerhardt."

"Was he in the cavalry? What regiment?"

"My—cavalry—Twenty-first—"

"What year did you serve together? What year are we in now?"

"Seventy-four."

"Where are you stationed?"

Sybil was completely immersed in the past now, with her face no longer hers; instead, we were watching a man in deep agony, struggling to speak again. Murray Burnett had his fingers at his lips, his eyes focused on the medium. It was clear he had never witnessed anything like it, and the extraordinary scene before him was bound to leave a deep and lasting impression, as indeed it did.

But the question went unanswered. Instead, Sybil was suddenly back again, or part of her, anyway. She seemed strangely distraught, however.

"Hands are asleep," she murmured, and I quickly placed her back into the hypnotic state so that the personality of Captain Ross might continue his testimony.

"Get me out, get me out," Sybil screamed now, "my hands . . . my hands are asleep. . . ."

I realized that the severed hand or hands of the Colonial soldier had left a strong imprint. Quickly I suggested that she go back into trance. I then recalled her to her own self, suggesting at the same time that no memory of the trance remain in her conscious mind.

Pearls of sweat stood on Sybil's forehead as she opened her eyes. But she was in the clear. Nothing of the preceding hour had remained in her memory. After a moment of heavy silence, we rose. It was time to return to the city, but Murray did not care. He knew that his producer, Ted Reinhart, would stall for time by playing a tape, if need be. The Robinsons offered us a quick cup of coffee, which tasted even more delicious than it must have been, under the circumstances. Everybody was very tense and I thought how wise it had been of Mrs. Robinson to keep the children away from the séance.

Hurriedly, we picked up our gear and drove back to the station. It took us about one-fifth of the time it had taken us to come out. Murray Burnett showed his skill behind the wheel as he literally flew along the expressway. Traffic was light at this hour and we managed to get back just as the announcer said, "And now, ladies and gentlemen, Murray Burnett and his guests. . . ."

As if nothing had happened, we strode onto the platform and did a full hour of light banter. By the time we left Philadelphia to return to New York, though, Sybil was exhausted. When we staggered out of our coaches in New York, it was well past one in the morning. The silence of the night was a welcome relief from the turbulent atmosphere of the early evening.

The following day I started to research the material obtained in the Robinson homestead.

To begin with, the Robinsons were able to trace previous ownership back only to 1841, although the local historical society assured her that it was built in 1732. The early records are often sketchy or no longer in existence because so many wars—both of foreign origin and Indian— have been fought around the area, not counting fire and just plain carelessness.

The Robinsons were the ninth family to own the place since the Civil War period. Prior to that the only thing known for certain was that it was a Quaker meeting house, and this fit in with the references Sybil had made in trance.

But what about Ross?

The gentleman had claimed that he was Captain John Ross, and the year, at the beginning of our conversation, was 1764.

In W. C. Ford's *British Officers Serving in America 1754–1774*, I found, on page 88, that there was a certain Captain John Ross, commissioned November 8, 1764. This man of course was a Tory, that is, he would have fought on the side of the British. Now the Revolutionary War started only in April 1775, and the man had expressed a dislike for the British and admiration for the "thirteen," the American colonies. Had he somehow switched sides during the intervening years? If he was a German mercenary, this would not have been at all surprising. Many of these men, often brought here against their desire, either left the British armies or even switched sides. Later on he referred to the date 1774, and Sybil had said it was important. At that time the war was already brewing even though no overt acts had happened. But the atmosphere in this area was tense. It was the seat of the Continental Congress, and skirmishes between Tories and Revolutionaries were not uncommon, although they were on a small or even individual level. What traumatic experience had happened to Captain Ross at that time? Did he lose his hands then?

I needed additional proof for his identity, of course. The name John Ross is fairly common. A John Ross was Betsy Ross's husband. He was guarding munitions on the Philadelphia water-front one night in 1776 when the munitions and Ross blew up. Another John Ross was a purchasing agent for the Continental Army, and he used much of his own money in the process. Although Robert Morris later tried to help him get his money back, he never really did, and only a year ago his descendants petitioned Congress for payment of this ancient debt of honor. Neither of these was our man, I felt, especially so as I recalled his German accent and the claim that he was born in a little place called Verruck in Holstein. That place name really had me stumped, but with the help of a librarian at the New York Public Library I got hold of some German source books. There is a tiny hamlet near Oldesloe, Holstein, called Viertbruch. An English-speaking person would pronounce this more like "Vertbrook." Although it is not on any ordinary map, it is listed in Mueller's *Grosses Deutsches Wortbuch*, published in Wuppertal in 1958, on page 1008.

Proser, his brother's name, is a German name. Why had he adopted an English name? Perhaps he had spent many years in England and felt it more expedient. He also mentioned belonging to the 21st Cavalry Regiment. The Captain John Ross I found in the records served in the 31st, not the 21st. On the other hand, there is, curiously enough, another Ross, first name David, listed for the 21st Regiment for the period in question, 1774.

I could not trace the superior named Albright or Albrecht, not knowing whether this was someone German or English. Since the first name given us by the communicator was unclear, I can't even be sure if the Philip Albright, a captain in the Pennsylvania Rifles 1776-1777, according to F. B. Heitman, *Historical Register of the Continental Army during the War of the Revolution*, is this man. This Philip Albright was a rebel, and if he was only a captain in 1776 he could not have been John Ross's commanding officer in 1774, unless he had changed sides, of course.

I was more successful with the fellow officer Lieutenant "Gerhardt," who also served in "his" 21st Regiment, Ross had claimed. Spellings of names at that period are pretty free, of course, and as I only heard the names without any indication as to proper spelling, we must make allowances for differences in the letters of these names. I did trace a Brevet Lieutenant Gerard (first name not given) of the Dragoons, a cavalry regiment, who served in the Pulaski Legion from September 3, 1778 to 1782.

Is this our man? Did he change sides after the Revolutionary War started in earnest? He could have been a regimental comrade of John Ross in 1774 and prior. The source for this man's data is F. B. Heitman's *Historical Register of the Continental Army*, Volume 1775-1783, page 189. The Pulaski Legion was not restricted to Polish volunteers who fought for the new republic, but it accepted voluntary help from any quarters, even former Britishers or mercenaries so long as they wanted to fight for a free America. Many Germans also served in that legion.

The Colonel Moss who was "bad" might have been Colonel Moses Allen, a Tory, who was from this area and who died February 8, 1779. He is listed in Saffell's *Records of the Revolutionary War*.

It was a confusing period in our history, and men changed their minds and sides as the need of the times demanded. Had the unfortunate soldier whom we had found trapped here in this erstwhile Quaker meeting house been one of those who wanted to get out from under, first to join what he considered "the good boys," and then, repelled by the continuing bloodshed, could he not even accept *their* war? Had he become religiously aware through his Quaker contacts and had he been made a pacifist by them? Very likely, if one is to judge the words of the colonial soldier from the year 1774 as an indication. His plea for peace sounds almost as if it could be spoken today.

Captain John Ross was not an important historical figure, nor was he embroiled in an event of great significance in the overall development of the United States of America. But this very anonymity made him a good subject for our psychometric experiment. Sybil Leek surely could not have known of Captain Ross, his comrades, and the Quaker connections of the old house on Byberry Road. It was her psychic sense that probed into the impressions left behind by history as it passed through and onward relentlessly, coating the house on Byberry Road with an indelible layer of human emotions and conflict.

I sincerely hope we managed to "decommission" Captain Ross in the process of our contact, to give him that much-desired "peace and silence" at last.

Mr. Hulse's Psychic Experiences

George Hulse is a quiet, soft-spoken gentleman who lives in Baltimore, Maryland, and deals in real estate. Now if there is any profession with its feet more firmly on the ground than real estate, I wouldn't know it. Mr. Hulse is a typical member of his profession, not given to guesswork or fantasy, but who had, nevertheless, learned to cope with some extraordinary facets of his personality, abilities which do not seem as substantial as his ability to appraise the value of a house or a piece of land, but which, nevertheless, partake of a higher reality, and he has learned to live with it.

Originally from Liverpool, England, he arrived in the United States in June, 1962. Hulse worked at a variety of professions; he's worked on ships, he's worked on the quays, in offices, as a salesman, and even as a truck driver. During World War II, he was a tail-gunner in the Royal Air Force and was wounded in August, 1941. Although he had some ESP experiences in his younger years, he would not accept them as valid. The first thing he remembers clearly happened when he was only a child.

He had been in bed asleep when he awoke and saw the figure of his grandmother standing at the side of the bed. The six-year-old George was his grandmother's favorite. He had given her a nickname, Pepper, because his grandmother used to take snuff and he thought she was taking pepper. From that evolved her peculiar nickname. Since George knew that his grandmother was dead, and yet he saw her standing next to his bed, he let out a yell and his mother came running into the bedroom. But she didn't persuade the little boy that he had dreamt it, but merely told him that if grandmother had come to see him, it was just to make sure that he was all right. As a matter of fact, she might have been telling the truth: shortly afterward, George contracted scarlet fever and had to go to a hospital.

Even when he was in his teens, George scoffed at the idea that there was anything to psychic phenomena. When his sister invited a medium to come to their house, George scoffed at the idea of a seance, and warned his sister not to meddle in such nonsense. However, in 1937, he awakened one night from deep sleep, and, still in a state bordering on sleep, but half-awke, he saw a vision of marching soldiers, with guns and other equipment. He was lying flat on his bed at the time, and as he looked up toward the ceiling, he saw this vision which reminded him of a television image. The soldiers wore British uniforms, of pre-World War II days, khaki, and puttees, which were still worn on the legs of British soldiers in those days. The men seemed to be advancing over rough ground, and, George thought, when he saw this vision, whether his mind was playing him tricks. But he had not been to any movies, not seen any war pictures, nor discussed the subject of war with anyone prior to having this vision.

During the year he had the same vision again; three times more, in fact, and always in total silence. The second time he had the vision, the word *war* seemed to be flashed across his mental horizon, like a newspaper headline. When it happened for the fourth time that year, it seemed more urgent. Yet, the vision was almost identical with the three previous ones.

Two years later George's vision became reality, when World War II broke out. But he was not one of the marching soldiers of his vision, since he joined the Royal Navy in September, 1939. He considered the visions a warning and at the time discussed them freely with his parents. During the War, when he was married, his wife was sharing a house with one of her sisters whose husband was also away in the Forces. But George wanted a house of his own, once he would be done with war, and so he decided to look for one in the Boodle section of Liverpool. He found just what he had in mind in a little row of houses right in the center of the district.

No sooner found than rented, she and his wife moved in on a Friday, and as soon as the movers had left, he and his wife worked like beavers to set up the beds and the rest of the furniture. But Saturday morning he had a terrible feeling that he had to get out of the house immediately. Giving in to his impulse, he jumped on his motorcycle, raced back to the people who had moved them in, and asked them to come back and take the furniture back where they had brought it from. The movers shook their heads, but did what he requested. That night there was a tremendous air raid on Liverpool; and, after it was over, Hulse jumped back on his motorcycle and went down to where the house stood. There was only rubble there now: the house had taken a direct hit.

Although Mr. Hulse's wife thought him crazy when he decided to move before even settling down in the house, she was no longer as skeptical after she learned that his psychic awareness had saved their lives. His psychic ability had been helpful to him many times in his life. One year, in October, he had a vision that his mother would die the following February; he saw the roads which the funeral procession would be taking, and the cemetery, and the kind of weather it would be on that day. Consequently, he was prepared for it and when it came to pass, exactly as he had foreseen it in his vision, he was able to withstand the emotional shock better. At the time, Mr. Hulse was living in Australia while his mother made her home in England: nevertheless, the impression of her impending passing was so strong it crossed both time and space without difficulty.

But not all of Mr. Hulse's psychic experiences were on the grim side. After he had become a widower in Australia, and returned to England, he had married again, this time an American. His wife's family wanted him to come to the United States, and since he had made quite a bit of money as a salesman in Australia, he decided to do so. But after he had figuredd out the fare for the family, he realized that there wouldn't be too much left beyond that. He was in the habit of going to Bingo games in Liverpool every Thursday evening. One particular Thursday evening, he left his sister after the Bingo, and went to his late mother's home. There he sat in what used to be her chair and suddenly had a vision, in which he saw himself win the following week's Bingo.

It was a very strange feeling, a picture suspended in front of the wall, lasting perhaps forty-five seconds, but clearly visible to his eyes. This gave him enough of a chance to study the vision in detail: he saw a man in a brown suit, with his face turned away from him, and he knew that this was the man in charge of handing out the prizes. He knew this was the Jackpot Night, next Friday, and as he looked closer, he saw the man in the brown suit put the amount of the winnings on a blackboard. Unfortunately, he was unable to make out whether the amount was three hundred forty or three hundred and four pounds, but he was sure it was beyond three hundred pounds.

The next morning Mr. Hulse telephoned his sister and told her that he was going to win the Bingo the following week. She laughed at this preposterous idea, but he assured her that he meant it. The following Friday the entire family went to the Bingo, instead of the usual Thursday night, since they wanted to be present when Mr. Hulse won the big prize. When they got on line for tickets, Mr. Hulse turned to one of the ushers and assured him that he was going to win the jackpot that evening. The man laughed, of course, but again Mr. Hulse assured him that he would.

When he got to the ticket window, and picked up the tickets to play Bingo, they felt very hot in his hand. Quickly he looked at the girl selling tickets and said, "Now look at me very close, miss, because I'm going to win the jackpot this evening." It never occurred to him that he might be accused of fixing the game, but then there was no possibility of that, since an ordinary player like himself had no access to the machinery where the game was decided.

When he returned to his seat, he realized that he had forgotten to buy some tickets for his sister, and he was about to hand her two of those he had bought for himself. At that moment he had the feeling of a tremendous roaring in his ears, and he heard a voice saying to him, "No! Do not do this." He recognized the voice as that of his late wife. Even though the ticket line was by now several blocks long, he went back on line to get two new tickets for his sister. Then they settled down to play the game. The last game of the evening was to be the jackpot, and when the man came out to put the figures on the board, there he was, the man of his vision: brown suit and all. The actual amount of the jackpot was 347.17 pounds.

Sure enough, Mr. Hulse had the winning ticket. When he walked out into the aisle to claim his prize, the usher looked at him in complete surprise, and said, "This is the man who said he was going to win," and when he passed the girl who had sold him the tickets, she, too, recognized him and shook her head. Fate had been kind to him: now he had all the money he needed to go to America.

After Mr. Hulse had settled down in Baltimore, it happened that he had to work half a day on a warm Saturday. His wife had gone to the beach with a sister and another friend and their children, and had left a note informing him that they would be home by four o'clock in the afternoon. Mr. Hulse likes punctuality, so promptly at four o'clock he telephoned his home, but received no answer. When he called back ten minutes later and again at half-past four, there still was no answer, so he became somewhat annoyed, if not worried. He slammed down the phone and became angry, and as he was sitting in his office, he had a

vision of his living room as big as a picture. It seemed as if he were looking at a giant TV screen. He saw the beach and his wife sitting on it,
and to her left was the friend, and the children were playing around
them; but lying on the sand in front of them were two men with their
chins resting on their hands, and talking to the ladies. He even observed
that his wife was wearing a black bathing suit and that one of the men
had on a red speckled pair of shorts.

Ten minutes to five, he telephoned his home again, and this time
his wife answered. When he informed her as to what she had been
doing the previous hour, she accused him of spying on her. But all the
details of his vision checked out correctly. At the time, Mr. Hulse's wife
found it difficult to accept the psychic explanation, and continued to
suspect that her husband was spying on her. However, she changed her
mind about this some time thereafter, when they were sitting in the
kitchen one evening, having a cup of tea before going to bed.

Suddenly the kitchen turned into an icebox, for no apparent reason,
and as they noticed the sudden chill, Mr. Hulse saw a vision appearing
in the doorway, out of nowhere, and pointed it out to his wife. There,
in their doorway, stood a woman, and he went on to describe her face
and apparel in great detail. As he did so, his wife turned white with
emotion, the apparition he had described was that of her late mother,
who had passed away several years before. Hulse had never met her.

Hulse uses his psychic gift whenever it can be useful; for instance,
he knows way ahead of time whether he's going to make a sale or not.
In each instance, his hunches have been correct. When he finds that a
certain transaction will not jell, he doesn't try to push it through, but
walks away from it, letting another salesman handle it. In July of 1971
he heard a warning voice in his ear, telling him not to let his wife use
the car. He tried to confirm the inner voice by using the Ouija board,
and a communicator identifying himself as Mr. Hulse's late father, confirmed the fact that the car should not be used.

So Mrs. Hulse used her sister's car that afternoon, but they had an accident just the same. When the spirit advisor had said, don't use the car that afternoon, he meant don't go at all, but the Hulses thought it merely meant their particular car. Fortunately, no one was seriously hurt.

A Visit With The Spirited Jefferson

"This typical pre-Revolutionary tavern was a favorite stopping place for travelers," the official guide to Charlottesville says. "With its colonial furniture and china, its beamed and paneled rooms, it appears much the way it did in the days when Jefferson and Monroe were visitors. Monroe writes of entertaining Lafayette as his guest at dinner here, and General Andrew Jackson, fresh from his victory at New Orleans, stopped over on his way to Washington."

The guide, however, does not mention that the tavern was moved a considerable distance from its original place to a much more accessible location where the tourist trade could benefit from it more. Regardless of this comparatively recent change of position, the tavern is exactly as it was, with everything inside, including its ghosts, intact. At the original site, it was surrounded by trees which framed it and sometimes towered over it. At the new site, facing the road, it looks out into the Virginia countryside almost like a manor house. One walks up to the wooden structure over a number of steps and enters the old tavern to the left or, if one prefers, the pub to the right, which is nowadays a coffee shop. Taverns in the eighteenth and early nineteenth centuries were not simply bars or inns; they were meeting places where people could talk freely, sometimes about political subjects. They were used as headquarters for Revolutionary movements or for invading military forces. Most taverns of any size had ballrooms in which the social functions of the area could be held. Only a few private individuals were wealthy enough to have their own ballrooms built into their manor houses.

What is fortunate about Michie Tavern is the fact that everything is pretty much as it was in the eighteenth century, and whatever restorations have been undertaken are completely authentic. The furniture and cooking utensils, the tools of the innkeeper, the porcelain, the china, the metal objects are all of the period, whether they had been in the house or not. As is customary with historical restorations or preservations, whatever is missing in the house is supplied by painstaking historical research, and objects of the same period and the same area are substituted for those presumably lost during the intervening period.

On my first visit to Charlottesville in 1964, Virginia Cloud had wanted me to visit the tavern, but somehow the schedule did not permit it then. This time the four of us arrived in mid-morning, in order to see the tavern before the tourists came—the luncheon crowd might make an interview with the current manager of the coffee shop difficult. The tavern has three floors and a large number of rooms, so we would need the two hours we had allowed ourselves for the visit. After looking at the downstairs part of the tavern, with its "common" kitchen and the over-long wooden table where two dozen people could be fed, we mounted the stairs to the second floor.

Ingrid kept looking into various rooms, sniffing out the psychic presences, as it were, while I followed close behind. Horace Burr and Virginia Cloud kept a respectable distance, as if trying not to "frighten" the ghosts away. That was all right with me, because I did not want Ingrid to tap the unconscious of either one of these very knowledgeable people.

Finally we arrived in the third-floor ballroom of the old tavern. I asked Ingrid what she had felt in the various rooms below. "In the pink room on the second floor I felt an argument or some sort of strife but nothing special in any of the other rooms."

"What about this big ballroom?"

"I can see a lot of people around here. There is a gay atmosphere, and I think important people came here; it is rather exclusive, this room. I think it was used just on special occasions."

By now I had waved Horace and Virginia to come closer, since it had become obvious to me that they wanted very much to hear what Ingrid was saying. Possibly new material might come to light, unknown to both of these historians, in which case they might verify it later on or comment upon it on the spot.

"I'm impressed with an argument over a woman here," Ingrid continued. "It has to do with one of the dignitaries, and it is about one of their wives."

"How does the argument end?"

"I think they just had a quick argument here, about her infidelity."

"Who are the people involved?"

"I think Hamilton. I don't know the woman's name."

"Who is the other man?"

"I think Jefferson was here."

"Try to get as much of the argument as you can."

Ingrid closed her eyes, sat down in a chair generally off limits to visitors, and tried to tune in on the past. "I get the argument as a real embarrassment," she began. "The woman is frail, she has a long dress on with lace at the top part around the neck, her hair is light brown."

"Does she take part in the argument?"

"Yes she has to side with her husband."

"Describe her husband."

"I can't see his face, but he is dressed in a brocade jacket pulled back with buttons down the front and breeches. It is a very fancy outfit."

"How does it all end?"

"Well, nothing more is said. It is just a terrible embarrassment."

"Is this some sort of special occasion? Are there other people here?"

"Yes, oh, yes. It is like an anniversary or something of that sort. Perhaps a political anniversary of some kind. There is music and dancing and candlelight."

While Ingrid is speaking, in an almost inaudible voice, Horace and Virginia were straining to hear what she was saying but not being very successful at it. At this point Horace waved to me, and I tiptoed over to him. "Ask her to get the period a little closer," he whispered in my ear.

I went back to Ingrid and put the question to her. "I think it was toward the end of the war," she said, "toward the very end of it. For some time now I've had the figure 1781 impressed on my mind."

Since nothing further seemed to be forthcoming from Ingrid at this point, I asked her to relax and come back to the present, so that we could discuss her impressions freely.

"The name Hamilton is impossible in this connection," Horace Burr began. But I was quick to interject that the name Hamilton was fairly common in the late eighteenth and early nineteenth centuries and that Ingrid need not have referred to *the* Alexander Hamilton. "Jefferson was here many times, and he could have been involved in this," Burr continued. "I think I know who the other man might have been. But could we, just for once, try questioning the medium on specific issues?"

Neither Ingrid nor I objected, and Horace proceeded to ask Ingrid to identify the couple she had felt in the ballroom. Ingrid threw her head back for a moment, closed her eyes, and then replied, "The man is very prominent in politics, one of the big three or four at the time, and one of the reasons this is all so embarrassing, from what I get, is that the other man is of much lower caliber. He is not one of the big leaders; he may be an officer or something like that."

While Ingrid was speaking, slowly, as it were, I again felt the strange sense of transportation, of looking back in time, which had been coming to me more and more often recently, always unsought and usually one of fleeting duration. "For what it is worth," I said, "while Ingrid is speaking, I also get a very vague impression that all this has something to do with two sisters. It concerns a rivalry between two sisters."

"The man's outfit," Ingrid continued her narrative, "was sort of gold and white brocade and very fancy. He was the husband. I don't see the other man."

Horace seemed unusually agitated at this. "Tell me, did this couple live in this vicinity or did they come from far away on a special anniversary?"

"They lived in the vicinity and came just for the evening."

"Well, Horace?" I said, getting more and more curious, since he was apparently driving in a specific direction. "What was this all about?"

For once, Horace enjoyed being the center of attraction. "Well, it was a hot and heavy situation, all right. The couple were Mr. and Mrs. John Walker—he was the son of Dr. Walker of Castle Hill. And the man, who wasn't here, was Jefferson himself. Ingrid is right in saying that they lived in the vicinity—Castle Hill is not far away from here."

"But what about the special festivity that brought them all together here?"

Horace wasn't sure what it could have been, but Virginia, in great excitement, broke in here. "It was in this room that the waltz was danced for the first time in America. A young man had come from France dressed in very fancy clothes. The lady he danced with was a closely chaperoned girl from Charlottesville. She was very young, and she danced the waltz with this young man, and everybody in Charlottesville was shocked. The news went around town that the young lady had danced with a man holding her, and that was just terrible at the time. Perhaps that was the occasion. Michie Tavern was a stopover for stagecoaches, and Jefferson and the local people would meet here to get their news. Downstairs was the meeting room, but up there in the ballroom the more special events took place, such as the introduction of the waltz."

I turned to Horace Burr. "How is it that this tavern no longer stands on the original site? I understand it has been moved here for easier tourist access."

"Yes," Horace replied. "The building originally stood near the airport. In fact, the present airport is on part of the old estate that belonged to Colonel John Henry, the father of Patrick Henry. Young Patrick spent part of his boyhood there. Later, Colonel Henry sold the land to the Michies. This house was then their main house. It was on the old highway. In turn, they built themselves an elaborate mansion which is still standing and turned this house into a tavern. All the events we have been discussing took place while this building was on the old site. In 1926 it was moved here. Originally, I think the ballroom we are standing in now was just the loft of the old Henry house. They raised part of the roof to make it into a ballroom because they had no meeting room in the tavern."

In the attractively furnished coffee shop to the right of the main tavern, Mrs. Juanita Godfrey, the manager, served us steaming hot black coffee and sat down to chat with us. "Had anyone ever complained about unusual noises or other inexplicable manifestations in the tavern?" I asked.

"Some of the employees who work here at night do hear certain sounds they can't account for," Mrs. Godrey replied. "They will hear something and go and look, and there will be nothing there."

"In what part of the building?"

"All over, even in this area. This is a section of the slave quarters, and it is very old."

Mrs. Godfrey did not seem too keen on psychic experiences, I felt. To the best of her knowledge, no one had had any unusual experiences in the tavern. "What about the lady who slept here one night?" I inquired.

"You mean Mrs. Milton—yes, she slept here one night." But Mrs. Godfrey knew nothing of Mrs. Milton's experiences.

However, Virginia had met the lady, who was connected with the historical preservation effort of the community. "One night when Mrs. Milton was out of town," Virginia explained, "I slept in her room. At the time she confessed to me that she had heard footsteps frequently, especially on the stairway down."

"That is the area she slept in, yes," Mrs. Godfrey confirmed. "She slept in the ladies' parlor on the first floor."

"What about yourself, Virginia? Did *you* hear anything?"

"I heard noises, but the wood sometimes behaves very funny. She, however, said they were definitely footsteps. That was in 1961."

What had Ingrid unearthed in the ballroom of Michie Tavern? Was it merely the lingering imprint of America's first waltz, scandalous to the early Americans but innocent in the light of today? Or was it something more—an involvement between Mrs. Walker and the illustrious Thomas Jefferson? My image of the great American had always been that of a man above human frailties. But my eyes were to be opened still further on a most intriguing visit to Monticello, Jefferson's home.

"You're welcome to visit Monticello to continue the parapsychological research which you are conducting relative to the personalities of 1776," wrote James A. Bear, Jr., of the Thomas Jefferson Memorial Foundation, and he arranged for us to go to the popular tourist attraction after regular hours, to permit Ingrid the peace and tranquility necessary to tune in on the very fragile vibrations that might hang on from the past.

Jefferson, along with Benjamin Franklin, has become a popular historical figure these days: a play, a musical, and a musical film have brought him to life, showing him as the shy, dedicated, intellectual architect of the Declaration of Independence. Jefferson, the gentle Virginia farmer, the man who wants to free the slaves but is thwarted in his efforts by other Southerners; Jefferson, the ardent but bashful lover of his wife; Jefferson, the ideal of virtue and American patriotism—these are the images put across by the entertainment media, by countless books, and by the tourist authorities which try to entice vistors to come to Charlottesville and visit Jefferson's home, Monticello.

Even the German tourist service plugged itself into the Jefferson boom. "This is like a second mother country for me," Thomas Jefferson is quoted as saying while traveling down the Rhine. "Everything that isn't English in our country comes from here." Jefferson, compared the German Rhineland to certain portions of Maryland and Pennsylvania and pointed out that the second largest ethnic group in America at the time were Germans. In an article in the German language weekly *Aufbau*, Jefferson is described as the first prominent American tourist in the Rhineland. His visit took place in April 1788. At the time Jefferson was ambassador to Paris, and the Rhine journey allowed him to study agriculture, customs, and conditions on both sides of the Rhine. Unquestionably, Jefferson, along with Washington, Franklin, and Lincoln, represents one of the pillars of the American edifice.

Virginia Cloud, ever the avid historian of her area, points out that not only did Jefferson and John Adams have a close relationship as friends and political contemporaries but there were certain uncanny "coincidences" between their lives. For instance, both Jefferson and Adams died within hours of each other, Jefferson in Virginia and Adams in Massachusetts, on July 4, 1826—exactly fifty years to the day they had both signed the Declaration of Independence. Adams's last words were, "But Jefferson still lives." At the time that was no longer true, for Jefferson had died earlier in the day.

Jefferson's imprint is all over Charlottesville. Not only did the talented "Renaissance man" design his own home, Monticello, but he also designed the Rotunda, the focal point of the University of Virginia. Jefferson, Madison, and Monroe were members of the first governing board of the University, which is now famous for its school of medicine—and which, incidentally, is the leading university in the study of parapsychology, since Dr. Ian Stevenson teaches here.

On our way to Monticello we decided to visit the old Swan Tavern, which had some important links with Jefferson. The tavern is now used as a private club, but the directors graciously allowed us to come in, even the ladies, who are generally not admitted. Nothing in the appointments reminds one of the old tavern, since the place has been extensively remodeled to suit the requirements of the private club. At first we inspected the downstairs and smiled at several elderly gentlemen who hadn't the slightest idea why we were there. Then we went to the upper story and finally came to rest in a room to the rear of the building. As soon as Ingrid had seated herself in a comfortable chair in a corner, I closed the door and asked her what she felt about this place, of which she had no knowledge.

"I feel that people came here to talk things over in a lighter vein, perhaps over a few drinks."

"Was there anyone in particular who was outstanding among these people?"

"I keep thinking of Jefferson, and I'm seeing big mugs; most of the men have big mugs in front of them."

Considering that Ingrid did not know the past of the building as a tavern, this was pretty evidential. I asked her about Jefferson.

"I think he was the figurehead. This matter concerned him greatly, but I don't think it had anything to do with his own wealth or anything like that."

"At the time when this happened, was there a warlike action in progress?"

"Yes, I think it was on the outskirts of town. I have the feeling that somebody was trying to reach this place and that they were waiting for somebody, and yet they weren't really expecting that person."

Both Horace Burr and Virginia Cloud were visibly excited that Ingrid had put her finger on it, so to speak. Virginia had been championing the cause of the man about whom Ingrid had just spoken. "Virginians are always annoyed to hear about Paul Revere, who was actually an old man with a tired horse that left Revere to walk home," Virginia said, somewhat acidly, "while Jack Jouett did far more—he saved the lives of Thomas Jefferson and his legislators. Yet, outside of Virginia, few have ever heard of him."

"Perhaps Jouett didn't have as good a press agent as Paul Revere had in Longfellow, as you always say, Virginia," Burr commented. I asked Virginia to sum up the incident that Ingrid had touched on psychically.

"Jack Jouett was a native of Albermarle County and was of French Huguenot origin. His father, Captain John Jouette, owned this tavern."

"We think there is a chance that he also owned the Cuckoo Tavern in Louisa, forty miles from here," Burr interjected.

"Jouett had a son named Jack who stood six feet, four inches and weighed over two hundred pounds. He was an expert rider and one of those citizens who signed the oath of intelligence to the Commonwealth of Virginia in 1779.

"It was June 3, 1781, and the government had fled to Charlottesville from the advancing British troops. Most of Virginia was in British hands, and General Cornwallis very much wanted to capture the leaders of the Revolution, especially Thomas Jefferson, who had authored the Declaration of Independence, and Patrick Henry, whose motto, 'Give me liberty or give me death,' had so much contributed to the success of the Revolution. In charge of 250 cavalrymen was Sir Banastre Tarleton. His mission was to get to Charlottesville as quickly as possible to capture the leaders of the uprising. Tarleton was determined to cover the seventy miles' distance between Cornwallis's headquarters and Charlottesville in a single twenty-four-hour period, in order to surprise the leaders of the American independence movement.

"In the town of Louisa, forty miles distant from Charlottesville, he and his men stopped into the Cuckoo Tavern for a brief respite. Fate would have it that Jack Jouett was at the tavern at that moment, looking after his father's business. It was a very hot day for June, and the men were thirsty. Despite Tarleton's orders, their tongues loosened, and Jack Jouett was able to overhear their destination. Jack decided to outride them and warn Charlottesville. It was about ten P.M. when he got on his best horse, determined to take short cuts and side roads, while the British would have to stick to the main road. Fortunately, it was a moonlit night; otherwise he might not have made it in the rugged hill country.

"Meanwhile the British were moving ahead too, and around eleven o'clock they came to a halt on a plantation near Louisa. By two A.M. they had resumed their forward march. They paused again a few hours later to seize and burn a train of twelve wagons loaded with arms and clothing for the Continental troops in South Carolina. When dawn broke over Charlottesville, Jouette had left the British far behind. Arriving at Monticello, he dashed up to the front entrance to rouse Jefferson; however, Governor Jefferson, who was an early riser, had seen the rider tear up his driveway and met him at the door. Ever the gentleman, Jefferson offered the exhausted messenger a glass of wine before allowing him to proceed to Charlottesville proper, two miles farther on. There he roused the other members of the government, while Jefferson woke his family. Two hours later, when Tarleton came thundering into Charlottesville, the government of Virginia had vanished."

"That's quite a story, Virginia," I said.

"Of course," Burr added, "Tarleton and his men might have been here even earlier if it hadn't been for the fact that they first stopped at Castle Hill. Dr. and Mrs. Walker entertained them lavishly and served them a sumptuous breakfast. It was not only sumptuous but also delaying, and Dr. Walker played the perfect host to the hilt, showing Tarleton about the place despite the British commander's impatience, even to measuring Tarleton's orderly on the living-room door jamb.

This trooper was the tallest man in the British army and proved to be six feet, nine and one-quarter inches in height. Due to these and other delaying tactics—and there are hints that Mrs. Walker used her not inconsiderable charms as well to delay the vistors—the Walkers made Jack Jouett's ride a complete success. Several members of the legislature who were visiting Dr. Walker at the time were captured, but Jefferson and the bulk of the legislature, which had just begun to convene early in the morning, got away.

"You see, the legislature of Virginia met in this building, and Ingrid was entirely correct with her impressions. The members of the legislature knew, of course, that the British were not far away, but they weren't exactly expecting them here."

After Thomas Jefferson had taken refuge at the house of a certain Mr. Cole, where he was not likely to be found, Jouett went to his room at his father's tavern, the very house we were in. He had well deserved his rest. Among those who were hiding from British arrest was Patrick Henry. He arrived at a certain farmhouse and identified himself by saying, "I'm Patrick Henry." But the farmer's wife replied, "Oh, you couldn't be, because my husband is out there fighting, and Patrick Henry would be out there too." Henry managed to convince the farmer's wife that his life depended on his hiding in her house, and finally she understood. But it was toward the end of the Revolutionary War and the British knew very well that they had for all intents and purposes been beaten. Consequently, shortly afterward, Cornwallis suggested to the Virginia legislators that they return to Charlottesville to resume their offices.

It was time to proceed to Monticello; the afternoon sun was setting, and we would be arriving just after the last tourists had left. Monticello, which every schoolboy knows from its representation on the American five-cent piece, is probably one of the finest examples of American architecture, designed by Jefferson himself, who lies buried here in the family graveyard. It stands on a hill looking down into the valley of

Charlottesville, perhaps fifteen minutes from the town proper. Carefully landscaped grounds surround the house. Inside, the house is laid out in classical proportions. From the entrance hall with its famous clock, also designed by Jefferson, one enters a large, round room, the heart of the house. On both sides of this central area are rectangular rooms. To the left is a corner room, used as a study and library from where Jefferson, frequently early in the morning before anyone else was up, used to look out on the rolling hills of Virginia. Adjacent to it is a very small bedroom, almost a bunk. Thus, the entire west wing of the building is a self-contained apartment in which Jefferson could be active without interfering with the rest of his family. On the other side of the round central room is a large dining room leading to a terrace which, in turn, continues into an open walk with a magnificent view of the hillside. The furniture is Jefferson's own, as are the silver and china, some of it returned to Monticello in recent years by history-conscious citizens of the area who had purchased it in various ways.

The first room we visited was Jefferson's bedroom. Almost in awe herself, Ingrid touched the bedspread of what was once Thomas Jefferson's bed, then his desk and the books he had handled. "I feel his presence here," she said, "and I think he did a lot of his work in this room, a lot of planning and working things out, till the wee hours of the night." I don't think Ingrid knew that Jefferson was in the habit of doing just that, in this particular room.

I motioned Ingrid to sit down in one of Jefferson's chairs and try to capture whatever she might receive from the past. "I can see an awful lot of hard work, sleepless nights and turmoil. Other than that, nothing."

We went into the library next to the study. "I don't think he spent much time here really, just for reference." On we went to the dining room to the right of the round central room. "I think that was his favorite room, and he loved to meet people here socially." Then she added, "I get the words plum pudding and hot liquor."

"Well," Burr commented, "he loved the lighter things of life. He brought ice cream to America, and he squirted milk directly from the cow into a goblet to make it froth. He had a French palate. He liked what we used to call floating island, a very elaborate dessert."

"I see a lot of people. It is a friendly gathering with glittering glasses and candlelight," Ingrid said. "They are elegant but don't have on overcoats. I see their white silken shirts. I see them laughing and passing things around. Jefferson is at the table with white hair pulled back, leaning over and laughing."

The sun was setting, since it was getting toward half past six now, and we started to walk out the French glass doors onto the terrace. From there an open walk led around a sharp corner to a small building, perhaps twenty or twenty-five yards distant. Built in the small classical American style as Monticello itself, the building contained two fair-sized rooms, on two stories. The walk led to the entrance to the upper story, barricaded by an iron grillwork to keep tourists out. It allowed us to enter the room only partially, but sufficiently for Ingrid to get her bearings. Outside, the temperature sank rapidly as the evening approached. A wind had risen, and so it was pleasant to be inside the protective walls of the little house.

"Horace, where are we now?" I asked.

"We are in the honeymoon cottage where Thomas Jefferson brought his bride and lived at the time when his men were building Monticello. Jefferson and his family lived here at the very beginning, so you might say that whatever impressions there are here would be of the pre-Revolutionary part of Jefferson's life."

I turned to Ingrid and asked for her impressions. "I feel everything is very personal here and light, and I don't feel the tremendous strain in the planning of things I felt in the Monticello building. As I close my eyes, I get a funny feeling about a bouquet of flowers, some very strong and peculiar exotic flowers. They are either pink or light red and have a funny name, and I have the feeling that a woman involved in this impression is particularly fond of a specific kind of flower. He goes out of his way to get them for her, and I also get the feeling of a liking for a certain kind of chinaware or porcelain. Someone is a collector and wants to buy certain things, being a connoisseur, and wants to have little knick-knacks all over the place. I don't know if any of this makes any sense, but this is how I see it."

"It makes sense indeed," Horace Burr replied. "Jefferson did more to import rare trees and rare flowering shrubs than anyone else around here. In fact, he sent shipments back from France while he stayed there and indicated that they were so rare that if you planted them in one place they might not succeed. So he planted only a third at Monticello, a third at Verdant Lawn, which is an old estate belonging to a friend of his, and a third somewhere else in Virginia. It was his idea to plant them in three places to see if they would thrive in his Virginia."

"The name Rousseau comes to mind. Did he know anyone by that name?" Ingrid asked.

"Of course, he was much influenced by Rousseau."

"I also get the feeling of a flickering flame, a habit of staying up to all hours of the morning. Oh, and is there any historical record of an argument concerning this habit of his, between his wife and himself and some kind of peacemaking gesture on someone else's part?"

"I am sure there was an argument," Horace said, "but I doubt that there ever was a peacemaking gesture. You see, their marriage was not a blissful one; she was very wealthy and he spent her entire estate, just as he spent Dabney Carr's entire estate and George Short's entire estate. He went through estate after estate, including his own. Dabney Carr was his cousin, and he married Jefferson's sister, Martha. He was very wealthy, but Jefferson gathered up his sister and the children and brought them here after Carr's death. He then took over all the plantations and effects of Mr. Carr.

"Jefferson was a collector of things. He wrote these catalogues of his own collection, and when he died it was the largest collection in America. You are right about the porcelain, because it was terribly sophisticated at that time to be up on porcelain. The clipper trade was bringing in these rarities, and he liked to collect them."

Since Ingrid had scored so nicely up to now, I asked her whether she felt any particular emotional event connected with this little house.

"Well, I think the wife was not living on her level, her standard, and she was unhappy. It wasn't what she was used to. It wasn't grand enough. I think she had doubts about him and his plans."

"In what sense?"

"I think she was dubious about what would happen. She was worried that he was getting too involved, and she didn't like his political affiliations too well."

I turned to Horace for comments. To my surprise, Horace asked me to turn off my tape recorder since the information was of a highly confidential nature. However, he pointed out that the material could be found in *American Heritage*, and that I was free to tell the story in my own words.

Apparently, there had always been a problem between Jefferson and his wife concerning other women. His associations were many and varied. Perhaps the most lasting was with a beautiful young black girl, about the same age as his wife. She was the illegitimate natural child of W. Skelton, a local gentleman, and served as a personal maid to Mrs. Jefferson. Eventually, Jefferson had a number of children by this girl. He even took her to Paris. He would send for her. This went on for a number of years and eventually contributed to the disillusionment of this girl. She died in a little room upstairs, and they took the coffin up there some way, but when they put it together and got her into the coffin, it wouldn't come downstairs. They had to take all the windows out and lower her on a rope. And what was she doing up there in the first place? All this did not contribute to Mrs. Jefferson's happiness. The irony is that, after Jefferson's death, two of his mulatto children were sent to New Orleans and *sold* as prostitutes to pay his debts. There are said to be some descendants of that liaison still alive today, but you won't find any of this in American textbooks.

Gossip and legend intermingle in small towns and in the countryside. This is especially true when important historical figures are involved. So it is said that Jefferson did not die a natural death. Allegedly, he committed suicide by cutting his own throat. Toward the end of Jefferson's life, there was a bitter feud between himself and the Lewis family. Accusations and counteraccusations are said to have gone back and forth. Jefferson is said to have had Merriweather Lewis murdered and, prior to that, to have accused Mr. Lewis of a number of strange things that were not true. But none of these legends and rumors can be proved in terms of judicial procedure; when it comes to patriotic heroes of the American Revolution, the line between truth and fiction is always rather indistinct.

A Visit with Woodrow Wilson

The Washington *Post* may have published an occasional phantom story over the years, but not too many ghost stories. Thus it was with a degree of skepticism that I picked up a copy of that ebullient newspaper dated May 4, 1969. It had been sent to me by a well-meaning friend and fan living in Washington. Mrs. Charles Marwick, herself a writer and married to a medical writer, is of Scottish ancestry and quite prone to pick up a ghost story here and there.

The piece in question had attracted her attention as being a little bit above the usual cut of the journalistic approach to that sort of material. Generally, my newspaper colleagues like to make light of any psychic report, and if the witnesses are respectable, or at least rational on the surface of it, they will report the events but still add a funny tag line or two to make sure that no one takes their own attitude toward the supernatural too seriously.

Thus, when I saw the headline, "Playing Host to Ghosts?" I was worried. This looked like one of those light-hearted, corny approaches to the psychic, I thought, but when I started to read the report by Phil Casey I realized that the reporter was trying to be fair to both his editor and the ghosts.

The Woodrow Wilson House at 2340 S St. NW is a quiet, serene place most of the time, with only about 150 visitors a week, but sometimes at night there's more noise than Jose Vasquez, the house man, can stand.

Vasquez has been hearing queer, and sometimes loud, noises in the night a couple of times a year for the past four years, but they didn't bother him much until the stroke of midnight, Saturday, April 5.

"It was depressing, " he said. "If I were a nervous man, it would be very bad."

Vasquez, who is 32, is from Peru, speaks four languages, plays the piano and is a student at D. C. Teachers College, where he intends to major in psychology. He doesn't believe in ghosts, but he's finding it hard to hold that position, the way things are going around that house.

He was downstairs playing the piano that night, he said, and he was all alone (his wife, a practical nurse, was at work at the National Institutes of Health).

"I felt that someone was behind me, watching me," he said. "My neck felt funny. You know? But there was no one there. I looked."

Later, Vasquez was walking up to his fourth floor apartment when he heard something behind him on the third floor, near the bedrooms of the World War I President and his wife.

"The steps were loud," he said, "and heavy, like a man."

The footsteps went into Mrs. Wilson's bedroom, and Vasquez went in, too. He kept hearing the steps in the room, and was in a state of almost total unhappiness.

"I go to this corner," he said, going to the corner, "and I stand here and wait. I waited a long time and then I hear the steps again, going into the hall and to Mr. Wilson's bedroom. I follow."

At that point, listening to the heavy footsteps at the foot of the President's four-poster bed, Vasquez decided to hurry upstairs.

"And when I do, the steps they came running behind me," he said, "and they follow me, bump, bump, bump, up the stairs. I am very nervous."

The backstairway is iron, and noisy, which didn't help any, Vasquez said, but he went on up to this apartment.

And then, he heard no more footsteps and he was glad about that.

Once, some time back, Vasquez was in his tub when he heard some knock-

ing noises on the tub.

"I knock right back, like this," he said, thumpting the tub, "and the noise stops."

His wife has never heard the footsteps or the tub knocking, but she hears an occasional noise and sometimes she wakes up in the night under the impression that someone is standing at the foot of the bed. There never is anyone she can see.

I talked to Mr. Vasquez, and he sounded like a very nice, rational fellow. He had nothing to add to the story that had appeared in the *Post*, but he referred me to the curator of the Wilson House for permission to visit.

I contacted Ruth Dillon and patiently explained the purpose of my investigation. As much as I tried to stress the historic aspects of it, she already knew from my name what I was after, and to my surprise did not object; so long as I did not publish anything untrue, but she did not mind my talking about any specters that might be on the premises, famous or otherwise.

I knew very little about the late Woodrow Wilson myself, except what one generally knows of any President of the United States, and I made it a point not to read up on him. Instead I called Ethel Johnson Meyers, my good friend and many times my medium, and arranged for her to accompany me to Washington in the near future. Due to a sudden cancellation in Mrs. Meyers' busy schedule, the date we were able to set was May 6, 1969, three days after the reporter had written his article. A good friend of mine, Mrs. Nicole Jackson, offered to drive us around since I did not drive a car, and the three of us arrived at the Woodrow Wilson House at the appointed hour.

That hour was 11 A.M., on a sunny and very warm May 6. The house was majestic, even from the outside. It looked the very essence of a presidential mansion. It looked that way to me today, although I gather that in the days when this house was built, such houses were not considered ostentatious but rather ordinary elegant town houses for those who could afford them.

Now the property of the National Trust, the house has been turned into a museum, and visitors are admitted at certain hours of the day. Four stories high, it also boasts a magnificent garden in the back and offers the privacy of a country estate along with the convenience of a town house. It is difficult to accurately describe the style of this building. Built for Henry Parker Fairbanks in 1915, the red-brick Georgian house was designed by the late architect Waddy B. Wood. Late in 1920, as President Wilson's second term neared its end, Mrs. Wilson searched for an appropriate residence. She happened to be passing the house on S Street, which she is later quoted as describing as "an unpretentious, comfortable, dignified house, fitted to the needs of a gentleman." On December 14 of that year, according to the brochure published by the National Trust about the Woodrow Wilson House, Mr. Wilson insisted that his wife attend a concert, and when she returned, presented her with the deed to the property. The next day they visited the house, where Mr. Wilson gave her a piece of sod, representing the land, and the key to one of the doors, representing the house—telling her this was an old Scottish custom.

The Wilsons made certain changes, such as the installation of an elevator and the addition of a billiard room. They also constructed a brick garage and placed iron gates at the entrance to the drive. Some of the rooms were changed, and a large library was constructed to hold Mr. Wilson's eight thousand books. Today the library contains a large collection of items connected with President Wilson and his contemporaries. There are mainly presentation copies of books and documents.

President Wilson lived in the house with his second wife, Edith Bolling Wilson. She was a devoted companion to him during his last years, went to Europe with him to attend peace conferences, and generally traveled with the President. She liked to read to him and he, conversely, liked to read to her, and in general they were a very close and devoted couple.

At the end of his second term he retired to this house, and died here three years later on February 3, 1924. Mrs. Wilson, who later presented the house to the American People under the guardianship of the National Trust, also lived and died there on December 28, 1961, which happened to be the 105th anniversary of President Wilson's birth.

By and large the rooms have been kept as they were during their tenancy, with the sole addition of certain items such as furniture, antiquities, and documents pertaining to the Wilsons' careers and lifetimes. If the house is a museum, it doesn't look like one. It is more like a shrine—but not an ostentatious one—to what many consider a great American.

As is my custom, I let Ethel Meyers—who did not know she was in the Wilson House—roam the premises under investigation at will, so that she could get her psychic bearings. She walked to and fro, puzzled here, sure of something or other there, without saying anything. I followed her as close as I could. Finally, she walked up the stairs and came down again in a hurry, pointing up towards the top floors.

"What is it?" I asked Ethel.

"Someone up there," she mumbled, and looked at me.

"Let us go in here," I suggested, as some visitors were coming in through the front door. I did not want to create a sensation with my investigation, as I had promised to do the whole thing quietly and unobtrusively.

We stepped into a parlor to one side of the main entrance. There I asked Ethel to take a seat in one of the old chairs and try to give me her impressions of what she had just experienced upstairs.

At this point, the medium's control personality, Albert, took over.

"So many detached things are coming in. I'm getting the *presence* of an individual here. I haven't had an impression like this before, it seems. Heed kindly the light which we throw on this to you now. *That is a hymn*—'Lead, Kindly Light.'"

"Is there anything in this house that is causing disturbances?"

"There is restlessness, where those who remember certain things. They are like fertile fields, to create over a past that is not understood."

"Who is the communicator, do you think?"

Albert replied: "I would say it is *himself*, in the picture on the mantelpiece."

"What does he want you to do or say?"

"I heard him distinctly say that the family rows should not be made public. That those are thought levels in the house. Angry voices sometimes rise. There are also others who have things to say for themselves, beyond that."

"What is the row?"

"Let them speak for themselves."

"What is there that he wants to do—is there anything specific he would like us to know?"

"That the world going forward is more pleasant now than going for me backwards, because true statements are coming forth to make wider reach for man *when he shakes his hands across oceans with his neighbors.* So now they are, not before; they were in your back yard so to speak under the shade of other threes."

The "resident spirit" was now talking directly to us.

"I want to say, if you will give me audience while I am here, that this in my pleasurable moment, to lift the curtain to show you that the mortal enemy will become the great friend, soon now. That my puny dream of yesteryear has been gradually realized—the brotherhood of man. And it becomes clear, closer to the next century. It is here, for us on our side. I see it more clearly from here. I am not sure about that designated time. But it is the brotherhood of man, when the religious problem is lifted and the truth is seen, and all men stand equal to other men, neighbors, enemies."

"Who are you referring to?"

"I come back again to tell you, that the hands that will reach over the mighty ocean will soon clasp! Hands lean forward to grasp them. My puny dreams, my puny ideal, takes form, and I look upon it and I am proud as a small part but an integral part of that. It will bloom, the period of gestation is about over, when this will come to light. And I give great thanks to the withinness that I have had a small a part in the integral whole. I tell you it is all a part of the period of gestation before the dawn."

"When will the dawn come?"

"Just before the turn of the century. Eighty-eight, -nine."

"And until then?"

"The period of gestation must go through its tortuous ways. But it will dawn, it will dawn and not only on this terra firma. It will dawn even over this city, and it will be more a part of world-state as I saw it in my close view of the world. I was given this dream, and I have lived by it."

"Do you want us to do anything about your family, or your friends? Tell them anything specifically?"

"That my soul lives on, and that it will return when I see the turn of the century, and that I may look face to face with that which I saw; that which was born within my consciousness."

"Whom should we give this message to?"

"The one living member of my family."

"What is this member's name?"

"Alice."

"Anything else?"

"Just mundane moments of the lives of many fallible mortals are inconsequential. Posterity has no need for it. It has only the need for that which is coming—the bright new dawn. We live to tell you this too. God rest the soul of man; it will win. Science will win. Man's soul will be free to know its own importance. I have forgotten the future; I look upon it all, here, as my integral part of the world."

"We will then go and have a look at that which was your house. Thank you for telling me what you did."

"God bless you—that is, the God that is your own true God."

"Thank you."

"Hello—Albert."

"Albert—is everything all right?"

"She's fine. I will release her."

"Thank you."

"I guess you know with whom you were speaking."

"Yes."

"It was difficult for him to take over."

Now Ethel came out of trance, none the worse for it. I questioned her about the room we were in.

"Deals have been made in this room."

"What kind of deals?"

"Political deals. There is a heavy-set man with sideburns here."

"Is he somebody of importance?"

"I would say so, He has not too much hair up here. Could have a beard."

"What would he be doing here?"

"Well he seems to take over the room. To make a deal, of some kind."

"What kind of deal?"

"I don't think he's an American."

"If you saw him would you recognize him?"

"I think I would, yes."

I walked Ethel into the hugh room with the fireplace, pointing at various photographs lined up on top of it.

"Would this be the man?"

"Oh, that's George isn't it?"

"No. Could this be the man?"

"That's Richard then."

"No, it's not Richard and it's not George, but is it the man that you saw?"

"He's a little more gray here than he was when I—if that's the man. But it could be, yes." She had just identified a world-famous statesman of World War I vintage.

We had now arrived on the third floor. A guide took us around and pointed out the elevator and the iron stairs. We walked down again and stopped at the grand piano.

"Ethel," I asked, "do you think that this piano has been used recently?"

"I would say it has. Ghostly, too. I think this is a whirlpool right here. I don't know whether Wilson was a good pianist or not, but he has touched it."

"Do you feel he is the one that is in the house?"

"I don't think that he is *haunting* it, but present, yes."

I carefully checked into the history of the house, to see whether some tragedy or other unusual happenings might have produced a genuine ghost. There was nothing in the background of the house to indicate that such an event had ever taken place. How then was one to explain the footsteps? What about the presence Mr. Vesquez had felt? Since most of the phenomena occurred upstairs, one is led to believe that they might be connected with some of the servants or someone living at that level of the house. At the period when the Wilsons had the house, the top floor was certainly used as servants' quarters. But the Wilson's own bedroom and living quarters were also upstairs, and the footsteps and the feeling of a presence was not restricted to the topmost floor, it would appear.

Then, too, the expressions used by the entranced medium indicate a person other than an ordinary servant. There are several curious references in the transcript of the tape taken while Ethel Johnson Meyers was in trance, and afterwards when she spoke to me clairvoyantly. First of all, the reference to a hymn, "Lead, Kindly Light," would indeed be in character for President Wilson. He was a son of a Presbyterian minister, and certainly grew up under the influence of his father as far as religion and expressions were concerned. The references to "hands across the sea" would be unimportant if Ethel Johnson Meyers had known that she was in the Wilson House. However, she did not connect the house with President Wilson at the time she made the statement. The "puny dream" referred to of uniting the world was certainly President Wilson's uppermost thought and desire. Perhaps Woodrow Wilson will be known as the "Peace President" in future history books—even though he was in office during a war, he went into that war with a genuine and sincere desire to end all wars. "To make the world safe for democracy" was one of his best-known slogans. Thus, the expressions relayed by the medium seem to me to be entirely in keeping with that spirit.

True, the entity speaking through the medium did not come forward and say, "I am Woodrow Wilson." I would not have expected it. That would have been ostentatious and entirely out of character for the quiet, soft-spoken gentleman Wilson was.

Is the Woodrow Wilson House haunted? Is the restless spirit of the "Peace President" once more about, because of what is transpiring in his beloved Washington? Is he aroused by the absence of peace even in his own homeland, let alone abroad? Truly, the conditions to cause a restless entity to remain disturbed are all present.

Why is he trying to make contact with the physical world at this time? The man who reported his experiences to the Washington *Post* evidently is mediumistic. There are very few people staying overnight in the house at the present time. Very likely the restless spirit of President Wilson—if indeed it is his spirit—found it convenient to contact this man, despite his comparatively unimportant position. But because he was psychic he presented a channel through which the President—if it was indeed he—could express himself and reach the outer world, the wold that seems to be so much in need of peace today.

In a sense he has succeeded in his efforts. Because of the experiences of Mr. Vasquez I became aware of the hauntings at the Wilson House. My visit and the trance condition into which I played Ethel Johnson Meyers resulted in a certain contact. There is every reason to believe that this contact was the President himself.

As we left the house, I questioned Mrs. Meyers once again about the man she had clairvoyantly seen walking about the house. Without thinking, she described the tall dignified figure of Woodrow Wilson. It may not constitute absolute proof in terms of parapsychology, of course, but I have the feeling that we did indeed make contact with the restless and truly perturbed spirit of Woodrow Wilson, and that this spirit somehow wants me to tell the world how concerned he is about the state it is in at present.

The Ghost at the Altar

I had heard rumors for some time of a ghost parson in a church near Pittsburgh, and when I appeared on the John Reed King show on Station KDKA-TV, one of the crew came up to me after the telecast and told me how much he enjoyed hearing about ghosts.

"Have you ever visited that haunted church in M——?" he asked, and my natural curiosity was aroused. A ghost here in Pittsburgh, and I haven't met him? Can't allow that. But my stay was over and I had to return to New York.

Still, the ghostly person of M—— was very much on my mind. When I returned to Pittsburgh in September of that year, I was determined to have a go at that case.

With the help of Jim Sieger and his roving reporter, John Stewart, at Station KDKA, we got together a car, a first-class portable tape recorder, and photographer Jim Stark. Immediately following my telecast, we set out for Milvale.

Fate must have wanted us to get results, for the attendant of the first gasoline station we stopped at, directed us to the Haunted Church. Both the name of the church and its current pastor must remain hidden at their own request, but the story is nevertheless true.

The Haunted Church is an imposing Romanesque building of stone, erected at the turn of the century on a bluff overlooking the Pittsburgh River. It is attached to a school and rectory and gives a clean and efficient impression, nothing haunted or mysterious about it.

When I rang the doorbell of the rectory, a portly, imposing man in sweater and slacks opened the door. I asked to talk to him about the history of the church. Evidently he had more than a share of the Sixth Sense, for he knew immediately what I was after.

"I am priest," he said firmly, with a strong Slavic accent. I was somewhat taken aback because of his casual clothes, but he explained that even priests are allowed to relax now and then. Father X., as we shall call him, was a well-educated, soft-spoken man of about forty-five or fifty, and he readily admitted he had heard the rumors about "spirits," but there was, of course, nothing to it. Actually, he said, the man to talk to was his superior, Father H.

A few moments later, Father H. was summoned and introduced to me as "the authority" on the subject. When the good Father heard I was a parapsychologist and interested in his ghost, he became agitated. "I have nothing to say," he emphasized, and politely showed us the door. I chose to ignore his move.

Instead, I persisted in requesting either confirmation or denial of the rumors of hauntings in his church. Evidently, Father H. was afraid of the unusual. Many priests are not and discuss freely that which they know exists. But Father H. had once met with another writer, Louis Adamic, and apparently this had soured him on all other writers, like myself.

It seems that Adamic, a fellow Croatian, had mentioned in one of his books the story about the ghost at the altar—and seriously at that— quite a feat for a nonbeliever as Adamic was said to have been. Father H. had nothing to say for publication.

"No, no, no—nothing. I bless you. Good-bye." He bowed ceremoniously and waited for us to depart. Instead, I turned and smiled at Father X., the assistant pastor.

"May we see the church?" I said and waited. They couldn't very well refuse. Father H. realized we weren't going to leave at once and resigned himself to the fact that his assistant pastor would talk to us.

"Very well. But without me!" he finally said, and withdrew. That was all Father X. had needed. The field was clear now. Slowly he lit a cigarette and said, "You know, I've studied parapsychology myself for two years in my native Croatia."

After his initial appearance, nothing about Father X. surprised me. As we walked across the yard to the church, we entered into an animated discussion about the merits of psychic research. Father X. took us in through the altar door, and we saw the gleaming white and gold altar emerging from the semidarkness like a vision in one of Raphael's Renaissance paintings.

There was definitely something very unusual about this church. For one thing, it was a typically European, Slavonically tinged edifice and one had the immediate feel of being among an ethnic group of different origin from one's own. The large nave culminated in a balcony on which an old-fashioned—that is, nonelectric, nonautomatic—organ was placed in prominent position. No doubt services at this church were imposing and emotionally satisfying experiences.

We stepped closer to the altar, which was flanked on either side by a large, heavy vigil light, the kind Europeans call Eternal Light. "See this painting," Father X. said and pointed at the curving fresco covering the entire inner cupola behind the altar, both behind it and above it. The painting showed natives of Croatia in their costumes, and a group of Croatians presenting a model of their church.

These traditional scenes were depicted with vivid colors and a charming, primitive style not found elsewhere. I inquired about the painter. "Maxim Hvatka," the priest said, and at once I recognized the name as that of a celebrated Yugoslav artist who had passed on a few years ago. The frescos were done in the early part of the century.

As we admired the altar, standing on its steps and getting impressions, Father X. must again have read my mind, for he said without further ado, "Yes, it is this spot where the 'spirits were seen.'"

There was no doubt in my mind that our assistant pastor was quite convinced of the truth of the phenomena.

"What exactly happened?" I asked.

"Well, not so long ago, Father H. and this painter Hvatka, they were here near the altar. Hvatka was painting the altar picture and Father H. was here to watch him. Suddenly, Hvatka grabbed Father's arm and said with great excitement, 'Look, Father—this person—there is someone here in the church, in front of the altar!'

"Father H. knew that the church was locked up tight and that only he and the painter were in the building. There *couldn't* be another person. 'Where? Who?' he said and looked hard. He didn't see anything. Hvatka insisted he had just seen a man walk by the altar and disappear into nothing. They stepped up to the vigil light on the left and experienced a sudden chill. Moreover, *the light was out.*

"Now to extinguish this light with anything less than a powerful blower or fan directly above it is impossible. Glass-enclosed and metal-covered, these powerful wax candles are meant to withstand the wind and certainly ordinary drafts or human breath. Only a supernormal agency could have put out that vigil light, gentlemen."

Father X. paused. I was impressed by his well-told story, and I knew at once why Father H. wanted no part of us. How could he ever admit having been in the presence of a spirit without having seen it? Impossible. We took some photographs and walked slowly towards the exit.

Father X. warmed up to me now and volunteered an experience from his own youth. It seems that when he was studying theology in his native Croatia, he lived among a group of perhaps a dozen young students who did not share his enthusiasm for psychic studies—who, in fact, ridiculed them.

One young man, however, who was his roommate, took the subject seriously, so seriously in fact that they made a pact—whoever died first would let the other know. A short time later, Father X., asleep on a warm afternoon, suddenly woke up. He *knew* his friend had died that instant, for he saw him sitting on a chair near his bed, laughing and waving at him. It was more than a mere dream, a vividly powerful impression. Father X. was no longer asleep at that moment; the impression had actually awakened him.

He looked at his watch; it was just three in the afternoon. Quickly, he made inquiries about his friend. Within a few hours he knew what he had already suspected—his friend had died in an accident at precisely the moment he had seen him in his room, back at the seminary!

"You're psychic then," I said.

Father X. shrugged. "I know many psychic cases," he said obliquely. "There was that nun in Italy, who left her hand prints on the church door to let her superiors know she was now in purgatory."

Father X. spoke softly and with the assurance of a man who knows his subject well. "There are these things, but what can we do? We cannot very well admit them."

A sudden thought came to my mind. Did he have any idea who the ghost at the altar was? Father X. shook his head.

"Tell me," I continued, "did anyone die violently in the church?"

Again, a negative answer.

"That's strange," I said. "Was there another building on this spot before the present church?"

"No," Father X. said nonchalantly.

"That's even stranger," I countered, "for my research indicates there was a priest here in the nineteenth century, and it is his ghost that has been seen."

Father X. swallowed hard.

"As a matter of fact," he said now, "you're right. There was an earlier wooden church here on this very spot. The present stone building only dates back to about nineteen one. Father Ranzinger built the wooden church."

"Was that around eighteen eighty-five," I inquired. That is how I had it in my notes.

"Probably correct," the priest said, and no longer marveled at my information.

"What happened to the wooden church, Father?" I asked, and here I had a blank, for my research told me nothing further.

"Oh, it burned down. Completely. No, nobody got hurt, but the church, it was a total loss."

Father Ranzinger's beloved wooden church went up in flames, it appeared, and the fifteen years he had spent with his flock must have accumulated an emotional backlog of great strength and attachment. Was it not conceivable that Father Ranzinger's attachment to the building was transferred to the stone edifice as soon as it was finished?

Was it his ghost the two men had seen in front of the altar? Until he puts in another appearance, we won't know, but Pittsburgh's Haunted Church is a lovely place in which to rest and pray—ghost or no ghost.

John Wilkes Booth's Tavern
Clinton, Maryland

A number of people have seen Abraham Lincoln's ghost walk the corridors of the White House, and others have reported unusual experiences at Ford's Theatre in Washington, where the actor John Wilkes Booth shot President Lincoln. Less known is an historical tavern in what is now Clinton, Maryland.

Thirteen miles south of Washington, in a small town now called Clinton but once known as Surrattville, stands an eighteenth-century building nowadays used as a museum. Mary Surratt ran it as an inn at the time when the area was far enough removed from Washington to serve as a way station to those travelling south from the nation's capital. When business fell off, however, Mrs. Surratt leased the eighteenth-century tavern to John Lloyd and moved to Washington where she ran a boardinghouse on H Street between Sixth and Seventh Streets. But she remained on close and friendly relations with her successor at the tavern at Surrattville, so that it was possible for her son, John Surratt, to use it as an occasional meeting place with his friends. These friends included John Wilkes Booth, and the meetings eventually led to the plot to assassinate President Lincoln.

After the murder, Booth escaped on horseback and made straight for the tavern. By prearrangement, he and an associate hid the guns they had with them in a cache in the floor of the tavern. Shortly after, he and the associate, David Herald, split up, and John Wilkes Booth continued his journey despite a broken foot. Eventually, he was discovered hiding at Garrett's barn and was shot there.

The connection between Booth and the tavern was no longer public knowledge as the years went by. Some local people might have remembered it, but the outside world had lost interest. At one time, it appears, the structure was acquired by John's brother, the actor Edwin Booth. In the 1950s it passed into the hands of a local businessman named B. K. Miller. By now the village was known as Clinton, since the Surrattville name had been changed shortly after the infamous trial of Mary Surratt.

The hauntings observed here include the figure of a woman thought to be the restless spirit of Mary Surratt herself, whose home this had been at one time. Strange men have been observed sitting on the back stairs when there was no one but the occupants of the house around. Muffled voices of a group of men talking in excited tones have also been reported, and seem to indicate that at the very least an imprint from the past has been preserved at the Surratt Tavern. Many meetings of the conspirators had taken place in the downstairs part of the building, and when I brought Sybil Leek to the tavern she immediately pointed out the site of the meetings, the place where the guns had been hidden, and, in trance, established communication with the former owner of the tavern, Edwin Booth himself.

Although the building is now a museum and open to visitors, one should first obtain permission from Mr. Miller, at Miller's Supermarket, in Clinton, Maryland. Clinton itself is less than an hour's drive from downtown Washington. As far as I know there is no fee attached to a visit at Surratt Tavern. At the time when I made my investigation, Mr. Miller had thought of selling the building to a museum or an historical trust, and by the time this appears in print, it may well have changed hands.

Anyone who is psychic and visits the old tavern might very well hear the same voices, or have some kind of psychic experience because the phenomena themselves have not faded away, nor are they likely to, since no formal exorcism has ever been attempted there.

The Case of the Buried Miners

In the second half of August of 1963, every newspaper in the United States was filled with the day-to-day accounts of a mining cave-in at Hazleton, Pennsylvania. Two men, David Fellin and Henry Throne, survived fourteen days at the bottom of a caved-in mine shaft and were finally rescued through a specially drilled funnel.

On August 28, Fellin gave the Associated Press an interview, in which he said:

> Now they're trying to tell me those things were hallucinations, that we imagined it all.
>
> We didn't. Our minds weren't playing tricks on us. I've been a practical, hardheaded coal miner all my life. My mind was clear down there in the mine. It's still clear.
>
> We saw what we say. These things happened. I can't explain them. I'm almost afraid to think what might be the explanation.
>
> For example, on the fourth or fifth day, *we saw this door,* although we had no light from above or from our helmets. *The door was covered in bright blue light. It was very clear, better than sunlight.*
>
> Two men, ordinary-looking men, not miners, *opened the door.* We could see beautiful marble steps on the other side. We saw this for some time and then we didn't see it. We saw other things I *can't explain.*

One thing I was always sure of. I was convinced we'd get out even if I had to dig us out myself.

A funny thing occurred on that very first day. We [*Henry Throne and Louis Bova*] hadn't been down in the mine five minutes that morning when my stomach started feeling a little out of whack.

I said, "Let's go out for an hour or so."

But the boys persuaded me to stay and get some work done first.

So we stayed, down at the tunnel's bottom, more than 300 feet down. Louis was on one side and me and Hank on the other.

Louis reached up to press the buzzer for the buggy *a small wagon which carries coal on tracks up to the surface*. He pressed the buzzer and stepped back. Then it happened.

Suddenly everything was coming down—timber, coal, rocks. The stuff was rushing down between us and Louis. Then it was quiet for maybe half a minute. Then the rush started again. It went on like this, starting and stopping for some time.

We sat there, listening as hard as we could for more rushes in the dark. We sat there against the wall that way 14 to 16 hours in a place about 6 feet long, 5 feet wide and about 3 feet high.

Now, you asked me about the strange things Hank saw. I actually saw more of them than he did. But I find it hard to talk about that.

I'm positive we saw what we saw. We weren't imagining them. Even before we heard from the men on the top, we had some light now and then. How else can you explain all the work we did down there? We couldn't have done it entirely in darkness.

The only time I was really *scared was when we saw two men dressed like power linemen. Don't ask me what men like that were doing down on the bottom.* But I *saw them.*

Hank asked me two or three times to ask the men for some light. This idea scared me down to my toes. I had the feeling this was something outside of our reach, that we shouldn't talk or do anything.

But Hank did not. Hank said to the men, "Hey, buddy, how about showing us some light?"

They didn't answer, and after a while we didn't see them any more.

Well, similar descriptions have been given from time to time by people close to death; Arthur Ford was once in that position in a hospital, and described vividly the door and the men operating it, before he was able to return to this side of the Veil once more.

Did David Fellin have a glimpse of the Other Side of Life, the Unseen World, the world of the psychic? Perhaps he did. Perhaps, too, he was being helped by these forces to return to the surface. In a television interview Fellin also claimed to have been given a message by the men, but he could not discuss it.

About the same time this happened, a millworker named Guy de Maggio had a vision of Fellin and his visitors from Beyond, and actually heard the words spoken by Fellin. So vivid was the impression that he took pains to tell people about it. This was many miles away from the scene and could be confirmed only later, after Fellin was rescued. Did both men tune in on the same supernormal wave length?

The local psychiatrists have done their best to convince Fellin that he had a hallucination. But Fellin is convinced of his experience. And so am I.

I tried to coax the two miners to come on Pittsburgh television with me. They refused. They were afraid of being laughed at. Then a reporter from the *Philadelphia Sunday Bulletin* went to interview them on the anniversary of the event.

Yes, it was true that David Fellin had seen a door with beautiful marble steps, but there were also the people, apparently human, walking up and down the stairs. Yet somehow he and Hank Throne feared to go through the door.

"Did you see what was on the other side of the door?" the reporter asked.

"A beautiful garden, just as far as you can see. The flowers were more beautiful, the grass greener, than here on earth. I knew that was some special place."

"Did the man hold the door open?"

"No, Hank shouted for him to hold it, but the door slammed."

"What happened then?"

"Hank got mad. He said: 'Give me that hammer. I'll open that door.' The hammer was lying next to me, and I just handed it to him. He took it and ran at the door, then swung the hammer at it. That's when he broke a bone in his hand. And he bruised himself on the right cheek."

"What happened to the door?"

"It disappeared, and the light went out."

"What light? What did it look like?"

"It was a bluish light, not like daylight."

"Both you and Hank saw this door and the light?"

"Yes. Also Pope John. But Hank didn't know it was Pope John, not until we got to the hospital and the priest brought me a book with a picture of Pope John on the cover." (Pope John XXIII died June 3, 1963.)

"Let's start at the beginning."

"I was sitting here, and Hank was sitting like where you are *facing him*. He kept looking up over my shoulder. I looked up one time and saw Pope John there. He had his arms crossed and was just looking down at us. He didn't say anything."

"Did you and Hank speak to him?"

"I would say, 'Is our friend still there?' or 'How's our friend today?' Hank would grin and say he was still there."

"Didn't you tell him this was Pope John?"

"I figured Hank was a Protestant, and wouldn't know who he was anyway."

"How did he find out then?"

"When they took us to the hospital, my priest brought me a book with a picture of the Pope on it. And Hank points to the book and said, 'Hey, there's that guy we saw, Dave.'"

"Did you and Hank discuss these things while you saw them?"

"No, not too much. When we saw those people on the steps I told him we stumbled onto something. I had nicknamed the mine where we were trapped 'The Graveyard of Souls.' And I told him that we stumbled onto the graveyard of souls."

The reporter later talked to Throne, who said that he saw the door, stairway and Pope John.

Pope John XXIII was, of course, on the spiritual side of the Veil at the time the two buried miners saw his apparition.

The London *Psychic News* also picked up the story and featured it. They headlined it:

ENTOMBED MINER
IS NOT AFRAID
TO DIE ANY MORE

Not after they saw where they'd be going.

New York Area

Hungry Lucy

"June Havoc's got a ghost in her townhouse," Gail Benedict said gaily on the telephone. Gail was in public relations, and a devoted ghost-finder even since I had been able to rid her sister's apartment of a poltergeist the year before.

The house in question was 104 years old, stashed away in what New Yorkers call "Hell's Kitchen," the old area in the 40s between Ninth and Tenth Avenues, close to the theater district. Built on the corner of Forty-fourth Street and Ninth Avenue, it had been in the possession of the Rodenberg family until a Mr. Payne bought it. He remodeled it carefully, with a great deal of respect for the old plans. He did nothing to change its quaint Victorian appearance, inside or out.

About three years later, glamorous stage and television star June Havoc bought the house, and rented the upper floors to various tenants. She herself moved into the downstairs apartment, simply because no one else wanted it. It didn't strike her as strange at the time that no tenant had ever renewed the lease on that floor-through downstairs apartment, but now she knows why. It was all because of *Hungry Lucy*.

The morning after Gail's call, June Havoc telephoned me, and a séance was arranged for Friday of that week. I immediately reached British medium Sybil Leek, but I gave no details. I merely invited her to help me get rid of a noisy ghost. Noise was what June Havoc complained about.

"It seems to be a series of *insistent* sounds," she said. "First, they were rather soft. I didn't really notice them three years ago. Then I had the architect who built that balcony in the back come in and asked him to investigate these sounds. He said there was nothing whatever the matter with the house. Then I had the plumber up, because I thought it was the steam pipes. He said it was not that either. Then I had the carpenter in, for it is a very old house, but he couldn't find any structural defects whatever."

"When do you hear these tapping noises?"

"At all times. Lately, they seem to be more insistent. More demanding. We refer to it as 'tap dancing,' for that is exactly what it sounds like."

The wooden floors were in such excellent state that Miss Havoc didn't cover them with carpets. The yellow pine used for the floorboards cannot be replaced today.

June Havoc's maid had heard loud tapping in Miss Havoc's absence, and many of her actor friends had remarked on it.

"It is always in this area," June Havoc pointed out, "and seems to come from underneath the kitchen floor. It has become impossible to sleep a full night's sleep in this room."

The kitchen leads directly into the rear section of the floor-through apartment, to a room used as a bedroom. Consequently, any noise disturbed her sleep.

Underneath Miss Havoc's apartment, there was another floor-through, but the tenants had never reported anything unusual there, nor had the ones on the upper floors. Only Miss Havoc's place was noisy.

We now walked from the front of the apartment into the back half. Suddenly there was a loud tapping sound from underneath the floor as if someone had shot off a machine gun. Catherine and I had arrived earlier than the rest, and there were just the three of us.

"There, you see," June Havoc said. The ghost had greeted us in style.

I stepped forward at once.

"What do you want?" I demanded.

Immediately, the noise stopped.

While we waited for the other participants in the investigation to arrive, June Havoc pointed to the rear wall.

"It has been furred out," she explained. "That is to say, there was another wall against the wall, which made the room smaller. Why, no one knows."

Soon *New York Post* columnist Earl Wilson and Mrs. Wilson, Gail Benedict, and Robert Winter-Berger, also a publicist, arrived, along with a woman from *Life* magazine, notebook in hand. A little later Sybil Leek swept into the room. There was a bit of casual conversation, in which nothing whatever was said about the ghost, and then we seated ourselves in the rear portion of the apartment. Sybil took the chair next to the spot where the noises always originated. June Havoc sat on her right, and I on her left. The lights were very bright since we were filming the entire scene for Miss Havoc's television show.

Soon enough, Sybil began to "go under."

"Hungry," Sybil mumbled faintly.

"Why are you hungry?" I asked.

"No food," the voice said.

The usually calm voice of Sybil Leek was panting in desperation now.

"I want some food, some food!" she cried.

I promised to help her and asked for her name.

"Don't cry. I will help you," I promised.

"Food . . . I want some food . . ." the voice continued to sob.

"Who are you?"

"Lucy Ryan."

"Do you live in this house?"

"No house here."

"How long have you been here?"

"A long time."

"What year is this?"

"Seventeen ninety-two."

"What do you do in this house?"

"No house . . . people . . . fields . . ."

"Why then are you here? What is there here for you?"

The ghost snorted.

"Hm . . . men."

"Who brought you here?"

"Came . . . people sent us away . . . soldiers . . . follow them . . . sent me away. . . ."

"What army? Which regiment?"

"Napier."

"How old are you?"

"Twenty."

"Where were you born?"

"Hawthorne . . . not very far away from here."

I was not sure whether she said "Hawthorne" or "Hawgton," or some similar name.

"What is you father's name?"

Silence.

"Your mother's name?"

Silence.

"Were you baptized?"

"Baptized?"

She didn't remember that either.

I explained that she had passed on. It did not matter.

"Stay here . . . until I get some food . . . meat . . . meat and corn . . ."

"Have you tried to communicate with anyone in this house?"

"Nobody listens."

"How are you trying to make them listen?"

"I make noise because I want food."

"Why do you stay in one area? Why don't you move around freely?"

"Can't. Can't go away. Too many people. Soldiers."

"Where are your parents?"

"Dead."

"What is your mother's name?"

"Mae."

"Her maiden name?"

"Don't know."

"Your father's first name?"

"Terry."

"Were any of your family in the army?"

Ironical laughter punctuated her next words.

"Only . . . me."

"Tell me the names of some of the officers in the army you knew."

"Alfred . . . Wait."

"Any rank?"

"No rank."

"What regiment did you follow?"

"Just this . . . Alfred."

"And he left you?"

"Yes. I went with some other man, then I was hungry and I came here."

"Why here?"

"I was sent here."

"By whom?"

"They made me come. Picked me up. Man brought me here. Put me down on the ground."

"Did you die in this spot?"

"Die, die? I'm not dead. *I'm hungry.*"

I then asked her to join her parents, those who loved her, and to leave this spot. She refused. She wanted to walk by the river, she said. I suggested that she was not receiving food and could leave freely. After a while, the ghost seemed to slip away peacefully and Sybil Leek returned to her own body, temporarily vacated so that Lucy could speak through it. As usual, Sybil remembered absolutely nothing of what went on when she was in deep trance. She was crying, but thought her mascara was the cause of it.

Suddenly, the ghost was back. The floorboards were reverberating with the staccato sound of an angry tap, loud, strong, and demanding.

"What do you want?" I asked again, although I knew now what she wanted.

Sybil also extended a helping hand. But the sound stopped as abruptly as it had begun.

A while later, we sat down again. Sybil reported feeling presences.

"One is a girl, the other is a man. A man with a stick. Or gun. The girl is stronger. She wants something."

Suddenly, Sybil pointed to the kitchen area.

"What happened in the corner?"

Nobody had told Sybil of the area in which the disturbances had always taken place.

"I feel her behind me now. A youngish girl, not very well dressed, Georgian period. I don't get the man too well."

At this point, we brought into the room a small Victorian wooden table, a gift from Gail Benedict.

Within seconds after Sybil, June Havoc, and I had lightly placed our hands upon it, it started to move, seemingly of its own volition!

Rapidly, it began to tap out a word, using a kind of Morse code. While Earl Wilson was taking notes, we allowed the table to jump hither and yon, tapping out a message.

None of us touched the table top except lightly. There was no question of manipulating the table. The light was very bright, and our hands almost touched, so that any pressure by one of us would have been instantly noticed by the other two. This type of communication is slow, since the table runs through the entire alphabet until it reaches the desired letter, then the next letter, until an entire word has been spelled out.

"L-e-a-v-e," the communicator said, not exactly in a friendly mood.

Evidently she wanted the place to herself and thought we were the intruders.

I tried to get some more information about her. But instead of tapping out another word in an orderly fashion, the table became very excited—if that is the word for emotional tables—and practically leapt from beneath our hands. We were required to follow it to keep up the contact, as it careened wildly through the room. When I was speaking, it moved toward me and practically crept onto my lap. When I wasn't speaking, it ran to someone else in the room. Eventually, it became so wild, at times entirely off the floor, that it slipped from our light touch and, as the power was broken, instantly rolled into a corner—just another table with no life of its own.

We repaired to the garden, a few steps down an iron staircase, in the rear of the house.

"Sybil, what do you feel down here?" I asked.

"I had a tremendous urge to come out here. I didn't know there was a garden. Underneath my feet almost is the cause of the disturbance."

We were standing at a spot adjacent to the basement wall and close to the center of the tapping disturbance we had heard.

"Someone may be buried here," Sybil remarked, pointing to a mound of earth underneath our feet. "It's a girl."

"Do you see the wire covering the area behind you?" June Havoc said. "I tried to plant seeds there, and the wire was to protect them— but somehow nothing, nothing will grow there."

"Plant something on this mound," Sybil suggested. "It may well pacify *her.*"

We returned to the upstairs apartment, and soon after broke up the "ghost hunting party," as columnist Sheila Graham called it later.

The next morning, I called June Havoc to see how things were. I knew from experience that the ghost would either be totally gone, or totally mad, but not the same as before.

Lucy, I was told, was rather mad. Twice as noisy, she still demanded her pound of flesh. I promised June Havoc that we'd return until the ghost was completely gone.

A few days passed. Things became a little quieter, as if Lucy were hesitating. Then something odd happened the next night. Instead of tapping from her accustomed corner area, Lucy moved away from it and tapped away from above June's bed. She had never been heard from that spot before.

I decided it was time to have a chat with Lucy again. Meanwhile, corroboration of the information we had obtained had come to us quickly. The morning after our first séance, Bob Winter-Berger called. He had been to the New York Public Library and checked on Napier, the officer named by the medium as the man in charge of the soldier's regiment.

The *Dictionary of National Biography* contained the answer. Colonel George Napier, a British officer, had served on the staff of Governor Sir Henry Clinton. How exciting, I thought. The Clinton mansion once occupied the very ground we were having the séance on. As far as I knew, the place was still not entirely free of the uncanny, for reports continued to reach me of strange steps and doors opening by themselves.

Although the mansion itself no longer stands, the carriage house in the rear was now part of Clinton Court, a reconstructed apartment house on West Forty-sixth Street. How could Sybil Leek, only recently arrived from England, have known of these things?

Napier was indeed the man who had charge of a regiment on this very spot, and the years 1781–1782 are given as the time when Napier's family contracted the dreaded yellow fever and died. Sir Henry Clinton forbade his aide to be in touch with them, and the Colonel was shipped off to England, half-dead himself, while his wife and family passed away on the spot that later became Potter's Field.

Many Irish immigrants came to the New World in those years. Perhaps the Ryan girl was one of them, or her parents were. Unfortunately, history does not keep much of a record of camp followers.

On January 15, 1965, precisely at midnight, I placed Sybil Leek into deep trance in my apartment on Riverside Drive. In the past we had succeeded in contacting *former* ghosts once they had been pried loose in an initial séance in the haunted house itself. I had high hopes that Lucy would communicate and I wasn't disappointed.

"Tick, tock, tickety-tock, June's clock stops, June's clock stops," the entranced medium murmured, barely audibly.

"Tickety-tock, June's clock stops, tickety-tock . . ."

"Who are you?" I asked.

"Lucy."

"Lucy, what does this mean?"

"June's clock stops, June's clock stops, frightened June, frightened June," she repeated like a child reciting a poem.

"Why do you want to frighten June?"

"Go away."

"Why do you want her to go away?"

"People there . . . too much house . . . too much June . . . too many clocks . . . she sings, dances, she makes a lot of noise . . . I'm hungry, I'm always hungry. You don't do a thing about it . . ."

"Will you go away if I get you some food? Can we come to an agreement?"

"Why?"

"Because I want to help you, help June."

"Ah, same old story."

"You're not happy. Would you like to see Alfred again?"

"Yes . . . he's gone."

"Not very far. I'll get you together with Alfred if you will leave the house."

"Where would I go?"

"Alfred has a house of his own for you."

"Where?"

"Not very far."

"Frightened to go . . . don't know where to go . . . nobody likes me. She makes noises, I make noises. I don't like that clock."

"Where were you born, Lucy?"

"Larches by the Sea . . . Larchmont . . . by the Sea . . . people disturb me."

Again I asked her to go to join her Alfred, to find happiness again. I suggested she call for him by name, which she did, hesitatingly at first, more desperately later.

"No . . . I can't go from here. He said he would come. He said *wait*. Wait . . . here. Wait. Alfred, why don't you come? Too many clocks. Time, time, time . . . noisy creature. Time, time . . . three o'clock."

"What happened at three o'clock?" I demanded.

"He said he'd come," the ghost replied. "I waited for him."

"Why at three o'clock in the middle of the night?"

"Why do you think? Couldn't get out. Locked in. Not allowed out at night. I'll wait. He'll come."

"Did you meet any of his friends?"

"Not many . . . what would I say?"

"What was Alfred's name?"

"Bailey . . . Alfred said 'Wait, wait . . . I'll go away,' he said. 'They'll never find me.'"

"Go to him with my love," I said, calmly repeating over and over the formula used in rescue circle operations to send the earthbound ghost across the threshold.

As I spoke, Lucy slipped away from us, not violently as she had come, but more or less resignedly.

I telephoned June Havoc to see what had happened that night between midnight and 12:30. She had heard Lucy's tapping precisely then, but nothing more as the night passed—a quiet night for a change.

Was Lucy on her way to her Alfred?

We would know soon enough.

In the weeks that followed, I made periodic inquiries of June Havoc. Was the ghost still in evidence? Miss Havoc did not stay at her townhouse all the time, preferring the quiet charm of her Connecticut estate. But on the nights when she did sleep in the house on Forty-fourth Street, she was able to observe that Lucy Ryan had changed considerably in personality—the ghost had been freed, yes, but had not yet been driven from the house. In face, the terrible noise was now all over the house, although less frequent and less vehement—*as if she were thinking things over.*

I decided we had to finish the job as well as we could and another séance was arranged for late March, 1965. Present were—in addition to our hostess and chief sufferer—my wife Catherine and myself; Emory Lewis, editor of *Cue* magazine; Barry Farber, WOR commentator; and two friends of June Havoc. We grouped ourselves around a table in the *front room* this time. This soon proved to be a mistake. No Lucy Ryan. No ghost. We repaired to the other room where the original manifestations had taken place, with more luck this time.

Sybil, in trance, told us that the girl had gone, but that Alfred had no intention of leaving. He was waiting for *her* now. I asked for the name of his commanding officer and was told it was Napier. This we knew already. But who was the next in rank?

"Lieutenant William Watkins."

"What about the commanding general?"

He did not know.

He had been born in Hawthorne, just like Lucy, he told Sybil. I had been able to trace this Hawthorne to a place not far away in Westchester County.

There were people all over, Sybil said in trance, and they were falling down. They were ill.

"Send Alfred to join his Lucy," I commanded, and Sybil in a low voice told the stubborn ghost to go.

After an interlude of table tipping, in which several characters from the nether world made their auditory appearance, she returned to trance. Sybil in trance was near the river again, among the sick.

But no Lucy Ryan. Lucy's gone, she said.

"The smell makes me sick," Sybil said, and you could see stark horror in her sensitive face.

"Dirty people, rags, people in uniform too, with dirty trousers. There is a big house across the river."

"Whose house is it?"

"Mr. Dawson's. Doctor Dawson. Dr. James Dawson . . . Lee Point. Must go there. Feel sick. Rocks and trees, just the house across the river."

"What year is this?"

"Ninety-two."

She then described Dr. Dawson's house as having three windows on the left, two on the right, and five above, and said that it was called Lee Point—Hawthorne. It sounded a little like Hawgton to me, but I can't be sure.

Over the river, she said. She described a "round thing on a post" in front of the house, like a shell. For messages, she thought.

"What is the name of the country we're in?" I asked.

"Vinelands. Vinelands."

I decided to change the subject back to Hungry Lucy. How did she get sick?

"She didn't get any food, and then she got cold, by the river.
. . . Nobody helped them there. Let them die. Buried them in a pit."

"What is the name of the river?"

"Mo . . . Mo-something."

"Do you see anyone else still around?"

"Lots of people with black faces, black shapes."

The plague, I thought, and how little the doctors could do in those days to stem it.

I asked about the man in charge and she said "Napier" and I wondered who would be left in command after Napier left, and the answer this time was, "Clinton . . . old fool. Georgie."

There were a Henry Clinton and a George Clinton, fairly contemporary with each other.

"What happened after that?"

"Napier died."

"Any other officers around?"

"Little Boy Richardson . . . Lieutenant."

"What regiment?"

"Burgoyne."

Sybil, entranced, started to hiss and whistle. "Signals," she murmured. "As the men go away, they whistle."

I decided the time had come to bring Sybil out of trance. She felt none the worse for it, and asked for something to drink. *Hungry*, like Lucy, she wasn't.

We began to evaluate the information just obtained. Dr. James Dawson may very well have lived. The A.M.A. membership directories aren't that old. I found the mention of Lee Point and Hawthorne interesting, inasmuch as the two locations are quite close. Lee, of course, would be Fort Lee, and there is a "point" or promontory in the river at that spot.

The town of Vinelands does exist in New Jersey, but the river beginning with "Mo-" may be the Mohawk. That Burgoyne was a general in the British army during the Revolution is well known.

So there you have it. Sybil Leek knows very little, if anything, about the New Jersey and Westchester countryside, having only recently come to America. Even I, then a New York resident for 27 years, had never heard of Hawthorne before. Yet there it is on the way to Pleasantville, New York.

The proof of the ghostly pudding, however, was not the regimental roster, but the state of affairs at June Havoc's house.

A later report had it that Lucy, Alfred, or whoever was responsible had quieted down considerably.

They were down, but not out.

I tactfully explained to June Havoc that feeling sorry for a hungry ghost makes things tough for a parapsychologist. The emotional pull of a genuine attachment, no matter how unconscious it may be, can provide the energies necessary to prolong the stay of the ghost.

Gradually, as June Havoc—wanting a peaceful house, especially at 3 A.M.—allowed practical sense to outweigh sentimentality, the shades of Hungry Lucy and her soldier-boy faded into the distant past, whence they came.

The Town-House Ghost

The remarkable thing about this case is that it introduced my wife to the realities of physical phenomena, just as Grandma Thurston's restless ghost had brought a firsthand experience to me for the first time.

Of course that is not the most important thing about this case by a long shot—the quality of the persons reporting the ghost is very high and their power of observation keen. By the same token, they were not overanxious for publicity and for that reason I will withhold the actual location of the Town House. But the names and everything else about this case are true.

In November, 1963, I received an urgent telephone call from Mrs. Jan Bryant Bartell, who occupies part of a very old house in New York's Greenwich Village. I asked her to put her experiences into a report, which arrived the following morning:

> I live with my husband and dog in a converted mansion off lower Fifth Avenue which was the turn-of-the-century Town House of Lillian Nordica, the opera diva. I have heard, too, that at one time or another, the house was owned and occupied by the Thomas Fortune Ryan family. In addition to its own distinction, the house is flanked by one of the former Mark Twain residences and the erstwhile family home of the poetess, Emma Lazarus. I live on the very top floor, which in the era of Mauve Decade elegance had been the servants' quarters. From the day

I took up abode here, despite the quaint charm of the apartment, I have sensed *something dark and brooding*, something of unrest enveloping the premises.

Now, I no longer merely sense this amorphous, but pervasive quality. I know. Briefly, this knowledge has been built up, during a five-year residence, upon the following:

1. The sound of something having been dropped (often quite loudly) which upon investigation discloses—nothing. And always, always, the sound of footsteps, sometimes tentatively, sometimes furtively, but always audibly and ceasing suddenly to be followed by the *faint rustling* in a room that announces another presence.

2. The appearance one evening at a recently vacated dinner table of a small, dried grape, neatly centered upon a dessert plate whose contents had quite thoroughly been consumed a few moments before.

3. The fright of a cleaning girl upon claiming to have seen a woman in white go quickly through a small room. The girl assumed it was I until she found *me* in another part of the apartment. This same room having a vague sound of activity in it around two-thirty and three o'clock in the morning and too often for my shredded nerves; the sense of a tangible presence having come to *stand beside my bed* to jerk me fearfully awake from a pre-sleep state.

4. The agitated actions of a dog whom we lost a year and a half ago, who would stare into apparently empty space and then, cautiously stalk something, or someone out of the room.

5. A new dog is strongly reacting to things my material vision cannot penetrate. Two weeks ago, this highly sensitive and intelligent puppy was drawn in the small hours of the morning to an empty (?) chair at which she sniffed violently,

raised her head, laid back her ears and quickly retreated.

6. A few evenings ago, my husband and I were having a quiet conversation when, suddenly, a wild weird sound came from the puppy who was lying facing the disturbed and disturbing small room. We looked in amazement to see her mouth opened wide, with the half-wail, half-moan sounds coming from her throat, all the while she quite plainly followed the progress of someone (or something).

When we rose to investigate, she entered the room gingerly, sniffed hard at the pillows upon my bed—and retreated.

There have been other things which I shan't attempt to catalogue here—little things and yet they loom large in creating the overall motif in psychic tapestry.

By profession, I am an actress and writer—and an ardent amateur archaeologist. I seem to have a rather peculiar magnetism which prompts people to stare at me unabashedly and which often draws quite perfect strangers to me with unsolicited confidences. For some time, I have become increasingly aware that I am endowed with the psychic gift for precognition and for evoking a potpourri of odd little occurrences which more mundane personalities are content to label "coincidences" and dismiss at that.

My husband and I are trying to find other quarters, but until they materialize, we need help.

My wife and I went to the Bartell home on November 22, 1963, and found it a charming, moody Victorian apartment, furnished with impeccable taste and embued with a timelessness that belied its disturbed state.

We received a most cordial welcome from Contessa, the large, brown "puppy." She was a most exuberant dog and it seemed hard to think that she could lie on the floor frozen stiff with fear of the Unknown.

Mr. Bartell, who was present, is the manager of a large chain of restaurants. He is not as emotional as is his wife, but he too has been impressed with the strange atmosphere of the house.

"Is there anything else you haven't told me in your letter?" I asked Mrs. Bartell.

"I have frequently been fingered lightly over my face and arms," she said.

"You mean, lightly touched by someone you could not see?"

She nodded.

"In the larger room—there is a sitting room leading into a large dining room—in the larger room I've smelled scents I never use," Mrs. Bartell added, "and of course there was that shadow of a person I saw, and always those footsteps without explanation."

"Quite," I said, and walked about the apartment. The bedroom was separated from the other two rooms by a wall, and one had to enter it from the common corridor. Evidently the apartment had once been the living quarters of servants, as was the custom with the top-floor apartments of town houses in the nineteenth century. Also, I felt very strongly that structural changes had taken place, and that perhaps the wall had been taken out and doors rearranged. Later, Mrs. Bartell confirmed this.

"Let us sit down and go over your experiences once more," I suggested. "And please start at the beginning."

Mrs. Bartell, a vivacious young lady with dark hair and sparkling eyes, thought for a moment, as if to put her recollections into proper sequence.

"The beginning was in October five years past, when we moved into the apartment. I had not been living here more than two weeks when it came to my attention that there was a certain book I wanted to own which was being handled by Samuel Weiser, who specializes in books on occult phenomena. I called the book store and I asked if he had the book and he said no, but that it would take only a few days to get it.

"In a few days he called me and said, 'Can you come in? I have the book you wanted.' It was a day on which I couldn't make that particular visit and he offered to send a delivery boy over with it. I opened the door to a wildly disheveled, pale, quaking little fellow who stood outside with my book. Without saying hello, he said, 'Lady, is this house haunted?' I looked at him in amazement and said, 'Why do you ask?' 'Because *somebody* followed me up the stairs!'

"This was after I had been here two weeks, and I had already heard footsteps. Constantly I had told my husband and was accused of having great imagination. It was quite a shock to have a perfect stranger confirm all this.

"During the entire time I've lived here, there have been the sounds of footsteps. They come down the hall and appear to stop at the little door of that small room. I usually sleep in that room, since my husband snores a little and it makes me nervous.

"I stay up reading quite late. At 2:30 or 3:00 A.M. every morning, there is constant movement behind the couch, and the hair in back of my neck stands up. Sometimes I say 'For God's sake, God bless you, please I'm exhausted, I want to get some sleep,' and it stops; it always stops."

"Always at the same time?" I asked.

"Yes, between 2:30 and 3:00 A.M. Also I became very ill the first week we moved in here, and I have been ill on and off more than I have ever been in my life since we came to this apartment. I have almost never quite been well in this place.

"We were here about two weeks and we had no curtains at the windows, we hadn't yet had a chance to have them made, and it was a very bright moonlit night. I was lying on the divan just ready to fall asleep. There were no lights whatsoever in the apartment, and I was ready to turn over on my left side, that would be facing the wall. Just as I turned over and was ready to sink into sleep, *a huge black shadow* went right across that wall and I screamed. My dog almost jumped up to the ceiling, my husband came running out of his room and I was sitting there, a shaking wreck. My husband insisted I'd seen the reflection of the trees outside, but the trees stop at the third floor and it could not very well have been a tree.

"Then there are sounds as though things have been crashed to their destruction in this apartment. I look about and think that I am going to find one of my pieces of Wedgwood shattered, a perfume bottle or something, yet nothing has been touched, nothing has been disturbed, nothing is broken."

"Do you ever feel a human presence?" I asked.

"Mainly in this small room. There have been any number of occasions when I have just been ready to fall asleep. Times without number I have lain there and felt, and sensed, and heard all at once this sudden *presence*, which kept me awake and, of course, there is nothing to be seen.

"After this has gone on long enough I sleep with all the lights on."

"Anything else?"

"Many times I would be in the kitchen and I would turn around very quickly because I felt somebody behind me. Of course there wasn't. I discussed this with a friend of mine who is a highly intuitive person. She got very pale, and said, 'Well, I wasn't going to frighten you, Jan, but now I'm going to tell you.

"'You recall when I came up to visit you. We had been talking and you were going to show me something and had left the room, but I wasn't aware that you had gone. I was standing there reading something when I thought I heard you directly behind me and I turned around to say, "Jan, this is very interesting." Of course you were in the bedroom at the time.'"

"Who was the person?" I asked.

"A very close friend of mine, Mrs. Mary Dietch; she lives on the East Side in the Mid-fifties. She said this has happened several times in the apartment, when I leave the room and she'll be busy with something and think that I have returned and start to speak, and of course there is nobody there."

I pointed at the kitchen door. "What about the time your maid saw a whitish form?"

"My cleaning girl comes in the afternoon. She is a very charming girl. We became very friendly and very fond of each other and we chattered all the time; we got more chatter then cleaning done on some days.

"Well, one afternoon I was in this small kitchenette, she was in the bathroom, and we were talking back and forth, when Dorothy came out of the bathroom and started to go into that room to tell me something, but in the midst of talking she suddenly just stopped. I poked my head out of the kitchen and said, 'Well, what were you going to say? She turned with a look of complete shock on her face and said, 'Mrs. Bartell, did you just leave that room?' I said, 'No, I did not.' She said, 'You've been in the kitchen all the time?' I said, 'Yes, yes.'

"She shook her head. 'Lord me, I saw a woman in white just come through there!' I was wearing a white blouse, it was summertime, so she thought it was me."

"Did your husband ever hear anything?" I asked.

"He just hears footsteps. The footsteps go on at all hours, early morning, early afternoon, late afternoon, early evening—I'm forever running into that long hall and saying, 'Who is it?' and of course there is nobody there."

"Are they the footsteps of a man or a woman?"

"I'm not able to tell you that, they are tentative, very tentative and very light, walking very slowly."

"There was this very strange Sunday evening. We had an early supper and then we went into the bedroom to watch a television program. Later I remembered I had the dishes on the table and I came in to do them. We had eaten a particularly delicious dessert in which we practically licked the plates clear, there just wasn't anything left on them. Yet, there right in the center of *my* plate, very precisely centered, was a small dried grape. We had no grapes in the house.

"When was the last time you saw anything or heard anything unusual?" I asked.

"Well, the most recent occurrences took place last week and about a week or so before that. I'll take you back to the earlier one. I was asleep and was awakened out of a sound sleep for no reason I'm aware of. I sat bolt upright in bed and looked around and felt very nervous. I got out of bed and came into the kitchen for a glass of water. Contessa, my dog, followed me in. I put the light on in the kitchen—it was about 3:30 or 4:00 in the morning—and was looking around, *when I heard this movement*. There was Contessa at this blue chair, she sat bolt upright at the side and sniffed and peered at the seat, and then backed away."

"You mean, as if she had seen someone?"

"As if she had seen a figure sitting in that chair. I hurried back to bed. When I lay down in my bed, my pillows and my sheets were cold as ice."

"The footsteps were heard at one particular location at night, near the bed?"

"Footsteps are heard mainly during the day and in the hall, and I have gone to great trouble to ascertain that nobody was home, because it's an old building and the partitions are thin and many times you can hear footsteps from the apartment downstairs. But at these times there was nobody home next door, there was nobody home downstairs in either apartment."

"When you heard the footsteps and your husband heard the foot-steps, did they both seem to come from the same direction?"

"Yes, they appear to come from this area, down the hall."

"Mrs. Bartell, one more question," I said. "In your earlier years did you ever have any psychic experiences before you moved to this house?"

"When I was a little girl of nine, I lived in Washington, D.C. One day I went with my parents to Mount Vernon, it was our first trip there. Mother and Dad had not seen the tomb of Martha and George Washington. It began to rain and we took refuge in the 'cook house,' thereby getting hopelessly lost in the vast grounds.

"The rain stopped and we set out from the wharf to the tombs and in those days there were no markers to the grave. We became hopeless-ly lost when I suddenly heard myself say, 'I know where it is, just follow me.' And of course, I was laughed at; most children are when they make statements like this.

"Well, I did lead them directly to the tomb, and I'd never been there in this life at all."

When we left that evening, I was hopeful that I had calmed the house. I had turned towards the empty room and quietly spoken to the Unseen Visitor, telling her to leave the living alone and that her world was no longer the world of the flesh. Sometimes this will do it, some-times not.

A day later, Mrs. Bartell was on the telephone again. The footsteps were continuing. Could I come again? This time I decided to bring my favorite medium, Ethel Johnson Meyers.

On November 27, we ascended the by-now-familiar old stairs to the top floor of the old town house.

On arriving, Mrs. Meyers, who had no idea of our plans for that evening, remarked that she felt the apartment full of great activity. It was at this moment, when we were all quietly seated around the dark-ened room—the Bartells, Ethel, my wife and I, and a Mr. Rockefeller, a friend of the Bartells—it was at this moment that a small table next to my wife's chair jumped. It did not jump high or far, but she had her eyes on it at the time, and she says it moved of its own volition as if some unseen hand had touched it.

Mrs. Meyers observed a feeling of jealousy in the atmosphere and added, "I was touched; there is someone sitting on the settee between us."

She felt a woman's presence almost at once. "She wants to go somewhere, there is urgency. But the apartment has been changed," she added, "and now the woman can't go.

"I have a feeling the piano area is the center of activities here."

"Correct," Mrs. Bartell nodded.

"I feel a very young person, and an aborted child, whose remains have been here at one time."

I thought of the nineteenth-century servant girl and the rigid code of that time, and the many affairs quietly perpetrated in the fashionable town houses of that day.

Ethel Meyers was now in a state halfway between clairvoyance and trance.

"Mallison," she murmured, "Renée, or Reney. The third person is the child. There is a pungent odor here."

Fred Bartell also noticed the scent, and my wife confirmed it, too. I did not sense it myself.

"A pretty young blonde, with large blue eyes and a tiny nose . . . Renée . . ."

Trance became more noticeable now.

"He put it on my finger . . . the ring . . . Mrs. John J. Mallison. I was born here . . . twenty-nine years. . . . March sixteenth, eighteen forty-eight . . . Where is my husband?"

"What is his name?" I asked softly.

"Henry . . . Henry McDermott," the entranced medium replied.

"Is he here now?"

"No, no . . . saw him last two years, now no more."

"What about a child?"

"No, NO!"

I decided to try and see if she knew in what year her tragedy occurred.

"Who is President of the United States?"

"They killed him."

"Whom?"

"Abraham."

"Who is now President?"

"Andrew Johnson."

Suddenly, the entity started to speak of the other man.

"John comes to play with me now, I can't go to him."

I firmly insisted she tell me about this John.

"He went, but he never came back. I lied to you, there was a child, but she died. I like it very much here. I can play with the little one. I lost a little one."

"What did your husband do for a living?"

"He made jewelry. He made my ring."

"Where was his shop?"

"Twenty-three . . . Twenty-three . . . Twenty-three . . ." She seemed hopelessly lost for the moment.

"What did your father do?"

"Supply restaurant . . ."

"Why are you here?"

"Papa did not know. . . . he's at the window, with blood . . . I lied, I'm nineteen not twenty-nine . . . married with ring now . . . Papa did not believe me . . . John has gone . . . they took him, Abraham took him, they killed him. . . ."

The emotions overcame the entranced medium at this point, and the entity slipped out, leaving the medium momentarily lifeless. Within a moment, though, control Albert took over and in his usual crisp voice announced that all was well.

"There was a miscarriage previous to the marriage," he explained, "and the father did not approve of the match. But they were married.

"The little girl died. She did abort the first child; there were two children; mother and child died together in childbirth. The husband was killed in battle. Reeny is really Irene, but the name Mallison is correct. Irene's mother also died in childbirth; there were four older girls and three boys."

"What about the name McDermott?"

"It is not quite correct."

With that, he bade us release "the instrument" as it was half past ten and she seemed visibly tired.

The next day, November 28, I received a phone call from Mrs. Bartell.

Somehow she was impressed with the correct name. Not McDermott, but McDevitt, she felt. But she was not sure.

On November 29, she called again, to report some chills, but she remembered my farewell speech to the ghost the previous time, and asked her gently to go away. The chills passed quickly.

As I always do, I tried to corroborate some of the material obtained in this manner. The Civil War period is particularly difficult as many of the records no longer exist. I could not find Mr. Mallison in the few sources available to me, namely Trow's city directories and commercial listings. But I did encounter a Henry McDermott who lived nearby, at 203 1/2 West Nineteenth Street, in the year 1868.

I have checked with Mrs. Bartell several times since, but things are well in hand. Once in a while, Contessa will sniff at something only she can see or sense, but nobody has seen any lady in white of late, and the town house has settled into a period of calm.

Quite possibly the young servant girl has found peace with both her men in a world where these things aren't taken so literally.

New York Is Full of Ghosts

Ghosts walk the streets of Manhattan or the parkways of its suburbs with the same regularity as they do in lonely Midwestern farmhouses or English manors. Subways and noisy buses seem to have no ill effect on the spectres, who have other business on their etheric minds, it seems.

What is more prosaic than a brownstone house on West Eighty-seventh Street? About a year ago, Mrs. William DeGeldern moved to an old house on that block, along with her husband, their young child, and her mother-in-law, Mrs. Worm. The house was built in 1894 and consists of five floors connected by heavy wooden stairs in the elegant manner of that time. It had been the property of one family until 1925, when it passed into the hands of an artist, followed by a Mr. Judd, who in turn was followed by the DeGeldern family. To the best of the DeGelderns' knowledge, nobody had reported anything unusual about the house before. Mrs. Worm had had some psychic experiences in Europe, but her daughter-in-law was completely untouched by the hand of the Sixth Sense.

On moving in, during the summer of 1962, Mrs. DeGeldern, working busily, had her back towards the entrance door downstairs. It was twilight, around the end of the afternoon, when she suddenly felt someone watching her. It was that indefinable feeling that you're not alone.

"What did you do?" I asked, as we sat in front of the downstairs fireplace.

"I looked around and I saw a young girl standing up on the staircase leading to the first floor and watching me very seriously. She seemed about sixteen years of age, had blonde hair in braids and wore a blue dress—nothing current, you understand, but something women might have worn in the last century."

"What did you do then?"

"She was standing there, motionless, with her hand on the wooden rail. I got up and walked towards her. But as I got real close to her she just faded away before my eyes."

"Did you ever seen anything, Mrs. Worm?" I asked the elder lady.

"Not see, but I've felt a presence a number of times. And last Christmas, while we were having dinner in the dining room downstairs, I felt a hand on my shoulder, as if someone were trying to get my attention! Many times I feel someone brush by me without talking—still, I can feel the rush of air."

"And you, sir?" I turned to the husband. "Have you ever seen anything unusual?"

"No, nothing," he replied casually, "but I do hear noises—strange noises I cannot readily explain."

The way things are nowadays in New York, the West Side is no place for a young girl ghost, but there you are.

Mrs. Rose Margolies now lives in Florida, but some years ago she made her home on Snyder Avenue, in Brooklyn. This is a section primarily consisting of small homes. The time had come to have the apartment, which was part of a small house, done over and the landlord was in the process of having Mrs. Margolies' ceiling fixed. But as happens so often, the workmen doing the job left some gaping holes in the ceiling. Mrs. Margolies was rather disappointed, especially as the landlord had personally promised her that the job would be done properly. There she sat, contemplating the holes in her living room ceiling.

"Then what happened?" I asked the peppery lady, who remembers the incident well.

"Towards evening I heard a knock on the door. I said come in, and heard nothing at first. But then I heard my landlord's voice—only it sounded odd, as if he were far, far away. I got up to let him in, but before I reached the door I saw a black shadow come right through it—a shadow in the shape of a man. It lasted only a second, then I had reached the door and opened it. My landlord walked in. He told me the men would return the next morning to finish the ceiling."

"Was there anything unusual about that?" I inquired.

"There was. Again he seemed a million miles away from me. After he left, I sat there thinking about it. Later that evening the superintendent came to call on me. He had sad news. The landlord had had a stroke that afternoon and had died instantly."

Recently I had the pleasure of meeting Miss Boyd down on Charles Street in the Greenwich village section of Manhattan. Miss Boyd is a ghost. But let me explain. Barrie Gaunt is an English designer of fashions and an actor but recently arrived in our midst. Although he is very English, he knows nothing about ghosts. He moved into a small ground-floor apartment on Charles Street a few weeks before and ghosts were the farthest thing from his mind.

Our mutual friend, writer Elizabeth Byrd, tipped me off that all was not as it should be with the old house and asked if I would please have a go at it.

It was Halloween night, when Catherine and I descended on the haunted apartment in the company of Sybil Leek, the English lady-witch, who also happens to be a good trance medium. The fire was licking the logs in the fireplace, the wind was howling outside in the back yard, and the setting could not have been more appropriate for a ghost hunt if Cecil B. DeMille had arranged it.

"The first time I heard about the place being haunted was in mid-September," Elizabeth Byrd explained, "when Barrie Gaunt had a house guest visiting here. She was a Mexican lady named Adriana de Sola and had come to stay here for ten days. But on the third or fourth night she was awakened in bed by a rather violent push on her arm. At the same time she felt herself compelled to burst into tears, and she wept profusely, although she is not given to weeping at all. She felt an enormous grief here.

"Somebody had been badly hurt here and she felt it. A few nights later, she was awakened again by a push as if someone were trying to rouse her. Again, she had to cry uncontrollably.

"However, she decided not to tell her host about it. He had been here only a short time and she did not wish to upset him."

"What about you, Barrie?" I asked. "When did you notice anything unusual about your place?"

Barrie Gaunt is a quiet man in his middle or late twenties, and not easily given to hysterics.

"I arrived home around one o'clock one night and I heard this crying—my friend Miss De Sola weeping away. Since she left, things have happened to me also. One night I could not sleep. I woke up sure there was someone else in the place watching me. I saw a peculiar sort of mist, but I shrugged it off and went back to sleep. Another time I felt sure there was a presence in the room. I discussed it with Miss Byrd and she finally told me about Adriana's experiences here."

"Something happened just a few hours ago, didn't it?" I inquired. Elizabeth Byrd had told me we should come right away.

"Last night I woke up at ten to four, sure I was not alone. Up to the time I came here, I had always slept well without waking up in the middle of the night. But lately I can't get any sleep here."

Neither Barrie Gaunt nor Elizabeth Byrd had any knowledge of the background of the house. Barrie had gotten the apartment from a friend, and made no inquiries whatever.

I then asked Sybil Leek, who had come dressed in her witches' best, complete with purple stockings and cape, to sit on the bed near the spot where Barrie had seen the misty cloud.

"Somebody's kept chickens here," Sybil said, gradually slipping into trance.

"There is a woman here with us all the time," she added with a faltering voice not quite her own any longer. "Her name's Boyd! B-o-y-d."

I like a medium who spells things out for you. But then Sybil is very British.

"Chickens, chickens—I don't know why there are these chickens here."

"What does this Miss Boyd look like?"

"She is wearing a cotton pink dress, high neck, long sleeves."

"What does she want?"

"She wants to be here."

"Why?"

"Because she lived here. Her home. Died here. Not in this room, though. There are chickens in this room. She is looking for something. Something she lost here. I think a Spanish girl did not like her. There was some foreign person here with her. Austa. A-us-ta. Ay-u-sta."

I asked Miss Boyd not to disturb the living with her pushes and tears, then turned to Sybil Leek again and asked what Miss Boyd was looking for in this room.

"It's a paper," Sybil, entranced, replied after a moment's hesitation. "It's got something to do with this house."

"How long ago did all this happen?"

"Eighteen eighty-six."

"Did she own this house?"

"No."

"Who owned the house?"

"A-NU-SSI. A-nu-ssi."

The medium seemed to repeat a name she was hearing.

I asked, "Did this person have a first name?"

"She called him Mr. Anussi, she says," the medium replied.

"Why is she so unhappy?"

"Wants the paper."

"Go in peace," I said, "never to be drawn back here by your unhappy memories. Your loved ones await you on the Other Side of the Veil. Go in peace."

Confident that we had dispatched Miss Boyd to the nether world, we brought Sybil Leek out of trance and went out into the cold October night, as Allhallow's Eve faded into the mist of morning.

But Miss Boyd wasn't going to be satisfied that quickly. A few nights later, Barrie awakened when he saw in the middle of the room a rainbowlike light for which there was no explanation.

About that time a call from radio station WINS, asking me if I knew of any good haunt on which they could come along with me, brought back Barrie Gaunt's apartment. Again I summoned Sybil Leek—by telephone, not magic—and we assembled at the Charles Street place. By we, I mean Elizabeth Byrd, Mr. Gaunt, Sybil and Westinghouse's Squire Rushnell of Boston, Stan Bernard and Mrs. Bernard, Paul Rohrer, M.C. and producer of "Contact" and myself. It was a Sunday night in December, and again a fire was burning lustily in the old fireplace.

I questioned Barrie Gaunt about the misty shape he had observed in the apartment. He admitted that he had experienced a similar misty cloud when he was fourteen years old, at the very moment when his father died.

Between these two sessions Elizabeth Byrd had gone down to the Hall of Records, the place where the City of New York keeps the records of all buildings and parcels of land within its boundaries. After going through several volumes of material along the lines suggested by me, she found that the house on Charles Street had indeed belonged to the Boyd family for many years! In 1827 Samuel Boyd appears as the owner of the parcel of land on which the house stands, in 1850 John T. Boyd is named, and in 1861 the house passed into the hands of the latter's heirs.

"We did not get a first name for Miss Boyd in the seance," Elizabeth Byrd said, "but there is no doubt that the house was in the Boyd family in the year mentioned, eighteen eighty-six, and in those days many people kept chickens in their back yard. In eighteen eighty-six, a lawyer named William Boyd was living here. The records bear this out. A Mary Boyd was living right next door. As far as the landlord Anussi is concerned, there was a Moeslin *pronounced Muslin* connected with this house. He and his wife Emma rented it to Mary Boyd in eighteen eighty-six."

"Fascinating," said Sybil, to whom all this was, of course, news.

Since our last seance, Barrie had had some more unusual experiences. Several times when he and Miss Byrd were talking on the telephone, both distinctly heard a deep breathing sound above Barrie Gaunt's voice, as if another person were breathing close to him. "I heard heavy breathing," Elizabeth confirmed, "but I simply thought Barrie was coming down with a cold." He wasn't though.

It was time to put Sybil into trance, to see what Miss Boyd had to say to us today.

Within a few moments, Sybil's own personality was gone, and, in her stead, I was speaking to a stranger.

"Go away!" the strange voice said. "This is my house!"

"What is your name?"

"Boyd. Miss Boyd."

"Your first name?"

"Mary Elizabeth Boyd." This without a moment's hesitation.

"How can we help you?"

The voice was almost crying. "Find the paper. My house."

"Who wrote the paper?"

"My father."

"What is your father's name?"

"Billy. Billy Boyd."

"Where was the paper left?"

"I don't know! Musli took the house. Did not like us. Father owed him a lot of money."

"Where did Musli live?"

"Here."

"What did he do for a living?"

"He bought things—houses, land."

"Your father's profession?"

"Lot of papers. Business."

"Where was his office?"

"In this street. Number 37."

Next door, I thought. How convenient! But people did have their offices near their homes, even then, at times.

"Father signed. They don't need my house. . . ."

"Did you have any sisters or brothers?"

"They're all dead. Jane—Jane died."

"Was she married?"

"Yes."

"Her husband's name?"

"Stephen Muslin."

"Then he was related to you?"

"My house," she cried, and I calmed her down.

"Then the man who took your house was your brother-in-law. What was his profession?"

"Bought land."

"Who is the Spanish woman you talked about?"

Derisive laughter. "Stayed here."

"Who brought her here?"

"Musli."

"Who was she?"

"A friend."

"Her name?"

"Alexi."

"What profession did she have?"

Derisive laughter was my answer. Words were not needed.

"If we found the paper, what would you do?"

"Live here."

I then explained that much time had gone by, that the papers had been found and the house was again rightfully hers. I did this to rest her distorted mind. "Go and join your father, who is waiting for you," I suggested. "Eighty years have gone by."

I then brought Sybil Leek out of trance. She was fine, albeit a bit tired. Eighty years can be a long journey. She remembered nothing.

Immediately, I pointed out a small but significant factor: In discussing her research, Elizabeth Byrd had mentioned only *a Mary Boyd.* Yet, in trance, Miss Boyd, speaking through Sybil Leek, identified herself as *Mary Elizabeth Boyd.* The records, we discovered, had her down as *Mary E. Boyd.* But neither Sybil nor, for that matter, I, had any way of knowing this prior to the second seance!

"William Boyd lived on Block 611—that is this house," Elizabeth Byrd said, "and Mary Boyd had Number 612, next door! So she must have been moved out of here sometime around eighteen eighty-six—her wanting to get back into her father's house makes sense."

Then she added, "About that Spanish lady—" and I suddenly remembered the intruder the ghost described with a sneer. "There is a court case on record between William Boyd and one Isabella Haviland.

Could she be that woman? At any rate, in eighteen eighty-seven, Isabella was in firm possession of this house. This is a matter of record."

When we left the house, we recommended Miss Boyd to Barrie Gaunt, but I had a feeling this was merely a polite gesture. Miss Boyd had left her chickens far behind and had joined her father, Billy, in the world where land grants mean very little.

The Teen-Agers and the Staten Island Ghost

I receive a great many letters from people between the ages of twelve and eighteen who have a serious, often very inquisitive interest in extrasensory perception. Sometimes they have a case of their own to report.

Such was the case when I first heard from Carolyn Westbo, who lived on Staten Island. It seemed that her aunt, Mrs. Carol Packer, had lived in a house on Staten Island where a poltergeist had also taken up residence. Poltergeists are ghosts who like to make noises or move objects around.

Carolyn's aunt no longer lived at the house. I asked the new owners, a family by the name of Goetz, for permission to visit.

What I liked about Carolyn Westbo, who was seventeen and very serious, was that she herself was doubtful about her experiences and wondered if they weren't all due to imagination or, as she put it, "self-delusion." But deep down she knew she was psychic, and had already accepted this knowledge.

"When were you at the house on Henderson Avenue the last time, Carolyn?" I asked.

"The last time I was at the house was in January of 1965," she answered. "My aunt was in the process of moving out, and the house was in an uproar. I stood against the wall and watched the proceedings. My left side was turned to the wall, and I was reminiscing about the wonderful times I had had on New Year's Eve, and somehow smiled to myself. All of a sudden, my *right side*, the right side of my head, felt very

depressed and a feeling of great despair came over me. I felt like wringing my hands and was very distraught. It only stayed with me a few
moments, but I had the distinct feeling of a woman who was very worried, and I could almost feel something or someone pressing against the
right side of my head. And then I saw a mist, in the large downstairs
dining room of the house."

"A mist? What sort of mist?"

"It had a shape, rather tall and thin. It did not have a face, and
looked kind of ragged. *But I did see hands wringing.*"

Carolyn had told her aunt about her uncanny experience, even
though she was afraid she would be laughed at. Her own family had
pooh-poohed the whole thing, and Carolyn did not like to be laughed
at, especially when she *knew* she had seen what she had seen. But her
aunt did not laugh. She, too, had observed the misty shape when she
was alone in the house, yet she had always felt great comfort with the
ghost, whoever it was.

It was then that Carolyn learned about the poltergeist on
Henderson Avenue. Objects were moving by themselves, her aunt
admitted, such as things falling from a table and other objects that had-
n't been touched. On one occasion she heard a loud crash downstairs—
the house had three stories—and found a freshly baked pie upside down
on the floor. She had placed it far back on the shelf in the pantry. Pots
and pans around the pie had not been touched, and no trucks were
passing by outside that might account for the vibration that could have
caused the pie to fall. There had been nobody else in the house at the
time. The aunt, Carol Packer, now lives in upstate New York. She had
never accepted the idea of a ghost, and yet could not offer any explanation for the strange happenings in the house.

"Have you had other experiences of a psychic nature?" I asked the
young girl.

"Nothing really great, only little things, such as knowing what my teacher would ask the next day, or what people are wearing when I talk to them on the telephone or dream about them. I see things happening and a week later or so, they do happen."

Carolyn and her aunt had looked into the history of the house. They found that three families prior to Mrs. Packer's stay in the house, a woman had dropped dead on the front porch. They never knew her name or anything else beyond this bare fact.

There the matter stood when our little expedition consisting of Sybil Leek and myself, book editor Evelyn Grippo, and CBS newscaster Lou Adler and his wife, arrived at the Victorian structure where the ghost was presumably awaiting us. Mr. Adler brought along a CBS radio car and an engineer by the name of Leon, who we almost lost on the way over the Verrazano Bridge. It was a humid Sunday evening in May of 1965. Fifteen people had assembled at the Goetzes' to celebrate some kind of anniversary, but I suspect they were very curious about our investigation as an added attraction. We could hear their voices as we mounted the steep wooden steps leading to the house from Henderson Avenue, a quiet street lined with shade trees.

While the CBS people set up their equipment, I politely put the celebrants into the front room and collected those directly concerned with the haunting around a heavy oak table in the dining room on the first floor of the sturdy old house. Carolyn Westbo, her younger sister Betsy, Mr. and Mrs. Goetz, their son and a married daughter, Mrs. Grippo of Ace Books, the Adlers, and I formed a circle around the table. I had asked Sybil to wait in another room, where she could not possibly overhear a single word that was said in the dining room. Afterwards, skeptical reporter Lou Adler admitted that "unless she had some sort of electronic listening device by which she could listen through walls, or unless you and Sybil set this up to trick everybody— there is no alternative explanation for what occurred this evening." Needless to say, we did not use electronic devices. Sybil could not hear anything, and neither she nor I knew anything of what would happen later.

As soon as Sybil Leek was out of earshot, I started to question the witnesses among those present. Carolyn Westbo repeated her testimony given to me earlier. I then turned my attention, and my microphone, to Betsy Westbo.

Betsy had been to the house a number of times. Had she ever felt anything unusual in this house?

"One time I walked in here," the serious young girl said in response. "My mother and my cousin were in the kitchen downstairs, in the rear of the house, and I walked into the hall. It was dark, about sunset, and I suddenly felt as if someone were staring at me, just looking at me. I was sure it was my cousin, so I asked him to come out. He had played tricks on me before. But he wasn't there, and I went into the kitchen, and he had not left it at all."

"Any other experiences bordering on the uncanny?" I asked.

This 15-year-old girl was calm and not at all given to imagination, I felt, and she struck me as mature beyond her years.

"The time my aunt moved out, I was here, too. I felt as if someone were crying and I wanted to cry with them. I was just walking around then, and it felt as if someone were next to me crying and saying, 'What's going to happen to me?'"

Betsy had also had psychic experiences in her young life. Not long before in her family's house, just down the street from the haunted house her aunt used to call home, Betsy was asleep in bed around 11 pm, when she awoke with a start.

"I heard a screech and a dog yelping, as if he had been hurt. I was sure there had been an accident, and we looked out the window, but there was nothing, no car, no dog."

"What did you do then?"

"We couldn't figure it out," Betsy answered, "but the very next evening, again at eleven o'clock, we heard the same noises—my sister was with me in the room this time. We checked again, and this time there was a dog. I had seen the entire accident happen, *exactly as it did, twenty-four hours before!*"

"Amazing," I conceded. "Then you are indeed clairvoyant."

Mrs. Mariam Goetz, a pleasant-looking, vivacious woman in her middle years, had been the lady of the house since February of 1965. She had not seen or heard anything uncanny, and she felt very happy in the house. But then there was this strange business about the silver—

"My silver spoons disappeared, one by one, and we searched and searched, and we thought someone was playing a prank. Each blamed the other, but neither Mr. Goetz, nor my son, nor my young married daughter, Irene Nelson, who lives with us, had hidden the spoons. The wedding gifts were displayed in Grandmother's room upstairs, including some pretty silver objects. One evening, after about a week of this, we discovered in each bowl—a silver spoon! Of course we thought Grandmother had been playing a trick on us, but she assured us she had not."

The rest of the spoons turned up in the drawers of the room, carefully hidden in many places. Although the grandmother was quite aged, she was in good mental condition, and the Goetzes really had no proof that she hid the spoons.

"Irene, my married daughter, had come to sleep with me several nights, because she hadn't felt very secure in her own bedroom," Mrs. Goetz added.

Mrs. Irene Nelson was a young woman with dark eyes and dark hair, not the dreamer type, but rather factually minded and to the point. She had been in the house as long as her parents, four months to the time of my investigation.

Had she noticed anything unusual?

"Yes," the young woman said. "One night I was sitting in the kitchen at the table, with two friends of mine, and as we sat there and talked, some screws were falling to the floor from the kitchen table, by themselves, one by one. My friends left. I got up to gather my things, and the table collapsed behind me. One of its legs had come off by itself. But the table was not wobbly, or any of the screws loose, just before we used it, or we would have noticed it. There was nobody else in the house who could have loosened the screws as a prank, either."

"And poor Grandmother can't be blamed for it, either," I added. The octogenarian did not get around very much any more.

"Anything else?" I asked, crisply.

"One night, about four in the morning," Mrs. Nelson said, "I woke up with a sudden start and I opened my eyes and could not close them again. Suddenly, I felt pin-prickles all over my body. I felt chilly. I felt there was someone in the room I could not see. I heard a strange sound, seemingly outside, as if someone were sweeping the sidewalk. This was in my bedroom directly above the living room. The feeling lasted about ten minutes, and I just lay there, motionless and frightened. I had several bad nights after that, but that first time was the worst."

"Have you ever felt another presence when you were alone?"

"Yes, I have. In different parts of the house."

The house, along with the building next door, was built at the turn of the century. It was Victorian in architecture and appointments. Heavy wooden beams, many small rooms on the three floors, high ceilings, and solid staircases characterized the house on Henderson Avenue.

It was time to bring Sybil Leek into the dining room and start the trance.

Had anything happened to her while she was waiting outside in the kitchen? Sybil seemed somewhat upset, a very unusual state for this usually imperturbable psychic lady.

"I was standing by the refrigerator," she reported, "and the kitchen door opened about two inches. It disturbed me, for I did not want any-one to think I was opening the door to listen. There was someone there, I felt, and I could have easily gone into trance that moment, but fought it as I never do this without you being present."

Imagine—a ghost too impatient to wait for the proper signal!

"I wanted to run outside, but restrained myself," Sybil added. "I never moved from the spot near the refrigerator. I was terrified, which I rarely am."

We sat down, and soon Sybil was in deep trance. Before long, a faint voice made itself heard through Sybil's lips.

"What is your name?" I asked.

"Anne Meredith." It came with great difficulty of breathing.

"Is this your house?"

"Yes . . . I want to get in. I live here. *I want to get in!*"

"What's wrong?"

"I . . . have . . . heart trouble . . . I can't get up the steps."

Sybil's breathing was heavy and labored.

"How long have you lived here?"

"Thirty-five."

"What year did you move in?"

"Twenty-two."

"Were you alone in this house?"

"No . . . James . . . these steps . . . James . . . son."

"What is it you want?"

"I can't stay here . . . want to get in . . . the steps . . . can't get to the door . . . *door must be opened.*"

"How old are you?"

"Fifty-two."

"Where did you go to school?"

"Derby . . . Connecticut."

"Your father's name?"

"Johannes.

"Mother's?"

"Marguerite."

"Where were you baptized?"

"Derby . . . my lips are sore . . . I bite them . . . I have pain in my heart."

I started to explain her true status to her.

"You passed out of the physical life in this house," I began. "It is no longer your house. You must go on and join your family, those who have passed on before you. Do you understand?"

She did not.

"I have to get up the stairs," she mumbled over and over again.

As I repeated the formula I usually employ to pry an unhappy ghost away from the place of emotional turmoil in the past, Sybil broke out of trance momentarily, her eyes wide open, staring in sheer terror and lack of understanding at the group. Quickly, I hypnotized her back into the trance state, and in a moment or two, the ghost was back in control of Sybil's vocal apparatus. Heavy tears now rolled down the medium's cheeks. Obviously, she was undergoing great emotional strain. Now the voice returned slowly.

"I want to come in . . . I have to come back!"

"You died on the steps of this house. You can't come back," I countered.

"Someone's there," the ghost insisted in a shaky voice. "I have to come back."

"Who is it you want to come back to?"

"James."

I assured her James was well taken care of, and she need not worry about him anymore.

"Don't leave me outside, I shall die," she said now.

"You *have* died, dear," I replied, quietly.

176

"Open the door, open the door," she demanded.

I took another tack. Suggesting that the door was being opened for her, I took her "by the hand" and showed her that someone else lived here now. No James. I even took her "upstairs" by suggestion. She seemed shocked.

"I don't believe you."

"This is the year 1965," I said.

"Fifty-five?"

"No, sixty-five."

There was disbelief. Then she complained that a dog kept her up, and also mentioned that her mother was living upstairs.

What was the dog's name?

"Silly dog . . . Franz." A dog named Franz was unusual even for a ghost, I thought. Still, people do like to give their pets strange names. The Goetzes had named their aged spaniel Happy, and I had never seen a more subdued dog in my life.

Why was she afraid of the dog? I asked the ghost.

"I fall over him," she complained. "My heart . . . dog is to blame."

"But this happened in 1955, you say."

"Happened *today*," she answered. To a ghost, time stands still. She insisted this was 1955. I strongly insisted it was 1965. I explained once more what had happened to her.

"Not dead," she said. "Not in the body? That's silly."

Unfortunately, very few ghosts know that they are dead. It comes as a shock when I tell them.

"I'm going upstairs and neither you nor that dog will stop me," she finally said resolutely.

I agreed to help her up the stairs.

"Lift me," she pleaded.

Mentally, we opened the door and went upstairs.

"Where is my mother?" she said, obviously realizing that her mother was not there. I explained she had died. The truth of the situation began to dawn on Anne Meredith.

I took advantage of this state of affairs to press my point and suggest her mother was awaiting her outside the house.

"May I come back sometime?" the ghost asked in a feeble voice.

"You may if you wish," I promised, "but now you must join your mother."

As the ghost faded away, Sybil returned to her own body.

She felt fine, but, of course, remembered nothing of what had come out of her mouth during trance. Just before awakening, tears once more rolled down her face.

I thought it rather remarkable that Sybil, in her trance state, had brought on a female personality who had died of a heart attack on the outside steps leading to the house. Sybil had no way of knowing that such a person actually existed and that her death had indeed taken place some years ago as described.

What about the names Anne Meredith and James?

Carolyn Westbo checked with the lady who had owned both houses and who lived in the one next door, a Miss Irving. Quite aged herself, she did not recall anyone with the name of Anne Meredith. By a strange coincidence, her own first names were Anne Adelaide. Derby, Connecticut, exists.

Checking church registers is a long and doubtful job at best. Finding a record of Anne Meredith would be wonderful, of course, but if I didn't find such a record, it didn't mean she never existed. Many tenants had come and gone in the old house atop the hill on Henderson Avenue. Perhaps Anne and Meredith were only her first and middle names.

Time will tell.

Meanwhile, it is to be profoundly hoped that the hand-wringing lady ghost of Staten Island need not climb those horrible stairs any longer, nor cope with dogs who have no respect for ghosts—especially ghosts who once owned the house.

Come and Meet My Ghost!

Margaret Widdemer was a spirited lady in her sunny years, a famed author and prize winner, who had for years made her home in the New York studio building on West Sixty-seventh Street called the Hotel des Artistes. It was the sort of place that cries out for a ghost, modeled on European studios and full of eerie, half-lit corridors and nooks. The tenants are painters, writers, and teachers.

Miss Widdemer lived in a roomy duplex, with a pleasantly crammed living room downstairs, and a wooden staircase winding to the upper story, which was divided unevenly between her workroom and a small bedroom.

All her life, Margaret Widdemer, poet and novelist, had had psychic experiences of one kind or another. Pennsylvania-born, she had visions of the dead many times.

Miss Widdemer bought her apartment in the mid-1940s, from a Mrs. Gertrude F., who had since passed on. Mrs. F. had another apartment a few doors away herself; she, her husband, and a daughter were among the original shareholders of the building, built around 1910.

Elizabeth Byrd, a mutual friend, had told me of her uncanny feelings in Margaret Widdemer's apartment.

It intrigued me sufficiently to make an appointment for a visit, but I did not feel that the presence of a medium was required—the evidence was too slender. Thus I arrived at the Hotel des Artistes on a damp night in February, 1965, accompanied only by my tape recorder and immense good will toward whoever it was who was present in the place!

I asked Miss Widdemer what her unusual experiences in the apartment had been.

"There have been unexplained noises, hangings of doors and such, and my cleaning woman would say, 'I thought you were in.' She would say 'I just saw someone walk up the stairs'—but, of course, I was not in. The same thing would happen to me. I was here alone, and I thought my maid had come in, because I heard footsteps going up and down the stairs, but on checking I found she hadn't come in at all."

Present were Elizabeth Byrd, Mrs. L. (a psychic neighbor from across the hall), and Barrie Gaunt, the young English designer and actor whose own haunted apartment we had visited not long before down on Charles Street.

For the past few minutes, Barrie had been restless and I saw him wandering about the place, up and down the stairs, as if searching for something or someone. The house was strange to him, of course, and I thought he was just exploring with the natural curiosity of the artist. But he seemed perplexed, and I began to wonder if he had sensed anything out of the ordinary.

"Someone came up these stairs," he finally said, "stopped about here and turned around—hate in the eyes. It's a woman."

His left hand felt strangely stiff, he added. And he had a feeling that someone was murdered here.

Elizabeth Byrd, too, had had an unusual experience in the apartment in April.

"I was having dinner with Margaret, and at one point wanted to go to the powder room. I went up the stairs, and the minute I got to the top of the stairs, I was seized with fear. I blundered into the other rooms before I could get my bearings. I didn't want to yell for help, because Margaret walks with a cane and would have had to scramble up the stairs to help me. I couldn't get down again fast enough. I was really scared, and I don't scare easily."

I turned my attention once more to Barrie Gaunt.

"I feel a great tragedy here," he said, "especially on the staircase where the curve is. I feel an agonizing screaming. In the room directly above this, there is a complete turmoil. A very beautiful woman, I feel, also a man, and I feel there's been a death here, a death by violence. The woman is fighting for her life, but not physically. Rather, she is fighting for *her mentality*. The person who is dead in this apartment is the man."

Everybody stared at Barrie now, as it turned out that we had a medium among us, after all, even though I had not brought one.

"Go on," I said, but it was hardly necessary. Barrie was engrossed in his impressions.

"The tragedy involved both people in this apartment. I just know it." Still shaken with the eerie feelings that had beset him on the stairs, Barrie reiterated his conviction of a terrible struggle going on and the woman's agony stood vividly etched on his expressive face.

I decided it was time to break up our meeting, and thanked our hostess. A few days later, Margaret Widdemer was able to supply some of the answers to the questions raised by Barrie Gaunt.

"The F. girl, Christy, was a tall, very beautiful blonde with great blue eyes," she said. "When she was around seventeen, she suddenly went raving mad, and became so violent that she had to be removed. There was a history of disturbance on both sides of the family, it is alleged, and her hatred directed itself, for reasons unknown, against her own mother. She was placed in an insane asylum at Middletown, New York. Her mother could not even visit her, so violent was the poor girl's reaction."

"Then the girl lived here for a while, before they removed her?" I asked.

"Evidently so," Miss Widdemer said, and explained that Mrs. L., her neighbor, had helped her gather this information.

Was it the father restraining his raving daughter that Barrie had sensed on the stairs? He was dead now, and no information on how he died was available.

The question now: Was the girl still living at the asylum? A few days later, that question, too, was answered. She had died some time ago, still raving mad.

Barrie Gaunt, of course, could not have known any of these facts. I took a series of photographs in the apartment, none of which showed anything unusual. Was it an etheric impression then that Barrie had sensed, a re-enactment of the emotional events of the past? Or was the ghost of the poor girl still holding on to her one-time home, struggling against the brute force that was to take her away from it forever?

Henny from Brooklyn

C linton Street, Brooklyn is one of the oldest sections of that borough, pleasantly middle-class at one time, and still amongst Brooklyn's best neighborhoods, as neighborhoods go. The house in question is in the 300 block, and consists of four stories. There was a basement floor, then a parlor floor, a few steps up as is the usual custom with brownstone houses, and a third and fourth floor above it. If one preferred, one could call the third floor the fourth floor, in which case the basement becomes the first floor; but no matter how one called it, there were four levels in this brownstone, all of them capable of serving as apartments to those who wished to live there. The house was more than 100 years old at the time the events herein described happened, and the records are somewhat dim beyond a certain point.

In the 1960's, the house was owned by some offbeat people, about whom little was known. Even the Hall of Records isn't of much help, as the owners didn't always live in the house, and the people who lived in it were not necessarily the owners, not to mention tenants although sharing a part of the house with people legitimately entitled to live there. However, for the purpose of my story we need only concern ourselves with the two top floors; the third floor contained two bedrooms and a bath, while the fourth or top floor consisted of a living room, dining room, kitchen and a second bath.

At the time when my account begins, the first two floors were rented to an architect and his wife, and only the two top floors were available for new tenants. It was in the summer of 1970 when two young ladies in their early 20's, who had been living at the Brooklyn YWCA decided to find a place of their own. Somehow they heard of the two vacant floors in the house on Clinton Street and immediately fell in love with it, renting the two top floors without much hesitation. Both Barbara and Sharon were 23 years old at the time, still going to college, and trying to make ends meet on what money they could manage between themselves. Two years later, Barbara was living in San Francisco with a business of her own in independent merchandising of clothing. Brooklyn was only a hazy memory by then. But on August 1, 1970 it was very much her world.

Immediately after moving in, they decided to clean up the house, which needed a good deal of cleaning up indeed. The stairway to the top floor was carpeted all the way up, and it was quite a job to vacuum clean it because there were a lot of outlets along the way and one had to look out for extension cords in order to clean it. Sharon got to the top floor and was cleaning it and removed the extension cord to plug it in further up. Instead she just used the regular cord of the vacuum cleaner, about 12 feet long, using perhaps 3 feet of it which left 9 feet of cord lying on the floor.

All of a sudden the plug just pulled out of the wall. Sharon couldn't believe her eyes; the plug actually pulled itself out of the socket, and flew out onto the floor. She shook her head and put it back in, and turned the vacuum cleaner on again. Only then did she realize that she had turned the switch on the cleaner back on, when she had actually never turned it off in the first place. She couldn't figure out how that was possible. But she had a lot more work to do, so she continued with it. Later she came downstairs and told her roommate who thought she was out of her mind. "Wait till something happens to you," Sharon said, "there is something strange about this house."

During the next five months the girls heard strange noises all over the house, but they attributed it to an old house settling, or to the people living downstairs in the building. Five months of "peace" were rudely shattered when Sharon's younger brother came to visit from New Jersey. He was still in high school and liked to listen to music at night, especially when it was played as loud as possible. The young people were sitting in the living room, listening to music and talking. It was a nice, relaxed evening. All of a sudden the stereo went off. The music had been rather loud rock and roll, and at first they thought the volume had perhaps damaged the set. Then the hallway light went out, followed by the kitchen light. So they thought a fuse had blown. Barbara ran down four flights of stairs, into the basement to check. No fuse had blown. To be on the safe side, she checked them anyway, and switched them around to make sure everything was fine. Then she went back upstairs and asked the others how the electricity was behaving.

But everything was still off. At this point Sharon's brother decided to go into the kitchen and try the lights there. Possibly there was something wrong with the switches. He went into the hallway where there was an old Tiffany type lamp hanging at the top of the stairway. It had gone off, too, and he tried to turn it on and nothing happened. He pulled again, and suddenly it went on. In other words, he turned it off first, then turned it on, so it had been on in the first place.

This rather bothered the young man, and he announced he was going into the kitchen to get something to eat. He proceeded into the kitchen and when he came back to join the others he was as white as the wall. He reported the kitchen was as cold as an icebox, but as soon as one left the kitchen the temperature was normal in the rest of the house. The others then got up to see for themselves and, sure enough, it was icy cold in the kitchen. This, despite the fact that there were four or five radiators going and all windows closed.

That night they knew they had a ghost, and for want of a better name they called her Hendrix—it happened to have been the anniversary of Jimi Hendrix's death, and they had been playing some of his records.

Shortly afterward Toby joined the other two girls in the house. Toby moved in on April 1, 1971. It had been relatively quiet between the incident in the kitchen and that day. But somehow Toby's arrival was also the beginning of a new aspect of the haunting.

About a week after Toby moved in, the girls were in the living room, talking. It was about 11:00 o'clock at night and they had dimmers on in the living room. Toby was sitting on the couch, and Barbara and some friends were sitting on the other side of the room, when all of a sudden she felt a chilly breeze pass by her. It didn't touch her, but she felt it nonetheless, and just then the lights started to dim, back and forth, back and forth, and when she looked up, she actually saw the dial on the dimmer moving by itself. As yet, Toby knew nothing about the haunting, so she decided to say nothing to the others, having just moved in, and not wishing to have her new roommate think her weird.

But things kept happening night after night, usually after 11:00 o'clock, when the two girls and their friends sat around talking. After a couple of weeks, she could not stand it any longer and finally asked the others whether they could feel anything strange in the room. Barbara looked at Sharon and a strange look passed between them; finally they decided to tell Toby about the haunting, and brought her up to date from the beginning of their tenancy in the house.

Almost every day there was something new to report: cooking equipment would be missing, clothing would disappear, windows were opened by themselves, garbage cans would be turned over by unseen hands. Throughout that period, there was continued walking of an unseen person in the living room located directly over the third floor bedroom. And the girls heard it at any hour of the night and once in a while even during the day. Someone was walking back and forth, back and forth. They were loud, stomping footsteps, more like a woman's, but they sounded as if someone were very angry. Each time one of them went upstairs to check if anyone was in the house, only to find absolutely nothing.

The girls held a conference and decided that they had a ghost, make no mistake about it. Toby offered to look into the matter and perhaps find out what might have occurred at the house at an earlier age. Barbara kept hearing an obscure whistling, not a real tune or song that could be recognized, but a human whistling nevertheless. Meanwhile Toby heard of a course on witchcraft and the occult being given at New York University, and started to take an interest in books on the subject. But whenever there were people over to visit them and staying in the living room upstairs past eleven o'clock at night, the ghost would simply run them out of the room with all the tricks in her ghostly trade.

"She" would turn the stereo on and off, or make the lights go on and off. By now they were convinced it was a woman. There were heavy shutters from the floor to the ceiling, and frequently it appeared as if a wind were coming through them and they would clap together, as if the breeze were agitating them. Immediately after that they heard footsteps walking away from them, and there was an uncomfortable feeling in the room, making it imperative to leave and go somewhere else, usually downstairs into one of the bedrooms.

As yet, no one had actually seen her. In June, 1971 Bruce, Toby's boy friend, moved into the house with her. They had the master bedroom, and off the bedroom was a bathroom. Since Barbara would frequently walk through in the middle of the night, they left the light in the bathroom on all night so that she would not trip over anything. That particular night in June, Toby and her boy friend had just made love and she was looking up, not at the ceiling, but at the wall, when suddenly she saw a girl looking at her.

It was just like an outline, like a shadow on the wall, but Toby could tell that she had long hair arranged in braids. Somehow she had the impression that she was an Indian, perhaps because of the braids. Toby looked up at her and called the apparition to her boy friend's attention, but by the time he had focused on it she had disappeared.

He simply did not believe her. Instead, he asked Toby to go upstairs to the kitchen and make him a sandwich. She wasn't up there for more than five or ten minutes, when she returned to the bedroom and found her boy friend hidden under the covers of the bed. When she asked him what was wrong, he would shake his head, and so she looked around the room, but could find nothing unusual. The only thing she noticed was that the bathroom door was now wide open. She assumed that her boy friend had gone to the bathroom, but he shook his head and told her that he had not.

He had just been lying there smoking a cigarette, when all of a sudden he saw the handle on the door turn by itself, and the door open. When he saw that he simply dived under the covers until Toby returned. From that moment on he no longer laughed at her stories about a house ghost. The following night, her boy friend was asleep when Toby woke up at two o'clock in the morning. The television set had been left on and she went to shut it off, and when she got back into bed she happened to glance up at the same place on the wall where she had seen the apparition the night before. For a moment or two she saw the same outline of a girl, only this time she had the impression that the girl was smiling at her.

Two weeks after that, Toby and her boy friend broke up, and this rather shook her. She had come back home one day and didn't know that he had left, then she found a note in which he explained his reasons for leaving, and that he would get in touch with her later. This very much upset her, so much so that her two roommates had to calm her down. Finally, the two other girls went upstairs and Toby was lying on her bed trying to compose herself.

In the quiet of the room, she suddenly heard someone sob a little and then a voice said, "Toby." Toby got up from bed and went to the bottom of the stairs and called up, demanding to know what Barbara wanted. But no one had called her. She went back to the room and lay down on the bed again. Just then she heard a voice saying "Toby" again and again. On checking, she found that no one had called out to her— no one of flesh and blood, that is.

Toby then realized who had been calling her, and she decided to talk to "Henny," her nickname for Hendrix, which was the name given by the others to the ghost since that night when they were playing Jimi Hendrix records. In a quiet voice, Toby said, "Henny, did you call me?" and then she heard the voice answer, "Calm down, don't take it so hard, it will be all right." It was a girl's voice, and yet there was no one to be seen. The time was about five o'clock in the afternoon, and since it was in June, the room was still fairly light.

Toby had hardly recovered from this experience, when still another event took place. Sharon had moved out and another girl had moved in by the name of Madeline. One day her brother came to visit them from Chicago, and he brought a friend along who had had some experience of a spiritual nature. His name was Joey, and both boys were about 20 or 21 years old.

Madeline and her brother were much interested in the occult, and they brought a Ouija board to the house. On Saturday, December 19, 1971, while it was snowing outside and the atmosphere was just right for a seance, they decided to make contact with the unhappy ghost in the house. They went upstairs into the living room and sat down with the board. At first, it was going to be a game, and they were asking silly questions of it, such as who was going to marry who, and other romantic fluff. But halfway through the session they decided to try to contact the ghost in earnest. The three girls and Madeline's brother sat down on the floor with their knees touching and put the board on them. Then they invited Henny to appear and talk to them, if she was so inclined. They were prepared to pick up the indicator and place their hands on it, so it could move to various letters on the board.

But before their hands ever touched it, the indicator took off by itself! It shot over to the word yes on the board, as if to reassure them that communication was indeed desired. The four of them looked at each other, dumbfounded, for they had seen only too clearly what had just transpired. By now they were all somewhat scared. However, Toby decided, since she was going to be interested in psychic research, she might as well ask the questions. She began asking why the ghostly girl was still attached to the house. Haltingly, word for word, Henny replied and told her sad story.

It was a slow process, since every word had to be spelled out letter by letter, but the young people didn't mind the passage of time—they wanted to know why Henry was with them. It appears that the house once belonged to her father, a medical doctor. Her name was Cesa Rist and she had lived in the house with her family. Unfortunately she had fallen in love with a boy and became pregnant by him. She wanted to marry him and have the baby but her father would not allow it and forced her to have an abortion. He did it in the house itself, and she died during the abortion.

Her body was taken to Denver, Colorado and buried in the family plot. She realized that her boy friend was dead also, because this all happened a long time ago. Her reasons for staying on in the house was to find help: she wanted her remains to be buried near her lover's, in New York.

"Do you like the people who live in this house?" "Yes," the ghost replied. "Is anyone who lives here ever in any danger?" "Yes, people who kill babies." This struck the young people as particularly appropriate: A close friend, not present at the time, just had an abortion. "Will you appear to us?" "Cesa has," the ghost replied, and as if to emphasize this statement, there suddenly appeared the shadow of a cross on the kitchen wall, for which there was no possible source, except of course from the parapsychological point of view.

The girls realized they did not have the means to go to Denver and exhume Cesa's remains and bring it to New York, and they told the ghost as much. "Is there anything else we can do to help you?" "Contact Holzer." By that time, of course, Toby had become familiar with my works, and decided to sit down and write me a letter, telling me of their problem. They could not continue with the Ouija board or anything else, that night, they were all much too shaken up.

On Monday Toby typed up the letter they had composed, and sent it to me. Since they were not sure the letter would reach me, they decided to do some independent checking concerning the background of the house, and if possible, try to locate some record of Cesa Rist. But they were unsuccessful, even at the Hall of Records, the events having apparently transpired at a time when records were not yet kept, or at least not properly kept.

When I received the letter I was just about to leave for Europe and would be gone two and a half months. I asked the girls to stay in touch with me and after my return I would look into the matter. After Toby had spoken to me on the telephone, she went back into the living room and sat down quietly. She then addressed Henny and told her she had contacted me and it would be a couple of months before I could come to the house because I had to go to Europe.

Barbara decided not to wait, however; and one night she went upstairs to talk to Henny. She explained the situation to her, and why she was still hanging around the house; she explained that her agony was keeping her in the house, and that she must let go of it in order to go on and join her boy friend in the Great Beyond. Above all, she should not be angry with them because it was their home now. Somehow Barbara felt that the ghost understood, and nothing happened, nothing frightening at all. Relieved, Barbara sat down in a chair facing the couch. She was just sitting there smoking a cigarette and wondering whether Henny really existed, or whether perhaps she was talking to thin air.

At the moment an ethereal form entered the room, standing near the couch. It looked as if she were leaning on the arm of the couch, or holding on to the side of it. She saw the outline of the head and what looked like braids around the front of her chest. For half a minute, she was there, and then she suddenly disappeared. It looked to Barbara as if the girl had been 5'4", weighing perhaps 120 pounds. Stunned, Barbara sat there for another ten or fifteen minutes, trying to believe what she had seen. She smoked another five cigarettes and then walked downstairs to try to go to sleep. But sleep would not come; she kept thinking about her experience.

At the time Sharon left, they were interviewing potential room mates to replace her. One particularly unpleasant girl came over and fell in love with the house. Both Barbara and Toby didn't like her to move in, but she seemed all set to join them, so Toby decided to tell her about the ghost. She hoped it would stop the girl from moving in. As Toby delineated their experiences with Henny, the would-be room mate became more and more nervous.

All of a sudden there was a loud crash in the kitchen, and they went to check on it. The garbage can had turned itself over and all the garabage was spilled all over the kitchen even though no one had been near it. The new girl took one look at this and ran out as fast as she could. She never came back.

But shortly afterward Toby went on vacation to California. There she made arrangements to move and found employment in the market research department of a large department store. Under the circumstances the girls decided not to renew the lease, which was up in July, but to move to another apartment for a short period. In September, 1972, they moved to California. Under the circumstances, they did not contact me any further, and I assumed that matters had somehow been straightened out, or that there had been a change in their plans. It was not until a year later that we somehow met in California and I could fill in the missing details of Henny's story.

On the last day of the girls' stay at the house on Clinton Street, with the movers going in and out of the house, Toby went back into the house for one more look and to say goodby to Henny. She went up to the living room and said a simple goodbye, and hoped that Henny would be all right. But there was no answer, no feeling of a presence.

For awhile, the house stood empty, then it was purchased by the father of an acquaintance of the girls. Through Alan, they heard of the new people who had moved in after the house was sold. One day when they had just been in the house for a few days, they returned to what they assumed to be an empty house.

They found their kitchen flooded with water: There were two inches of water throughout the kitchen yet they knew they had not left the water taps on. Why had Henny turned the water on and left it run? Perhaps Henny didn't like the new tenants after all. But she had little choice, really. Being a ghost, she was tied to the house.

Following her friends to San Francisco was simply impossible, the way ghosts operate. And unless or until the new tenants on Clinton Street call for my services, there is really nothing I can do to help Henny.

The Fifth Avenue Ghost

Some cases of haunted houses require but a single visit to obtain information and evidence, others require two or three. But very few cases in the annals of psychic research can equal or better the record set by the case I shall call The Fifth Avenue Ghost. Seventeen sessions, stretching over a period of five months, were needed to complete this most unusual case. I am presenting it here just as it unfolded for us. I am quoting from our transcripts, our records taken during each and every session; and because so much evidence was obtained in this instance that could only be obtained from the person these events actually happened to, it is to my mind a very strong case for the truth about the nature of hauntings.

It isn't very often that one finds a haunted apartment listed in the leading evening paper.

Occasionally, an enterprising real-estate agent will add the epithet "looks haunted" to a cottage in the country to attract the romanticist from the big city.

But the haunted apartment I found listed in the New York *Daily News* one day in July 1953 was the real McCoy. Danton Walker, the late Broadway columnist, had this item—

"One for the books: an explorer, advertising his Fifth Avenue Studio for sublet, includes among the attractions 'attic dark room with ghost.' . . ."

The enterprising gentleman thus advertising his apartment for rent turned out to be Captain Davis, a celebrated explorer and author of many books, including, here and there, some ghost lore. Captain Davis was no skeptic. To the contrary, I found him sincere and well aware of the existence of physical research. Within hours, I had discussed the case with the *study group* which met weekly at the headquarters of the Association for Research and Enlightenment, the Edgar Cayce Foundation. A team was organized, consisting of Bernard Axelrod, Nelson Welsh, Stanley Goldberg and myself, and, of course, Mrs. Meyers as the medium. Bernard Axelrod and I knew that there was some kind of "ghost" at the Fifth Avenue address, but little more. The medium knew nothing whatever. Two days *after* the initial session, a somewhat fictional piece appeared in the *New York Times* (July 13, 1953) by the late Meyer Berger, who had evidently interviewed the *host*, but not the *ghost*. Mr. Berger quoted Captain Davis as saying there was a green ghost who had hanged himself from the studio gallery, and allegedly sticks an equally green hand out of the attic window now and then.

Captain Davis had no idea who the ghost was. This piece, it must be re-emphasized, appeared two days *after* the initial sitting at the Fifth Avenue house, and its contents were of course unknown to all concerned at the time.

In order to shake hands with the good Captain, we had to climb six flights of stairs to the very top of 226 Fifth Avenue. The building itself is one of those big old town houses popular in the mid-Victorian age, somber, sturdy, and well up to keeping its dark secrets behind its thick-set stone walls. Captain Davis volunteered the information that previous tenants had included Richard Harding Davis, actor Richard Mansfield, and a lady magazine editor. Only the lady was still around and, when interviewed, was found to be totally ignorant of the entire ghost tradition, nor had she ever been disturbed. Captain Davis also told of guests in the house having seen the ghost at various times, though he himself had not. His home is one of those fantastic and colorful apartments only an explorer or collector would own—a mixture of comfortable studio and museum, full of excitement and personality, and offering more than a touch of the Unseen. Two wild jungle cats completed the atmospheric picture, somewhat anticlimaxed by the host's tape recorder set up on the floor. The apartment is a kind of duplex, with a gallery or balcony jutting out into the main room. In the middle of this balcony was the window referred to in the *Times* interview. Present were the host, Captain Davis, Mr. and Mrs. Bertram Long, the Countess de Sales, all friends of the host's, and the group of researchers previously mentioned—a total of eight people, and if you wish, two cats. As with most sittings, tape recordings were made of the proceedings from beginning to end, in addition to which written notes were taken.

Meeting a Ghost

Like a well-rehearsed television thriller, the big clock in the tower across the square struck nine, and the lights were doused, except for the one medium-bright electric lamp. This was sufficient light, however, to distinguish the outlines of most of the sitters, and particularly the center of the room around the medium.

A comfortable chair was placed under the gallery, in which the medium took her place; around her, forming a circle, sat the others, with the host operating the recorder and facing the medium. It was very still, and the atmosphere seemed tense. The medium had hardly touched the chair when she grabbed her own neck in the unmistakable manner of someone being choked to death, and nervously told of being "hung by the neck until dead." She then sat in the chair and Bernard Axelrod, an experienced hypnotist, conditioned her into her usual trance condition, which came within a few minutes.

With bated breath, we awaited the arrival of whatever personality might be the "ghost" referred to. We expected some violence and, as will

197

be seen shortly, we got it. This is quite normal with such cases, especially at the first contact. It appears that a "disturbed personality" continuously relives his or her "passing condition," or cause of death, and it is this last agony that so frequently makes ghostly visitations matters of horror. If emotional anxiety is the cause of death, or was present at death, then the "disturbed personality," or entity, will keep reliving that final agony, much like a phonograph needle stuck in the last groove of a record. But here is what happened on that first occasion.

Sitting of July 11th 1953, at 226 Fifth Avenue

The Medium, now possessed by unknown entity, has difficulty in speaking. Entity breaks into mad laughter full of hatred.

Entity: . . . curry the horse . . . they're coming . . . curry the horse! Where is Mignon? WHERE IS SHE?

Question: We wish to help you. Who is Mignon?

Entity: She should be here . . . where is she . . . you've got her! Where is she? Where is the baby?

Question: What baby?

Entity: What did they do with her?

Question: We're your friends.

Entity: (in tears) Oh, an enemy . . . an enemy . . .

Question: What is your name?

Entity: Guychone . . . Guychone. . . . (express pain at the neck; hands feeling around are apparently puzzled by finding a woman's body)

Question: You are using someone else's body. (Entity clutches throat.) Does it hurt you there?

Entity: Not any more . . . it's whole again . . . I can't see . . . All is so different, all is very strange . . . nothing is the same.

I asked how he died. This excited him immediately.

Entity: (hysterical) I didn't do it . . . I tell you I didn't do it, no . . . Mignon, Mignon . . . where is she? They took the baby . . . she put me away . . . they took her. . . . (Why did she put you away?) So no one could find me (Where?) I stay there (meaning upstairs) all the time.

At this point, tapes were changed. *Entity,* asked where he came from, says Charleston, and that he lived in a white house.

Question: Do you find it difficult to use this body?
Entity: WHAT?? WHAT?? I'm HERE . . . I'm here. . . . This is my house . . . what are YOU doing here?
Question: Tell me about the little room upstairs.
Entity: (crying) Can I go . . . away . . . from the room?

At this point, the entity left, and the medium's *control,* Albert, took over her body.

Albert: There is a very strong force here, and it has been a little difficult. This individual here suffered violence at the hands of several people. He was a Confederate and he was given up, hidden here, while they made their escape.
Question: What rank did he hold?
Albert: I believe that he had some rank. It is a little dubious as to what he was.
Question: What was his name?
Albert: It is not as he says. That is an assumed name, that he likes to take. He is not as yet willing to give full particulars. He is a violent soul underneath when he has opportunity to come, but he hasn't done damage to anyone, and we are going to work with him, if possible, from

this side.

Question: What about Mignon and the baby?

Albert: Well, they of course are a long time *on this side,* but he never knew that, what became of them. They were separated cruelly. She did *not* do anything to him.

Question: How did he leave this world?

Albert: By violence. (Was he hanged?) Yes. (In the little room?) Yes. (Was it suicide or murder?) He says it was murder.

The *control* then suggests to end the trance, and try for results in "open" sitting. We slowly awaken the medium.

While the medium is resting, sitter Stanley Goldberg remarks that he has the impression that Guychone's father came from Scotland.

Captain Davis observes that at the exact moment of "frequency change" in the medium, that is, when Guychone left and Albert took over, the control light of the recording apparatus suddenly blazed up *of its own accord,* and had to be turned down by him.

A standing circle was then formed by all present, holding hands, and taking the center of the room. Soon the medium started swinging forward and back like a suspended body. She remarked feeling very stiff "from hanging and surprised to find that I'm whole, having been cut open in the middle."

Both Axelrod and I observed a luminescent white and *greenish glow* covering the medium, creating the impression of an older man without hair, with high cheekbones and thin arms. This was during the period when Guychone was speaking through the medium.

The seance ended at twelve-thirty. The medium reported feeling exhausted, with continued discomfort in the throat and stomach.

Captain Davis, unfortunately, left on a worldwide trip the same week, and the new tenant was uncooperative. I felt we should continue the investigation. Once you pry a "ghost" loose from his place of unhappy memories, he can sometimes be contacted elsewhere.

Thus, a second sitting took place at the headquarters of the study group, on West 16th Street. This was a small, normally-furnished room free of any particular atmosphere, and throughout this and all following sittings, subdued light was used, bright enough to see all facial expressions quite clearly. There was smoking and occasional talking in low voices, none of which ever disturbed the work. Before the second sitting, Mrs. Meyers remarked that Guychone had "followed her home" from the Fifth Avenue place, and twice appeared to her at night in a kind of "whitish halo," with an expression of frantic appeal in his eyes. Upon her admonition to be patient until the sitting, the apparition had vanished.

Sitting of July 14th, 1953, at 125 West 16th Street

Question: Do you know what year this is?

Guychone: 1873.

Question: No, it is 1953. Eighty years have gone by. You are no longer alive. Do you understand?

Guychone: Eighty years? EIGHTY YEARS? I'm not a hundred-ten years?

Question: No, you're not. You're forever young. Mignon is on your side, too. We have come to help you understand yourself. What happened in 1873?

Guychone: Nobody's goddamn business . . . mine . . . mine!

Question: All right, keep your secret then, but don't you want to see Mignon? Don't you want justice done? (mad, bitter laughter) Don't you believe in God? (more laughter) The fact you are here and are able to speak, doesn't that prove that there is hope for you? What happened in 1873? Remember the house on Fifth Avenue, the room upstairs, the horse to be curried?

201

Guychone: Riding, riding . . . find her . . . they took her away.

Question: Who took her away?

Guychone: YOU! (threatens to strike interrogator)

Question: No, we're your friends. Where can we find a record of your Army service? Is it true you were on a dangerous mission?

Guychone: Yes.

Question: In what capacity?

Guychone: That is my affair! I do not divulge my secrets. I am a gentleman, and my secrets die with me.

Question: Give us your rank.

Guychone: I was a Colonel.

Question: In what regiment?

Guychone: Two hundred and sixth.

Question: Were you infantry or cavalry?

Guychone: Cavalry.

Question: In the War Between the States?

Guychone: Yes.

Question: Where did you make your home before you came to New York?

Guychone: Charleston . . . Elm Street.

Question: What is your family name, Colonel?

Guychone: (crying) As a gentleman, I am yet not ready to give you that information . . . it's no use, I won't name it.

Question: We will abide by your wishes.

Guychone: (relieved) I am very much obliged to you . . . for giving me the information that it is EIGHTY YEARS. Eighty years!

I explain about the house on Fifth Avenue, and that Guychone's "presence" had been felt from time to time. Again, I ask for his name.

Apparently fumbling for paper, he is given paper and fountain pen; the latter seems to puzzle him at first, but he then writes in the artistic, stylized manner of the mid-Victorian age—"Edouard Guychone."

Question: Is your family of French extraction?

Guychone: Yes.

Question: Are you yourself French or were you born in this country?

Guychone: In this country . . . Charleston.

Question: Do you speak French?

Guychone: No.

Question: Is there anything you want us to do for you? Any unfinished business?

Guychone: Eighty years makes a difference . . . I am a broken man . . . God bless you . . . Mignon . . . it is so dark, so dark. . . .

I explain the reason for his finding himself temporarily in a woman's body, and how his hatred had brought him back to the house on Fifth Avenue, instead of passing over to the "other side."

Guychone: (calmer) There IS a God?

I ask when was he born.

Guychone: (unsure) 1840 . . . 42 years old. . . .

This was the most dramatic of the sittings. The transcript cannot fully convey the tense situation existing between a violent, hate-inspired and God-denying personality fresh from the abyss of perennial darkness, and an interrogator trying calmly to bring light into a disturbed mind. Toward the end of the session, Guychone understood about God, and began to realize that much time had passed since his personal tragedy had befallen him. Actually, the method of "liberating" a "ghost" is no different from that used by a psychiatrist to free a flesh-and-blood person from obsessions or other personality disturbances. Both deal with the mind.

It became clear to me that many more sessions would be needed to clear up the case, since the entity was reluctant to tell all. This is not the case with most "ghosts," who generally welcome a chance to "spill" emotions pent up for long years of personal hell. Here, however, the return of reason also brought back the critical faculty of reasoning, and evaluating information. We had begun to liberate Guychone's soul, but we had not yet penetrated to his conscience. Much hatred, fear, and pride remained, and had to be removed, before the true personality could emerge.

Sitting of July 21st, 1953

Albert, the medium's control, spoke first.

Question: Have you found any information about his wife and child?

Albert: You understand that this is our moral code, that that which comes from the individual within voluntarily is his sacred development. That which he wishes to divulge makes his soul what it should eventually be.

I asked that he describe Guychone's appearance to us.

Albert: At the moment he is little developed from the moment of passing. He is still like his latter moments in life. But his figure was of slight build, tall . . . five feet nine or ten . . . his face is round, narrow at the chin, high at the cheekbones, the nose is rather prominent, the mouth rather wide . . . the forehead high, at the moment of death and for many years previous very little hair. The eyes set close to the nose.

Question: Have you learned his *real* name?

Guychone: It is not his wish as yet. He will tell you, he will develop his soul through his confession. Here he is!

Guychone: (at first grimacing in pain) It is nice to come, but it is hell . . . I have seen the light. It was so dark.

Question: Your name, sir?

Guychone: I was a gentleman . . . my name was defiled. I cannot see it, I cannot hear it, let me take it, when it is going to be right. I have had to pay for it; she has paid her price. I have been so happy. I have moved about. I have learned to right wrongs. I have seen the light.

Question: I am going to open your eyes now. Look at the calendar before you, and tell me what is the date on it? (placing calendar)

Guychone: Nineteen fifty-three. . . . (pointing at the tape recorder in motion) Wagon wheels!

Question: Give us the name of one of your fellow officers in the war. Write it down.

Guychone: I am a poor soul. . . . (writes: Mignon my wife . . . Guychone) Oh, my feet, oh my feet . . . they hurt me so now . . . they bleed . . . I have to always go backwards, backwards. What shall I do with my feet? They had no shoes . . . we walked over burning weed . . . they burned the weed . . . (Who?) The Damn Yankees . . . I wake up, I see the burning weed. . . . (Where? When?) I have to reach out, I have so much to reach for, have patience with me, I can only reach so far— I'll forget. I will tell you everything. . . . (Where?) Georgia! Georgia! (Did you fight under General Lee?) I fell under him. (Did you die under him?) No, no.

Question: Who was with you in the regiment?

Guychone: Johnny Greenly . . . it is like another world . . . Jerome Harvey. (Who was the surgeon?) I did not see him. Horse doctors. (Who was your orderly?) Walter . . . my boy . . . I can't tell the truth, and I try so hard. . . . I will come with the truth when it comes, you see the burning weeds came to me . . . I will think of happier things to tell . . . I'd like to tell you about the house in Charleston, on Elm Street. I think it is 320, I was born in it.

Question: Any others in the family?

Guychone: Two brothers. They died. They were in the war with me. I was the eldest. William, and Paul. (And you're Edward?) Yes. (Your mother?) Mary. (Your father?) Frederick. (Where was he born?) Charleston. (Your mother's maiden name?) Ah . . . ! (Where did you go to college?) William . . . William and . . . a white house with green grass. (When did you graduate?) Fifty-three . . . ONE HUNDRED YEARS. . . . It is hard to get into those corners where I can't think any more.

"I never had my eyes open before, in trance," observed Mrs. Meyers afterwards. "While I could look at you and you looked like yourself, I could almost look through you. That never happened before. I could only see what I focused on. This machine . . . it seemed the wheels were going much, much *faster* than they are going now."

On July 25th, 1953, a "planchette" session was held at the home of Mrs. Meyers, with herself and the late Mrs. Zoe Britton present, during which Guychone made himself known, and stated that he had a living son, eighty-nine years old, now living in a place called Seymour, West Virginia.

Evidential material begins to pile up

By now we knew we had an unusual case. I went through all the available material on this period (and there is a lot), without turning up anyone named Guychone.

These were extremely hot afternoons, but the quest went on. Rarely has any psychic researcher undertaken a similarly protracted project to hunt down psychic evidence.

Sitting of July 28th, 1953

Finding a St. Michael's medal around my neck, Guychone says it reminds him of a medal of St. Anne, which his "Huguenot mother," Marie Guychone, had given him.

Question: Do you remember the name of your college?

Guychone: Two colleges. St. Anne's in Charleston, South Carolina . . . Only one thought around another, that's all I had—curry the horses. Why? I know now. I remember. I want to say my mother is here, I saw her, she says God bless you. I understand more now. Thank you. Pray for me.

Sitting of August 4th, 1953

This sitting repeated previous information and consisted in a cat-and-mouse game between Guychone and myself. However, toward the end, Guychone began to speak of his son Gregory, naming him for the first time. He asked us to find him. We asked, "What name does Gregory use?" Guychone casually answered: "I don't know ... Guychone ... maybe McGowan. ...." The name McGowan came very quietly, but sufficiently distinct to be heard by all present. At the time, we were not overwhelmed. Only when research started to yield results did we realize that it was his real name at last. But I was not immediately successful in locating McGowan on the regimental rosters, far from it! I was misled by his statement of having served in the cavalry, and naturally gave the cavalry rosters my special attention, but he wasn't in them. Late in August I went through the city records of Charleston, West Virginia, on a futile search for the Guychone family, assuming still that they were his in-laws. Here I found mention of a "McGowan's Brigade."

Sitting of August 18th, 1953

Question: Please identify yourself, Colonel.

McGowan: Yes . . . Edward . . . I can stay? I can stay?

Question: Why do you want so much to stay? Are you not happy where you are?

McGowan: Oh yes. But I like to talk very much . . . how happy I am.

Question: What was your mother's name?

McGowan: Marie Guychone.

Question: What is your own name?

McGowan: Guychone.

Question: Yes; that is the name you *used*, but you really are . . . ?

McGowan: Edward Mac . . . Mac . . . curry the horses! (excited, is calmed by me) Yes, I see . . . Mac . . . McGowan! I remember more now, but I can only tell what I know . . . it is like a wall . . . I remember a dark night, I was crazy . . . war on one hand, fighting, bullets . . . and then, flying away, chasing, chasing, chasing . . .

Question: What regiment were you with?

McGowan: Six . . . two . . . sometimes horse . . . oh, in that fire. . . .

Question: Who was your commanding general?

McGowan: But—Butler.

He then speaks of his service in two regiments, one of which was the Sixth South Carolina Regiment, and he mentions a stand on a hill, which was hell, with the Damyankees on all sides. He says it was at Chattanooga.

Question: The house on Fifth Avenue, New York . . . do you remember the name of your landlord?

McGowan: A woman . . . Elsie (or L. C.) . . . stout. . . .

Actually, he says, a man collected the rent, which he had trouble paying at times. He knew a man named Pat Duffy in New York. He was the man who worked for his landlady, collecting the rent, coming to his door.

During the interrogation about his landlord, McGowan suddenly returns to his war experiences. "There was a Griffin," he says, referring to an officer he knew.

Sitting of August 25th, 1953

"The Colonel," as we now called him, came through very clearly. He introduced himself by his true name. Asked again about the land-lady in New York, he now adds that she was a widow. Again, he speaks of "Griff . . . Griff. . . ." Asked what school he went to, he says "St. Anne's College in Charleston, South Carolina, and also William and Mary College in Virginia, the latter in 1850, 51, 52, 53, 54." What was his birthday? He says "February 10, 1830." Did he write any official letters during the war? He says, "I wrote to General Robert E. Lee." What about? When? "January, 1864. Atlanta. . . . I needed horses, horses, wheels to run the things on." Did you get them? "No." What regiment was he with then? "The Sixth from South Carolina." But wasn't he from West Virginia? Amazed, McGowan says, "No, from South Carolina."

I then inquired about his family in New York.

McGowan explained that his mother did live with him there, and died there, but after his own death "they" went away, including his sister-in-law Gertrude and brother William. Again, he asks that we tell his son Gregory "that his father did *not* do away with himself."

I asked, "Where is there a true picture of you?" McGowan replied, "There is one in the courthouse in Charleston, South Carolina." What kind of a picture? "Etch . . . etch . . . *tintype!*"

All through these sittings it was clear that McGowan's memory was best when "pictures" or scenes were asked for, and worst when precise names or dates were being requested. He was never sure when he gave a figure, but was very sure of his facts when he spoke of situations or relationships. Thus, he gave varying dates for his own birthday, making it clear that he was hazy about it, not even aware of having given discrepant information within a brief period.

But then, if a living person undergoes a severe shock, is he not extremely hazy about such familiar details as his name or address? Yet, most shock victims can *describe* their house, or their loved ones. The human memory, apparently, is more reliable in terms of associations, when under stress, than in terms of factual information, like names and figures.

By now research was in full swing, and it is fortunate for the sake of the Survival View that so much prima-facie evidence was obtained *before* the disclosure of McGowan's true name started the material flowing. Thus, the old and somewhat tiring argument of "mental telepathy" being responsible for some of the information, can only be applied, if at all, to a part of the sittings. No one can read facts in a mind *before* they get into that mind!

The sittings continued in weekly sessions, with Colonel McGowan rapidly becoming our "star" visitor.

Sitting of September 1st, 1953

Question: What was your rank at the end of the war?

McGowan: That was on paper . . . made to serve.

Question: Did you become a general?

McGowan: Naw . . . honors . . . I take empty honors. . . .

Question: When you went to school, what did you study?

McGowan: The law of the land.

Question: What happened at Manassas?

McGowan: Oh . . . defeat. Defeat.

Question: What happened to you personally at Manassas?

McGowan: Ah, cut, cut. Bayonets. Ah. Blood, blood.

Question: What happened at Malvern Hill?

McGowan: Success. We took the house. Low brick building. We wait. They come up and we see right in the mouth of a cannon. 1864. They burned the house around our ears. But we didn't move.

Question: What was under your command at that time?

McGowan: Two divisions.

Question: How many regiments?

McGowan: Four . . . forty . . . (Four?) TEEN!

Question: What did you command?

McGowan: My commander was shot down, I take over. (Who for?) John . . . Major. . . .

Question: Listen, Colonel, your name is not Edward. Is there any other first or middle name you used? (Silence) Did anyone of high rank serve from South Carolina? (My brother William) Anyone else? (Paul)

McGowan: Do you think of Charles McGowan? That was no relation of mine. He was on the waterfront. He was . . . exporter.

Question: Were you at Gettysburg, Colonel? (Yes.) What regiments were under your command then?

McGowan: I had a wound at Gettysburg. I was very torn. (Where did you get the wound?) Atlanta . . . change of rank. Empty honors (About his son Gregory) Seymour . . . many years Lowell, Massachusetts, and then he went back down South, Seymour, South Carolina, and sometimes West Virginia . . . he was in a store, he left and then he came into property, mother also had property, down there near Charleston in West Virginia . . . that is where he is, yes.

Question: You say your father was Frederick? (Yes.) Who was William. (My brother.) Who was Samuel? (Long pause, *stunned,* then: *I* wrote that name!) Why didn't you tell us? (Crying: I didn't want to tell. . . .) Tell us your true rank, too. (I don't care what it was). Please don't evade us. What was your rank? (Brigadier . . . General). Then you are General Samuel McGowan?

McGowan: You made me very unhappy . . . such a name (crying) . . . blood, empty honors. . . .

Question: Who was James Johnson? (My commander.) What happened to him? (Indicates he was shot.) Who took over for Johnson? (I did.) What regiment was it?

McGowan: I don't know the figures . . . I don't know.

Question: Your relative in New York, what was his name?'

McGowan: Peter Paul.

Question: What was his profession?

McGowan: A doctor. (Any particular kind of doctor?) Cuts. (What kind?) (McGowan points to face.) (Nose doctor?) (McGowan points to mouth and shakes head.) (Mouth doctor?) (McGowan violently grabs his teeth and shakes them.) (Oh, teeth? A dentist) (McGowan nods assent.)

Question: I will name some regiments, tell me if any of them mean anything to you. The 10th . . . the 34th . . . the 14th . . . (McGowan reacts.) The 14th? Does it mean anything to you?

McGowan: I don't know, figures don't mean anything on this side. . .

Some interesting facts brought out by research

In the sitting of August 18th, McGowan stated his landlord was a woman and that her name was "Elsie" or L. C. *The Hall of Records* of New York City lists the owner of 226 Fifth Avenue as "Isabella S. Clarke, from 1853 to (at least) March 1, 1871." In the same sitting, McGowan stated that Pat Duffy was the man who actually came to collect the rent, working for the landlady. Several days *after* this information was *voluntarily* received from the entity, I found in *Trow's New York Directory for 1869/70:*

Page 195: "Clark, Isabella, wid. Constantine h. (house) 45 Cherry."

Page 309: "Duffy, Patrick, laborer, 45 Cherry."

This could be known only to someone who actually *knew* these people, eighty years ago; it proved our ghost was *there* in 1873!

The sitting of September 1st also proved fruitful.

A "Peter McGowan, dentist, 253 W. 13 St." appears in *Trow's New York City Directory for 1870/71.*

J. F. J. Caldwell, in his *"History of a Brigade of South Carolinians known first as Gregg's, and subsequently as McGowan's Brigade."* (Philadelphia, 1866) reports:

Page 10: "The 14th Regiment South Carolina Volunteers selected for field officers . . . Col. James Jones, *Lt. Col. Samuel McGowan* . . . (1861)."

Page 12: "Colonel Samuel McGowan commands the 14th Regiment."

Page 18: "McGowan arrives from the Chickahominy river (under Lee)."

Page 24: "Conspicuous gallantry in the battle of Malvern Hill."

Page 37: ". . . of the 11 field officers of our brigade, seven were wounded: Col. McGowan, etc. (in the 2nd battle of Manassas)."

Page 53: "Col. Samuel McGowan of the 14th Regiment (at Fredericksburg)."

Page 60: "The 13th and 14th regiments under McGowan. . . ."

Page 61: "Gen. Gregg's death Dec. 14, 1862. McGowan succeeds to command."

Page 66: "Biography: Born Laurens district, S. C. 1820. Graduated 1841 South Carolina College, Law; in Mexican War, then settled as lawyer in Abbeville, S.C. Became a Brig. Gen. January 20, 1863, assists in taking Ft. Sumter April 1861; but lapsing commission as General in State Militia, he becomes Lt. Col. in the Confederate Army, takes part at Bull Run, Manassas Plains, under Gen. Bonham. Then elected Lt. Col. of 14th Regiment, S.C.; Spring 1862, made full Col. *succeeding Col. Jones who was killed.* McGowan is *wounded* in battle of Manassas." Biographer Caldwell, who was McGowan's aide as a lieutenant, says (in 1866) "he still lives."

Page 79. "April 29, 1863, McGowan's *Brigade* gets orders to be ready to march. Gen. McGowan commands the brigade."

Page 80: "Wounded again (Fredericksburg)."

Page 89: "Gen. Lee reviews troops including McGowan's. Brigade now consists of 1st, 12th, 13th, 14th Regiments and Orr's Rifles. Also known as 'McGowan's Sharpshooters.'"

Page 91: "McGowan takes part in battle of Chancellorsville."

Page 96: "Battle of Gettysburg: McGowan commands 13th, 12th, 14th, and 1st."

Page 110: "McGowan near Culpepper Courthouse."

Page 22: "Gen. McGowan returned to us in February (1864). He had not sufficiently recovered from the wound received at Chancellorsville to walk well, but remained with us and discharged all the duties of his office."

Page 125: *About Butler:* "Butler to lead column (against McGowan) from the Eastern coast." Another Butler (Col.) commanded the Confederate 1st Regt. (Battle of Chickamauga)

Page 126sq.: "Battle of Spottsylvania, May 1864."

Page 133: "Gen. Lee and Gen. Hill were there (defeat)."

Page 142: "McGowan wounded by a 'minie ball,' in the right arm, quits field."

But to continue with our sittings, and with McGowan's personal recollections—

Sitting of September 8th, 1953

McGowan: (speaking again of his death) "It was in the forties . . . they killed me on the top floor. They dragged me up, that 'man of color' named Walter. He was a giant of a man. She was a virtuous woman, I tell you she was. But they would not believe it."

I wanted to get his reaction to a name I had found in the records, so I asked, "Have you ever met a McWilliams?"

McGowan: You have the knowledge of the devil with you. *Her* family name.

Question: Did you stay in New York until your passing?

McGowan: 1869, 1873. Back and forth. I have written to Lee, Jackson, James, and Beaufort. 1862–63, March.

Question: What did you do at the end of the war?

McGowan: Back and forth, always on the go. Property was gone, ruined. Plantations burned. I did not work. I could not. Three or four bad years. I quit. My wits, my wits. My uncle. The house burned in Charleston. Sometimes Columbia. (Then, of Mignon, his wife, he says) She died in 1892 . . . Francois Guychone . . . he was so good to little boys, he made excursions in the Bay of Charleston—we sailed in boats. He was my uncle.

Sitting of September 15th, 1953

I asked, what did he look like in his prime.

McGowan: I wasn't too bad to look at, very good brow, face to the long, and at one time I indulged in the whiskers . . . not so long, for the chin . . . colonial . . . I liked to see my chin a good deal, sometimes I cover (indicates mustache). . . .

Question: What can you tell us about the cemetery in Abbeville?

McGowan: There is a monument, the family cemetery . . . nobody cared . . . my father was born the fifth of January. . . . (What was on your tombstone?) Samuel Edward McGowan, born . . . 32? . . . died 1883? 1873? 1-8-7 hard to read so dirty . . . age 40 . . . 41 . . . gray-brown stars . . . battered. . . . I go between the bushes, I look at the monument, it's defaced. . . .

Question: What news did your family give out of your death?

McGowan: Foul play. (What happened to the body?) Cremated I guess, I think in this city. The remains were destroyed: not in the grave, a monument to a memory. . . . (What did they tell the public?) Lost forever . . . I could have been at sea . . . house was destroyed by fire. . . . (Do you mean there is no official record of your death?) No. *Not identical to passing,* they never told the exact month or day . . . I see . . . 1879 . . . very blurred . . . September 4th. . . .

Question: Were you ever injured in an argument?

McGowan: I spent much time on my back because of a wound . . . on my head. (An argument?) Yes. (With whom?) A man. Hand to hand. Rapier. . . . Glen, Glen . . . Ardmore.

Sitting of September 22nd, 1953

"Mother" Marie Guychone spoke briefly in French and was followed by McGowan. He said he was at one time "An Associate Justice" in the city of Columbia.

Here again do I wish to report some more research information bearing on this part of the investigation. Evans, in his *Confederate Military History*, 1899[1] has a picture of the General which became available to us *after* the September 22nd sitting. His biography, on page 414, mentions the fact that "he was associate Justice of the (State) Supreme Court." Curiously, this author also states that McGowan died in "December 1893." Careful scrutiny of two major New York dailies than existing (*Post* and *Times*) brought to light that the author of the *Confederate Military History* made a mistake, albeit an understandable one. A certain Ned McGowan, described as a "notorious character, aged 80" had died in San Francisco on December 9, 1893. This man was also a Confederate hero. (*The New York Times*, XII/9). However, the same source (*The New York Times*, August 13, 1897) reports General McGowan's death as having occurred on the ninth of August, 1897. The obituary contains the facts already noted in the biography quoted earlier, plus one interesting additional detail, that McGowan *received a cut across the scalp in a duel.*

Another good source, *The Dictionary of American Biography*, says of our subject: "*McGowan, Samuel*. Son of William and Jeannie McGowan, law partner of William H. Parker. Died August 9, 1897 in Abbeville. Buried in Long Cane Cemetery in Abbeville. Born Oct. 9, 1819 in Crosshill section of Laurens district, S. C. *Mother's name was McWilliams*. Law partner of *Perrin* in Abbeville. Representative in State House of South Carolina. Elected to Congress, *but not seated.*"

A *Colonel at Gettysburg*, by Varina Brown, about her late husband Colonel Brown, contains the following: "In the battle of Jericho Mills, '*Griffin's Division*' of Federals wrought havoc against McGowan's Brigade."

Correspondence with Mrs. William Gaynes, a resident of Abbeville, revealed on October 1st, 1953—"The old general was a *victim of the failing mind* but he was doctored up until the date of his death. He was attended by his cousin *Dr. F. E. Harrison*."

---

1. Vol. V., p. 409.

Eminent & Representative Men of South Carolina by Brant & Fuller (Madison, Wisconsin, 1892) gives this picture:

"Samuel McGowan was born of *Scotch* Irish parents in Laurens County S.C. on October 9th 1819. Graduated with distinction from the South Carolina College in 1841. Read law at Abbeville with T. C. Perrin who offered him a partnership. He entered the service as a private and went to Mexico with the Palmetto Regiment. He was appointed on the general Quartermaster's Staff with the rank of Captain. After the war he returned to Abbeville and resumed the practice of Law with T. C. Perrin. He married Susan Caroline, eldest daughter of Judge David Lewis Wardlaw and they lived in Abbeville until some years after the death of Gen. McGowan in 1897. The home of Gen. McGowan still stands in Abbeville and was sold some time ago to the Baptist Church for 50,000 dollars. . . . After the war he entered law practice with William H. Parker (1869/1879) *in Abbeville.* He took an interest in political affairs . . . member of the Convention that met in Columbia in September, 1865. Elected to Congress but not allowed to take his seat. Counted out on the second election two years later. In 1878 he was a member of the State Legislature and in 1879 he was elected Associate Justice of the State Supreme Court.

"General McGowan lived a long and honorable life in Abbeville. He was a contributing member of the Episcopal Church, Trinity, and became a member later in life. At his death the following appeared in the *Abbeville Medium,* edited by Gen. R. R. Hemphill who had served in McGowan's Brigade. 'General Samuel McGowan *died at his home in this city* at 8:35 o'clock last Monday morning August 8th. Full of years and honors he passed away surrounded by his family and friends. He had been in declining health for some time and suffered intense pain, though his final sickness was for a few days only and at the end all was Peace. Impressive services were held in *Trinity Church* Tuesday afternoon, at four o'clock, the procession starting from the residence. At the

Church, the procession . . . preceded by Dr. Wm. M. Grier and Bishop Ellison Capers who read the solemn service . . . directly behind the coffin old Daddy Willis Marshall, a colored man who had served him well, bore a laurel wreath. Gen. McGowan was buried at *Long Lane* cemetery and there is a handsome stone on the plot."

Mrs. William Gaynes further reports:

"Gen. McGowan had a 'fine line of profanity' and used it frequently in Court. He was engaged in a duel once with Col. John *Cunningham* and was wounded behind one ear and came near passing out. Col. Cunningham challenged Col. *Perrin who refused* the challenge on the ground that he did not approve of dueling, and Gen. McGowan took up the challenge and the duel took place at Sand Bar Ferry, near Augusta, with McGowan being wounded.

"As far as I know, there was never any difficulty between Mr. McGowan and the old General. His father-in-law, Judge Wardlaw, married *Sarah* Rebecca Allen, and *her* mother was Mary Lucia *Garvey*."

In other words, Judge Wardlaw married *Sarah Garvey*.

Mrs. Gaynes continues: "I have seen him frequently on his way to his law office, for he had to pass right by *our* office. If he ever was out of town for any length of time, Abbeville *did not know it*."

The inscription on Samuel McGowan's tombstone in Long Cane Graveyard reads as follows:

"Samuel McGowan, born Laurens County 9 October 1819. Died in Abbeville 9 August 1897. Go soldier to thy honored rest, thy trust and honor valor bearing. The brave are the tenderest, the loving are the daring."

Side 2: "From humble birth he rose to the highest honor in Civic and military life. A patriot and a leader of men. In peace his country called him, he waited not to her call in war. A man's strength, a woman's tenderness, a child's simplicity were his and his a heart of charity fulfilling the law of love. He did good and not evil all the days of his life and at its end his country his children and his children's children rise up and call him blessed. In Mexican War 1846–1848. A Captain in United States Army. The Confederate War 1861–1865. A Brigadier General C.S.A. Member of the Legislature 1848–50. Elected to Congress 1866. Associate Justice of Supreme Court of South Carolina 1878–1894. A hero in two wars. Seven times wounded. A leader at the Bar, a wise law giver a righteous judge. He rests from his labors and his works do follow him."

MCGOWAN BECOMES A "REGULAR" OF THE WEEKLY SITTINGS.

General McGowan had by now become an always impatient weekly "guest" at our sittings, and he never liked the idea of leaving. Whenever it was suggested that time was running short, McGowan tried to prolong his stay by becoming suddenly very talkative.

Sitting of September 29th, 1953

A prepared list of eight names, all fictitious but one (the sixth is that of Susan Wardlaw, McGowan's wife) is read to him several times. McGowan reacts to two of the nonexistent names, but not to the one of his wife. One of the fictitious names is John D. Sumter, to which McGowan mumbles, "Colonel." Fact is there was a Colonel Sumter in the Confederate Army!

McGowan also described in detail the farm where his son Gregory now lives. Asked about the name Guychone, he says it comes from Louisiana; Mignon, on her mother's side, had it. He identifies his hometown newspapers as "Star-Press." ("*Star-Press,* paper, picture, Judge, Columbia, picture in paper. . . .")

Question: Who was Dr. Harrison?
McGowan: Family doctor.

Question: Is your home in Abbeville still standing?

McGowan: It isn't *what it was*. Strange pictures and things. (Anyone live in it?) No. Strange things, guns and cannons.

Sitting of October 14th, 1953

McGowan says he had two daughters. Trying again to read his tombstone, he says, "1887, or is it 97?" As to his birthyear, he reads, "1821 . . . 31?"

Sitting of October 20th, 1953

When the control introduces McGowan, there is for several moments intense panic and fear brought on by a metal necklace worn by the medium. When McGowan is assured that there is no longer any "rope around his neck," he calms down, and excuses himself for his regression.

Question: Who was the Susan you mentioned the last time?

McGowan: The mother of my children.

Question: What was her other name?

McGowan: Cornelia.

Question: Were you elected to Congress?

McGowan: What kind of Congress? (The U. S. Congress.) I lost. Such a business, everybody grabs, everybody steals. . . . Somebody always buys the votes and it's such a mess.

Question: Are Mignon and Susan one and the same person or not?

McGowan: I don't wish to commit myself. (I insist.) They are *not!*

Question: Let us talk about Susan. What profession did your father-in-law follow?

McGowan: Big man . . . in the law.

Question: What was your mother-in-law's first name?

McGowan: Sarah.

Question: Did she have another name?

McGowan: Garvey. . . .

Question: Coffee? Spell it.

McGowan: Not coffee. *Garvey!*

At a sitting on October 28th, 1953, at the home of Mrs. Meyers, McGowan's alleged grandson, Billy, manifested himself as follows:

"My name is William, I passed in 1949, at Charleston. I'm a grandson of General McGowan. I was born in Abbeville, January 2nd, 1894. Gregory is half-brother, son of the French bitch. He (McGowan) would have married her, but he had a boss, grandfather, who held the purse strings. Susan's father of Dutch blood, hard-headed."

Sitting of October 29th, 1953

McGowan: You must find Gregory. He may be surprised about his father, but I must let him know I wanted for him, and they took for *them* . . . all. And they gave him nothing. Nothing! I had made other plans. (Was there a will?) There was . . . but I had a judge in the family that made other plans . . . THEY WERE NOT MINE! You must tell Gregory I provided. . . . I tell you only the truth because I was an honest man . . . I did the best for my family, for my people, for those I considered my countrymen, that what you now call posterity . . . I suffer my own sins. . . . For you maybe it means nothing, for me, for those who remember me, pity . . . they are now aware of the truth, only now is my son unaware of the truth. Sir, you are my best friend. And I go into hell for you. I tell you always the truth, Sir, but there are things that would not concern you or anybody. But I will give you those names yet!

Question: I ask again for the name of McGowan's father-in-law.

McGowan: Wida . . . Wider.

THE "GHOST" IS FREED

One of the functions of a "rescue circle" is to make sure a disturbed entity does not return to the scene of his unhappiness. This mission was accomplished here.

Sitting of November 3rd, 1953

McGowan: I see the house where I lived, you know, where you found me. I go there now, but I am not anymore disturbed. I found my mother and my father. They could not touch me, but now, we touch hands. I live over my life, come back to many things. Herman! He was a good soul, he helped me when I was down in Atlanta. He bathed my feet, my legs were scorched, and he was good to me, and he is over here. I thank him. I thanked him then, but I was the big man, and he was nothing, but now I see he is a fine gentleman, he polished my boots, he put my uniform in order.

Sitting of November 6th, 1953

I was alone with the medium, Mrs. Meyers, at her home, when I had a chance to question McGowan about his apparent murder, and the "conspiracy of silence" concerning it.

McGowan: The Judge protected them, did not report my death. They had devised the kidnapping. I was murdered downstairs, strangled by the kidnapper Walter. He took her (Mignon) all the way to Boston. I wore the uniform of Damyankees (during the war), rode a horse *every night* to Boston . . . no, I made a mistake. I came to my Uncle Peter Paul in New York, I had a letter from Marie Guychone, she was in New York. Begged me to find Mignon and Gregory. I come to New York. I can't find her, she was in Boston then, but I didn't know that until later. Marie Guychone remained with my uncle, and I gave up the chase, and like a thief crawled back to Confederate grounds. That was in 1863. After the war, there was a struggle, property was worthless, finally the Union granted that we withdraw our holdings, and with that I came to New York. My mother and father came also, until rehabilitation was sufficient for their return.

I continued to live with my wife, Susan, and the children, and I found Mignon. She had escaped, and came to her mother in New York.

I made a place for them to live with my uncle and when my wife returned to stay with her father (the judge), I had Mignon, but she was pregnant and she didn't know it, and there was a black child—there was unpleasantness between us, I didn't know if it were mine and Mignon was black, but it was not so, it was his child (Walter's), and he came for it and for her, he traced her to my house (on Fifth Avenue); my father-in-law (the Judge) was the informer, and he (Walter) strangled me, he was a big man.

And when I was not dead yet, he dragged me up the stairs. Mignon was not present, not guilty. I think . . . it was in January 1874. But I may be mistaken about time. Gregory had two sons, William and Edward. William died on a boat in the English Channel in 1918. Gregory used the name *Fogarty*, not McGowan. The little black boy died, they say. It was just as well for him.

McGowan then left peacefully, promising more information about the time lag between his given date and that officially recorded. I told him the difference was "about twenty years." For the first time, McGowan had stated his story reasonably, although some details of it would be hard to check. No murder or suicide was reported in the newspapers of the period, similar to this case. But of course anyone planning a crime like this might have succeeded in keeping it out of the public eye. We decided to continue our sittings.

Sitting of November 10th, 1953

McGowan talked about the duel he fought, which cost him his hair, due to a wound on the left side, back and top of his head. It was over a woman and against a certain Colonel C., something like "Collins," but a longer name. He said that Perry or Perrin *did* so make a stand, as if someone had doubted it!

MORE PROOF TURNS UP!

Leading away from personal subjects, the questioning now proceeded toward matters of general interest about New York at the time of McGowan's residence here. The advantage of this line of questioning is its neutral value for research purposes; and as *no research* was undertaken until after the sittings of November 17th, mental telepathy must be excluded as an alternate explanation!

Sitting of November 17th, 1953

McGowan: You don't have a beard. They called them *milksops* in my days, the beardless boys!

Question: What did they call a man who was a nice dresser and liked ladies?

McGowan: A Beau Brummel.

Question: What did they call a gentleman who dressed too well, too fancifully?

McGowan: A fop.

Question: What was your favorite sport?

McGowan: Billiards (He explains he was good at it, and the balls were *made of cloth.*)

Question: What was the favorite game of your day?

McGowan: They played a *Cricket* kind of game. . . .

Question: Who was mayor of New York?

McGowan: Oh . . . Grace. Grace . . . *Edmond* . . . Grace . . . something like it.

William R. Grace was mayor of New York, 1881–1882, and Franklin Edson (not Edmond) followed, 1883–1884. Also, plastic billiard balls as we know them today are a comparatively recent invention, and billiard balls in the Victorian era were indeed made of cloth. The cricket kind of game must be baseball. Beau Brummel, fop, milksop are all authentic Victorian expressions.

Sitting of November 26th, 1953

I asked the General about trains in New York in his time.

McGowan: They were smoke stacks, up in the air, smoke got in your eyes, they went down to the Globe Building near City Hall. The *Globe* building was near Broadway and Nassau. The train went up to Harlem. It was a nice neighborhood. I took many strolls in the park.

Question: Where was the Hotel Waldorf-Astoria?

McGowan: Near Fifth Avenue and 33rd, near my house . . . and the Hotel Prince George. Restaurants were Ye Olde Southern, Hotel Brevoort. You crack my brain, you are worse than that boss in the Big House, Mr. Tammany and Mr. Tweed. (I discussed his house, and he mentioned doing business with—) Somebody named *Costi* . . . I paid $128.50 a month for the entire house. A suite of clothes cost $100.00.

Question: Who lived next door to you?

McGowan: Herman . . . *was a carriage smith.* He had a business where he made carriages. He lived next door, but his business was not there, the shop was on Third Avenue, Third Street, near the river.

Question: Any other neighbors?

McGowan: Corrigan Brown, *a lawyer* . . . lived three houses down. The editor of the *Globe* was White . . . Stone . . . White . . . the editor of the Globe was not good friends with the man in the Big House. THey broke his house down when he lived on Fifth Avenue. *He was a neighbor.* Herman the carriage maker made good carriages. I bought one with fringes and two seats, a cabrio. . . .

Question: Did you have a janitor?

McGowan: There was a black boy named Ted, mainly colored servants, we had a gardener, white, named Patrick. He collects the rent, he lives with the Old Crow on Cherry Street. Herman lives next door. He had a long mustache and square beard. He wore a frock coat, a diamond tie pin, and spectacles. I never called him Herman . . . (trying to remember his true name) . . . Gray . . . I never called him Herman. He had a wife named Birdie. His wife had a sister named Finny who lived there too . . . Mrs. Finny . . . she was a young widow with two children . . . she was a good friend to my Susan.

McGowan then reluctantly signs his name as requested.

Research, undertaken *after* the sitting, again excluded mental telepathy. The facts were of a kind not likely to be found in the records, *unless* one were specifically looking for them!

The *New York Globe* building, which McGowan remembers "near Broadway and Nassau," was then (1873) at 7 Spruce Street and apparently also at 162 Nassau Street.[2] The *Globe* is on Spruce, and *Globe and Evening Press* on Nassau, around the corner.

McGowan describes the steam-powered elevated railroad that went from City Hall to Harlem. Steam cars started in 1867 and ran until 1906, according to the New York Historical Society, and there were two lines fitting his description, "Harlem, From Park Row to . . . E. 86th Street" and "Third Avenue, from Ann Street through Park Row to . . . Harlem Bridge."[3]

McGowan was right in describing Harlem as a nice neighborhood in his day. Harlem did not become a low-rent, colored section until the present century.

McGowan also acknowledged at once that he had been to the Waldorf-Astoria, and correctly identified its position at Fifth Avenue and 33rd Street. The Waldorf-Astoria came into being on March 14th, 1893. Consequently, McGowan *was alive then*, and evidently sane, if he could visit such places as the Waldorf, Brevoort, and others.

McGowan refers to a (later) landlord as Costi. In 1895, a real-estate firm by the name of George and John Coster was situated at 173 Fifth Avenue, a few houses down the street from McGowan's place.[4]

---

2. "*Trow's New York City Directory for 1872/73*, p. 448 regular section and p. 38 City Register section.
3. *Ibid.* City Register, p. 18, under "City Railroads.
4. *Trow*, 1895/96, p. 550.

As for the carriage smith named Herman, a little later referred to as Herman Gray, there was a carriage maker named William H. Gray from 1872 or earlier, and existing beyond the turn of the century, whose shop was at first at 20 Wooster Street,[5] and who lived at 258 West Fourth Street, until at least 1882. In 1895 he is listed as living at 275 West 94th Street. Not all Trow volumes in between are available, so that residence in McGowan's neighborhood can neither be confirmed nor denied. At one time, Gray's shops were on West Broadway. As for Corrigan Brown, the lawyer neighbor, McGowan's mispronouncing of names almost tripped me up. There was no such lawyer. There was, however, one Edmond Congar Brown, lawyer, listed for the first time as such in 1886, and before that only as a clerk. No home is, unfortunately, listed for his later years.[6] McGowan stated that the editor of the *Globe* was named White-and-something, and that he lived near his (McGowan's) house on Fifth Avenue.

Well, one Horace P. Whitney, editor, business, 128 Fulton Street, home, 287 Fifth Avenue, is listed in Trow.[7] And 128 Fulton Street is the place of the *Globe's* competitor, the *New York Mercury*, published by Cauldwell and Whitney.[8]

That McGowan did not die in 1873 seems certain to me, as the above information proves. But if he did not die in 1873, something very traumatic must have been done to him at that time. Or perhaps the murder, if such it was, took place in 1897?

It could well be that General McGowan will take this ultimate secret with him into the Great Land where he now dwells safely forever.

---

5. *Trow,* 1872/73, City Register, p. 27.
6. *Trow,* 1895/96, p. 174, list his office as 132 Nassau.
7. 1872, p. 1287, regular section.
8. *Trow,* 1872, City Register section, p. 39.

South

The Gray Man of Pawley's Island

One of the best known ghosts of South Carolina's low country is the so-called Gray Man of Pawley's Island. A number of local people claim they have seen him gazing seaward from the dunes, especially when a hurricane is about to break. He is supposed to warn of impending disaster. Who the Gray Man of Pawley's Island is is open to question. According to *A Perceptive Survey of South Carolina Ghosts* by Worth Gatewood, published in 1962, he may be the original Percival Pawley who so loved his island that he felt impelled to watch over it even after he passed on. But Mr. Gatewood gives more credence to a beautiful and romantic account of the origin of the specter. According to this story a young man who was to be married to a local belle left for New York to attend to some business but on his way back was shipwrecked and lost at sea. After a year's time the young woman married his best friend and settled down on Pawley's Island with her new husband. Years later the original young man returned, again shipwrecked and rescued by one of his former fiancée's servants.

When he realized that his love had married in the meantime, he drowned himself at the nearby shore. All this happened, if we believe it happened, a long time ago, because the Gray Man has been seen ever since 1822, or perhaps even earlier than that. A Mrs. Eileen Weaver, according to Mr. Gatewood's account, saw the specter on her veranda and it was indeed a dim outline of a man in gray. There had been unexplained footsteps on her veranda and doors opening and closing by themselves, untouched by human hands.

A businessman by the name of William Collins who did not believe in ghosts, not even in South Carolina ghosts, found himself on the lookout to check on the rising surf on the morning of famed Hurricane Hazel. As he was walking down the dunes he noticed the figure of a man standing on the beach looking seaward. Collins challenged him, thinking that perhaps he was a neighbor who had come out to check on the rising tide, but the stranger paid no attention. Busy with his task, Collins forgot about this and by the time he looked up the stranger had gone. According to the weather forecast, however, the hurricane had shifted directions and was not likely to hit the area, so Collins and his family went to bed that night, sure that the worst was over. At five o'clock in the morning he was aroused from bed by heavy pounding on his door. Opening it, he could feel the house shake from the wind rising to tremendous force. On his veranda stood a stranger wearing a gray fishing cap and a common work shirt and pants, all of it in gray. He told Collins to get off the beach since the storm was coming in. Collins thanked him and ran upstairs to wake his family. After the excitement of the storm had passed Collins wondered about the man who had warned him to get off the island. Intelligently he investigated the matter, only to find that no one had seen the man, nor had any of his neighbors had a guest fitting his description. The state highway patrolman on duty also had not seen anyone come or go, and there is only one access road, the causeway over the marshes.

*   *   *

Mrs. G. lives in the state of Kansas. She is a respectable real estate operator who has been in business for many years. She and her husband share a lovely, upper-middle class home in one of the finer residential areas.

The occult was the furthest thing from her mind when someone laughingly suggested they try their hands at a ouija board rather than continue playing bridge as was their custom on slow afternoons. As so many others, Mrs. G. not for a moment took the ouija board seriously nor did she think that anything could come of it she couldn't handle. To her surprise there was an immediate response. The indicator moved under her hands, and this surprised Mrs. G. very much since she knew very well that she was not doing the moving.

Before long the disconnected letters made sense and spelled out words. Imagine her surprise and subsequent horror when Mrs. G. discovered that she was receiving a message from a man she had once known and who was now dead! Her former suitor had dropped dead of a heart attack some years before, but they had been estranged ever since she had refused his offer of marriage. Mrs. G. was quite happy in her present marriage and had given William, the man she once knew well, no further thought for years. All of a sudden there he was communicating with her through a piece of wood. At first she tried to laugh off the whole thing and explained the resurgence of her old suitor by some trick of the memory. Perhaps she had liked him better than she was consciously aware of and in some unknown fashion his name surfaced again while she was playing with this board. But the discarnate personality showed that it was indeed he, the man she had known some years before, who was sending her those messages, moving her hands against her wishes over the board. Before long she was made to write down his messages with a pencil. They were clear and concise. William wanted to make up for lost time. He didn't care that he had been dead and gone for several years. He had never stopped loving her, had hated her husband for marrying her, and was now quite prepared to take his rightful place with her, the way he saw it.

Mrs. G. protested, taking the entity seriously now, but the more she protested, the stronger he became. He was no longer satisfied to send her messages through the ouija board or automatic writing. A few days later she felt him in her bed. There was no mistaking it: William, in some unspeakably horrible way, was making love to her. She could sense the outlines of his body, even though she could not see it. There was definite weight and pressure against her body, as he lay upon her.

She cried out in horror and begged him to go away. She took her refuge in replying that hell would await William if he did not cease and desist, but it was of no avail. Eventually she found her way to me and a session with hypnosis. I reasoned with William. I asked him to leave the body of the unwilling Mrs. G. but this didn't do any good either. Shortly after her return to Kansas, the phenomena recommenced.

Almost every psychiatrist would say that since this case involved a woman in the change of life, such a phenomena could not be caused by possessing entities but by some form of sexually connected hysteria. It is always possible that cases of this kind are indeed due to internal biological changes in a woman's body and personality. But from the practical point of view, it is of little difference whether the possessing entity is an outsider or a split-off, alienated part of the individual's own personality. In either case, possession exists and must be dealt with.

In the case of Mrs. G., much depended upon her own attitude. I became convinced that the possessing entity was not entirely unwelcome. The evil fascination of this dead man, who had been her suitor and whom she had rejected, somehow had triggered within her a sense of reverse frustration which allowed her to reject his physical advances from the beyond while at the same time wallowing in the very evil force they represented.

I advised Mrs. G. to leave ouija boards and other occult gadgets alone in the future and to find emotional outlets in other quarters. Presumably, she had done so, or perhaps she has come to terms with William. At any rate, I have heard nothing further from her.

There are many cases where the possessor could not be part of the person's own personality. The evil one possessing the flesh-and-blood person can be identified as a real person who once lived, but of whom the victim knows nothing or had no connection with. I do not think it likely that a rational, well-adjusted individual could invent a relationship with a person who once lived but is now dead, and of whom the victim has no knowledge beforehand. If anything, an individual might invent a nonexistent personality and mask it as a possessor. But when we have proof that the personality existed as a human being, we must look to true possession as the only answer.

*   *   *

David G. is a prominent broadcaster and writer in a major city. His career had been going well for years, but lately there had been difficulties with management, and in the end he had resigned his position. For several months prior to the events I'm about to describe, Mr. G. had been in a highly nervous condition, depressed, and generally not quite himself.

He and his wife and children lived in a modernized town-house in the heart of the city. They had spent considerable time and effort to create from an ordinary brownstone house a jewel of a modern residence three stories high, filled with fine furniture and the technical apparatus Mr. G. required for his broadcasting activities. It was a happy house, as houses went. They had been in it for some time without noticing anything unusual.

Then they noticed that the atmosphere seemed strangely charged. Little things began to bother them. Doors would not stay shut. Footsteps would reverberate when no one was walking. The G.'s had no interest or belief in the supernatural, but one day Mr. G. himself saw a hairbrush fly of its own volition off its shelf in the bathroom and hit the wall so hard that the brush broke in two.

He had built himself a tool shop down in the cellar. Tools would disappear from one corner and reappear in another spot where they did not belong. As he turned around in puzzlement, he found the tool gone from its incorrect location, only to see it back where it should have been in the first place, a moment later. It was as if someone were trying to play games with him. At night, lights would turn themselves on. In several instances the G.'s saw the switch being turned by unseen fingers. The footsteps indicated some sort of presence in the house.

At first they thought it was a young person, but they couldn't be sure. Mr. G. hastily consulted books on parapsychology and realized that the presence of his son Michael, age thirteen, might furnish the energies in some as yet little understood way. This knowledge calmed him considerably, since there was now a seemingly natural explanation for the phenomena. He, of course, did not tell Michael anything about this. A few days later, towards four o'clock in the morning, Mr. G. could not sleep so he decided to do some work in his tool shop downstairs. As he approached the shop, unseen hands flung the door open for him. In the subsequent weeks this happened at least twenty times. On one occasion a taxi driver who had come to fetch him for an early-morning broadcast also witnessed the amazing performance.

Mr. G. had bought the house in 1958 from a local man initialed L. But L. only owned the house for a few short years. The man who would know more about it than anyone else was the late Dr. D., who was born in it and had lived there for fifty years. The house itself was considerably older, though no one knew exactly when it had been built. Since G. had remodeled it completely, using only the original walls, it would be hard to determine its age merely from appearances. As the phenomena continued to plague the G's, Mr. G. thought several times of consulting someone like myself to get rid of the problem but his busy career and other problems did not allow him to follow through. Then one fine day the need to do something about the phenomena was graphically brought into focus again. One afternoon in 1961, Mr. G's wife was found dead. The verdict was suicide, but Mr. G. could never accept this as final. There had been no quarrel, no disagreements whatever, and no unhappiness between them. Why would Mrs. G. have wanted to take her own life? The horrible tragedy made Mr. G.'s own condition even worse than it had been due to professional reverses of the past months.

For a few weeks the house fell strangely silent; then the phenomena began again, more urgently, more sinister than ever before. Mr. G. however was in no mood to cope with them now. His own nervous condition was such that he felt himself at the breaking point. It was precisely at this moment that he called me to help him. I took Ethel Johnson Meyers with me and in June of 1962, we visited Mr. G. in his townhouse. After she had looked the place over for a few minutes, Mrs. Meyers confirmed that there was "a presence" in the house. She had no idea where she was or who her famous host was. In trance, her own personality was replaced by someone filled with hatred, complaining bitterly that he had been deceived by his friends and by his wife. His best friend had taken his money and his wife, Helen. His name was Henry, he had been in Wall Street and he had been sold short. "I am Titus Andronicus, Titus the Fool," he said with a fine sense of satire, referring to Shakespeare's unfortunate hero. Somehow, in the strange way in which these things seem to work in the world beyond, the confused entity staying on in what was once his house mistook Mr. G.'s wife for the unfaithful wife who had left him with his best friend. In a moment of hatred he had caused her death.

The emotional impact of all this seemed almost too much for the medium. Shortly after, she broke from her trance and had to be calmed down for several minutes. As soon as she was fully herself again, she looked around the room as if she were only now conscious of her surroundings, and remarked—"Somebody fell to death here of a broken neck." Nobody said a word. Mr. G. was visibly upset by all this, but he thanked us for having come to make things a little easier for him. Twice more I returned to Mr. G.'s house with Mrs. Meyers. On those occasions the earlier material was confirmed and broadened but nothing essentially new was found. What was different, however, was the very personal contact Mrs. Meyers was able to make for Mr. G. with his late wife in the house she had loved so much.

Immediately after the first séance I went to work trying to research the house. I could only go back to 1879 for the house itself, but the building lot had been in use continuously since 1760, according to the records in the Hall of Records, Conveyances and Deeds. I then discovered that there had been a protracted will fight between the heirs of one particular owner, and that for years two branches of the family, the Joneses and the Masons, had been pitted one against the other. Bitterness had marked this period during which petition after petition was filed with the supreme court. Finally, the court handed down a partition rule in July, 1855. The man who received the lot on which Mr. G.'s house stood *had the first name of Henry.*

Several months passed, and the house seemed quieter. Then I received another call from Mr. G. Even though the entity had had a chance to express himself and was aware of having taken the wrong life, apparently he was not fully satisfied. What did Henry want of him now? Mr. G. wondered. I realized that the continued presence of young people in the house and of the highly nervous Mr. G. himself might be supplying the energies on which the disturbed mind of the discarnate Henry M. feasted. Under the circumstances I advised Mr. G. to sell the house as soon as he could. This was done, and Mr. G. moved to another neighborhood. He has had no problems, either personal or professional, ever since.

North Carolina

Since I published my findings regarding the famous Maco Light near Wilmington, North Carolina, people have come to me with new information and others have asked me to shed additional light on the very mysterious light that has puzzled people for many, many years. There are other mysterious lights all over the world, to be sure, such as the Brown Mountain Lights in Tennessee and similar mysterious luminous bodies frequently observed in Washington state. Some of these lights are unquestionably of natural origin and have nothing whatsoever to do with the psychic. Others may be of a parallel nature to the famous Maco Light. I investigated this railroad crossing and published my findings and the testimony of all witnesses I had met. Under the title "The Case of the Lost Head," I described what had happened to lure me down South to look for an elusive light along a railroad track.

One of the most famous ghosts of the South is railroad conductor Joe Baldwin. The story of Joe and his lantern was known to me, of course, and a few years ago *Life* magazine even dignified it with a photograph of the railroad track near Wilmington, North Carolina, very atmospherically adorned by a greenish lantern, presumably swinging in ghostly hands.

Then one day in early 1964, the legend became reality when a letter arrived from Bill Mitcham, Executive Secretary of the South Eastern North Carolina Beach Association, a public relations office set up by the leading resort hotels in the area centering around Wilmington. Mr. Mitcham proposed that I have a look at the ghost of

Joe Baldwin and try to explain once and for all—scientifically—what the famous Maco Light was or is.

In addition, Mr. Mitcham arranged for a lecture on the subject to be held at the end of my investigation and sponsored jointly by the Beach Association and Wilmington College. He promised to roll out the red carpet for Catherine and me, and roll it out he did.

Seldom in the history of ghost hunting has a parapsychologist been received so royally and fully covered by press, television, and radio, and if the ghost of Joe Baldwin is basking in the reflected glory of all this attention directed toward his personal Ghost Hunter, he is most welcome to it.

If it were not for Joe Baldwin, the bend in the railroad track which is known as Maco Station (a few miles outside of Wilmington) would be a most unattractive and ordinary trestle. By the time I had investigated it and left, the spot had almost risen to the prominence of a national shrine, and sightseeing groups arrived at all times, especially at night, to look for Joe Baldwin's ghostly light.

Bill Mitcham had seen to it that the world knew about Joe Baldwin's headless ghost and Hans Holzer seeking same, and no fewer than seventy-eight separate news stories of one kind or another appeared in print during the week we spent in Wilmington.

Before I even started to make plans for the Wilmington expedition, I received a friendly letter from a local student of psychic phenomena, William Edward Cox, Jr., and a manuscript entitled *The Maco Light*. Mr. Cox had spent considerable time observing the strange light, and I quote:

A favorite "ghost story" in the vicinity of Wilmington, N.C., is that of "Joe Baldwin's Ghost Light," which is alleged to appear at night near Maco, N.C., 12 miles west of Wilmington on the Atlantic Coast Line Railroad.

On June 30–July 1, 1949, this writer spent considerable time investigating the phenomenon. The purpose was to make an accurate check on the behavior of the light under test conditions, with the view toward ascertaining its exact nature.

This light has been observed since shortly after the legend of the Joe Baldwin ghost light "was born in 1867." It is officially reported in a pamphlet entitled "The Story of the Coast Line, 1830–1948." In its general description it resembles a 25-watt electric light slowly moving along the tracks toward the observer, whose best point of observation is on the track itself at the point where the tracks, double at that point, are crossed by a branch of a connecting roadway between U.S. Highway 74-76 and U.S. Highway 19.

The popular explanation is that Conductor Baldwin, decapitated in an accident, is taking the nocturnal walks in search of his head. . . .

After testing the various "natural" theories put forward for the origin of the nocturnal light, Mr. Cox admits:

Although the general consensus of opinion is that the lights stem from some relatively rare cause, such as the paranormal, "ignis fatuus," etc., the opinions of residents of the Maco vicinity were found by this observer to be more detailed. The proprietor of the Mobilgas Service Station was noncommittal, and a local customer said he had "never seen the light." A farmer in the area was quite certain that it is caused by automobile headlights, but would not express an opinion upon such lights as were customarily seen there before the advent of the automobile.

The proprietress of the Willet Service Station, Mrs. C. L.

Benton, was firmly convinced that it was of "supernatural origin," and that the peculiar visibility of automobile headlights to observers at Maco must be more or less a subsequent coincidence.

She said that her father "often saw it as he loaded the wood burners near there over 60 years ago."

The basic question of the origin and nature of the "Maco Light," or the original light, remains incompletely answered. The findings here reported, due as they are to entirely normal causes, cannot accurately be construed as disproving the existence of a light of paranormal origin at any time in the distant past (or, for that matter, at the present time).

The unquestionable singularity of the phenomenon's being in a locale where it is so easily possible for automobiles to produce an identical phenomenon seems but to relegate it to the enigmatic "realm of forgotten mysteries."

So much for Mr. Cox's painstaking experiment conducted at the site in 1949.

The coming of the Ghost Hunter (and Mrs. Ghost Hunter) was amply heralded in the newspapers of the area. Typical of the veritable avalanche of features was the story in the *Charlotte Observer:*

Can the Spook Hunter De-Ghost Old Joe? The South Eastern N.C. Beach Association invited a leading parapsychologist Saturday to study the ghost of Old Joe Baldwin.

Bill Mitcham, executive director of the association, said he has arranged for Hans Holzer of New York to either prove or disprove the ghostly tales relating to Old Joe.

Holzer will begin his study May 1.

Tales of Joe Baldwin flagging down trains with false signals, waving his lantern on dark summer nights have been repeated since his death in 1867.

Baldwin, a conductor on the Wilmington, Manchester and Augusta Railroad, was riding the rear coach of a train the night of his death. The coach became uncoupled and Baldwin seized a lantern in an effort to signal a passenger train following.

But the engineer failed to see the signal. In the resulting crash, Baldwin was decapitated.

A witness to the wreck later recalled that the signal lantern was flung some distance from the tracks, but that it burned brightly thereafter for some time.

Soon after the accident, there were reports of a mysterious light along the railroad tracks at Maco Station in Brunswick County.

Two lanterns, one green and one red, have been used by trainmen at Maco Station so that engineers would not be confused or deceived by Joe Baldwin's light.

Most helpful in a more serious vein was the Women's Editor of the Wilmington *Star-News*, Theresa Thomas, who had for years taken an interest in the psychic and probably is somewhat sensitive herself. On April 8, 1964, she asked her readers:

Have you ever seen the Maco Light? Have you ever seen Old Joe Baldwin? Or his light, that is? As far as we know, nobody has actually seen Joe himself.

But if you have seen his lantern swinging along the railroad track at Maco, you can be of great help to Hans Holzer, Ghost Hunter, who will be in Wilmington April 29th.

Either write out your experience and send it to us, or call and tell us about it.

Then the feminine point of view crashed the scientific barrier a little as Miss Thomas added:

> His *Mr. Holzer's* wife is just as fascinating as he. She is a painter and great-great-great-granddaughter of Catherine the Great of Russia. Mrs. Holzer was born Countess Catherine Buxhoeveden in a haunted castle in Meran, the Tyrol, in the Italian Alps. And she paints—haven't you guessed?—haunted houses.

My visit was still three weeks away, but the wheels of publicity were already spinning fast and furiously in Wilmington.

Theresa Thomas's appeal for actual witnesses to the ghostly phenomenon brought immediate results. For the first time people of standing took the matter seriously, and those who had seen the light, opened up. Miss Thomas did not disguise her enthusiasm. On April 12 she wrote:

> It seems a great many people have seen old Joe Baldwin's light at Maco and most of them are willing—even eager—to talk about it.

> Among the first to call was Mrs. Larry Moore, 211 Orange Street, who said she had seen the light three or four times at different seasons of the year.

> The first time it was a cloudy, misty winter night and again in the summer, misty again. Her description of the light was "like a bluish yellow flame." She and her companions walked down the track and the light came closer as they approached the trestle. When they reached the center of the trestle with the light apparently about 10 feet away, it disappeared.

> Mrs. Thelma Daughty, 6 Shearwater Drive, Wrightsville Beach, says she saw it on a misty spring night. It was about 7

or 8 o'clock in the evening and the reddish light appeared to swing along at about knee height.

Mrs. Margaret Jackson, 172 Colonial Circle, a native of Vienna, Austria, saw it about seven years ago on a hazy night, a "glary shine" steady and far away but always the same distance ahead of them.

Dixie Rambeau, 220 Pfeiffer Avenue, saw it about 1 a.m. Friday morning. She says it was "real dark" and the light appeared as a red pinpoint at a distance up the track, as it neared it became yellowish white, then closer still it was a mixed red and white.

She recalls that she and her companions watched it come closer to the left side of the track and that as it came close the reflection on the rail almost reached them. At about 10 feet away it reversed its process and as they walked toward it, it disappeared. Once it appeared to cross over. They watched it five or six times, she said.

Mrs. Marvin Clark, 406 Grace Street, a practical nurse, states that she and her husband saw the light 15 years ago. It was about midnight on a cloudy, rainy night. They were standing in the middle of the tracks and "it looked like a light on a train coming at full speed."

Mrs. Clark described the light as "the color of a train light."

"We picked up our little girl and ran. All of us have always seen reflections of automobiles but beyond a doubt it was the Maco Light."

Mrs. Lase V. Dail of Carolina Beach also has a story to tell. It seems she and her husband came home late one night from Fayetteville.

She writes, "As we left the cut off and headed into 74-76 Highway, I shall never forget the experience we had. . . . " She goes on, "All at once a bright light came down the road towards us, first I figured it was a car. But decided if so it had only one light. On it came steadily toward us.

"Then I figured it was a train, yet I heard nothing, and as suddenly as it appeared it vanished. I can say it was quite a weird feeling. I have often thought of it. I have heard many versions, but never one like this."

Three days later, Miss Thomas devoted still another full column to people who had witnessed the ghost light.

Mrs. Marjorie H. Rizer of Sneads Ferry writes: "I have seen the light three times. The last and most significant time was about a year and a half ago. My husband, three young sons and a companion from the United States Naval Hospital at Camp Lejeune were with me and we saw the same thing. It was about 10:30 p.m. and we were returning from a ball game. We decided to go to Maco since we were so near and the young man with us didn't believe there was anything to our story.

"The sky was cloudy and a light mist was falling. We parked the car beside the track and sure enough, there was the light down the track. I stayed in the car with my sons, and my husband and the corpsman walked down the track toward the light.

"The light would alternately dim and then become very bright. The two men walked perhaps a quarter of a mile down the track before they returned. They said the light stayed ahead of them, but my sons and I saw the light between them and us.

"It looked as if the light would come almost to where we were parked and then it would wobble off down the track and disappear. In a moment it would reappear and do the same time after time.

"When we had been there for about an hour and started to leave, a train approached going toward Wilmington. The light was a short distance away from us. As the train passed the light, it rose and hovered over the train. We could clearly see the top of the train as the light became very bright.

"It stayed over the train until it had passed then disappeared back down the track and finally it looked as if someone had thrown it off into the woods.

"As we pulled away from the track the light came back on the track and weaved backward and forward down the track as it had been doing."

And still the letters poured in. On April 22, after half a column devoted to my imminent arrival in the area, Miss Thomas printed a letter from a young man who had taken some interesting pictures:

He is J. Everett Huggins, home address 412 Market Street, Wilmington. The letter is addressed to Bill Mitcham and reads in part: "I read with interest the articles on your 'ghost survey,' especially since I saw the Maco light less than two weeks ago and was actually able to catch Old Joe on film.

"On the nights of April 1 and 2 a schoolmate of mine and I went to Maco Station in the hopes of seeing the light. We saw nothing on Friday, April 1, but we had more success on Saturday, when it was a little darker. Around 10:30 we saw a yellow light about 100 yards down the track from us (this distance is only a guess). It seemed to be about 10 feet above the tracks and looked as if it were moving slowly toward us for a while, then it went back and died out.

"The light appeared maybe three times in succession for

periods up to what I would estimate to be about thirty seconds.

"I attempted to take two time exposures with my camera. Unfortunately I did not have a tripod, and so I had to hold the camera in my hands, which made clear results impossible. The pictures are not spectacular—just a small spot on each of the color transparencies—but they are pictures. If you are interested I will have some copies made.

"My friends had kidded me about the light, so I noted some details to try to end their skepticism. The headlights of cars traveling west on Highway 74 could be seen in the distance, and no doubt many who think they see Old Joe only see these lights. Old Joe could be distinguished in several ways, however. First, the light had a yellower tone than did the auto headlights.

"Secondly, unlike the headlights which grow brighter and brighter and then suddenly disappear, the Maco light would gradually grow brighter and then gradually fade out. Thirdly, the Maco light produced a reflection on the rails that was not characteristic of the headlights.

"More interesting was the fact that the reflection on the rails was seen only on a relatively short stretch of track. By observing the reflection, we could tell that the light moved backward and forward on the rails. It always remained directly above the tracks.

"I had seen the light once before, in 1956. It was on a cold winter night, and the light was brighter."

As the day of our arrival grew nearer, the tempo of the press became more hectic. On April 26, Arnold Kirk wrote in the Wilmington *Star-News:*

This tiny Brunswick County village, nestled in a small clearing a few miles west of Wilmington off U.S. Highway 74, is rapidly gaining acclaim as the "Ghost Capital" of North Carolina.

Its few dozen inhabitants, mostly farmers of moderate means, have suddenly found their once-peaceful nights disturbed by scores of vehicles sparring for vantage points from which to view the famous "Maco Light."

While the legend of the light and Old Joe Baldwin, the "Ghost" of Maco, has long been known, its popularity has become intense only in recent months.

Elaborate plans have already been made to welcome Holzer to the Port City. The mayors of all the towns in New Hanover and Brunswick counties, in addition to county commissioners from both counties, have agreed to be at New Hanover County Airport Wednesday at 7:43 pm when the "ghost hunter's" plane arrives.

Also on hand to greet the noted parapsychologist will be 1,000 high-school students, carrying, appropriately enough, lighted lanterns! The lanterns were purchased by the city years ago to offer warmth to trees and plants during blustery winter months.

Adding to the fanfare of the event will be the first public offering of "The Ballad of Old Joe Baldwin," written by the senior English class of New Hanover High School.

The reception was a bash that would have made Old Joe Baldwin feel honored. A little later, we tried to sneak out to Maco and have a first glance at the haunted spot. The results were disappointing.

It was not so much that the ghost did not show, but what did show up was most disturbing. The Wilmington *Star-News* summed it up like this:

An unwilling Old Joe Baldwin exercised his ghostly prerogative Wednesday night by refusing to perform before what may have been his largest audience.

Huddled in small clusters along the railroad tracks near the center of this tiny Brunswick County village, an estimated 250 persons stared into the gloomy darkness in hopes of catching a glimpse of the famous "Maco Light."

But the light would not offer the slightest flicker.

Holzer's announced visit to the scene of Baldwin's ghastly demise gave no comfort to the few dozen residents of Maco. By 10 o'clock, dozens of cars lined both sides of the narrow Maco road and scores of thrill-seeking teenagers had spilled onto the railroad track.

If Joe Baldwin had decided to make an appearance, his performance no doubt would have been engulfed in the dozens of flashlights and battery-powered lanterns searching through the darkness for at least a mile down the track.

Several times, the flashlights and lanterns were mistaken for the "Maco Light," giving hope that the mysterious glow would soon appear.

A large portion of the track was illuminated by the headlights of a jeep and small foreign car scurrying back and forth along both sides of the track. A young girl created an anxious moment when she mistook a firefly for the "Maco Light" and released a penetrating scream that sliced through the pitch-darkness.

Holzer's visit to Maco on Wednesday night was mostly for the benefit of photographers and reporters who met the noted parapsychologist at the New Hanover County airport earlier that night.

His second visit to the crossing will be kept a closely guarded secret in hopes the "ghost hunter" will be able to conduct his investigation of the light without being interrupted by pranksters and playful teenagers.

Soon I realized that it would be impossible for us to go out to the tracks alone. Crowds followed us around and crowds were ever present at the spot, giving rise to a suspicion in my mind that these people were not in a working mood while we were visiting their area. Evidently we were the most exciting thing that had happened to them for some time.

Finally, the day of a scheduled press conference arrived, and at ten o'clock in the morning, before a battery of klieg lights and microphones set up at the magnificent Blockade Runner Hotel on the beach, I started to talk in person to those who had come to tell me about their encounters with Joe Baldwin's ghost.

In addition to those who had written to Miss Thomas and reaffirmed their original stories, others came forward who had not done so previously. There was William McGirt, an insurance executive, who called the light "buoyant," flicking itself on and off, as it were, and fully reflected on the iron rails. But you cannot see it looking east, he told me, only when you look toward Maco Station.

Margaret Bremer added to her previously told story by saying the light looked to her "like a kerosene lantern swaying back and forth."

Her husband, Mr. Bremer, had not planned on saying anything, but I coaxed him. He admitted finally that twelve years ago, when his car was standing straddled across the tracks, he had seen a light coming toward him. It flickered like a lamp, and when it came closer it flared up. As an afterthought he added, "Something strange—suddenly there seemed to be a rush of air, as if a train were coming from Wilmington."

"Was there?" I inquired cautiously.

"No, of course not. We wouldn't have had the car across the track if a train were expected."

Mrs. Laura Collins stepped forward and told me of the time she was at the trestle with a boy who did not believe in ghosts, not even Joe Baldwin's. When the light appeared, he sneered at it and tried to explain it as a reflection. Six feet away from the boy, the light suddenly disappeared and reappeared in back of him—as if to show him up! Mrs. Collins, along with others, observed that misty weather made the light appear clearer.

Next in the parade of witnesses came Mrs. Elizabeth Finch of Wilmington, who had offered her original testimony only the day before.

"It appeared to me many times," she said of the light; "looked like a lantern to me. Two years ago, we were parked across the tracks in our car—we were watching for a train of course, too—when I saw two dazzling lights from both sides. It was a winter evening, but I suddenly felt very hot. There was a red streak in front of the car, *and then I saw what was a dim outline of a man walking with a lantern and swinging it.* Mind you, it was a bare outline," Mrs. Finch added in emphasis, "and it did have a head . . . just kept going, then suddenly he disappeared inside the tracks."

"Did you ever have psychic experiences before, Mrs. Finch?" I wanted to know.

"Yes, when we lived in a house in Masonborough, I used to hear noises, steps, even voices out of nowhere—later, I was told it was haunted."

I thanked Mrs. Finch, wondering if the local legend had impressed her unconscious to the point where she did see what everyone had said was there—or whether she really saw the outline of a man.

I really have no reason to doubt her story. She struck me as a calm, intelligent person who would not easily make up a story just to be sensational. No, I decided, Mrs. Finch might very well have been one of the very few who saw more than just the light.

"I tell you why it can't be anything ordinary," Mr. Trussle, my next informant, said. "Seven years ago, when I saw the light on a damp night about a mile away from where I was standing, I noticed its very rapid approach. It disappeared fast, went back and forth as if to attract attention to something. *It was three feet above the track about the height of where a man's arm might be.*

"At first, it seemed yellowish white; when I came closer, it looked like kind of pinkish. Now an ordinary car headlight wouldn't go back and forth like that, would it?"

I agreed it was most unlikely for an automobile headlight to behave in such an unusual manner.

Mrs. Miriam Moore saw it three times, always on misty, humid nights. "I had a funny ringing in my ears when I reached the spot," she said. She was sure what she saw was a lamp swinging in a slow motion. Suddenly, she broke into a cold sweat for no reason at all. I established that she was a psychic person and had on occasion foretold the deaths of various members of her family.

E. S. Skipper is a dapper little man in the golden years of life, but peppery and very much alert. He used to be a freight skipper on the Atlantic Coast Line and grew up with the Maco Light the way Niagara kids grow up with the sight of the Falls.

"I've seen it hundreds of times," he volunteered. "I've seen it flag trains down—it moved just like a railroad lantern would. On one occasion I took my shot gun and walked toward it. As I got nearer, the light became so bright I could hardly look. Suddenly, it disappeared into the old Catholic cemetery on the right side of the tracks."

"Cemetery?" I asked, for I had not heard of a cemetery in this area.

Mr. Skipper was quite certain that there was one. I promised to look into this immediately. "Since you came so close to the light, Mr. Skipper," I said, "perhaps you can tell me what it looked like close up."

"Oh, I got even closer than that—back in 1929. I remember it well.

It was two o'clock in the morning. I got to within six foot of it."

"What did you see?"

"I saw a flame. I mean, in the middle of the light, there was, unmistakably, a flame burning."

"Like a lantern?"

"Like a lantern."

I thanked Mr. Skipper and was ready to turn to my last witness, none other than Editor Thomas herself, when Mrs. E. R. Rich, who had already given her account in the newspaper, asked for another minute, which I gladly gave her.

"Ten years ago," Mrs. Rich said, "we were at the track one evening. My son Robert was in the car with me, and my older son went down to the track to watch for the light. Suddenly not one but two lights appeared at the car. They were round and seemed to radiate and sparkle—for a moment they hung around, then one left, the other stayed. My feet went ice cold at this moment and I felt very strange."

"Miss Thomas," I said, "will you add your own experiences to this plethora of information?"

"Gladly," the Women's Editor of the *Star-News* replied. "There were three of us, all newspaper women, who decided a few weeks ago to go down to the trestle and not see anything."

"I beg your pardon?"

"We'd made up our minds not to be influenced by all the publicity Joe Baldwin's ghost was getting."

"What happened?"

"When we got to the track, dogs were baying as if disturbed by something in the atmosphere. We parked on the dirt road that runs parallel to the track and waited. After a while, the light appeared. It had a yellow glow. Then, suddenly, there were two lights, one larger than the other, swaying in the night sky.

The lights turned reddish after a while. There was no correlation with car lights at all. I thought at first it was a train bearing down on us, that's how big the lights appeared. Just as suddenly the lights disappeared. One light described an arc to the left of the track, landing on the grass."

"Just as those old tales say Joe's lantern did, eh?"

"It seems so, although it is hard to believe."

"What else did you notice?"

"I had the feeling I was not alone."

And there you have it. Mass hysteria? Self-hypnosis? Suggestion? Could all these people make up similar stories?

Although the Maco Light is unique in its specific aspects, there are other lights that have been observed at spots where tragedies have occurred. There are reports of apparitions in Colorado taking the form of concentrated energy, or light globes. I don't doubt that the human personality is a form of energy that cannot be destroyed, only transmuted. The man who heard the sound of a train, the psychic chill several people experienced, the flame within the light, the two lights clearly distinguished by the newspaper women—possibly Joe's lantern and the headlight of the onrushing train—all these add up to a case.

That evening, at Bogden Hall, before an audience of some five hundred people of all ages, I stated my conviction that the track at Maco Station was, indeed, haunted. I explained that the shock of sudden death might have caused Joe Baldwin's etheric self to become glued to the spot of the tragedy, reenacting the final moments over and over again.

I don't think we are dealing here with an "etheric impression" registered in the atmosphere and not possessing a life of its own. The phantom reacts differently with various people and seems to me a true ghost, capable of attempting communication with the living, but not fully aware of his own status or of the futility of his efforts.

I was, and am, convinced of the veracity of the phenomenon and,

by comparing it to other "weaving lights" in other areas, can only conclude that the basic folklore is on the right track, except that Joe isn't
likely to be looking for his head—he is rather trying to keep an imaginary train from running into his uncoupled car, which of course exists
now only in his thought world.

And until someone tells Joe all's well on the line now, he will continue to wave his light. I tried to say the right words for such occasions,
but I was somewhat hampered by the fact that I did not have Mrs.
Ethel Meyers, my favorite medium, with me; then, too, the
Wilmington people did not like the idea of having their town ghost go
to his reward and leave the trestle just another second-rate railroad
track.

The folks living alongside it, though, wouldn't have minded one bit.
They can do without Joe Baldwin and his somewhat motley admirers.

Suddenly the thought struck me that we had no proof that a Joe
Baldwin had ever really existed in this area. The next morning I went
to the Wilmington Public Library and started to dig into the files and
historical sources dealing with the area a hundred years ago. Bill
Mitcham and I started to read all the newspapers from 1866 onward,
but after a while we gave up. Instead, I had a hunch which, eventually,
paid off. If Joe Baldwin was physically fit to work on the railroad in so
hazardous a job as that of a train man, he must have been well enough
to be in the Armed Forces at one time or another.

I started to search the Regimental Records from 1867 on backward.
Finally I found in volume V, page 602, of a work called *North Carolina
Regiments,* published in 1901, the following entry:

"Joseph Baldwin, Company F, 26th N. C. T, badly wounded in the
thigh. Battle of Gettysburg. July 1, 1863."

It was the only Joseph Baldwin listed in the area, or, for that matter, the state.

I also inquired about the old Catholic cemetery. It was, indeed, near the railroad track, but had been out of use for many years. Only oldsters still remembered its existence. Baldwin may have been Catholic, as are many residents of the area. Time did not permit me to look among the dilapidated tombstones for a grave bearing the name of Joe Baldwin.

But it would be interesting to find it and see if all of Joe Baldwin lies buried in sacred ground!

On November 17, 1964, the Wilmington *Morning Star* in their Letter to the Editor column published a communication from one Curtis Matthews in which Mr. Matthews stated he knew all about the Maco Light and what it really was. He assured the readers of the Wilmington *Morning Star* that, when he was going to New Hanover High School back in 1928 through 1933, they would make a sport out of fooling their dates so they would be real scared and cling to their arms. This was accomplished by getting out of the car and walking along the tracks and watching the mysterious Maco Light come toward them. "The light would startle you as it came down the tracks and the reflection off the tracks made it more eerie. Afterward we checked on it and determined it to be cars coming toward Wilmington at that point and encountering hills before passing Maco itself. This caused the lights to flicker off and come back on again. We thought the reflection of the lights off the tracks made it look as scary as it did. If no automobiles came by some of the fellows went up ahead and waved lights or lanterns. No one was disappointed then. We never told our dates of our findings. It would have ruined everything." Mr. Matthews, of course, makes it all sound just too easy. He was, of course, unaware of the extensive work done those lines by Mr. Cox and other scientists with or without dates clinging to their arms.

I had thought no more about Wilmington and the Maco Light when a communication reached me on October 28, 1968. An alert young man by the name of Mack Etheridge, then age fifteen, wanted me to hear of his experiences with the Maco Light. He had been interested in the occult for many years prior to his contacting me but had never had any actual psychic experiences even though other members of his family had. Mack's family, including himself, was traveling from Maryland to South Carolina to visit his grandmother that summer. They decided to route their trip through Wilmington to have a look at the fabled Maco Light.

The family arrived in Wilmington on August 7,1968, around 2:30 in the morning. They didn't intend to stay but only ride through. They had difficulty finding the bend in the railroad track where the Maco trestle is located, due to the darkness and the lack of signs. Nevertheless, disregarding the late hour, they continued to look for it. They knocked on doors, but no one answered. Finally they were riding back toward Wilmington on Route 74-76 when they noticed a new road parallel to it under construction. They decided to stop at a dimly lit trailer as a last try to obtain some information. A young woman directed them back down the highway from where they had just come and told them how to continue toward the track. There was a dirt road parallel to it which they assumed was the road to take. With their eyes wide open and directed toward the track, they followed the dirt road slowly till it came to a small house and ended. They realized they had gone down the wrong road. Retracing their steps they suddenly noticed a small sign reading *Maco, two miles*. They followed the sign and exactly two miles later arrived at the proper spot. The moment they arrived Mr. Etheridge, Sr., parked the car across the track and shut off the lights, and the family stayed in the car quietly and expectantly, hopefully awaiting some sort of glimpse of the light.

It was an exceptionally clear night with a full moon. Nevertheless, a moment later Mr. Etheridge, Sr., noticed a very bright light and pointed it out to his family. The light was not moving up the track toward them. At first it did not appear to be very bright and Mack immediately dismissed it as being a train and not the Maco Light because it seemed to him to be far too bright. But several minutes later the light approached and remained constant. Mack was no longer sure that the light belonged to an approaching train since there was absolutely no sound. Now the light would alternately dim and become bright again. He could observe it with the naked eye and noted that it was a yellowish light one foot in diameter and extremely bright. It would flare up to its brightest intensity for two seconds and then slowly fade out. Sometimes when it faded out it would appear to be farther up the track. There were times when the light would pulsate and he also noticed that there was a hazy luminosity around it when it faded out. At its closest point the light seemed about two hundred feet away. He noticed with mounting excitement that when it was very close the light would slowly swing at knee level as a lantern would in the hands of a man. When the light was closest it appeared to him that it shone on a relatively short stretch of track.

At this point Mr. Etheridge, Sr., reminded his family that they had brought binoculars, and immediately they put them to good use observing the phenomenon for several minutes through them. The binoculars had a seven by thirty-five power and were in excellent condition. "The following," Mack Etheridge explained, "was seen wholly by me and will be totally new to you and to your writings."

As he was gazing at the light through the binoculars about a quarter mile up the track it faded out again and he quite naturally expected it to reappear as the same, but instead it reappeared accompanied by two other lights. These additional lights appeared instantly to the side of the track. There was a red light to the far left; a few feet to the right of that was a small green light, and several feet to the right of that was the usual yellow light, the largest of them. Mack could clearly see the center green light float into the red one and become part of it, which was then all red. Then the red moved into the yellow by way of a yellow cord. This connecting link first appeared in the yellow light, then shot forward to the red one, connecting the two. Gradually it drew the red light into itself to form the usual bright light observed as the Maco Light.

Mack was amazed at what he had just seen. He followed the light as it moved up the track to perform various maneuvers, only to move back down to repeat the previous procedure. He saw it happen twice and described what he observed to his family. They, however, could only see two of the lights due to the distance and faintness. But as seen through the binoculars the single light seemed to rise up in the air above the track, possibly to the height of a telephone pole. After the three lights had formed Mack also noticed the colors visible together a few times. At this point a train was approaching from the opposite direction and it became necessary to move the car off the track. When the train went by, the light faded out, only to return after the train had passed. At that time of night Highway 74 and 76, the crucial point in the observation of the Maco Light, was virtually desolate. They had passed only a few cars in the hours they spent searching for the station. I had surmised that the lights represented Joe Baldwin's lantern and the headlights of an onrushing train, but Mack Etheridge took issue with that explanation. He assured me that in his estimation no train could have been in sight of the track a quarter of a mile away. The two lights to him were completely separate, and as one would fade out another would continue its strange behavior.

Assuming that the Etheridges were sober and sane people, and their observation correct, it would bear out some of the previous testimony reported by me. What is fascinating in this additional report is the fact that some sort of human agency seems behind the movements of the lights.

This was by no means the end of Joe Baldwin and his lost head. In 1970 I received another communication from a certain Daniel Harrington of Flushing, Long Island. Mr. Harrington had visited the

Maco Light, inspired by my account of it. He had brought along a camera, since he was somewhat of a camera fan, in the hopes of capturing the elusive light on film. His black and white pictures were taken with time exposure, 5 or 6 seconds, but unfortunately without tripods. Thus the results would, of necessity, be somewhat blurred. He had clearly seen a large light on the track circling, bobbing and weaving about. In one of the two photographs submitted to me the light seems extremely large in relation to the track. That, however, as Mr. Harrington pointed out, is due to the angle of the camera. In the first photograph there is a single light. In the second shot there are clearly three separate lights: round, brightly lit orbs of luminosity—two large ones and a small one. Mr. Harrington assured me there were no cars passing by when these pictures were taken.

So it would appear that today, seven years after my original visit to the spot, Joe Baldwin is still merrily walking along the track and holding up the lantern to stop an imaginary train. No one has yet come up with a better explanation.

Southern Mansion Ghosts

There is nothing as gracious as a Southern host or hostess, and nothing quite as colorful as a Southern ghost. Sometimes it is difficult to differentiate the true from the merely well told, but I have cut through the magnolia-scented curtain to ascertain what facts there are in a number of Southern houses, by no means more than a fraction of what there is, for the tragedies of the South, gentle though they may be in comparison with the violence of New England or the rugged West, have yielded their fair share of spectral characters.

My wife and I spent time in the Charlottesville, Virginia, area in May of 1963, and in North Carolina in April of 1964.

On both occasions we were fortunate enough to know the "right" people, so that we were received everywhere with open arms and—more important for a Ghost Hunter—open doors and secrets.

Take Castle Hill, Virginia, for instance. Its ghost isn't much of a ghost as spectres go, but it is authenticated and the names of witnesses are known. The house itself is magnificent and the only one of its kind.

Now the residence of Colonel Clark Lawrence, it has a colorful history, and I quote from information supplied to me by the Colonel:

> The estate of Castle Hill passed into possession of Dr. Thomas Walker in 1741 when he married the widow of Nicholas Meriwether. It then comprised 15,000 acres and was a grant from George II, King of England.

Miss Judith Page Walker, daughter of Dr. Walker's son Francis from whom she inherited Castle Hill, married William Cabell Rives, bringing Castle Hill into the possession of the Rives family, where it remained until purchased in September, 1947, by Colonel and Mrs. Clark J. Lawrence. The estate now comprises 1,183 acres.

The house is actually two houses: the first, built in 1765 by Dr. Thomas Walker, is a frame clapboard structure, one room deep and a story and a half high, exhibiting the charm and sturdiness of the eighteenth century. Its six dormer windows and small porch with floor of solid stone blocks, belonging to an earlier structure built by Dr. Walker, look out across the old Bowling Green to Walnut Mountain, part of the estate, a continuation of the Southwest Range.

Its entrance hall runs the length of the house and is flanked on either side by spacious pine-paneled rooms.

The front of the house then faced north. In 1820 Judith Page Walker and her husband, Senator William Cabell Rives, twice Minister to France, built the formal brick addition with twelve-foot ceilings and beautiful interior trim. In 1840 he added the one-story wings with the loggias.

The 1820 structure made the front of the mansion facing the south, and the hour-glass-shaped lawn and entrance box hedges were laid out and planted by Mrs. Rives and show a decided French influence.

It was at Castle Hill that Major Jack Jouett broke his famous ride, "hell for leather" from Louisa Court House to Charlottesville. He was on his way to warn Thomas Jefferson, then Governor of Virginia, and the members of the legislature there assembled that General Tarleton and his British troopers were coming to capture them.

Near Castle Hill Jouette's mount gave out. Dr. Walker remounted him on one of Castle Hill's fastest horses and bade him God Speed.

At daybreak the next morning, June 4, 1781, Tarleton and his troopers appeared at Castle Hill and demanded breakfast. Dr. Walker's potent mint juleps and an intentionally delayed breakfast made Jefferson's escape possible. Under the mellow effect of such liquid hospitality Tarleton seems to have unbent a good deal and he and Dr. Walker measured his orderly on the living-room doorjamb.

This trooper was the tallest man in the British army and proved six feet nine and one quarter inches in height. The notch cut by Dr. Walker is still visible on the old doorjamb now connecting the old part of the house with the 1820 stair hall.

The old house is full of interesting memories. The youthful Jefferson played the fiddle for the still younger Madison to dance in the old living room. General Washington, General Lafayette, Dolly Madison, and in later years Andrew Jackson, Martin Van Buren and John Tyler visited at Castle Hill.

It was long the house of Amélie Rives, the authoress, who lived there with her artist husband, Prince Pierre Troubetzkoy.

The ghost has appeared from time to time to guests using a certain bedroom, known as the Pink Bedroom. In the 1930's, author Julian Green, who did not profess any belief in the supernatural, slept in the haunted room. The next morning, he packed his bags and left, cutting short an expected long stay.

Princess Troubetzkoy, who lies buried in the private cemetery on the grounds, reported smelling a certain peculiar perfume associated with the ghostly lady. As the story goes, she appears to people she doesn't like and tells them to go away. Those she likes are permitted to stay in her bedroom, however.

I questioned Colonel Lawrence as to whether he himself might have had any unusual experiences at Castle Hill. He shook his head. Either he was not psychic, or preferred not to talk about it.

Southerners can be very politely negative if they want to be and, although the Colonel was only a fairly recent addition to the Southland, he had become very much like any other owner of a Southern mansion. But he did admit that the people sleeping in the Pink Room were generally restless and disturbed for no apparent reason, for the room with its subdued, dainty elegance is surely one of the prettiest and most restful rooms I have ever been in. It has a decidedly feminine appeal, of course, and the Colonel is keeping it exactly as it was.

Not far from Castle Hill is one of America's most venerated historical shrines, the country house once owned by President Monroe, where he and Thomas Jefferson frequently exchanged small talk and also big decisions. The modest-appearing house is now in private hands, but is open to visitors at certain hours.

For unexplained reasons, photography is frowned upon, and I was told in no uncertain terms by those in the know, that I should not try to take any pictures. Also, I could not have a private visit, for the very word "ghost" was unwelcome to the present owners of Ash Lawn, as the house is called.

The ghostly goings on center around a certain wooden rocking chair which is said to rock without benefit of human hands. With historian Virginia Cloud momentarily distracting the attention of the guide, I photographed the chair several times. It did not rock for me, but any self-respecting ghost would run for the woods, so to speak, if he had to listen to the talk of a professional museum guide every hour on the hour.

This was Monroe's favorite house even after he moved to a bigger place later in his career. Here he could "get away from it all" and, with friend Jefferson only a couple of miles away at Monticello, could really relax.

Has anyone ever seen the ghostly chair rock? Mrs. Joseph Massey, a resident of the area, whose mother once owned the house and gardens, is most emphatic about it:

"I will tell anyone, and have no objection to its being known, I have seen, not once but time and time again, the rocking chair in my bedroom rocking exactly as though someone were in it. My brother John has seen it, too. If we touched it, it stopped."

Horace Burr is a collector as well as an expert on art. His house in Charlottesville, Virginia, is filled to the rafters with art and fine furniture. Carrsgrove, as the rambling country place is called, is a wooden structure, the oldest part of which dates back at least a hundred fifty years. Soon after acquiring the property, about 1956, the Burrs realized that there was something the matter with their house.

It was haunted. In the oldest part of the house, dead center, they kept hearing a "sighing" ghost.

Mrs. Helen Burr had just given birth to a child when she first reported hearing the uncanny noise. At 3:45 A.M. every morning she heard the mournful sighing of a woman no one could see. At first only she heard it, but one day she woke her husband and insisted that he accompany her to the spot near the inner wall. Then he heard it, too.

Burr's curiosity was aroused and he made some inquiries about the house. The previous owner, whose name was McCue, had died, but his faithful nurse was still living. She reported what had happened one terrible morning, about 1910.

McCue's daughter was staying at the house at the time with her young child. She started to imagine that the baby was not going to be normal, and in a fit of postnatal depression, she took poison. At exactly 3:45 A.M., the nurse told Burr, the father awoke and heard his daughter's *dying gasp*. By the time he raced to her bedroom on the other side of the house, she was dead.

It was that identical dying gasp that the Burrs had been hearing. However, once the explanation was given and the reasons for the noise in the house had been discussed, something happened to the ghost. The Burrs have not heard the noise lately, but with *ghosts* one never knows.

The area is full of ghostly tales. Many of them cannot be traced to a point where a scientific inquiry would yield tangible results in terms of believability. But now and then a tale sounds so real, and the people involved are so honest and free of ulterior motives that I cannot help but feel they ought to be at least mentioned here. For the following tale, as for other invaluable help, I am indebted to Virginia Cloud, librarian and author, who lives in Charlottesville.

Not far from Castle Hill in a less pretentious house lived a family with a ten-year-old daughter.

One night, when the child was supposed to be asleep in her upstairs room, the mother found her wide awake when she herself was going to bed.

"Why aren't you asleep?" the mother sternly asked. The little girl pointed to a corner of the room and replied, "I've been watching the little old man in the bed in the corner."

The mother insisted there was no bed in the corner, and the daughter, with equal determination, insisted that the old man was there and that he was very short of stature and had a very white beard.

All this upset the parents so much that they looked into the background of their house. To their amazement they discovered that the previous occupants had had a grandfather staying with them until his death. The room now occupied by their daughter had been his room, and the bed was exactly as the child had described it. The old man had

had a very white beard and had not been very tall. He had, however, passed on long before the little girl was even born!

Some people consider Washington, D.C., neither Northern nor Southern, but the truth is that, in a historical and cultural sense, it really is a Southern city.

Our expedition to the nation's capital was aimed primarily at The Octagon, but I had read of still another haunted house and decided to pursue the matter.

On April 21, 1963, the *Boston Sunday Globe* ran a story signed by one Nick Roper and entitled, "I Lived in a Haunted House." The story was illustrated by four photographs showing Mr. Roper, his sister Anne, the police in one of the corridors, and an outside view of the famous old Georgian mansion known as Halcyon House in Georgetown.

Mr. Roper, whose family had moved into the sprawling mansion six months before, had been a nonbeliever in ghosts. Mr. Roper, Sr., was a real-estate broker who had first rented the house and then sold it to Georgetown University, which now owns it, although the Ropers still live in it.

Young Roper made it plain that his new-found enthusiasm for things spectral was not shared by the rest of the Ropers:

> Dad remains staunchly skeptical. But try as he will, even he can't explain the footsteps that tread the attics and run up and down the stairs, the lights that switch on and off without human hands, doors that open and shut themselves, ash trays that mysteriously fill with water, the Riddle of the Basement, and the Strange Affair of the Fallen Mirror—not to mention the voice in the Garden.
>
> My twenty-one-year-old sister Anne and the three girls who share Apartment 1214 will admit they've heard strange

things, too. The girls report that every Thursday between 1 and 2 in the morning they hear measured pacing in the attic over-head. The "ghost" is always on schedule.

Corinne Mitchell Poole reported in the *Sunday Star* of August 9, 1959, when writing about Halcyon House:

Perhaps the ghost of Benjamin Stoddert, the builder of Halcyon House, is responsible for the occasional mysterious opening and shutting of doors, and one likes to think it is the ghost of a twentieth century owner, Albert Clemens, which sometimes makes a clatter in the upper stories.

The house has 45 rooms plus numerous nooks and pas-sageways.

Of course the Ropers, Nick included, did not believe this story one bit. But they soon found out that ghosts aren't something you can sweep under the carpet. Nick writes, in the *Globe* account:

On two or three occasions my mother Mary, while brewing coffee in the kitchen, heard someone running down the stairs.

Convinced it was me, she poured a cup and waited. When I didn't show up, she came upstairs calling me. I was still in my room and hadn't left it.

Night after night, I have heard footsteps in the attic over my room, sometimes on the fire escape outside my French win-dow. They pace steadily, then stop abruptly. The first time this happened, thinking it might be a prowler, I sneaked up into the attic to check. The light was on, but no one was there. The only way out of the attic was through my bedroom. I shrugged off the burning light as an electrical quirk (though the switch worked perfectly) and the footsteps as the normal creakings of an old house.

Nick Roper still would not accept the fact the house was haunted. On one occasion he found the lights burning in the basement and the atmosphere surcharged with the presence of an Unseen Person. When he shouted "Who's there?" the light went out by itself.

On another occasion he was awakened by mysterious footsteps and found himself floating above his bed, the window in his room wide open, when he distinctly remembered having it shut before he went to bed. He was gently lowered into bed again by unseen hands, but the terror of it all was enough to change his attitude towards the Uncanny.

All sorts of nocturnal noises, heard by the entire family, added to the nervous tension in the house. When a heavy mirror fell off its iron spike all by itself during their absence from the house, and a black X mark showed in the center of the glass, the Ropers were no longer amused. But what could they do?

What they could do, they did not do. That is, get the help of someone like myself to come to terms with the haunting personalities and find out what they wanted. I offered my services, free of course, and in confidence, as early as August, 1963. Mr. Roper, Sr., refused to see me, or even to discuss the matter.

A long-time Washington resident, Eleanor Baumgardner, better known to her friends as "Lady," tried to arrange things, to no avail. But she did manage to get me some background information about Halcyon House. She asked an expert friend to get me all the data I needed. Here they are:

On August 24, 1961, Bowman Jeffries wrote:

One of Georgetown's great houses, Halcyon House, has been purchased by Georgetown University. The sale was arranged by George S. Roper, real-estate broker for the University, who bought the house from Mrs. Kondrup Gray and her daughter, Mrs. H. E. Kondrup, for a purchase price reported to be in the neighborhood of $250,000.

Halcyon House, situated in the lower part of town at 3400 Prospect Street, was built in 1783 by Benjamin Stoddert, the nation's first Secretary of the Navy and one of the 18 "proprietors" of the Federal City.

The mansion is as fabulous as the myth of the bird from which its name is derived. The classic belief about the halcyon bird was that, floating on the sea in its nest, it bred at the time of the winter solstice, magically causing the water to be especially calm at that time. Hence halcyon quietude, "Halcyon Days," and Halcyon House, a name aptly selected by Secretary Stoddert.

The original Georgian structure of the house was brick laid up Flemish bond, with handsome symmetry in its two-story wings, and a widow's walk at the top.

The beautiful front door—a seven-section fanlight flanked by fluted pilasters with a rounded arch and key-stone above—faced the River with Prospect Street at the back. The original façade is not visible from the street now (one can just glimpse it in winter, crossing Key Bridge), but it remains as constructed. Spreading from the front door toward the Potomac is a magnificent garden, said to be Major L'Enfant's plan.

Wisteria and boxwood are the triumphs here, with black-green magnolias, old rhododendron, mossy brick walls and walks, and ivy everywhere. The garden seems timeless, remotely walled and stranded high above Thirty-fourth Street. Various owners have added and subtracted a swimming pool, terraces, fountains, and Grecian colonnades; the dark gleaming greens of ivy, box and magnolias remain superb.

At the turn of the century Albert Clemens, eccentric *extraordinaire,* bought Halcyon House for the proverbial song. Clemens, a firm foe of electricity, refused to permit it to be installed. In addition to other changes, he had a large cigarstore Indian placed on the balcony overlooking the front door. He is said to have been buried under a chapel in the house. His ghost walks the long corridors at night.

Georgetown is the second university to have owned Halcyon House. Clemens willed it to Harvard and in 1943 the university sold it to Frederick Sterling, former Ambassador to Sweden. Not being subject to Mr. Clemens' antagonisms, he immediately installed electricity.

Georgetown University plans to turn the historic house, ghosts and all, into a dormitory for women students in the School of Foreign Service of the Graduate School and Institute of Foreign Language and Linguistics. Apartments for 60 women will be constructed.

September 13, 1963—Upon calling at Georgetown University, I found that because of zoning regulations, they were unable to turn Halcyon House into a dormitory for women students; however, it has been turned into apartments for men and women.

This latter admonition was superfluous as Mr. Roper, Sr., had already refused my help, advice and even a brief visit. When I requested the address of his son Nick, the one who had written the newspaper piece—or at any rate, signed it—in the *Boston Globe,* I was told, "My son Nicholas is no longer a resident in Washington."

But the Ghost Hunter is not that easily dismayed. Since we were already in the city, I tried to telephone the house and ask permission to see it for a few minutes, just as any scientist might ask under the circumstances. I could not reach the Ropers.

Catherine and I decided to take a chance, having heard about and experienced lots of Southern hospitality. We felt sure that the Ropers would at least spare us ten or fifteen minutes. It was a chilly night and we realized that we were far from the center of the city—a fact that caused us considerable unhappiness on our return, for taxis were nowhere to be had.

When I rang the bell at Halcyon House, a young man in his middle teens opened the gate. He was a cousin of the Ropers, and most friendly. I explained my reason for not announcing our visit and he asked my wife and me to step inside the house. We discussed Dr. Joseph Rhine and parapsychology for a few moments, then the young man led us farther into the house and began to show us around. We passed the kitchen where he decided to introduce us to his aunt, Mrs. Mary Roper.

I apologized for our unexpected visit, and asked whether we might have the privilege of seeing the historical portion of the house before flying back to New York.

All over the world such a request would have been honored, even though our visit was unexpected. And in other days people used to visit each other without telephone announcements when Mr. Bell had not yet become lucky.

Mrs. Roper practically threw us out of the house, and only the arrival of her husband prevented an embarrassing scene.

It was evident to me at once that Mrs. Roper was suffering from extreme nervousness, due no doubt to the ghostly goings on in the house, which had deprived her momentarily of her inbred good manners.

Mr. Roper, Sr., quietly explained that his home was his castle and that he would rather not discuss the matter of hauntings. He finally gave me the address of his son in Wheaton, Maryland, but young

Roper, to this very day, has not seen fit to either confirm or deny the material facts of the haunting, although I have written to him a number of times. No doubt he prefers to keep quiet about it.

A Washington psychiatrist I met through famed psychic Jeane Dixon also told us of young Roper's unusual interest in the extrasensory field, but in his view Roper's imagination was running away with him. I am inclined to accept Roper's testimony at face value. At any rate, anyone interested in finding out if ghostly Ben and Bert still haunt the corridors and rooms of Halcyon House need only go up and see. The ghosts won't object, I'm sure, but the Ropers probably will.

My sympathy, of course, is with the ghosts.

A Ghost's Last Refuge

Near Charlottesville, Virginia, stands a farmhouse built during Revolutionary days, now owned by Mary W., a lady in her early fifties, who, some years ago, had a fleeting interest in the work of Professor Rhine at Duke University.

Her own psychic talents are acknowledged, but she insists she has not done any automatic writing lately and isn't really very much interested any more. Later I realized that her waning interest must have some connection with the events at the house which we shall call Wickham, since the real name must at present remain veiled in deference to the owner's request.

Virginia Cloud had come along to serve as a combination guide and clairvoyant, and writer Booton Herndon also came along to observe what he had always found a fascinating subject. Thus a caravan of two cars made its way to Wickham one bright May morning when nature's brilliance belied the sober subject of our goal.

On arrival, my wife, Catherine, and I sat down with Mary W. to hear her tell of her own experiences in the haunted house. Only after she had done so did Virginia Cloud enter the house.

The oldest part of the house, rather skillfully connected to the rest, consists of a hall or main room and a small bedroom reached by a narrow winding staircase.

This portion, dating back to 1781, has been the location of some uncanny happenings beginning at the time when Mrs. W. acquired the house and acreage in 1951. Whether previous owners had had any experiences couldn't be ascertained.

Emotionally keyed up at the time, Mrs. W. recalls, she was in a small adjoining room downstairs, which has been turned into a small home bar, when she clearly heard footsteps in the main room, and a noise like that made by riding clothes, swishing sounds; she called out, but she knew it was not her husband; the steps continued; someone was walking up and down in the room. Mrs. W. took a look through the window and saw her entire family outside near the barn, some twenty yards away.

This alarmed her even more and she stepped into the main room. There was no one there. But the eerie thing was that even in her presence the steps continued, reached the doorway and then went back across the room to the stairway where they stopped abruptly at the landing leading to the old room above.

The previous owner, by the name of Deauwell, had told Mary W. that when his predecessor at the house, Mrs. Early, had died, there had been a strange noise *as if someone were falling downstairs.*

Two years later, Mrs. W.'s two girls, aged twelve and nine at the time, were playing in the upstairs room while the parents were entertaining some guests in the nearby cottage apart from the main house. It was 10 P.M., when the girls distinctly heard someone walk around downstairs in the empty house. They called out, but got no answer. They thought it was a friend of their parents, but later checking revealed nobody had left the party to return to the main house even for a moment.

Around 1960-61, Mrs. W. again heard the by-now-familiar footsteps in the same spot. They started, then stopped, then started up again. Although Mrs. W. admitted some psychic talent, her automatic writing had yielded no one claiming to be connected with the house except perhaps a slave girl named Rebecca, who claimed to have been captured by Indians who cut out her tongue; she was found by the Early sons, and became their servant since; Mrs. W. also claimed a guide or control named Robert.

The place had been in litigation for many years, and there are no less than three family cemeteries on the grounds. The house itself was built by one Richard Durrette in 1781. When the fireplace was rebuilt prior to 1938, before Mrs. W. owned the place, an inscription turned up explaining that Hessian-soldier prisoners from a nearby barracks had helped build the chimney in 1781. Three thousand prisoners were kept in barracks nearby. Some stayed afterwards and married local girls.

This was *not* discussed in the presence of Virginia Cloud, who soon went into semi-trance in the presence of Mary W. and myself. She "saw" an Albert or Alfred, in white shirt, boots, trousers, but not a uniform, dragging himself into the house; perhaps he was an injured Hessian entering an empty house, chased here by Redcoats. "The British are farther away . . . Something was burned near here." At this point, both Mary W. and I smelled smoke.

Independent of Virginia Cloud's testimony, both of us also heard a faint knock at the entrance door, two short raps.

Virginia, in her chair near the stairway, started to shiver. "The ghost remembers his mother and calls her, but she is not here any more . . . only a memory; he may have died here, since I don't see him leave again. His arm is hurt by metal, perhaps a shell."

Mary W. had lived through tragedy in her own life. Her husband, Kenneth, had committed suicide in the very house we were visiting. I had the feeling that Mary's interest in the occult coincided with this event, and that perhaps she thought the ghostly footsteps were actually her late husband's restless movements in the room he had called his own.

But the noises and disturbances go back farther than Mary's tenancy of the house. Premeditated suicide seldom yields ghosts. I am convinced that the ghost at Wickham is not Mary's husband, but the Hessian deserter who wanted to find refuge from the pursuing British.

Georgia

The state of Georgia, especially the area around Atlanta, is full of people interested in psychic research. Whether this has something to do with the fact that many cases exist in the area, or whether this is simply because Georgia has some fine universities and metropolitan centers where the interest in ESP has been high for many years, is hard to tell. But the fact is that I get far more cases of interest from the area of Atlanta and of Georgia in general than, for instance, Mississippi or Louisiana. The caliber of the people who have most of the experiences or are possessed of ESP talents is also quite high. A.W.C., a science teacher from rural Georgia, says he does not believe in ghosts as such; however, he is quick to admit that the experiences he has had will admit of no explanation other than a psychic one. When he was a teenager he was very close to his grandmother even though she lived 150 miles away. One night, while he was in bed, he awoke and saw his grandmother standing in the corner of his room. At first he thought he was imagining things. He closed his eyes and looked once again but she was still there. Now he covered his head and after a while looked back; grandmother was still standing there. At that point he heard footsteps in the kitchen and got up to see if anybody had entered the kitchen, but to his surprise he found no one there. When he returned to his bedroom he decided, in his logical mind, that what he had seen had been a dress or some other piece of material hanging on the wall and not his grandmother. In the morning he would make sure that that was so. Came the morning and he checked and there was nothing in the corner of that room. However, a few days later the family received a telegram advising them that grandmother had had a stroke and was at the point of death. Evidently the young man had seen a projected image of his dear relative at a time when partial dissolution had taken place. Shortly thereafter the grandmother died.

But Mr. C. not only has been the recipient of psychic impressions, he has also been able to send them, although not at will. During World War II he was with the Army in France. His family frequently discussed his fate abroad. One evening his wife, sister, and an aunt who had reared him and who was particularly close to the young man were sitting in front of a wooden stove in their home. Suddenly the aunt started to scream. Terror-stricken, the woman explained that she had just seen Mr. C.'s face appear to her in the flames of the stove. At that very moment Mr. C. was wounded in France.

Robert Mullinax of Atlanta, Georgia, is in his early twenties. When he was seventeen years old, in 1967, he had an experience he will never forget. His mother had often had premonitions of things to come and perhaps some of this talent had come down to him also. On that particular day in April, Mrs. Mullinax had been very restless all day long as if something were about to happen. She had the feeling she should telephone her sister-in-law, but somehow she never got around to it. They were not particularly close; in fact, they had visited each other only about three times in twenty-five years. That evening she knew why she had had the strange feeling of urgency to call her sister-in-law. The woman had committed suicide by shooting herself.

It was two days after her death when young Robert found himself standing in his home in front of a large mirror. This was in their living room and he was about to comb his hair when he saw his aunt in the mirror behind him. He turned around and, sure enough, there she was standing about six feet away. As he got a closer look at her she vanished.

In this fleeting moment young Robert had the impression that his aunt wanted to tell him something—perhaps express regret at what she had done and to send a message to her youngest son whom she loved very much, but she was gone before Robert could really make out the message. What is interesting about this case is the fact that the ghost was solid enough to be seen in a mirror, not merely a hallucination or a subjective vision.

Mrs. W. is a housewife living in Athens, Georgia. She is also a certified nursery school teacher, the mother of six children, and she has had ESP experiences for many years past. She is living proof that ESP messages can be very precise at times in giving the recipient an indication of what the message is all about and to prepare the recipient for any shock that might come his or her way. In 1946 Mrs. W. was living in another city in Georgia. At that time she had one son age two and a half years and another six months old. She was also pregnant with another child. During that period she had many vivid dreams of a psychic nature. But after the third child was born she was particularly disturbed one night by a dream which became so powerful that it awoke her. She found herself crying uncontrollably, so much so that her husband was genuinely concerned. When she became calmer she told her husband she had dreamed she saw her brothers and sisters and her mother looking at her through the glass of their front door, saying, "Call an ambulance." The dream had no meaning for her, so after a while she went back to sleep and didn't think about it again. Three months later the dream became a reality. Her brother appeared at her front door and standing outside the glass said, "Call an ambulance." He then explained that their father, who lived on the next street and who had no telephone, had suffered a heart attack while preparing for bed. The father died three days later. It was only after her grief ceased that Mrs. W. realized that in her dream she had seen all members of her family except one—her father was not in it. Had she understood this properly perhaps she would have been more prepared for the shock that was to come her way shortly.

The relationship with her father had been a close one, so she was not surprised that after his passing there were times when she felt him standing near her. She did not see him, yet she knew of his presence. She hesitated to discuss this with her husband out of fear of being ridiculed or worse. During that time she awakened her husband five or six separate times and asked him to get up and shut the door since Daddy had come in. Her husband didn't like it, but when she insisted he did get up in order to please his wife. They never discussed it until many years later when her husband admitted that each time she had asked him to close the door it was indeed open and there had been no reason for it to be open.

Mrs. W's husband is the editor of a county newspaper and a very logical man. He learned to accept his wife's special talent as the years rolled by, but there were times when he wished that she weren't as psychic as she was. One night she dreamed that a plane crash had taken place somewhere in back of their house and she saw some Army men drive up in a jeep and take away the bodies of those killed. In the morning she told her husband of this dream. He didn't say anything. Two weeks later, however, he told his wife to quit having "those crazy dreams." It appeared that Mr. W had been traveling away from home in the direction one might properly call "back of the house" when he saw that an Army plane had crashed and Army personnel in a jeep had driven up to the site and removed some bodies, just as his wife had told him. Mrs. W. realized that she had a very special talent and perhaps had been chosen by some superior intelligence as a communicator.

A month after her daughter Karen was born she happened to be lying down for an afternoon nap. She was facing the wall when she felt compelled to turn over in the opposite direction. There she saw the figure of a man in a white robe standing by her bed. Her first thought was that she still had in her system some of the drug that had been given her during the birth and that she was indeed hallucinating. She thought it best to turn back to the wall. Immediately, however, she felt a strong compulsion to turn back, and this time she saw the man pointing his finger at her with a stern look on his face. She got the impression she was to get up immediately and follow him. She did just that and walked straight into the next room. As if acting in a daze she saw herself dial her husband at his office. As soon as her husband came to the phone she told him not to ask questions but if he ever intended to do something that she had asked him for, this was the time to do it. She told him to go at once to a place called Curry's Creek to see if their son Joe was there. Her husband objected. He knew, he said, that the five-year-old was not there. Nevertheless Mrs. W. insisted. Her plea was so urgent she impressed her husband sufficiently that he did indeed go down to the creek. Ten minutes later he telephoned her asking her how she knew that the boy was indeed at the creek. It appeared that he had found the little boy at the edge of the water looking down into it. The creek furnished the town's water supply and is next to a busy highway a mile outside of town. The child had never been there before. Had Mr. W. not arrived in time the child might very well have drowned. Mrs. W then realized that the man in the white robe had come to save their child.

The warning of impending disaster is a recurrent theme in ghost lore. It appears that on occasion the departed are given the task of warning the living of impending difficulties or disaster but are not permitted to be specific. Evidently that would interfere with the exercise of free will under test conditions. A similar case involves a lady from Decatur by the name of Mrs L. E., who, when a child, was staying with her Aunt Mary in her house. Twenty years before that visit Mary's

Great-aunt Rev had passed on. With her cousins Mrs. E. then proceeded to one of the bedrooms in the house to fetch some of the tricycles they had stored in it to go outside and play. When they got to the door of the room they saw Great-Aunt Rev standing in the middle of the room right where the tricycles were. She was looking at the children rather sternly. She wore her long white nightgown and her nightcap, the clothing she was wearing when she died. The children stood there transfixed by shock. They spoke her name more in fear than in reverence. Then they ran out. When they described the apparition to the owner of the house, Mrs. E.'s Aunt Mary was very solemn. "She came back," she said and began to move all the furniture from the house, taking it out into the yard away from the house. This seemed like strange behavior, but the children were young and did not understand many things. Then Aunt Mary took the children and walked with them up the road to a neighbor's house. There she left them. Several hours later when they returned they found the house had burned down to ashes. No one has seen the ghost of Aunt Rev since.

Tucker, Georgia, is about an hour's ride due north of Atlanta, a pleasant, almost suburban community populated by pleasant, average people. The Stevens house, a landmark as early as 1854, was built of huge hand-hewn chestnut pine logs originally. The older part was added to by a Baptist minister around 1910. Finally another addition was made to the house in the late 1940s. When the Stevenses bought the house they were told that it was originally built by Indian settlers in the area around 1800, or even before. This is Cherokee Territory and according to the local tradition the Indians brought their sick to this house. They would stay with them overnight on their way to Decatur. Decatur was the town where the famed Dr. Chapman Powell lived. The Powell cabin has been restored and is now located in Stone Mountain Park, but originally it was in Decatur and was moved to the park to better preserve it as a landmark. The Stevens house stands about a mile off the High Tower Trail, which is the old Cherokee Indian trail, and four miles from Stone Mountain Park. Since Mrs. Stevens is herself about one thirty-second Cherokee, she has a vivid sympathy for all Indian lore and has always been interested in the Indian background of the house. When they first bought the house in May of 1960 the Steveneses lived in it for only a year. Then, for business reasons, they moved down to Florida and sold their house to their in-laws. However, two years later they returned from Florida and bought the house back. During that first year in the house they do not recall anything strange except for a recurrent dream Mrs. Stevens had right from the start when they took up residence at the house. In that dream she saw herself looking up through an opening in the ceiling into the darkness of a loft. She could clearly make out the rafters, wooden beams, and the chimneys. Somehow this dream seemed all very familiar. As soon as she had moved to the house she realized that her dream visions concerned the attic of their house. It looked exactly like the visions she had seen so many years prior to coming to the house. Evidently it was predestined that the Stevenses should take up residence in Tucker. On recollection Mrs. Stevens remembers that her in-laws had no special experiences in the house out of the ordinary during the two years in which they resided there. But then neither of her in-laws professed any particular interest in the occult or was possessed of psychic sensitivities.

As soon as the Stevenses had returned to their original home they noticed a strange feeling, perhaps more of a current all around the house. It affected the children as well. They would not want to take a nap or go to bed because they said someone kept touching them. Soon Mrs. Stevens experienced that too. Their smallest children reported seeing a man on the porch when there was no man about. Both Mr. and Mrs. Stevens have seen a man going across the porch. This has happened a number of times. Sometimes it is only a kind of quick flash and sometimes they can clearly make out a human form. Whenever they have seen something and their children have not, they try their best to keep it from them so as not to alarm them. Nevertheless the children on their own report similar occurrences. Gradually it has become clear to the Stevenses that the oldest part of the house, the log part, is the center of the psychic phenomena. In the living room/dining room area they have seen a form when there was certainly no one else but themselves in the house. On another occasion Mrs. Stevens has seen a hand materialize by her bed. In August of 1968 Mr. Stevens awoke from sound sleep because he had the feeling that there was someone in the house who should not be there. He sat up and looked into the room where their sons were sleeping across from the parents' bedroom. There he saw a gray form standing by their bunkbeds looking at the oldest boy. Fully awake now, Mr. Stevens looked closely at the form and realized it was female. The woman appeared to be wearing a cowl-type hood. When he made a move the form dissolved into thin air. Stevens discussed the appearance with his wife. She had seen a similar form in the boys' room reclining on the lower bunk beside the youngest boy. Moreover, the apparition was not alone. Mrs. Stevens could make out additional figures in the room. Footsteps up and down the stairs when there was no one around to make them had become a common occurrence in the house. The Stevenses thought that the repair work going on in the house might have offended one or the other of its former inhabitants. They were doing their level best to save the old part of the house, repairing what could be repaired and replacing what could not.

It was soon clear to them that they had more than one unearthly visitor in their house. The woman so concerned with the well-being of the children might have been someone left behind from the old days or perhaps the shade of a former owner of the house. None of them ever saw her clearly enough to make sure, but there was someone else. In 1966 Mr. Stevens had a strange dream. The dream was followed by similar dreams, continuing, as it were, the narrative of the first one. In these dreams his brother Bill communicated with him. Bill had been killed in a plane crash in North Carolina during World War II. However, in the dreams Bill explained that he was not dead and that he had returned home. In another dream he wanted his brother to accompany him on a trip. In all of these dreams Bill appeared to have aged. He was balding and wearing a tattered officer's khaki uniform. His overcoat in particular was tattered and faded. While the Stevenses discussed these dreams with each other, they made a special point of never talking about them with their children. So the children had no idea that dreams about Uncle Bill had indeed taken place.

About three weeks after the last of this series of dreams involving Bill, all the boys came into the kitchen very much alarmed and white as sheets. They insisted that they had seen a ghost. When questioned about the apparition they said they had seen a man walk across the front room, which is part of the 1910 addition of the house. Immediately the parents checked to see whether a trespasser had perhaps entered the house. There was no one to be seen. Skeptical, and at the same time alarmed, the parents demanded that the boys described what they had seen. Without a moment's hesitation they described the ghost as being a thin man, sort of crouched down and bald, with clothes rather torn and sort of a faded khaki. They did in effect describe exactly what Uncle Bill looked like in the series of dreams their father had had for so long. Only what they had seen was not in the dream state. Uncle Bill evidently had returned from the grave not as a resident ghost, for ghosts do not travel, but to look after the affairs of his brother's family.

Watkinsville is a small town of about five hundred people nine miles from the city of Athens and as quiet a place as you may want to visit. The people here are church-going, law-abiding citizens sho have no interest in such things as psychic phenomena. The entire village consists of two streets. Where the street divides one takes the left fork and past the railroad track one arrives at a stately house that once belonged to the town doctor. Built around 1960, the house stands about a mile from the tracks surrounded by a good deal of land. The doctor had built the house for himself in his middle years, but after he moved in something happened to his wife. For some reason she started to drink, and not long after they had come to live in the house she committed suicide by shooting herself in the head. Two years later the doctor remarried. Something happened to his second wife as soon as they had settled in the house. She became addicted to drugs and could not find any rest even at night. The house was lit up all through the night until the doctor could no longer cope with his ill wife and had her committed to an asylum. The tragedies took their toll on the doctor, however, and not much later he died of an overdose of drugs. The verdict was death due to heart failure caused by an overdose of drugs. Evidently the doctor knew just how much to take.

After some litigation and questions about the property, the house and grounds were sold at public auction in Clarke County, passing into the hands of Mr. and Mrs. J. B. The young couple had two children. He was a mechanic, and psychic phenomena didn't interest him at all; in fact he firmly considered them just so much fantasy. Not so for his wife. Carol had known about the unseen world all her life. At the time when she was living with her grandmother, who was bringing her up, she had her first psychic experience. She was only eight years at the time but the memory is still as fresh with her now as if it had happened yesterday. She awoke in the middle of the night for no apparent reason. Then she felt a familiar hand on her shoulder. The hand belonged to her grandmother but it seemed icy cold. The next morning she reported the experience to her grandmother, who assured her that she had not touched the child. Soon after, her grandmother passed away. At the time when this happened Carol was holding her hand and the hand was ice cold.

She was about twenty years of age when she and her husband moved into the former doctor's house at Watkinsville. Soon after they had moved in she realized that they were not alone in the house. It was a very hot day and her older son was asking for a glass of water. After the boy had drunk the water Carol took the glass and placed it securely on a shelf inside the house, about halfway from either edge. When she started to leave the room again the glass flung itself to the floor and shattered completely. There was no logical explanation for this. After her husband returned home from work she told him what had happened. He did not believe in ghosts. That very evening her husband had finished a piece of cake and his wife took the plate and fork and placed it on the range in their kitchen. The range was in full view through the doorway of the living room. While her husband was watching television Carol was looking toward the range for reasons she did not know at the time. Suddenly she saw the plate lift itself off the range and fall to the floor with a resounding crash. Again there was no possible logical explanation, since she had placed the plate well away from the edge of the range. There had been no earthquake or other movement of the house to account for the astonishing performance by the plate. Shortly thereafter she awoke at three-thirty in the morning because she heard a radio playing. Since she knew that the radio had been out of order for some time, she got up and went to the bathroom to see whether there was a neighbor's radio playing. She realized that the radio was on in the garage. As she looked out the bathroom window she also saw that the dashboard light on the car was on and the radio playing full blast. Her first thought was that her husband had left the glove compartment open and the radio on. He assured her he had not. In fact he remembered clearly that he had turned the radio off and closed the glove compartment. He knew better than to turn the radio on when the car was in the garage since it played on the batteries when the motor was shut off. This was something a mechanic would never do. Having no explanation for the strange behavior of their car, they dismissed it. About a week later they were standing by their fence looking at the neighbor's house when the radio in their car started playing again by itself. They were standing just a few yards away and there was no possible way in which anyone could have entered the garage without being seen by them. At this point her husband went to the house to fetch a shotgun. Carol took her little son and returned to the house. Just as her husband approached the car with the shotgun the door of the glove compartment flew open of its own volition. Feverishly Mr. B. searched everywhere, but there was no one about. He checked for a short in the radio and inspected the latch on the glove compartment. Both checked out fine.

Since they had only rented the house it was easy for them to move on. They explained to the owner that their child had contracted a rash and that they felt the area was too full of pollen and it would be better if they went to live in another part of the state. But when they became familiar with the history of the house they realized that the doctor's two mad wives were still playing pranks. Perhaps it was only the second wife who always liked the lights on all night, but one can't be entirely sure. They may have met in the world beyond and become fast friends.

The first time I heard of Mr. James Arthur Williams's haunted house in Savannah, Georgia, was when the advertising manager of Citroën cars told me about it. Mr. Leach assured me that as far as haunted houses went his friend's really was the McCoy. Not only did it look like one, the phenomena in it were countless and the owner, Williams, a man of impeccable judgment and taste. Since we drive a Citroën and know that it represents not only the unusual but also quality, I assumed that Mr. Leach's judgment in matters of haunted houses might also be thus oriented. Before I could put his opinion of haunted houses to a test, however, I received a letter from one of my readers, a

Mrs. Marjorie Bruce who lives in Savannah. The house had been in the morning news and she had taken the trouble of researching some of the reported phenomena for me.

The house in question is a five-story building with a good foundation and a wooden superstructure. On top of the slanting roof is a so-called widow's walk, a small platform near the chimney safeguarded by a wooden banister on all four sides. On the right side there is an entrance to the first floor of the house, which is actually two stories above ground. The strange occurrences may be due to the fact that the house was moved from its original location at 312 Bryan Street to its present location at 507 East St. Julian Street near Houston and Price. This happened in 1963 and the house survived the four-block ride rather well.

The house itself was built in 1796 by a planter from Sea Island, Georgia, as his town house. It was designed in so-called gambrel style, something not usually associated with the South, but the planter had come originally from Newport, Rhode Island, where this type of house is common. The present owner, James Arthur Williams, is a native Georgian and has lived in Savannah since 1952. He is a professional interior designer and a member of the American Institute of Designers as well as a dealer in eighteenth-century antiques. He is in his early forties and lives in the house alone. Prior to acquiring the house he had scant interest in the occult. Except for a minor ESP experience in a house across the street from the one he now lives in, there was little to make him wonder about the spirit world. All that changed after he moved into the house on Julian Street. He knew, of course, that a man had hanged himself from a tall fourposter and that others had died in it over the years under strange conditions. But that holds true of many old houses, and Mr. Williams paid little attention to these traditions and legends. Soon he realized that he had bought more than an empty old house.

Around three in the morning he would awaken to the sound of footsteps very close to his bed. It sounded as if someone were walking on sand or broken glass. Williams immediately assumed that he had to deal with an intruder and asked what the man wanted. There was no answer. Then someone ran toward the bedroom door and crashed into an open closet. Immediately Williams got out of bed and walked to the adjoining library to turn on the light. There was no intruder. He could still hear the sound of feet walking on the floor, yet there was no man to be seen to whom the feet might conceivably belong.

While he was restoring the old house he and four friends were looking over the day's work in the interior of the house. Suddenly they heard what sounded like a group of workmen moving about upstairs. Immediately they searched the house, floor by floor, and found no one. They decided to go up to the roof and stand on the widow's walk. They had not encountered a single living soul on the way up. When they reached the top of the house they heard the identical noises, below them this time.

Not much later Williams happened to be out of town when his friends decided to pay the strange house a visit on their own. Since they were well acquainted with the owner, they felt they were not doing anything wrong by inspecting the house in his absence, especially as it had not yet been fully restored. As they were walking about the garden-floor level they heard noises above them. It sounded as if people were moving about. One of the men went upstairs to investigate and, if necessary, challenge the intruder. When he reached the top floor he felt as if he had just walked into a pool of cold water. He lost control over his bodily movements and felt himself being drawn into an unfinished chimney shaft which dropped about thirty feet into the basement. When the man did not return, his friends began to worry about him. They went up the stairs and found him on the floor, face up, trembling and completely disheveled. He had thrown himself to the floor to break what he considered an evil spell. That was enough to convince the three men to leave the house. They decided to await the owner before venturing further into what they now knew was a haunted house. A mutual friend had an apartment directly across from the haunted house and they decided to await Williams's return there. As they were seated discussing the unnerving experience they had just gone through, they glanced across the street toward Williams's house. At that precise moment they all heard a woman scream in agony across the street. They were terrified and sat in silence. When the scream resounded once again one of the men ran outside and looked up at the haunted house. To his surprise he saw a tall, dark-haired man wearing a white shirt and black bow tie standing at a third-floor window. His first thought was that perhaps Williams had returned unbeknownst to them and was looking down into the street. He was so sure of this that he decided to call out to his friends to greet the returning Williams. Williams, however, was not there. When he returned later that evening he assured them that he was not wearing a bow tie such as one of the men had seen.

On one occasion Mr. Williams had the company of a policeman on some police business. Both men distinctly heard loud crashing noises from the area of the room where there was a pipe organ. The room was on the fourth floor and the policeman immediately rushed up to see who the intruder was. When he reached the pipe-organ room both men saw the door to an adjacent storeroom open by itself and shut itself of its own volition. The policeman confidently assured Williams that the intruder must be in that other room. He turned the doorknob and found it locked. Only after the key had been inserted in the lock did the door open, yet both men had seen it open and shut itself. Finally Williams consulted with William G. Roll of the American Psychical Research Foundation of North Carolina, and Roll came and conducted a thorough investigation of the phenomena. He interviewed some twenty or thirty people who had personally witnessed these occurrences and others. They were people from all walks of life, ranging from masons and construction workers to college men and scientists and in age from seventeen to sixty. From the testimony of these witnesses Mr. Roll concluded that genuine psychic phenomena were indeed taking place in the old house.

Some of the witnesses have seen a gray-haired man wearing a gray suit and a white tie. He may only be one of the ghosts in residence at 507 East St. Julian Street. Whether the ghosts have become active because of the move from their customary site a few years ago and are trying to let the owner know they preferred the original site is a moot question. Ghosts don't like to travel because it destroys memories tied to specific occasions.

Mr. Williams does not encourage visitors. Despite its reputation as a haunted house he considers this his home and, in the tradition of his Anglo-Saxon forebears, also his castle. The house is called the Hampton Lilly Bridge House, and when last reported, both Mr. Williams and the ghostly boarders were still in residence.

Florida

Fort Jefferson

About seventy miles west of Key West, Florida, is a group of small islands known as the Dry Tortugas. Today they are a wildlife paradise. In the eighteenth century pirates and smugglers used to hang out in the Tortugas because they were so difficult to reach from the mainland. They still are, but the trip is worth it. One of the islands boasted a very large prison fortification that in its heyday was called Fort Jefferson. Today the fort is an empty shell, but when it was built it was half a mile in circumference, and surrounded by a deep moat. Getting out of Fort Jefferson's clutches wasn't easy; it once resembled an American Devil's Island.

And that is precisely why the angry authorities dealing with the aftermath of the assassination of President Lincoln chose to send to this island prison a man whom they considered as guilty as the four conspirators who had been hanged. Dr. Samuel Mudd had become a convicted criminal for the sole humanitarian act of setting John Wilkes Booth's broken ankle! He had nothing whatever to do with the conspiracy, and he defended his action as something he would have done for anyone, even the devil himself.

Dr. Mudd was to spend most of the rest of his life in Fort Jefferson, and his anguish no doubt still clings to the walls of his cell—psychic impressions of it can often be felt there. Recently his grandson petitioned the United States government to set aside the unjust conviction of his ancestor. Unfortunately, in March 2001, his petition was rejected by a U.S. district court. John McHale, a Mudd family spokesman, said that an appeal would be filed.

As many historians (this one included) know, the so-called conspiracy to assassinate Abraham Lincoln wasn't a southern plot at all, but was hatched and manipulated by members of the president's own government. Any show of leniency toward Dr. Mudd was most unlikely; the prosecutors displayed excessive anger and an apparent thirst for revenge at every turn—perhaps to divert any suspicion that might arise concerning their own involvement in the plot.

* * *

Fort Matanzas

Measuring only forty by thirty feet, Fort Matanzas in St. Augustine, Florida, would hardly deserve to be noted in these pages were it not for a terrible crime committed there. The fort was built in 1737 as a secondary fortification of ancient St. Augustine. The spot where it now stands had witnessed the massacre of the French Huguenot settlers who had claimed Florida for France in 1565. As a result of this treachery by the Spanish regional commandant, General Menendez, Florida became a Spanish possession.

The Huguenot settlers, who had been forced to flee from their native France because they were Protestants, had come face-to-face with the ever increasing and ruthless power of the Spanish conquistadors. Commandant General Menendez invited them to discuss problems of coexistence, or so he claimed. When the settlers showed up in good faith, he had them massacred by his troops. The killing of these "heretics" enabled Menendez to simultaneously serve two masters: the Catholic Church and the Spanish Crown.

A sensitive person may well feel the anguish of this long-ago event here, not likely to have faded away completely over the centuries.

* * *

Henry Flagler was Florida's greatest booster—sometimes a hero to his people, sometimes a villain. Which attribution he was given depended on the eccentric millionaire's quixotic behaviors. As a partner of John D. Rockefeller, Flagler had made a fortune in grain and oil. After his first wife died, Flagler moved from Cleveland, Ohio, to New York with his small son. Soon thereafter he married his widow's nurse, Alice, and fired his sister Carrie, who had been acting as his housekeeper. On a vacation during the same period, Flagler "discovered" St. Augustine and decided to go into the hotel business there, first with the Ponce de Leon Hotel, which proved to be a raging success.

Just as he had "created" St. Augustine, making it into a fashionable resort frequented by the adventurous well-to-do, he then did the same for Palm Beach, where he opened the Royal Poinciana. In 1895, Flagler went to work to "create" Miami. Alas, Alice Flagler became ill and had to be confined to a mental institution. While his wife was firmly ensconced in her sanitarium, Henry Flagler met a young singer named Mary Kenan. Both he and his son were soon in love with Mary, an unfortunate coincidence that destroyed the relationship between father and son. Henry was able to divorce Alice even though she was institutionalized, by bribing the Florida legislature to pass a special law—the same law made it possible for him to then marry the youthful Mary Kenan.

In short order these scandalous events turned the people of Florida, who had once so admired Flagler for the prosperity he had brought them, firmly against him. He was forced to leave the state, moving with Mary to suburban New York. But his love for Florida was too strong to resist for long, and he decided to return. To regain his lost popularity he thought up a spectacular plan: He would build a railroad connecting the mainland with the keys, all the way down to Key West. And so he did. He was once more a hero, at age eighty-two. But he did not know that some thirty years later, after his death, a raging storm would wash his railroad right into the sea. Today, there is no railroad, but there is a causeway where it used to run.

Whitehall, his magnificent mansion in Palm Beach, is now mainly a museum. If you happen to get up to the top floor, under the roof, you may perhaps catch a glimpse of Henry himself. I have heard that he never really left his much-beloved Florida.

The Girl Ghost of Kentucky

Mrs. D. and her son Bucky lived in a comfortable house on a hill-top in suburban Kentucky, not far from Cincinnati, Ohio. It is a pleasant white house, not much different from other houses in the area. The surroundings are lovely and peaceful, and there's a little man-made pond right in front of the house. Nothing about the house or the area looks in the least bit ghostly or unusual. Nevertheless, Mrs. D. needed my help in a very vexing situation.

Six months after Mrs. D. had moved into the house, she began to hear footsteps upstairs, when there was no one about, and the sound of marble being rolled a across the hall. Anything supernatural was totally alien to Mrs. D.

Nevertheleass, she has a questioning and alert mind, and was not about to accept these phenomena without finding out what caused them. When the manifestations persisted, she walked up to the foot of the stairs and yelled, "Why don't you just come out and show yourself or say something instead of making all those noises?"

As if in answer, an upstairs door slammed shut and then there was utter silence. After a moment's hesitation, Mrs. D. dashed upstairs and made a complete search. There was no one about and the marble, which seemingly had rolled across the floor, was nowhere to be seen.

When the second Christmas in the new house rolled around, the D.'s were expecting Bucky home from the army. He was going to bring his sergant and the sergant's wife with him, since they had become very friendly. They celebrated New Year's Eve in style and high spirits (not the ethereal kind, but the bottled type).

Nevertheless, they were far from inebriated when the sergeant suggested that New Year's Eve was a particularly suitable night for a séance. Mrs. D. would have no part of it at first. She had read all about phony séances and remembered what her Bible said about such matters. But later, after her husband had gone to bed, the four of them decided to have a go at it.

They joined hands and sat quietly in front of the fireplace. Nothing much happened for a while. Then Bucky, who had read some books on psychic phenomena, suggested that they needed a guide or control from the other side of life to help them, but no one had any suggestions concerning to whom they might turn.

More in jest than as a serious proposal, Mrs. D. heard herself say, "Why don't you call your Indian ancestor, Little White Flower!" Mr. D. is part Cherokee, and Bucky, the son, would, of course, consider this part of his inheritance too. Mrs. D. protested that all this was nonsense, and they should go to bed. She assured them that nothing was likely to happen. But the other three were too busy to reply, staring behind her into the fireplace. When she followed the direction of their eyes she saw what appeared to be some kind of light similar to that made by a flashlight. It stayed on for a short time and then disappeared altogether.

From that day on, Mrs. D. started to find strange objects around the house that had not been there a moment before. They were little stones in the shape of Indian arrows. She threw them out as fast as she found them. Several weeks later, when she was changing the sheets on her bed, she noticed a huge red arrow had been painted on the bottom sheet—by unseen hands.

One afternoon she was lying down on the couch with a book trying to rest. Before long she was asleep. Suddenly she awoke with a feeling of horror which seemed to start at her feet and gradually work its way up throughout her entire body and mind. The room seemed to be permeated with something terribly evil. She could neither see nor hear anything, but she had the feeling that there was a presence there and that it was very strong and about to overcome her.

For a few weeks she felt quite alone in the house, but then things started up again. The little stone arrowheads appeared out of nowhere again, all over the house. Hysterical with fear, Mrs. D. called upon a friend who had dabbled in metaphysics and asked for advice. The friend advised a séance in order to ask Little White Flower to leave.

Although Little White Flower was not in evidence continually and seemed to come and go, Mrs. D. felt the Indian woman's influence upon her at all times. Later the same week, Little White Flower put in another appearance, this time visual. It was toward four o'clock in the morning, when Mrs. D. woke up with the firm impression that her tormentor was in the room. As she looked out into the hall, she saw on the wall a little red object resembling a human eye, and directly below it what seemed like half a mouth. Looking closer, she discerned two red eyes and a white mouth below. It reminded her of some clowns she had seen in the circus. The vision remained on the wall for two or three minutes and then vanished completely.

After several postponements, I was finally able to come to Kentucky and meet with Mrs. D. in person. On June 20, I sat opposite the slightly portly, middle-aged lady who had corresponded with me so voluminously for several months.

As I intoned my solemn exorcism and demanded Little White Flower's withdrawal from the spot, I could hear Mrs. D. crying hysterically. It was almost as if some part of her was being torn out and for a while it seemed that *she* was being sent away, not Little White Flower.

The house has been quiet ever since; Little White Flower has presumably gone back to her own people and Mrs. D. continues living in the house without further disturbances.

South Carolina

Susan D. of Columbia, South Carolina, was born in Texas and is presently twenty-eight years old. Her father was in the service at first and after the war her parents moved to South Carolina, where her father's family had lived for generations. Susan is the eldest of three sisters. They grew up in a small town in the upper section of the state and then moved to Columbia, where her father became the superintendent of a state boarding school for unusual students. At that point Susan was seventeen. Later she entered a local college and stayed for two years. She is presently living with her husband, who is also in education, and they have a little boy. Because of a background of premonitions she had some interest in studying psychic phenomena, but this interest was rather on the vague side.

The first complete incident Susan can remember happened when she was just twelve years old. At that time she had spent the night with her grandmother, also named Susan. During the night the little girl dreamed her grandmother had died. She was awakened from her dream by her cousin Kenneth with the sad news that her grandmother had indeed died during the night.

There had always been a close relationship between her and her father, so when her father was taken to the hospital with a heart attack in 1967 she was naturally concerned. After a while the doctors allowed him to return to his home life, and by the time her little boy was a year old in March of 1968 her father seemed completely well and there was no thought of further illness on the family's mind. Two days after they had all been together for the first birthday celebration of her little boy she awoke in the middle of the night with an overpowering anxiety about her father's well-being. She became convinced that her father would leave them soon. The next morning she telephoned her sister and started to discuss her concern for her father. At that moment her father interrupted her call by asking her sister to get her mother immediately. He died on the way to the hospital that very afternoon.

Susan's father had a very close friend by the name of Joe F. with whom he had shared a great love of college football games. Joe F. had passed on a short time before. A little later, Susan and her husband attended one of the games of the University of South Carolina. This was in the fall of 1968. On the way to their seats Susan looked up toward the rear section of the arena and quickly turned her head back to her husband. She was so upset at what she saw that it took her a moment to calm down and take her seat. There, not more than eight feet away from her, stood her late father just as he had looked in life. Moreover, she heard him speak to her clearly and in his usual tone of voice. Her husband had not noticed anything. She decided not to tell him about it. As she slowly turned her head back to where they had come from she noticed her father again. This time Joe F., his life-long friend, was with him. The two dead men were walking down the walkway in front of the seats and she had a good opportunity to see them clearly. They seemed as much alive then as they had ever been when she knew them both in the flesh.

Susan D. has an aunt by the name of Mrs. Fred V. They had frequently discussed the possibility of life after death and psychic phenomena in general, especially after the death of the aunt's husband, which had come rather unexpectedly. It was then that the two women realized that they had shared a similar extraordinary experience. Mrs. Fred V. had also gone to a football game at the University of South Carolina, but her visit was a week later, for a different game than

Susan's had been. Since the two women had not met for some time there had been no opportunity to discuss Susan's original psychic experience at the football game with her aunt. Nevertheless, Mrs. V. told her niece that something quite extraordinary had happened to her at that particular football game. She too had seen the two dead men watch the game as if they were still very much in the flesh. To Mrs. V. this was a signal that her own husband was to join them, for the three had been very good and close friends in life. As it happened she was right. He passed on soon afterwards.

Susan D. has heard the voice of her father since then on several occasions, although she hasn't seen him again. It appears that her father intercedes frequently when Susan is about to lose her temper in some matter or take a wrong step. On such occasions she hears his voice telling her to take it easy.

The Devil in Texas

I am frequently asked to comment on poltergeists, or noisy ghosts, a term derived from the German and somehow conjuring up the image of violent physical activity beyond the pale of ordinary understanding. Poltergeists have been generally considered the work of youngsters in a house—youngsters below the age of puberty, when their physical energies have not yet been channeled either sexually or occupationally and are therefore free to play pranks on others in the household. The majority of parapsychologists consider poltergeists the unconscious expression of such repressed feelings, attention getters on the part of young people, and do not connect them to supernormal beings such as spirit entities or any other form of outside influence. I, however, have investigated dozens of cases involving poltergeists where physical objects have been moved or moved seemingly by their own volition and found that another explanation might be the true one. In each case, to be sure, there were young people in the household, or sometimes retarded adults. I discovered, for instance, that a metally disabled adult has the same kind of suppressed kinetic energy that is capable of being tapped by outside forces to perform the physical phenomena as the unused energy of youngsters. I also discovered that in each and every case with which I came in contact personally there had been some form of unfinished business in the house or on the grounds on which the house stood. Sometimes this involved a previous building on the same spot. At other times it involved the same building in which the activities took place. But in each instance there was some form of psychic entity present, and it is my conviction that the entity from beyond the physical world was responsible for the happenings, using, of course, the physical energy in the young people or in the retarded adult. Thus, to me, poltergeists are the physical activities of ghosts expressed through the psychic powers within young people or retarded older people, but directed solely by outside entities no longer in the flesh. This link between the physical energies of living persons and the usually demented minds of dead persons produces the physical phenomena known as poltergeist activities which can be very destructive, sometimes threatening, sometimes baffling to those who do not understand the underlying causes.

The purpose of these physical activities is always to get the attention of living persons or perhaps to annoy them for personal reasons. The mentality behind this phenomenon is somewhere between the psychotic and the infantile, but at all times far from emotionally and mentally normal. But it can still be dealt with on the same basis as I deal with ordinary hauntings. That is to say, the cause of the activities must be understood before a cure for them can be found. Making contact with the troubled entity in the non-physical world is, of course, the best way. When that is not possible, a shielding device has to be created for the living to protect them from the unwanted poltergeist activities. In the well-publicized Seaford, Long Island, case a few years ago, a young boy in the household was held responsible for the movement of objects in plain daylight. Even so astute an investigator as Dr. Karlis Osis of the American Society of Psychical Research, who was then working for Parapsychology Foundation of New York City, could not discern the link between the boy's unconscious thought and the unseen, but very real, psychic entities beyond the world of the flesh. In his report he intimates that the activities were due to the unconscious desires of the youngster to be noticed and to get the sort of attention his unconscious self craved. I was not involved in the Seaford case personally although

I was familiar with it, having discussed the matter with Mr. Herman, the boy's father. I did not enter the case because certain aspects of it suggested publicity seeking on the part of the family, and at any rate others in my field had already entered the case. I saw no reason to crowd the scene, but I did go into the background of the house with the help of medium Ethel Johnson Meyers independently of the investigation conducted by Dr. Osis. For what it may be worth at this late date, my sitting with Mrs. Meyers disclosed that an Indian burial ground had existed on the very site of the Seaford house and that the disturbances were due to the fact that the house had been erected on the spot. They had not occurred earlier since no physical medium lived in the house. When the young man reached the age of puberty, or nearly so, his energies were available to those wishing to manifest, and it was then that the well-publicized movement of objects occurred.

Similarly, two years ago a case attracted public attention tn the city of Rosenheim, Bavaria. A young lady working for an attorney in that city was somehow able to move solid objects by her very presence. A long list of paranormal phenomena was recorded by reputable witnesses, including the attorney himself. Eventually Dr. Hans Bender of the University of Freiburg entered the case and after investigation pronounced it a classical poltergeist situation. He too did not link the activity with any outside entity that might have been present on the premises from either this house or a previous one standing on the spot. It seems to me that at the time great haste was taken to make sure that a physical or temporal solution could be put forward, making it unnecessary to link the phenomena with any kind of spirit activity.

But perhaps the most famous of all poltergeist cases, the classical American case, is the so-called Bell Witch of Tennessee. This case goes back to the 1820s and even so illustrious a witness as Andrew Jackson figures in the proceedings. Much has been written and published about the Bell Witch of Tennessee. Suffice it to say here that it involved the

hatred of a certain woman for a farmer named John Bell. This relationship resulted in a post-mortem campaign of hatred and destructiveness
ultimately costing the lives of two people. In the Bell Witch case of
Tennessee the entire range of physical phenomena usually associated
with poltergeistic activities was observed.

Included were such astounding happenings as the appearance or
disappearance of solid objects into and out of thin air; strange smells
and fires of unknown origin; slow deliberate movement of objects in
plain sight without seeming physical source; and voices being heard out
of the air when no one present was speaking. Anyone studying the proceedings of this case would notice that the phenomena were clearly the
work of a demented individual. Even though a certain degree of cun-
ning and cleverness is necessary to produce them, the reasoning behind
or, rather, the lack of reasoning, clearly indicates a disturbed mind. All
poltergeist activities must therefore be related to the psychotic, or, at the
very least, schizophrenic state of mind of the one causing them. As yet
we do not clearly understand the relationship between insanity and free
energies capable of performing acts seemingly in contradiction of physical laws, but there seems to be a very close relationship between these
two aspects of the human personality. When insanity exists certain
energies become free and are capable of roaming at will at times and of
performing feats in contradiction to physical laws. When the state of
insanity in the mind under discussion is reduced to normalcy these
powers cease abruptly.

I have, on occasion, reported cases of hauntings and ghostly activities bordering upon or including some poltergeist activities. Generally
we speak of them as physical phenomena. A case in point is the haunted house belonging to Mr. and Mrs. John Smythe of Rye, New York.
The phenomena in this house included such physical activities as doors
opening by themselves, footsteps, the sound of chains rattling, ashtrays
flying off the table by themselves, and, most frightening of all, a carv-

ing knife taking off by itself on a Sunday morning in full view of two adult sane people and flinging itself at their feet, not to hurt them but to call attention to an existing unseen entity in the house. These are, of course, the kind of activities present in poltergeist cases, but they are merely a fringe activity underlining the need for communication. They are not the entire case, nor are they as disorganized and wanton as the true poltergeist cases. In the case of Rye, New York, the physical activities followed long-time mental activities such as apparitions and impressions of a presence. The physical phenomena were primarily used here to make the message more urgent. Not so with the true poltergeist case, where there is no possibility of mental communication simply because the causing person is incapable of actual thinking. In such a case all energies are channeled toward destructive physical activity and there is neither the will nor the ability to give mental impressions to those capable of receiving them, since the prime mover of these activities is so filled with hatred and the desire to manifest in the physical world that he or she will not bother with so rational an activity as a thought message.

It is therefore difficult to cope with cases of this kind since there is no access to reasoning, as there is in true ghost cases when a trance medium can frequently make contact with the disturbed and disturbing entity in the house and slowly, but surely, bring it back to the realm of reason. With the true poltergeist case nothing of the sort can be established and other means to solve it have to be found. It is therefore quite natural that anyone who becomes the victim of such activities and is not familiar with them or with what causes them will be in a state of panic, even to the point of wanting to abandon his property and run for his life.

On September 1, 1968, I was contacted by a gentleman by the name of L. H. Beaird. He wrote to me from Tyler, Texas, requesting that I help him understand some of the extraordinary happenings that had made his life hell on earth during the period of three years between 1965 and 1968. Through his daughter who was married in Austin he learned of my work with ghosts and finally concluded that only someone as familiar with the subject as I could shed light on the mysterious happenings in his home. He had purchased their home in 1964, but after three years of living with a poltergeist and fighting a losing battle for survival he decided that his sanity and survival were more important, and in 1968 he sold it again, losing everything he had put into it. The move, however, was a fortuitous one, for the new home turned out to be quiet and peaceful. Once Mr. Beaird got his bearings again and learned to relax once more he decided to investigate what had occurred during the previous three years and find some sort of answer to this extraordinary problem.

I had never heard of Tyler before and decided to look it up on the map. It turned out to be a city of about 60,000 inhabitants also known as the "rose capital" because of the large number of horticultural activities in the area. Tyler is connected with Dallas and Houston by a local airline and lies about halfway between Dallas and Shreveport, Louisiana. It has one television station, one newspaper and some pleasant ordinary citizens going about their various businesses. The people of Tyler whom I got to know a little after my visit later on are not concerned with such things as the occult. In fact, anyone trying to lecture on the subject would do so in empty halls.

Howard Beaird works in a nearby hospital and also runs a rubber stamp shop in which he has the company of his wife and more orders than he can possibly fill. Their son, Andy, was enrolled in barber school at the time of my visit and presumably is now cutting people's hair to everyone's satisfaction somewhere in Texas. The big local hotel is called the Blackstone and it is about the same as other big hotels in small towns. Everything is very quiet in Tyler, Texas, and you can really sleep at night. There is a spirit of not wanting to change things, of letting sleeping dogs lie as much as possible, pervading the town, and I have the distinct impression that cases such as the poltergeist case were not exactly welcome subjects for discussion over a drink at the local bar.

It must be held to Mr. Beaird's credit that despite the indications of small-town life he felt compelled to make inquiries into the extraordinary happenings in his life, to look into them without fear and with great compassion for those involved—his wife and son. Others in his position might have buried the matter and tried to forget it. This is particularly important since Mr. Beaird is reasonably prosperous, does business with his neighbors and has no intention of leaving Tyler. To ask me for an investigation was tantamount to stirring things up, but Beaird took this calculated risk because he could not live with the knowledge of what he had observed and not know what caused it.

At the time of our correspondence in September of 1968 the phenomena had already ended, as abruptly as they had come. This too is typical of genuine poltergeist activities, since they depend solely on the available free energies of living people. As will be seen in the course of my investigation, that energy became no longer available when the principals were removed from the house. There are other factors involved, of course. It is not as simple as plugging in on a power line, but in essence poltergeist activities depend not only on the desire of the disturbing entity to manifest but also on the physical condition of the unconscious part of those whom they wish to use as power supplies.

The house which the Beairds had to leave under pressure from their poltergeists is on Elizabeth Street. It is a one-story ranch-type dwelling, pleasant enough to look at and about fourteen or fifteen years old. The new owners are not particularly keen on the history of their house, and it is for that reason that I am keeping confidential the actual location, but the house has not been altered in any way since it has been sold to Mr. M. and his family. One enters the house through a porch that is located somewhat above the road. There is a garage and a steep driveway to the right of the porch. Once one is inside the house one is in the living room with a den to the left and a dining area to the right. Beyond the living room are the kitchen and a rather long room leading directly to a breakfast room. On the extreme left are two bedrooms. To the right of the house behind the garage is the workshop, which, in the period when Mr. Beard owned the house, was used as such. There is also a concrete slab separating the shop from the garage proper, and the garage contains a ladder leading up to the attic.

Howard Beaird, sixty-five years of age, is a pleasant man with a soft Texas accent, polite, firm, and obliging in his manner. He was overjoyed when I expressed an interest in his case and promised to cooperate in every way. In order to get a better understanding of the extraordinary happenings at Tyler I asked that he dictate in his own words the story of those three years in the house that had come to be three years of unrelenting terror. The principals in this true account besides Howard Beaird are his wife, Johnnie, whom he has always called John; a daughter named Amy who lives in another city and was in no way involved in the strange experiences at Tyler; and a son, Andy, now nineteen, who shared all of the unspeakable horror of the experiences between 1965 and the early part of 1968 with his parents. Most of the others mentioned in his account have been dead for several years. A few are still alive, and there are some names in this account Mr. Beaird has never heard of. Here then is his own account of what occurred in the little house on Elizabeth Street in Tyler, Texas:

"My story begins late in 1962, which marked the end of nearly thirty-nine years of employment with the same company. During the last twenty years of that time John worked in the same office with me; in fact her desk was only a few feet from mine. We were both retired during September of 1962.

"John had always been an excellent employee, but devoted much more time to her work than the company required for any one person. She would never take a vacation, and was rarely away from her job for more than an occasional half-day at a time, mainly, I think, because she would trust no one with her work. I cannot say when her mind began to show signs of being disturbed, although as I think back on it today, she had acted a little strangely for several years prior to the time of our retirement. This, however, did not affect her work in any way; in fact she was even more precise in it than ever, and I suppose I just could not bring myself to admit that there was anything wrong with her mind. At any rate, during the next twelve months she began to act more abnormally than ever, especially when at home, until finally it was necessary that she enter a mental institution. Although the doctors there were reluctant to release her, they did not seem to be having any success in whatever treatment they were giving her, so I asked for her release after about three months. Being of very modest means I naturally had to obtain employment as soon as possible, but after working about three months in another city I felt that it was most urgent that I move my family from Grand Saline, Texas, to some other place, believing that the mere change of environment would play a big part in helping John to get well. So about the middle of 1964 we moved to Tyler, Texas, a place where John had always said she would like to live. We bought a house, and after about a month I obtained employment which, in addition to a sideline business I had begun a few years before, gave us a satisfactory, if not affluent, living. For almost a year John did seem to be better; she would go places with Andy and me, to the Little League baseball games in which Andy played, to the movies occasionally, sometimes to bowling alleys and a miniature golf course, but all of a sudden she stopped.

"She had not actually kept house since we made the move and had not cooked a single meal for Andy or me. About this time she started walking to a drugstore in a nearby shopping center for breakfast, and then in the late afternoon just before I would get home she would walk to a restaurant a few blocks away for the evening meal, usually by herself. A little later she began calling a taxi nearly every morning to go to a different place for breakfast; once to a downtown hotel; once way out on the other side of town to a roadside restaurant on the Mineola Highway, and to many other places within the course of a few weeks. Always in the evenings though she would go to the restaurant near our home. She would come home usually just after I arrived, and would change clothes and stay in her room from then on. She would get up very early in the morning, about five o'clock, something she had never done during our entire married life. For the past few years she insisted that people were spying on her, and finally, when I did not agree with her, she accused me of being at the head of this group set out to torment her, and even said that I had television cameras set up in the house to spy on her.

"John smoked almost incessantly, every kind of cigarette made, but later began to smoke little cigars the size of a cigarette, and still later started on the big regular ones that men smoke. Once she bought a small can of snuff. She had never used snuff before. This was a little while after she had begun to lay cigarettes down just anywhere, although there were plenty of ashtrays throughout the house. She also began putting lighted cigarettes on table tops, the arms of a divan, or even on the bed, and if Andy or I had not been there to put them out, no doubt the house would have eventually been burned down. She did burn holes in several sheets and in the mattress on her bed. When that happened I told her that she simply could not smoke any more. She did not protest. Andy and I searched the house and found cigarettes and matches everywhere. John had hidden them everywhere, inside a little table radio by removing the back, inside a flashlight where the batteries are supposed to be, in those little shoe pockets she had hanging in her closet, in a little opening at the end of the bathtub where a trap door in the closet exposes the pipes for repairs, under the mattress, inside pillow covers, and even in the dog house outdoors. We gathered up cigarettes, matches, and cigarette lighters every day when I got home and there is no telling how many we finally found and destroyed. Of course she would get more every day at the shopping center, and once we even found one of those little automatic rollers that a person can use to make his own cigarettes.

"Exactly what part John played in the frightening events that took place at our house I cannot say. I am convinced though, as is Amy, that there was some connection. The three years from late 1962 to the summer of 1965 preceded the most awesome, fantastic chain of events that the human mind can imagine. In fact, as these unbelievable episodes began to unfold before us I was beginning to doubt my own sanity. Andy, who was 13 at the time this began, shared with me every one of the horrible experiences, which started in midsummer of 1965 and lasted without interruption until near the end of 1966, when we were 'told' that they were over with, only to find that during the next fifteen months we were in for even worse things. If Andy had not been with me to substantiate these awful experiences I would have indeed considered myself hopelessly insane.

"The frightening events began to take place near the middle of 1965, about the time John quit going places with Andy and me. When at home she would stay in her bedroom and close the door and leave it closed after she went to bed. Andy and I slept in the same bed in another room.

"During our first year at this house we were not bothered by the usual summertime insects, so I did not bother to repair the screens needing fixing at that time. However, during July of 1965, Andy and I would go to bed, and as soon as we turned out the light we were plagued by hordes of June bugs of all sizes, which would hit us on our heads and faces, some glancing off on the floor, others landing on the bed, and some missing us entirely and smashing themselves against the metal window blinds. Night after night we fought these bugs in the dark, grabbing those that landed on the bed and throwing them against the blinds as hard as we could.

"Then we discovered that at least half of the bugs that hit us were already dead, in fact had been dead so long that they were crisp and would crumble between our fingers when we picked them up! I would get up and turn on the lights, and the raids would cease immediately; we could see no sign of them in the air . . . only those hundreds that littered the floor and bed. The instant I turned off the light, though, the air would be filled with bugs again, just as if someone were standing there ready to throw handfuls at us as soon as it was dark. One night I got up and swept and vacuumed the entire room, moved every piece of furniture away from the walls, dusted the backs of the dresser, chest and tables, and vacuumed the floor again. When I was through I could swear that there was not a living creature in that room other than Andy and me. I got some rags and stuffed them in the cracks beneath the closet door and the one leading from the room into the hall. The windows were closed. The room was absolutely clean. Andy was in bed, awake. I turned off the light. At that exact instant hundreds of bugs hit us!

"About this time John began to act more strangely than ever, doing things she would not dream of doing under ordinary circumstances. For example, I might look in my closet to get a shirt or a pair of trousers, and there would not be any there. I do not know what prompted me to do it, but I would go to John's closet, and there would be my clothes hanging alongside some of hers.

"At this time I had a rubber stamp shop in a room behind the garage, which was a part of the house, and I worked out there every night. There was no direct connection from the house. One had to go out the kitchen door into the garage and then through another door into the shop. On many occasions I would hear the kitchen door being opened, and would rush to the shop door to see who it was. No matter how hard I tried, though, I could never get there fast enough to see anybody . . . only my clothes, suits, shirts, etc., on hangers just as they landed in the middle of the garage floor.

"It was during the hottest part of summer while we had the air-conditioners running that other strange things took place for which we assumed John was responsible. Andy or I would suddenly find the bathroom wall heater lighted and the flames running out the top, with the door closed. The room would be hot enough to burst into flames. John insisted that she had not lit the heater . . . that one of us had. After this had happened several times, I removed the handle that turns on the gas. A short time later, while I was out in the shop, Andy came running out and called me in. There was a bunch of paper towels stuffed into the heater where the burners are and they were on fire, some of them on the floor, burning. I then decided to turn off all the pilot lights in the house. This was on the weekend before Labor Day, and I did not know how I could possibly go to work on Tuesday following the holiday and leave John at home alone, since Andy would be in school. I had talked with Dr. until I could determine what I would eventually be able to do with her, but the psychiatric wards were already running over, and he did not want to admit her as a patient. I decided to tell John that if she did 'any of those things again' I would have to put her in jail. Monday night she started waving a pistol around, so I called the police station and told them the predicament I was in. They said they would keep her until things could be settled and told me to bring her on down. She went without protest. When my lawyer returned he made appointments for her to be examined by two psychiatrists, after which I thought there would be no further question about the need for commitment, and she stayed at home that week. However, on the Monday following Labor Day she called her sister-in-law Mack in Daingerfield, Texas, about a hundred miles from Tyler, and asked if she could visit her at once. I was at work and knew nothing of this until Mack got to Tyler and asked if it would be all right for John to go with her. I objected, but my lawyer advised me that I should let her go, as she could be brought back for the commitment hearing, so they left that day for Daingerfield.

"A few days later John's lawyer had her examined by a psychiatrist again, and he finally said that she might benefit somewhat from getting a job, although she would have to undergo psychiatric treatment at various times in the future. It would be almost impossible to have her committed involuntarily, so we decided to just let things stand as they were. For the record, John's attorney insisted that I be examined by the same doctors who had examined her. The reports on me were favorable.

"Shortly after John had gone off to stay with Mack, Andy and I were lying in bed with the lights off, talking about the terrible things we had gone through. Suddenly I heard a voice calling my name . . . a high-pitched, falsetto voice that seemed to be coming from out in space. The voice said it was John, and although it sounded nothing at all like her, I am convinced it was, since she talked about several things that only she and I knew of. One was about some disagreeable words she had had with one of my sisters at the time of my father's death in 1950. She said that although my other sister had insulted her, she was good, and that she had forgiven her. Andy did not hear any part of this conversation. Apparently John, or the voice, could talk to either of us without the other listening to the voice. I even suspected that Andy was doing the talking, and I held my fingers to his lips while listening to the voice. I knew then it could not have been coming from his lips.

"One night while I was lying in bed and Andy was in the bathroom I heard his voice say 'goodbye,' though, just before he came to bed, and he told me he had been talking with his mother. During the following weeks we heard six other voices from right out of nowhere, all from people who had been dead for some time. I knew all but one of them while they were living. Two of them had always been friendly toward me, and both were old enough to be my mother. Andy also knew these two women and one of the men named George Swinney. This latter person was killed in an accident some time after he visited us 'by voice.' The other two women were mothers of friends of mine and both had died some time before we moved to Tyler. One was Mrs. Snow and the other was Mrs. Elliott, and theirs were the next two voices we heard after John had left, and they came to us about the time the visits by Henry Anglin started. He was the only one of the lot who gave us trouble to start with; in fact I am convinced that he is the one responsible for the bug raids and other awful things that happened to us.

"One of the work benches in my shop was against the wall dividing the shop and the kitchen, and at the bottom of the wall was an opening with a grill over it to handle the return air from the central heating system. For some reason the grill on the shop side had been removed, and by stooping down near the floor under the bench I could see much of what was going on in the kitchen. I worked in the shop every night, and when these 'ghosts' first began visiting us they would call my name, the voices seeming to come from the opening into the kitchen. I would stoop down and answer. At that time I would carry on lengthy conversations with all of them. Mrs. Snow and Mrs. Elliot were very friendly and seemed to want to give me all kinds of good advice. Henry Anglin was just the opposite. He was extremely mean and demanded that I do all sorts of things I would not do. When I refused, he would be very nasty. Once he got a can of insect spray we kept on the kitchen cabinet top and held it down at the opening to my shop. He would start spraying through the hole. He used a whole can of spray and in that little room I nearly suffocated. One cannot imagine what a feeling it is to see a can of insect spray suspended in midair with apparently nothing holding it and to have it sprayed right in one's face! When I went inside I could see the dents made by the edge of the can where he had banged it against the wall.

"About the middle of September 1965 the nightly bug raids began to taper off. We thought that we were going to get a few nights' sleep without fear. However, when we went to bed we would feel something moving on an arm or in our hair—after we had turned off the lights. We jumped up and found one or several slugs somewhere on us or on the bed. They are the ugliest, slimiest wormlike creatures that can be imagined, big at the head and tapering to a point toward their rear end. They have whiskers on each side of the head, and although they have eyes, they are not supposed to see very well, according to Andy, who, strangely enough, was studying them at school at that time. The large ones are as big as a Vienna sausage, about three inches long, and leave a silvery looking trail wherever they crawl. When the first few of these creatures appeared Andy thought they had clung to his shoes while he was playing in the yard and had gotten into the house that way. However, night after night the number of slugs increased, and we went through the same torture as with the bugs, only much worse. One cannot imagine how awful it is to wake up in the middle of the night and find oneself surrounded by a horde of slimy, ugly worms! Andy said that salt would dissolve the slugs. So we sprinkled salt all around the baseboard, around the bed legs, but still the slugs came as soon as the lights were out. A few nights later we were again bombarded with bugs . . . not June bugs this time, but the wood louse, the little bug about the size of a blackeyed pea. They have lots of tiny legs, will roll up into a round ball when touched, and are generally called pill bugs. I knew they could not fly, yet there they came, hitting us just as if they were shot out of a gun, at the exact moment we turned out the lights! Mixed in with these were some bugs I had never seen anywhere before, like a doodle bug but brown in color. I knew doodle bugs couldn't fly, and these things no more had wings than I did. Yet there they came, shooting through the air, and, just as the June bugs had done, they started out one or two at a time, until finally dozens began hitting us at once the moment the lights were out. I also found little pieces of clear material which looked like pieces of broken glass. I finally discovered that these pieces were making the loud noise against the blinds . . . some of them landed on the bed along with the peculiar bugs. I then washed off a piece about the size of a pea and tasted it; it was pure rock salt! I had not the slightest idea where it came from, as we certainly had had no use for any here. As baffling as the idea of bugs flying without wings was, it was no more so than rock salt sailing through the air with apparently nothing to propel it. There was absolutely no human being in the house except Andy and me.

"A day or two after John had left, I cleaned up her room thoroughly, moved every piece of furniture, swept, vacuumed, dusted, and made up the bed, putting on a spread that came nearly to the floor. A few days after the second series of bug raids, Andy called me into John's room. He raised up the spread, and there under the bed was a conglomeration of objects, among which was a ten-pound sack of rock salt, most of which had been poured in a pile on the carpet under the bed. There was an old hair net mixed with it, some burned matches, an unwrapped cake of hotelsoap, and on top of the pile was a note, printed the way a six-year-old child would do it,

'Evil spirit go away.'

"In the next few days we began looking through things in John's room and found lots of notes written in longhand, most of which were like those of a child just learning to write, although a few words were unmistakably John's handwriting. They were mainly of people's names, a date which might be the birthdate, and then another date some time in the future . . . some up past 1977. There were many names contained in the notes. One name was of a man I am sure John could not have known. He was Henry Anglin, a pitifully ignorant old man who used to farm just west of Grand Saline, and, like all farmers in the adjoining territory back in 1918, would come to town each Saturday to buy groceries and other supplies for the following week. When I was about fourteen years old I worked in a department store that also handled groceries. My job was to keep track of the farmers' stacks of groceries so that when they were ready to leave in the evening I could show them where their purchases were and help load their wagons. Henry Anglin was among the people I regularly waited on. He seemed old to me then and that was about fifty years ago. I have no doubt that he has long since died. I cannot imagine how his name entered John's mind. There were also some typewritten sheets in John's room which contained the same items as the notes we had found. One mentioned a certain 'Tink' Byford. There was a date that was probably his birthdate, then a date in 1964. We had moved to Tyler in July of 1964, and it was several months after that when I read in the paper that 'Tink' Byford had been killed in an auto accident while returning to Grand Saline from Dallas. Another name was 'Bill' Robertson, a friend of both of us. There was an early date, then 'Hosp. 1965, death 1967.' There were many other names, some now dead, but most still living, always with two dates! One day when I got home from work Andy and I found in the living room between the divan and table a new bar of soap which had been crumbled up and scattered over a two- or three-foot area. Andy found a potato masher in John's room with soap on it, so we assumed it was used in the living room where the soap was scattered. We did not clean it up right away. That night, after we went to bed, several pieces of soap about the size of a quarter hit our blinds like bullets, although the door to the living room was closed and the den and hallway are between the living room and our bedroom.

"I had had to wash some clothes that night, and it was after dark when I hung them on the line. While I was doing that, Andy came to the door and advised me that bugs and slugs were flying all over the house. I told him I thought I had heard something thud against the dog house near the clothesline. He checked and picked up a little leather wallet about the size of a billfold, which we had seen earlier in John's room, filled with loose tobacco. I told him to put it into the garbage can at the end of the house. The can had a lid on it. When I got through, it was time to take a bath and go to bed. While I was in the tub and Andy in the den, I heard something that sounded like a shotgun just outside the bathroom window. I called Andy to run out and see what he could find; he had heard the noise too . . . Just beneath the window he picked up the same leather purse he had put into the garbage can an hour earlier! It had hit the house flat, I suppose, near the bathroom window, to cause such a loud noise.

"During the preceding days we had found several other notes, all written or printed in the same peculiar way, as a little child might write. I had no idea what they meant, if anything, but some examples are:

Johnnie Beaird	Joe Bailey—1972	Amy Beaird
Red Lesser—1966	The End	Tink Byford—1964
1913 Murder		
Bill Robertson—1967	The dog—leave 1965	Die 1972

"In a little notebook we found:

Allie L. Lewis (This woman worked for the same company we did, and probably still does).

Luther Anderson (He owns a truck line that hauls salt).

Die 1980

Jeraldine Fail (This woman used to be a good friend of John's).

Die 1977

Louise Beaird (This is my sister, who would be 118 years of age in 2018.

Die 2018

"One day we found an old wooden box where John had kept her canceled checks. She had burned something in it, as the ashes were still in the box. The only thing left was one half of a calling card saying, 'burn spirit burn. On just a scratch of paper were the words, 'Johnnie Beaird—Death 1991.'

"There were many more. Note the peculiar use of capital letters. All of these notes were printed:

JoHN is goIN   Be NIce IN   There IS A   I pOisOned
to Die   FROnt Hertz in Mt   little FOOLS
    OF   PleaSant   white kittEn
    OLD FOOL- SnEak ShALL i
    ish MacK   AWAY From   poisOn The   Cat

(I checked, and there is not Hertz in Mt. Pleasant).

(Andy did have white kitten which had died for some reason, and at this time still had a Siamese cat).

"On a Canton bank blank check was written in the 'pay to' line: Johnnie B. Walker $1,000,000; in the 'for' line: Bill is NUTTY, and on the 'signature' line: ha ha.

"The ghastly events continued through October and into November, when they seemed to be letting up a little. One day early in the month when I got home from work Andy took me into John's room. Lined up under the edge of her bed but behind the spread were some pictures in little frames of various kinds. There was one of Amy, of John and Andy, of me, of Thelma Lowrie, who had been John's best friend and who had died in 1951, and several others. I don't know what significance they were supposed to have, but I left them right there. I assumed that John had been to the house that day. Bugs, dead and alive, continued to bombard us every night; even the slugs started flying through the air, smashing against the blinds and walls, making an awful mess wherever they hit.

"I decided to clean up both bedrooms as soon as I could, and to start taking up the carpets. While I was doing that Andy found a note in John's room saying: 'Bugs will end for ThursDay Dec. 29.'"

I think the 23rd was the day I cleaned up our room, and the bugs were worse than ever that night, so we decided that maybe it was meant that the 23rd would be the last night. The next night, strangely enough, was pretty quiet.

"On the 24th I took up the carpet in John's room. While doing that I was hit by hundreds of bugs, slugs, and even some of the nails I pulled out of the floor simply flew through the air and hit against the blinds. Finally I was able to completely clean the room, paint the walls and woodwork, put up curtains, and the room looked very nice when I was finished.

"On November 26 I cleaned the house thoroughly, and no unusual activity took place that night. On the 27th bugs were everywhere. Just before dark I was taking a bath, and when I was through, standing up in the tub, I saw something hit the screen but could not tell what it was. I called Andy from the den and told him to go out to see what it was. It turned out to be one of John's rubber gloves I had put out beside the garbage can to be hauled off.

"On Thanksgiving day I took all of our outside locks and had Andy take them to a locksmith in town the next morning to have them changed and get new keys, as I was convinced that John had been somehow coming from Daingerfield and using her keys to get in. I put the locks in place on Saturday. On Wednesday, December 1, 1965, somebody (I supposed it was John) punched a hole in the back screen door near the hook and unhooked the door. If it was John, though, her key would not fit.

"December 4 was the worst. It was Saturday, and we went to bed about 10:30. Something that sounded exactly like fingers drummed lightly on the bed. Although we were under the covers we could feel whatever it was tugging at the sheets, actually trying to jerk the covers off us! We would turn on the light and the tugging would stop. There were no bugs that night, but when the lights were off both Andy and I could feel something on our arms that seemed like small flying bugs bouncing up and down, sort of like gnats might do. We would slap at them, but there was absolutely nothing there. We would turn the lights on and see nothing. We sprayed the air everywhere with insect spray but it did no good. It felt exactly like someone lightly grabbing the hair on your arms with the thumb and forefinger, not actually pulling very hard at first, but later jerking the hair hard enough to hurt.

"While we were lying in bed with the light on, my shoes, weighing possibly two pounds each, flew right over our heads and landed on the other side of the bed. Andy's house shoes got up from the floor and flung themselves against the blinds. My clothes, which were hanging in the closet with the door closed, got out of there somehow without the door being opened and landed across the room. Finally we turned off the lights and heard a strange sound we could not identify. It was under the bed, and sounded like bed rollers being turned rapidly with the fingers; but the bed was not even on rollers! Suddenly something hit the blind like a bullet. We turned on the light and found that the handle from the gas jet under the bed had unscrewed itself, and both the bolt and the handle had flung themselves against the blind. Then the bed started moving away from the wall. We would roll it back again only to have it do the same thing over and over. That was about all we could stand, and as it was 2 a.m. Sunday, I told Andy to put on his clothes. We went to a motel to spend the rest of the night.

"As we were walking down the driveway, after closing and locking the door, a handkerchief still folded hit me on the back of the neck. Just as we got in the car another handkerchief I had left on the bedside table hit me on the back after I had closed the car doors.

"We were so weary that we were asleep almost by the time we were in bed at the motel, and nothing happened to us while we were there. We came home about 9:30 the next morning. Some of John's clothes were in my closet, and most of mine were in hers. All sorts of weird notes were flying all about the house. I cleaned the house, and just as I was through, a big cigar hit the back of my neck from out of nowhere. I put it in the kitchen waste basket. Andy wanted some soup, so I started to a Cabell grocery store a few blocks away. Just as I left the house Andy saw the cigar jump up out of the waste basket and land on the floor. He put it back in the basket. When he came to the door to tell me about it I was getting into the car parked at the foot of the driveway, and when I turned toward him I saw the cigar come sailing over his head and land at the side of the car, about sixty feet from the house. When I came back and stepped in the door from the garage to the kitchen I saw a clean shirt of mine coming flying from the den and land near the back door of the kitchen.

"By this time I had decided that it did absolutely no good to change the locks on the doors, although John had not broken in, if, indeed, this was John. Apparently whoever it was did not need a door, nor did he need to break in. Andy and I were standing in the kitchen watching things fly through the air, when all of a sudden his cap, which had been resting on the refrigerator, hit me in the back of the head. A roll of paper towels flew through the air; a can of soup on the cabinet top jumped off onto the floor several times after Andy picked it up and put it back.

"All of a sudden we heard a click. The toaster had been turned on, and the click meant it had turned itself off. There was a piece of soap in it, melted! A note nearby read 'clean toaster.' I felt something like a slight brush on my shoulder and heard Andy shout, 'Look out! He saw the faint outline of a hand which looked like his mother's vanish near my head.

"Later, while in the den, I began to ask questions aloud, such as:

'John, tell me where we stayed last night?' A few seconds late a note came floating down in front of us, reading: 'Motel on T. B. Road. Couldn't get in.' Got to go, you've ruined me.' We did spend the night before at a motel on the road to the Tuberculosis Hospital where I work. I then said aloud, trying to sound funny in a totally unfunny situation: 'With all that power, why don't you just drop $5,000 on us?' Almost immediately a check with nothing but $5,000 written on the face dropped from out of nowhere. I said, 'John, why don't you appear here before us right this minute?' In about five seconds a note came down saying, 'Can't come ToDay haPPy YuLeTide.' I then asked, 'Are we going to be able to sleep tonight?' This answer came down to us: 'CaN't maKE aNyTHing haPPen tONighT you BROKE MY POWER Call HOUsTon.'

"Previously she told me to call Houston police and ask them about a witch who had solved the murder of a man named Gonzales. I felt like a fool, but I did call the Houston police department. I told them they could think I was drunk, crazy, or anything they wished to, but I just wanted a yes or no answer, and asked if they had any record of a witch ever helping the Houston police solve a murder of a man named Gonzales. The man I talked to did not appear surprised and simply asked me to wait a moment, and a few seconds later said that he could find no record of any such event.

"John had also given us directions for breaking her power. It was to 'break an egg, mix with a little water and a dash of salt and then throw it out in the back yard.'

"I have never been superstitious before, and this sounded awfully silly to me, but I think I would have done absolutely anything I was told if it meant a chance to put an end to these uncanny events, so I told Andy to go ahead and follow the directions. That night we had a few bugs and a note came floating down reading, 'power will end at 10 o'clock give or take an hour.'

"For several days we received what seemed like hundreds of notes from right out of nowhere, simply materializing in midair, some folding themselves as they came toward us. Some time after he had seen the hand vanish near my head, Andy was sitting in the den facing the outside windows. For a few fleeting seconds he saw the outline of John in front of the windows. Her back was to him as she looked out the windows, and Andy heard a faint 'goodbye' just as the figure melted in the air.

"We heard other voices after talking with John. All seemed very strained, especially the female speakers, and they would often say that they had a 'mist' in their throat and could not continue talking to me, although they could always talk to Andy and he would hear them. I have dozens of notes that fell down to us from somewhere above, and most of them are from the same two people who stayed with us for the longest period of time. One of these was Mrs. Elliot, who had been dead for three or four years when all this began to happen. The other was from a Mr. Gree, of whom I had never heard, but who seemed eager to help Andy and me with advice, especially concerning the care of Andy's cats and dogs. We were 'visited' by a great variety of 'people,' some long since dead, some still living, most of whom we know, or knew, but also some well-known public figures whose names were often in the news. I dated the notes from then on, but at times so many descended on us at once that I did not try to record the exact order in which we received them.

"It was Henry Anglin who tormented us from the very beginning, and who caused us to move out of the house. One night Anglin came to our room after we had gone to bed and his voice asked if he could cook himself an egg. We heard nothing else from him that night, but the next morning when I went to the kitchen to prepare breakfast, there in a teflon-lined skillet on the stove burner which was turned down low was an egg burned to a crisp!

"Another night Anglin came to our room and insisted that I call Houston. This was about the time he was beginning to be so terribly mean. I told him that I had already made one silly call to the Houston police, and that I had no intention of doing it again. He countered that I had not questioned them enough, and for me to phone them again. I refused, and he tormented us relentlessly. Finally he said he would leave us alone if we would drive around the loop, which was a distance of a little over twenty miles around the city of Tyler. Andy and I put on our clothes and did just that. We drove completely around the town, and sure enough, when we got home we were able to sleep the rest of the night without further trouble.

"A few nights after this, both Mrs. Elliott and Mrs. Snow told me verbally, while I was working in my shop, that they had taken Henry Anglin 'back to his grave,' and had driven a stake, prepared by Mr. Gree, through Anglin's heart. They promised that he would not bother us again.

"About this time we received notes allegedly from people who were still living, and also some from persons other than those previously mentioned who had been dead for several years. Among those still living were Mrs. W. H. Jarvis, and Odell Young, who lives in Grand Saline at this time. I also had one note from Mr. W. H. Quinn, who had been dead for several years. He used to be a railroad agent in Grand Saline. For a number of years I had occasion to have him sign numerous shipping papers, so I had become familiar with his handwriting. The note I got from him was written in the same backhand fashion. I believe that this note was written by him:

Dear Howard and Andy,

I pay tribute to you. You have put up with a lot from old man Anglin. It is all over now. Friday I am going to my grave to join my wife, whom I love. I am going to Marion's house to see him once more. He

329

is my favorite child. I have always like you, John and the boy and hope someday you will be together again.

Hiram Quinn

P.S. I enjoyed hearing about John going with Marion to get new teeth.

"The P.S. about his son's false teeth refers to the time about thirty years ago when John and I went to see Marion just after he had received his first set of dentures. At that time we lived just across the street from Marion and his wife and were friendly with them.

"We also got notes allegedly from Marilyn Monroe, Dorothy Kilgallen, and former Governor Jim Allred, who sympathized with us for what Henry Anglin was doing to us and about John's condition. Mrs. Snow and Mrs. Elliot had previously told us that Anglin had caused many deaths, some by auto accident, and some by switching a person's pills, as they said he had done in the case of Dorothy Kilgallen. The note we received with her name also said that was the cause of her death. I am not certain, but I believe they also said Anglin caused Marilyn Monroe's death.

"None of the people still living, except John, ever spoke to me; they just dropped their notes from the air. Mrs. Jarvis actually spoke to Andy, though, and had him tell me to answer aloud each of the questions she put in her note to me. Mr. Quinn's note was stuck in the grate between the kitchen and my shop.

"For the first few weeks in January 1966 only Mrs. Elliott and Mr. Jack Gree 'visited' us. She and I had lots of conversations, but she gradually got so she could barely talk to me, although Andy could still hear her. The notes were written either on some note paper Andy kept in the kitchen or on some Canton, Texas, bank deposit slips in John's room. If I was working in the shop she would stick the notes in the grill and bang on the wall to attract my attention, and then I would stoop down under the work bench and retrieve the note. Mr. Gree, who told us we had never heard of him, had a very low, deep, gruff voice. Most of his communications to me were in the form of notes, however, but he and Andy carried on lengthy conversations nearly every day. He also used the grill 'post office' for depositing his notes, then banged on the wall to let me know they were there.

"At times, when Andy and I were in the car, Mrs. Elliott or Mr. Gree would be with us. They would ride along for a while and then suddenly say they were going to Canada, Russia, Minnesota, or some other far-off place, saying it took only two or three minutes for then to travel those distances, and then we might not hear anything else from them until the next day or night. Early in January of 1966 Andy came out to my shop and said Mr. Gree wanted to know if it was OK; for him to use the telephone, and of course I told him it was. I did not know what control I would have had over the situation anyway. That first time he said it was something personal and asked Andy if he would mind leaving the room. I could hear the phone being dialed, and stooped down near the floor so I could look through the grilled opening, but of course I could not see anyone there and could not quite see the phone itself. After that he used the phone many times while I was working and while Andy was studying at the kitchen table in full view of the telephone. It was really spooky to see the receiver stand up on end by itself, and then after a while put itself back down where it belonged, but always upside down. Some nights he would dial many times after we had gone to bed, and we could hear the sound plainly in our bedroom. The next morning I would find the receiver on the phone upside down. One night while Andy was taking a bath Mr. Gree called somebody and I hear him say in a low, deep voice, 'I'm weird . . . I'm unusual.' I thought to myself, 'You can say that again.' He repeated it several times and then all I could hear would be a series of low grunts, from which I could not make out any real words. One evening while we were in the car coming home from the post office I asked Andy whom he supposed Mr. Gree called on the phone. Without a moment's hesitation Mrs. Elliott, who we did not know was with us, spoke up and said he was calling her. We did not ask her where she was when she received the call!

"Both Mr. Gree and Mrs. Elliott certainly had Andy's welfare in mind. Practically every day for the whole month of January there was a note from one of them stuck in the screen door. It appeared to be Mrs. Elliott's job to help get John home and to take care of Andy. She said if she could do that she would probably go back to her grave early.

"After John had left home I felt sorry for Andy. He was lonely being at home alone so much of the time. He indicated a desire for a cat, and a little later for a dog. At the insistence and complete direction of Mrs. Elliott I spent quite a sum of money for such pets. Mr. Gree then took over completely the direction for our taking care of these dogs and cats.

"On January 29, 1966, while I was writing a letter, there was a pounding on the kitchen wall, indicating that there was a note in our 'post office.' It was from Mrs. Elliott. 'I love that beagle. Sorry the dogs have been sick. I feel responsible. Andy worries. He loves them so much. If something does happen I only hope it isn't the beagle. The beagle will be a better companion. Andy would give up one if you asked him to. Not that he wants to. But he would understand. He loves dogs. He understands. El. Reply to this note. Reply to every line I wrote.'

"The other dog she referred to was a brown dachshund, which did not look very healthy when we bought it. It never did gain any weight and after we had given away the black dachshund the brown one continued to get worse. During the next few days and nights some of the most unbelievable things happened in connection with this brown dachshund. I would be working in my shop and suddenly hear a slight noise on the roof of the house. It would be utterly impossible for the dog to jump up there from the ground, and there was nothing else around for him to get on in order to jump up on the house. Yet there he was clear up on the peak walking from one end to the other! We would get a ladder and finally coax him down into the eave where we could get hold of him and put him on the ground. This happened time after time. We finally decided to leave him up there and go on to bed. The next night Mrs. Elliott told us she knew about the dog. We asked her how it was possible and said we would like to see how the dog got up there. She said we could not see it . . . that it was just a case of 'now he's down here . . . now he's up there.' She said that even if we were watching him, he would just simply vanish from his spot on the ground and at the same instant be on the roof. Later that night Mrs. Elliott called Andy and me and said the dog was trying to commit suicide and for us to go to the back door and look in the flower bed on the south side of the back steps. Sure enough we looked, and the ground had been freshly dug and looked as if it had been loosely put back in place. We could see the dirt moving, and I told Andy to go and get the shovel from the garage. Mrs. Elliott said it was not in the garage, but for us to wait just a few seconds and we would find it out in the front yard under the tree, where it would be when it got back from 'Heaven.' Andy did go and found the shovel just where she said it would be and brought it to me. I dug down beside where the dirt was moving and pulled the dog out by the tail. He was barely breathing and looked very pitiful, but after a few seconds was able to feebly walk a little. Mrs. Elliott told us that we had better put it out of its misery that night. I told her I did not have anything to put it to sleep with, but she finally told me to just go ahead and kill it, using a hammer, a brick or anything that would put it to death. It was a sickening experience, but I did kill the dog with a brick, as I was certain that it was in pain and would be better off dead. We buried the dog where it had apparently dug its own grave! I cannot say that the dog actually dug this hole, crawled into it and covered itself up with dirt, as I find it hard to see how it could possibly have dragged the dirt in on top of it . . . I have only Mrs. Elliott's word for that. I am merely stating what she told us, although I did find the dog in the hole, covered with loose dirt, and barely breathing when I pulled it out.

"While John was away in Daingerfield, I had bought a little plastic toilet bowl cleaner on which a disposable pad is used. The handle had come apart the first time I tried to use it. It cost only a few cents, and ordinarily I would have just bought another and forgotten about it. However, I decided to write the manufacturer, and some time later I received a letter from them, advising me that they were sending me another handle. Eventually I received a notice that there was a package at the post office. I would have had to drive about ten miles from the place where I work to the post office and back during the noon hour to pick it up, and since it was of no importance I intended to just wait until Saturday to call for the package. That evening, though, when I went to my shop to start work there was a package on my work bench. The shop had been locked all day and was still locked when I started to work. I asked Andy if he knew anything about it and he assured me that he did not even know about the package being in the post office. At that moment Mrs. Elliott spoke up and admitted she had gotten it out of the post office and brought it home to me!

"Not long after John had gone to Daingerfield another mystifying thing happened. In one of the kitchen drawers where we kept some silverware in one of those little compartments made for that purpose, there was a space five or six inches behind that section clear across the drawer. In there I kept a few tools such as a screwdriver, pliers, tack hammer, where they would be conveniently available when I needed them. I had not had occasion to look in there for some time, and when I finally did I noticed a pistol. It was a .22 cal. and looked very real, and only when I picked it up did I discover it was just a blank pistol. I asked Andy where it came from, but he knew nothing whatever about it. Mrs. Elliott spoke and said she had brought it from Daingerfield. She told us that John had ordered it from some magazine and and had paid $12 for it. She said it was awfully hard for her to bring it to our house and that it had taken her several hours to do so. She did not say why she did it but intimated that she just wanted us to know about it. Later, when we were moving away from that house, the pistol was gone, and I have not seen it since.

"For many years I had owned a .25 cal. Colt automatic pistol. I always kept it in good condition but it had not been fired in thirty years at the time we moved to Tyler. John's mother also had had a pistol exactly like mine except for the handles, as I bought a pair of white, carved bone handles for mine. When she died we brought that pistol to our house, although we never had occasion to shoot it either. We still had them both when we moved to Tyler. With so many mysterious events taking place, I decided to keep a pistol out in ny shop, so I brought the one that had belonged to John's mother and left it on top of my work bench. It stayed there for several weeks. One night it was missing. My shop was always locked and I had the only key. I had wrapped my own gun in a polyethylene bag after cleaning it thoroughly, and put it in a little compartment between the two drawers in a chest in my room. One of the drawers had to be removed completely to get the gun, and even then one had to look closely to find it. I had told no one about the hiding place. When the gun in my shop suddenly disappeared I decided to get mine that I had hidden in the chest. However, when I looked in the hiding place my pistol was not there, but in its place was the one which had been in the shop! I did not take it to my shop then, but some time later when I did decide to, that gun too was gone, and we have seen neither of them since that time.

"Occasionally during all this time I would write to John, saying that I wished she would come home so that we might be able to get her well and be happy together again. She never replied to any of my letters, although she wrote Andy a note now and then when he would write her first. I talked to her on the phone a short while later. I do not remember whether I called her on the phone or whether she was the one who called, but she finally said she would be home on a given date in February 1967, and that Mack would bring her. When she got to Tyler she called me at work. She had taken a room in a private home for a few days before coming back to our house. Andy and I talked her into coming home that night, though, and during the remainder of 1967 things seemed to be more normal for us than they had been in many years.

"During March of 1967 I moved my shop to a building downtown. I was getting too crowded in the little room I had been using at the house, and when I got things all set up at the new location I thought that it would be good for John to run the shop during the day, or at least part of each day, which she agreed to do. Things went along very well throughout the rest of the year. Our daughter Amy came for a few days visit at Christmastime. A little while before this, though, John had begun to throw cigarettes all over the house again, and there were burned places everywhere. John, of course, insisted that she had not thrown them there.

"Some time in late 1967 Mrs. Elliott reappeared and began giving us more advice about how to handle John. By this time I believe Andy was about to go to pieces. One of the officials of the school Andy attended called me and asked why Andy had not been to school. Mrs. Elliott had said for him not to go to school any more, that he could take a correspondence course and get his high school diploma that way. I tried to convince him to return to school.

"I received all sorts of notes from Mrs. Elliott, telling me that Andy was becoming a nervous wreck, and that if I tried to make him go back to school she would take him with her. Andy also told me he would rather go with her than to return to school. Finally I asked her why she did not get away from us and never return. The last note I received from her read as follows:

Howard,

You might wish I wouldn't come back but I did. You can do whatever you want to with John. I won't ask Jr. if he wants to come with me, though he might kill himself. Taking John away will only make him worry more. You don't care. THERE IS ONE THING YOU CARE ABOUT AND THAT IS YOU. I wish you would leave Jr. alone. He can get a course to finish school and get a diploma and leave you. If you cause any trouble I'll take him or he'll kill himself. I could help him go to California but that wouldn't be good he be better off dead, which he probably will be. There's not going to be a world in 15 years so he doesn't care. He just wants to have some enjoyment. You are real silly. John's going to get violent. That's the silliest thing I ever heard. Now you are really going to hurt things when you send John away. All I asked was 1 week. You don't want John well you just want rid of her, so you cause trouble and get her mad. John doesn't cost you all that money you selfish fool. I can't make John love you but I could get her to clean house and if you had any sense (which you don't) you would leave her at Trumark. Now when you send her away and start giving Jr. trouble you are going to be sorrier than you have been or will ever be. I don't know Jr. is good at music and would be excellent and be able to make 3 times your money.

Maybe he will be better off gone. You silly old selfish idiot.

You can holler and anything else but it will be of no avail. When you see the nut doctor, tell him about me, maybe they ll put you away.

"During the last part of March and early February the most ghastly things yet began to happen at the house. Henry Anglin came back. I could not hear him, but Andy said he talked very little and what few words he did speak were barely understandable. Andy could hear his evil laughter. He began by putting an egg under the mattress about where my head would be. We would not have known at the time, of course, but he would tell Andy to have me look in certain places. There was an egg, broken, in one of my house shoes, one in a pocket of my robe, one in the shade of the ceiling light, one broken in the corner of the room where it was running down the wall, and one broken against the chest of drawers. There was even one inside my pillow case. Andy said that Anglin would just give a sort of insane-sounding laugh each time we would find another egg. We cleaned up the mess, and that was the end of the egg episode.

"A few days later when I got home from work, Andy called ne into our room and there in the middle of the bed was our dresser. It was not very heavy, and I was able to lift it down by myself. The next day the chest of drawers was on the bed. This was very heavy, and it took both Andy and me to set it on the floor again. The following day, when I got home, Andy was not there. I noticed that the door to the room he and I shared was closed. That was not unusual, though, as we often kept it closed during the day. However, when I started to open it, it simply came off the hinges in my hands. I could see that the pins had been removed from the hinges, so I just leaned the door against the wall. The next day I found the closet door wrenched from the opening, bringing most of the door facing with it. These were hollow doors and both of them had holes knocked in them about the size of a fist. The next night, about nine o'clock, while I was working at the shop, Andy telephoned me and said the refrigerator was in our room. He had heard a noise while he and John were watching television, and got up to see what it was. To reach the bedroom the refrigerator had had to go through the length of the breakfast room, the den, and a hallway before reaching our room. I knew we could not move it back that night so I told Andy to just leave it alone and we would decide what to do the next day. However, a little later he called and said the washing machine, which was located in the kitchen, had been pulled away from the wall and the faucets behind it were leaking and water was running all over the floor.

"I told him to cut off the hydrants, which he did. I then called the police and asked them to meet me at the house. When we got there the holes in the two doors in the bedroom had increased to about fifteen or twenty and some of them were through both sides of the doors and big enough to put one's head through.

"Pretty soon, the house was swarming with policemen and detectives. That is when I decided to tell them as briefly as I could what we had been going through. Some of them, I am certain, thought the whole thing was a hoax, and came right out and said they thought I was being hoodwinked by John, who had enlisted Andy's help. That was absolutely ridiculous, though, as practically all of the strange happenings occurred when Andy and I were together, and while John was staying with Mack about a hundred miles away. One of the chief detectives talked a long time with John, and later told me that she talked sensibly, but that he was amazed at her lack of concern about the strange things that had happened. I too had noticed that she was wholly indifferent to the entire 'show.'

"About the middle of February 1968 things got so bad that I made John give me her key to the shop, and told her that I was going to have to do one of three things. I was going to try and have her committed to a state hospital as I was not financially able to have her take psychiatric treatments, or she could take them and pay for them herself, or I was going to get a divorce. A divorce at my age I thought was ridiculous, but I felt as if I could not stand to go on as things were. Andy was going to move with me as soon as I found a suitable place. John did not seem perturbed one way or the other, and probably did not believe I would really do any of those things. However, on February 24, I did move out of the house, and had my attorney begin divorce proceedings, since he again stated that he did not think I would have a chance in trying to have her committed. I think that when the papers were served on John

THE GHOST HUNTER'S FAVORITE CASES

it was the first time she actually realized what was happening. I got an apartment only a few blocks from my shop. I told Andy to call me every night to let me know how things were at home. I met him at a nearby shopping center each Saturday and gave him enough money to buy food for himself and John during the following week.

"For several weeks we went on this way. One night Andy called me and said that the dining table was up in the attic. The only opening to the attic was a rectangular hole in the garage ceiling about 16 by 24 inches, through which it was absolutely impossible for the table to go. The next night the table was back in the house again. This happened several times. Other things also 'went to the attic, such as a small table, an ottoman and another kidney-shaped end table. Finally, the dining table came down and Andy found it in the garage, and after considerable work was able to get it inside the house, where it belonged.

"Eventually, John was beginning to believe that the strange things we had been talking about were really happening. Previously she had just made fun of us whenever we would mention them. Several weeks after I had left, Andy was sitting in the den, playing his guitar, when the lights went out. At first he thought that a bulb had burned out, but when he looked at the switch he could see that it had been turned off. This happened several times. Once when John was going through the den the light went out and she too saw that the switch had been turned; Andy was not anywhere near it, and there was nobody else who could have done it.

"It was well into the second month after I left home. I had just finished work in the shop. The telephone rang. It was John and she sounded hysterical. She said she was very sick and begged me to come home. I got there a few minutes later, and she could hardly talk. She continued to beg me to come home, but I told her I could never spend another night in that house. Finally I got her calmed down enough to talk seriously. I finally told her that I would come back, but that first we would have to find another place to live. I demanded that she never smoke again. Finally, on April 15, 1968, we moved out of the house of horrors, and I have not been there since.

"John has not smoked since that time. It has now been over three months since we left the house, and John does the normal things about the house except cook. She is again at my rubber stamp shop and seems to enjoy it."

In retrospect, as I read over these words, I realized how difficult it must have been for Mr. Beaird to report on his experiences, especially to a stranger. What had appeared completely impossible to him would, of course, have been even more unbelievable to someone who was not present when it happened, and he doubted his own sanity at times, which was not surprising.

Having met Howard Beaird I am sure that he is completely sane, in fact, so sane he could not even be called neurotic. Had I not heard of parallel cases before, perhaps I too would have wondered about it. None of the phenomena reported by Mr. Beaird are, however, impossible in the light of parapsychological research. We are dealing here with forces that seem to be in contradiction of ordinary or orthodox physical laws, but the more we learn of the nature of matter and the structure of the atom, the more it seems likely that poltergeist activities connect with physics in such a way as to make seeming de-materialization and re-materialization of solid objects possible practically without time loss. But the case was a question of studying not so much the techniques involved in the phenomena as the reasons behind them and those causing them.

I informed Mr. Beaird that I was eager to enter the case, especially as I wanted to make sure that the poltergeist activities had really ceased once and for all and would never recur at his new location. In cases of this kind there is always the possibility that the phenomena are attached to one or the other person in the household rather than to a location. Moving to another house seems to have stopped the activities, but as there had been pauses before that culminated in renewed and even stronger physical activities, I wanted to be sure that this would not be the case in this new location. I explained that I would have to interview all those concerned, even the police detectives who had come to the house on that fateful night. Mr. Beaird assured me that he would make all the necessary arrangements, and, after discussing my plans with his wife and son, they too agreed to talk to me. Mack, her sister-in-law, who had been hostess to Mrs. Beaird while most of the phenomena took place at the house, was unable to meet me in Tyler, but I was assured that Mrs. Beaird had never left her care during all that time. For a while Howard Beaird had thought that his wife had returned without his knowledge and done some of the things about the house that had startled him. This, of course, turned out to be a false impression. At no time did Mrs. Beaird leave her sister-in-law's house in Daingerfield, 75 miles away. Whether or not her astral self visited the home is another matter and would be subject to my investigation and verification as far as possible.

Mr. Beaird also went back to his former home to talk to the present owners. Somewhat suspicious of him, for no apparent reason, they were willing to see me if I came to Tyler. Mr. M. works for a local bakery and returns home at 5:30 p.m., and since his wife would not entertain strange visitors in the absence of her husband, my visit would have to be at such an hour as was convenient to the M.'s. Perhaps the somewhat battered condition of the house when the M.'s had bought it from Mr. Beaird might be the reason for their reluctance to discuss my visit. At any rate it was agreed that I could call briefly on them and talk to them about the matter at hand. Howard Beaird's daughter, who is now Mrs. Howard Wilson, lives in Austin, Texas. She has had some interest in the occult and mind development and had suggested that someone from the Silva Mind Center in Laredo should come up to Tyler to investigate the case. That was prior to my entering the situation, however, and now Mrs. Wilson wanted very much to come up to Tyler herself and be present during my investigation. Unfortunately it turned out later that she was unable to keep the date due to prior commitments. Thorough man that he is, Howard Beaird also talked to Detective Weaver at the police station to make sure I could see him and question hin about his own investigation of the house. I was assured of the welcome mat at the police station, so I decided to set the time when I could go down to Tyler and look for myself into what appeared to be one of the most unusual cases of psychic phenomena.

On February 5, 1969, I arrived at the Tyler airport. It was 5:42 in the afternoon and Howard Beaird was there to welcome me. We had made exact plans beforehand so he whisked me away to the Blackstone Hotel, allowed me to check in quickly, then went with me to see Detective Weaver at the police station.

As we passed through town I had the opportunity to observe what Tyler, Texas, was all about. Clean shops, quiet streets, a few tree-lined avenues, small houses, many of them very old well, old—anyway in terms of the United States—and people quietly going about their business seem to be characteristic of this small town. We passed by Howard Beaird's shop, a neat, tidy shop, the company name Trumark plainly written on the window pane. As in many small towns, the telephone wires were all above ground, strung in a lazy haphazard fashion from street to street. The police station turned out to be a modern concrete building set back a little from the street. Detective Weaver readily agreed to talk to me. Howard Beaird left us for the moment in a fine sense of propriety just in case the detective wanted to say something not destined for his ears. As it turned out, there wasn't anything he could not have said in front of him. Was there anything in the detective's opinion indicating participation by either the boy or Mrs. Beaird in the strange phenomena? The detective shrugged. There was nothing he could pinpoint along those lines. He then went to the files and extricated a manila envelope inscribed "pictures and letter, reference mysterious call at——Elizabeth, February 19, 1968, 11:00 p.m., case number 67273. Officer B. Rosenstein and officer M. Garrett." Inside the envelope there were two pictures, photographs taken at the time by a police photographer named George Bain. One picture was of the door, clearly showing the extreme violence with which a hole had been punched into it. The entire rim of the hole was splintered as if extremely strong methods had been employed to punch this hole through the door.

The other picture showed a heavy chest of drawers of dark wood sitting squarely upon a bed. Quite clearly the description given to me by Howard Beaird had been correct. What exactly did the two police officers find when they arrived at the house on Elizabeth Street? The house was in disorder, the detective explained, and furniture in places where it wasn't supposed to be. On the whole he bore out the description of events given by Howard Beaird.

Somehow he made me understand that the police did not accept the supernatural origin of the phenomena even though they could not come up with anything better in the way of a solution. Almost reluctantly, the officer wondered whether perhaps Andy wasn't in some way responsible for the phenomena although he did not say so in direct words. I decided to discuss the practical theories concerning poltergeists with him and found him amazingly interested. "Would you like to have the photographs?" the detective asked and handed me the folder. Surprised by his generosity, I took the folder and I still have it in my files. It isn't very often that a researcher such as I is given the original folder from the files of a police department. But then the mystery on Elizabeth Street is no longer an active situation—or is it?

After we had thanked Detective Weaver for his courtesies we decided to pay a visit to the house itself. After a moment of hesitation, the officer suggested that he come along since it might make things easier for us. How right he was. When we arrived at the house on Elizabeth Street and cautiously approached the entrance, with me staying behind at first, there was something less than a cordial reception awaiting us. Mr. M. was fully aware of my purpose, of course, so that we were hardly surprising him with all this.

After a moment of low-key discussion at the door between Howard Beaird and Detective Weaver on one hand and Mr. M. on the other, I was permitted to enter the house and look around for myself. The M. family had come to see me, if not to greet me, and looked at me with curious eyes. I explained politely and briefly that I wanted to take some photographs for the record and I was permitted to do so. I took black and white pictures with a high sensitivity film in various areas of the house, especially the kitchen area where it connects with the garage and the living room, both places where many of the phenomena have been reported in Mr. Beaird's testimony.

On developing these, under laboratory conditions, we found there was nothing unusual except perhaps certain bright light formations in the kitchen area where there should be none since no reflective surfaces existed. Then I returned to the living room to talk briefly with Mr. M. and his family.

Was there anything unusual about the house that he had noticed since he had moved in? Almost too fast he replied, "Nothing whatsoever. Everything was just fine." When Mr. M. explained how splendid things were with the house he shot an anxious look at his wife, and I had the distinct impression they were trying to be as pleasant and superficial as possible and to get rid of me as fast as possible. Did they have any interest in occult phenomena such as ghosts? I finally asked. Mr. M. shook his head. Their religion did not allow them such considerations, he explained somewhat sternly. Then I knew the time had come to make my departure.

I made inquiries with real estate people in the area and discovered a few things about the house neither Mr. Beaird nor Mr. M. had told me. The house was thirteen years old and had been built by a certain Terry Graham. There had been two tenants before the Beairds. Prior to 1835 the area had been Indian territory and was used as a cow pasture by the Cherokee Indians.

I also discovered that Mrs. M. had complained to the authorities about footsteps in the house when there was no one walking, of doors opening by themselves, and the uncanny feeling of being watched by someone she could not see. That was shortly after the M.'s had moved into the house. The M.'s also have young children. It is conceivable that the entities who caused such problems to the Beaird family might have been able to manifest through them also. Be that as it may, the matter was not followed up. Perhaps their religious upbringing and beliefs did not permit them to discuss such matters and they preferred to ignore them, or perhaps the activities died of their own volition. At any rate, it seemed pretty certain to me that the poltergeist activities did not entirely cease with the removal of the Beairds from the house. But did these activities continue in the new house the Beairds had chosen for their own? That was a far more important question.

I asked Howard Beaird to send me a report of further activities if and when they occurred at the new house. On February 23 he communicated with me by letter. I had asked him to send me samples of John's and Andy's handwriting so that I could compare them with the notes he had let me have for further study. In order to arrive at a satisfactory explanation of the phenomena it was, of course, necessary to consider all ordinary sources for them. Amongst the explanations one would have to take into account was the possibility of either conscious or unconscious fraud, that is to say, the writing of the notes by either John or Andy and their somehow manipulating them so that they would seem to appear out of nowhere in front of Mr. Beaird. For that purpose

I needed examples of the two handwritings to compare them with some of the handwritings on the notes.

There were a number of noises in the new home that could be attributed to natural causes. But there were two separate incidents which, in the opinion of Howard Beaird, could not be so explained. Shortly before I arrived in Tyler a minor incident occurred which makes Howard wonder whether the entities from beyond the veil are still with him in the new house. One evening he had peeled two hard-boiled eggs in order to have them for lunch the following day. He had placed them in the refrigerator on a paper towel. The following morning he discovered that both eggs were frozen solid even though they were still on the lower shelf of the refrigerator. This could only have been accomplished if they had spent considerable time in the freezer compartment during the night. Questioning his wife and son as to whether they had put the eggs in the freezer, he discovered that neither of them had done so. He decided to test the occurrence by repeating the process. He found that the two new eggs which he had placed in the refrigerator that night were still only chilled but not frozen the next day. What had made the first pair of eggs as hard as stone he is unable to understand, but he is satisfied that the occurrence may be of non-psychic origin.

Then there was the matter of a clock playing a certain tune as part of its alarm clock device. Through no apparent reason this clock went off several times, even though no one had been near it. Even though it had not been wound for a long time and had only a 24-hour movement, it played this tune several times from deep inside a chest of drawers. Eventually the clock was removed, and in retrospect Mr. Beaird does not think that a supernatural situation could have been responsible for it. But the two separate incidents did frighten the Beairds somewhat. They were afraid that the change of address had not been sufficient to free them from the influences of the past. As it turned out, the move was successful and the separation complete.

I had to work with two kind of evidence. There was, first of all, the massive evidence of mysterious notes which had fallen out of the sky and which showed handwriting of various kinds. Perhaps I could make something out of that by comparing them with the handwritings of living people. Then there was the question of talking personally and in depth with the main participants, the Beairds, and, finally, to see what others who knew them had to say about them. Howard Beaird's daughter, Amy, now Mrs. Howard C. Wilson, thought that the real victim of what she thought "a circus of horrors" was her brother Andy. "If you had known Andy when he was small, up to the time mother began to show real signs of her illness, it would be impossible for you to recognize him as the same person now. He was typically, for a little boy, simply brimming over with mischievous humor. He would do anything to make people laugh and would run simply hooting with joy through the house when he had done something devilish." That was not the Andy I met when I came to Tyler. The boy I talked to was quiet, withdrawn, painfully shy, and showed definite signs of being disturbed.

The following morning I went to see the Beairds at their new home. The home itself is pleasant and small and stands in a quiet, tree-lined street. As prearranged, Mr. Beaird left me alone with each of the two other members of his family so that I could speak to them in complete confidence. Andy, a lanky boy, seemed ill at ease at first when we sat down. In order to gain his confidence, I talked about songs and the records popular at the time, since I had seen a number of record albums in his room. Somehow this helped open him up; he spoke more freely after that. Now sixteen, he was studying at a local barber college. When I wondered how a young man, in this day and age, would choose this somewhat unusual profession, he assured me that the money was good in this line of work and that he really liked it. He felt he could put his heart and soul into it. After some discussion of the future as far as Andy was concerned, I brought the conversation around to the matter at hand.

"When these peculiar events took place you and your father lived alone in the other house. Did you ever see anyone?"

"Well, I had seen a vision of my mother this one time. It looked like her but nobody was there really . . . kind of like a shadow, or a form."

"Have you seen the notes?"

"Yes."

"Did you ever actually see anyone writing them?"

"No."

"Did you ever hear any voices?"

"Yeh. I talked to them."

"How did they sound?"

"Well, the women that were here all sounded alike . . . real high voices. The men were dead, you know . . . the spirits, or whatever you want to call them. They had real deep voices. They were hard to understand."

"Did they talk to you in the room?"

"From out of nowhere. No matter where I might be."

"You didn't see them anywhere?"

"Never saw them."

"Was your father with you at the time you heard the voices or were you alone?"

"He was with me at times and not at others."

"These voices . . . are they mostly in the daytime or are they at night?"

"At night . . . mostly at night, or afternoon, when I'd get home from school."

"Did it start right after you moved in?"

"No . . . it was two or three months after . . ."

"Did you see the insects?"

"Oh yes."

"Where did they come from?"

"It seemed like just out of the ceiling."

"Could they have come in any other way?"

"They couldn't have come in . . . not that many."

"Whose voices did you hear?"

"First of all my mother's."

"The time she was away at Daingerfield?"

"Yes."

"What did the voice sound like?"

"The same high voice. It sounded a little like her."

"What did she say?"

"She started to talk about my grandfather's funeral and about some-one being mean to her."

Clearly the boy was not at his best. Whether it was my presence and the pressure the questioning was putting on him or whether he genuinely did not remember, he was somewhat uncertain about a lot of the things his father had told me about. But he was quite sure that he had heard his mother's voice at a time when she was away at Daingerfield. He was equally sure that none of the insects could have gotten into the house by ordinary means and that the notes came down, somehow of their own volition, from the ceiling. I did not wish to frighten him and thanked him for his testimony, short though it was. I then asked that John, Mrs. Beaird that is, be asked to join me in the front room so we could talk quietly. Mrs. Beaird seemed quite at ease with me and belied the rather turbulent history I knew she had had. Evidently the stay at her sister-in-law's house and the prior psychiatric treatment had done some good. Her behavior was not at all unusual; in fact, it was deceivingly normal. Having seen one of her earlier photo-graphs I realized that she had aged tremendously. Of course I realized that her husband would have discussed many of the things with her so that she would have gained secondhand knowledge of the phenomena.

Nevertheless, I felt it important to probe into them because sometimes a person thinks she is covering up while, in fact, she is giving evidence.

"Now we are going to discuss the other house," I said pleasantly. "Do you remember some of the events that happened in the other house?"

"Well, I wasn't there when they took place. They told me about it . . . and actually, you will learn more from my son than from me because I don't know anything."

"You were away all that time?"

"Yes."

"Before you went, did anything unusual happen?"

"Nothing."

"After you came back did anything happen?"

"Well, I don't know . . . I don't remember anything."

"Before you bought the house, did you have any unusual experience involving extrasensory perception at any time?"

"Never. I know nothing whatever about it."

"You were living somewhere else for a while."

"I was with my sister-in-law."

"How would you describe that period of your life? Was it an unhappy one? A confusing one? What would you say that period was?"

"I have never been unhappy. I have never been confused."

"Why did you go?"

"I felt I needed to for personal reasons."

"During that time did you have contact with your husband and son? Did you telephone or did you come back from time to time?"

"I did not come back, but I had some letters from them and I believe that I talked some . . ."

"Did your husband ever tell you some of the things that had happened in your absence?"

"Yes. He told me."

"What did you make of it?"

"I didn't understand it. If I had seen it, I'd have gotten to the bottom of it somehow."

"The people who are mentioned in some of these notes, are you familiar with them? Were there any of them that you had a personal difficulty with or grudge against?"

"None whatever. They were friends."

"Now, you are familiar with this lady, Mrs. Elliott, who has, apparently, sent some notes."

"Oh yes. She was a very good friend of mine. Of course, she is much older. She had a daughter my age and we were very good friends."

"Did you have any difficulties?"

"I have no difficulties," she replied and her eyes filled with tears. "No? You had at the time you left here."

"Not real difficulties. For several reasons, I needed a change. I didn't intend to stay so long. She was living alone and she worked during the day. And we sort of got into a most enjoyable relationship whereby I took care of certain household chores while she was gone . . ."

"What made you stay so long?"

"I just really can't tell you what it was."

"You still have no answer to the puzzle as to what happened?"

"None. I have no idea."

"Do you remember having any treatments?"

"I'm just getting old. That is the difficulty."

It was clear that her mind had blocked out all memory of the unpleasant occurrences in her life. As often happens with people who have undergone psychiatric treatment, there remains a void afterwards, even if electric shock therapy has not been used. Partially this is, of course, due to the treatment, but sometimes it is selfinduced deliberately by the patient in order to avoid discussing the unpleasant. Mrs. Beaird had returned to her husband and son to resume life and try to

make the best of it. To go back over the past would have served no purpose from her point of view. This was not a matter of refusing to discuss these things with me. She did not remember them quite consciously and no amount of probing would have helped, except perhaps
in-depth hypnosis, and I was not prepared to undertake this with a former mental patient. Clearly then I could not get any additional material from the principal. I decided to re-examine the evidence and talk
again with the one man who seemed, after all, the most reliable witness
in the entire case, Mr. Beaird himself.

In particular, I wanted to re-examine his own personal observations
of certain phenomena, for it is one thing to make a report alone, quietly, filled with the memory of what one has experienced, and another to
report on phenomena while being interrogated by a knowledgeable,
experienced investigator. Quite possibly some new aspects might be
unearthed in this fashion. At the very least it would solidify some of the
incredible things that had happened in the Beaird household.

On the morning of February 6, 1969, I met with Howard Beaird at
my hotel and we sat down, quietly, to go over the fantastic events of the
past three years. In order to arrive at some sort of conclusion, which I
wanted very much to do, I had to be sure that Mr. Beaird's powers of
observation had been completely reliable. In going over some of his
statements once again I wasn't trying to be repetitive but rather to
observe his reaction to my questions and to better determine in my own
mind whether or not he had observed correctly. In retrospect I can only
say that Howard Beaird was completely unshaken and repeated, in
essence, exactly what he had reported to me earlier. I feel that he has
been telling the truth all along, neither embellishing it nor diminishing
it. Our conversation started on a calm emotional note which was now
much more possible than at the time he first made his report to me,
when he was still under the influence of recent events. Things had been
quiet at the house and seemed to continue to remain quiet, so he was

able to gather his thoughts more clearly and speak of the past without the emotional involvement which would have made it somewhat more difficult for me to judge his veracity.

"Now we had better start at the beginning. I am interested in discussing whatever you yourself observed. Your wife was still in the house when the first thing happened?"

"Yes."

"Were those real bugs?"

"Yes."

"When you turned the light on?"

"You could see thousands of bugs on the floor."

"How did you get rid of them?"

"We had a vacuum cleaner."

"Did they come from the direction of the windows or the door?"

"The door."

"Now, after the bugs, what was the next thing that you personally observed?"

"I heard my wife's voice. After my son and I had gone to bed we were lying there talking about these things that had happened. That was after she had left Tyler."

"Did it sound like her voice?"

"No. It didn't sound like her voice to me but it was her . . ."

"Well, how did you know it was her?"

"She told me it was and was talking about my sister having insulted her. Nobody else knew that except my wife and I."

"Where did the voice seem to come from? Was it in the room?"

"Yes."

"What happened after that?"

"Several nights after that, she appeared to Andy. I heard him talking in the bathroom. He talked for two or three minutes, and then I heard him say, well, goodbye."

"Didn't it make you feel peculiar? His mother was obviously not there and he was talking to her?"

"Well, I had already had my encounter with her."

"Did you call your wife in Daingerfield?"

"No."

"Why not?"

"Well, she wouldn't have believed me. I had thought about writing her sister-in-law and telling her that you've got to keep my wife in Daingerfield. I don't want her here. Yet, I thought, that's a foolish thing to do, because all she'll say is, she wasn't here. She wasn't in person. Her body wasn't here."

"After the voice, what came next?"

"Well, it was shortly after that we started hearing these other voices."

"Did you hear those voices?"

"All of them, yes. All four." "Did they sound alike or did they sound different?"

"The men had deep rough voices, but I could tell them apart. And the ladies were all subtle voices and I couldn't tell them apart, except when they told me."

"Did you ever hear two voices at the same time?"

"I don't believe so. However, Mrs. Snow and Mrs. Elliott were there at the same time. That is, they said they were. That was when Henry Anglin was giving us so much trouble and they had to carry him back to his grave."

"Let's talk about anything that you have actually seen move."

"I saw these notes that were folded. Sometimes as many as ten or fifteen notes a day."

"From an enclosed room?"

"Well, the doors weren't closed between the rooms, but I'd be sitting at the table eating something, and all of a sudden I'd see one fall.

I'd look up toward the ceiling and there'd be one up there."

"Most of these notes were signed 'Mrs. Elliott'?"

"Yes. Later she signed them. At first, Elie and then El. Now after my wife came back from Daingerfield she, too, would send me notes through Andy. I was working in my shop and Andy would bring me a note written with numbers, in code. 1 was A, 2 was B, and so forth. I hated to take the time to decipher those things, but I would sit down and find out what they said. In one note she asked me if I didn't 'lose' some weight?"

"Did your wife ever write you a note in longhand or in block letters?"

"No."

"Was there any similarity in the writing of your wife's note and those that later came down from the ceiling?"

"I can't say, but Mrs. Elliott had been after me to lose weight. I thought it was peculiar—that my wife came from Daingerfield and asked about my losing weight also."

"Mrs. Elliot was a contemporary of your wife?"

"She died in 1963. About a year before we moved here."

"Were those two women very close in life?"

"Not particularly. They were neighbors."

"What about Mrs. Snow?"

"She was peculiar."

"What objects did you see move in person?"

"I saw a heavy pair of shoes lift themselves off the floor and fly right over my bed and land on the opposite side of the bed."

"Did they land fast or did they land slowly?"

"It was just as if I'd picked them up and thrown them. Andy's house shoes came the same way. I've watched the cat being lifted up about a foot from where he was sitting and just be suspended for several seconds and it didn't fall on the floor. I saw a can of insect spray which was sitting on the cabinet come over and suspend itself right over that open-ing, and spray into that little room, and I was nearly suffocated. I had to open the doors or the insect spray would have got me."

"You weren't holding the can?"

"No."

"I am particularly interested in anything where you were actually present when movement occurred, or voices were heard."

"I've seen my clothes fly through the air as I was coming home."

"Did these things occur whether your wife was physically in the house or not?"

"Yes."

"Did anything ever happen while neither your son nor your wife was at home but you were alone?"

"I believe so."

"You wife had some personal shock in 1951, I believe. When her best friend died suddenly. Do you feel her mental state changed as a result?"

"Very gradually, yes. She was very happy, though, when she found out she was going to have another child, because she thought this would make up for the loss of her friend. She was just crazy about him."

"Now, when was the first time you noticed there was something wrong with her mentally?"

"In 1960 my wife took over her daughter's room. She stopped up all the windows with newspapers scotch-taped against the wall and hung a blanket in each window of the bedroom."

"Why did she do that?"

"She felt someone was spying on her. At the office, she took the telephone apart, and adding machines and typewriters, looking for microphones to see who was spying on her."

"But the phenomena themselves did not start until you moved into this house?"

"That's right."

I thanked Mr. Beaird for his honest testimony, for he had not claimed anything beyond or different from his original report to me. I took the voluminous handwritten notes and the letters pertaining to the case and went back to New York to study them. This would take some time since I planned to compare the handwriting by both Mrs. Beaird and Andy. I didn't, for a moment, think that the notes had been written consciously by either one of them and simply thrown at Mr. Beaird in the ordinary way. Quite obviously Mr. Beaird was no fool, and any such clumsy attempt at fake phenomena would not have gone unnoticed, but there are other possibilities that could account for the presence of either Mrs. Beaird's or Andy's handwriting in the notes, if indeed there was that similarity.

There were already, clearly visible to me, certain parallels between this case and the Bell Witch case of Tennessee. Vengeance was being wrought on Howard Beaird by some entity or entities for alleged wrongs, in this case his failure to execute minor orders given him. But there were other elements differing greatly from the classic case. In the Bell Witch situation there was not present, in the household, anyone who could be classed as psychotic. In Tyler we have two individuals capable of supplying unused psychic energies. One definitely psychotic, the other on the borderline, or at least psychoneurotic.

I then decided to examine the notes written in this peculiar style longhand, almost always in block letters but upper case letters in the middle of words where they do not belong. It became immediately clear to me that this was a crude way of disguising his handwriting and was not used for any other reason. It is of course a fact that no one can effectively disguise his handwriting to fool the expert. He may think so, but an expert graphologist can always trace the peculiarities of a person's handwriting back to the original writer provided samples are available to compare the two handwritings letter by letter, word for word. Some of the notes were downright infantile. For instance, on December 6, 1965, a note read "My power is decreasing. I'm going back to Mack. I must hurry. I would like to come home but I don't guess I will. I love you. Please give me a Yule gift. I can't restore my power. I am allowed only three a year. Phone police." What the cryptic remark, "I am allowed only three a year," is supposed to mean is not explained.

Sometimes Howard Beaird played right into the hands of the unknown writer. The Sunday morning after he and Andy had spent the night at a motel because of the goings-on in the house, he received the notice of a package at the post office. He knew that he couldn't get it except by noon on a week day, so he asked aloud, "Is this notice about anything important, as I don't want to come in from the hospital if it doesn't amount to anything?" A few seconds later a note fluttered down from the ceiling reading only "something." That of course was not a satisfactory answer such as an adult or reasonable person would give. It sounded more like a petulant child having a game. On December 6, 1965, a note materialized equally mysteriously, reading, "I don't want to admit to Mack that I'm nutty." Another note dated December 6, 1965, simply read, "Howard got jilted." Another note read "My powers were restored by the Houston witch. Call the police and ask about her." There doesn't seem to be any great difference between the notes signed by Henry Anglin or by Mrs. Elliott or not signed at all by someone intimating that they were the work of Mrs. Beaird. The letters and the formation of the words are similar. A note dated December 8, 1965, read: "Dear Howard, I love you. I have been wrong. I want to come home but I don't want stupid Mack to know I am unusual. I am really two people. If things end I won't remember nothin'. I can be in three places at one. I love you and Junior. Please dear."

The note signed "Dorothy Kilgallen," mentioned previously and received by Howard Beaird December 22, 1965, reads, "Dear Mr. Beaird: Mrs. Elliott told me about what all has happened to your family and what Henry Anglin is responsible for. It is very tragic. He is the reason I am dead because he changed my pills. Good night and good luck." Having been personally acquainted with the late Hearst columnist Dorothy Kilgallen, I am quite certain that she would not have expressed herself in this manner, dead or alive.

A note signed Pont Thornton dated December 23, 1965, reads, "Dear Howard P.S. an Andy: I no yu well. I no yu good. I don't drinck much do yu haf had hardships. Anglin is a mean man. I am smarter than Henry Lee. I am a distant kin of Abe Lincoln and Lewis Armstrong and Sam Davis. Junior and Jon F. Kenede." Not only was the note atrociously misspelled but it lists several quite improbable relationships. When writing as Mrs. Elliott the personality is much more concise and logical than when the writer is supposed to be Henry Anglin or Mrs. Beaird. But despite the difference in style the letters are very similar. Of course since the notes came down for almost three years it is to be expected that there are some differences in both style and appearance between them.

On September 17, 1967, Howard Beaird observed, "About 9 or 10 p.m. Andy heard Mrs. Elliott call. She told him he could talk to her and that mother could not hear so he did and apparently mother knew nothing of it. Just as I was getting ready for bed I heard Mrs. Elliott calling me. The sound seemed to come toward the kitchen and as Andy and Johnny were watching TV in her bedroom I went to the kitchen. Mrs. Elliott called me several more times and the sound then seemed to be coming from my room. She said that Johnny couldn't hear me so I tried to talk to her but Andy said she told him she never could hear me. Anyway before going to bed I found a very small piece of paper folded so small on the floor in the hall and also a South Side Bank deposit slip folded near it. The small note said 'Be very generous. Say hi to me. Mrs. Snow. The larger note said, 'Don't be stingy Sam be a generous Joe. George Swiney.' After I had gone to bed I heard Mrs. Elliott calling me several times but could never make her hear me answer. Just as I was about to go to sleep, Andy came in and said Mrs. Elliott told him she had left me a note on the floor. Just as I got up to look for it a note dropped in the chair next to my bed. I took it to the kitchen to get my glasses and it said, 'Howard, I hope there won't be any slugs. Try to be generous, you have a lot of money. There's so much you could get you, John and Andy.' This was followed by a list of objects, clothing primarily, which he could get for his family on her suggestion. Howard Beaird tried to talk to Mrs. Elliott to ask her where all that alleged money was but he could never get an answer to that.

On September 29, 1967, Howard Beaird noticed that Mrs. Elliott came to visit him around 7:30 p.m. He can't understand how she can make him hear her when she calls him by name and then make it impossible for him to hear the rest of her. Apparently the rest of the conversation has to be relayed through Andy. On the other hand, if he speaks loudly enough she can hear him. That night Mrs. Elliott informed him that a Mr. Quinn had been by earlier. A little later Mr. Quinn himself came back and Howard Beaird actually heard him call, but he could hear nothing else, and again Andy had to be the interpreter. Andy said that Mr. Quinn sounded like a robot talking, and that, of course, made sense to Mr. Beaird, since he knew that Quinn, who had lost his voice due to cancer prior to his death, used an instrument held to his throat to enable him to talk. The late Mr. Quinn apparently wanted to know how some of the people back in Grand Saline were, including a Mrs. Drake, Mr. and Mrs. Watkins, and the McMullens. This information, of course, could not have been known to Andy, who had been much too young at the time the Beairds knew these people in the town where they formerly lived.

Mrs. Elliott also explained the reason she and the other spirits were able to be with Mr. Beaird that evening was that they had been given time off for the holidays—because of Halloween, although that was a little early for All Hallow's Eve. Mr. Beaird thought it peculiar that spirits get furloughs from whatever place they are in.

On September 30, 1967, Beaird had heard nothing at all from Mrs. Elliott during the day. Andy had been out pretty late that night and Mr. Beaird was asleep when he came in. Sometime after, Andy woke him and said that Mrs. Elliott had left him a note. They found it on his bed. It read, "Howard, think about what I said. Are you going to do it Monday. Elliott." Just below it was a note reading, "John wants a vacuum cleaner and a purse. Junior wants a coat for school and some banjo strings. Hiram." Now the remarkable thing about this note is that the first part was definitely in the handwriting of Mrs. Beaird, while the second part was a crude note put together with a lot of capital letters where they did not belong and generally disorganized. Hiram Quinn, the alleged writer, was of course a very sick man for some time prior to his passing. When Howard Beaird confronted the alleged Mrs. Elliott with the fact that her note was written in the handwriting of his wife, she shrugged it off by explaining that she could write like anybody she wished.

On October 2, 1967, Mr. Beaird noted, "About 7:30 p.m. Mrs. Snow called my name. I was in the kitchen and the voice seemed to come from the back part of the house where Andy and John were. The voice sounded exactly like Mrs. Elliott's and although I could hear it plainly enough and answered aloud immediately I could hear nothing else and Andy had to tell me what she had said. She just wanted to tell me about my stamp business and how John had been. She barely could hear me and told Andy to turn off the attic fan and for me to go into my room and close the door so she could hear. She couldn't explain how I could hear her call my name and then hear nothing more and said it was some kind of 'law.'"

The notes signed by Mrs. Elliott from that period onward frequently looked as if they had been written by Mrs. Beaird. The handwriting is unquestionably hers. That is to say it looks like hers. Howard Beaird does not doubt that the notes were genuinely materialized in a psychic sense. On October 23 he had dozed off to sleep several times and on one occasion was awakened by the rustling of papers on the floor beside his bed. He was alone in the room at the time. He turned the light on and found a sort of pornographic magazine folded up on the floor. Andy came in at this point and explained that Mrs. Elliott had told him she had found this magazine in Mrs. Beaird's room. She said that Mrs. Beaird had gotten it at the beauty shop and the piece of paper was torn from it. On the note was printed "Somebody loves you," signed underneath, El.

On November 12, 1967, a Sunday, Howard Beaird heard Mrs. Elliott talk to him. She advised him that he should go to Mrs. Beaird's room and look for some nudist pictures and also some hand-drawn pictures of naked men and women. Mr. Beaird found all these things but his wife denied any knowledge of them. The following night, November 13, 1967, was particularly remarkable in the kind of phenomena experienced by Howard Beaird. "Mrs. Elliott came by before I left for the shop and told me to look for some more lewd pictures. I found some and destroyed them. Mrs. Elliott told me to be sure and tear them up in front of John and maybe she would quit drawing them, and also quit buying the nudist magazine pictures. Later that night, about 9:15, Mrs. Elliott called me on the telephone. That's the first time I ever talked to a ghost on the telephone. I could understand what she said on the phone, yet I could never hear anything except her calling my name when I was at home. Of course all she said on the phone was to come home. I then talked to Andy and he said she wanted me to come home right then and get some more drawings and nudist magazines from John's hiding places. I did go home and got the pictures and went back to the shop after I had destroyed them."

Some of the notes showed the underlying conflict, imagined or real, between the young boy and his father which was of much concern to "guardian angel" Mrs. Elliott. On January 11, 1968, a note read, "Howard, I need to write you notes. Junior has had to worry so much. Why do you mind him coming with me? He would be happy. It would be right for him not to worry. I agree he must get an education but at seventeen he could get a course and then to college. In the meantime I will help John and him. He could play music and he would be great at seventeen. He would also like to take care of the house. John would get so much better. You would be better financially and Junior could get better. This is the only thing I will allow or I will take him with me if he wants to . . . He said he would tell me to go and wouldn't go but that wouldn't change him from wanting to. You had better pay attention cause he wants to come. I have all the divine right to take him. El." This threat by the spirit of Mrs. Elliott to take the young boy with her into the spirit world did not sit lightly with his father, of course. Analyzed on its face value, it has the ring of a petulant threat a retarded youngster would make against his parents if he didn't get his way. If Mrs. Elliott was the spirit of a mature and rational person then this kind of threat didn't seem, to me, to be in character with the personality of the alleged Mrs. Elliott.

The following night, January 12, 1968, the communicator wrote, "Howard, I have the divine right. I will prove it by taking Junior and I take him tonight. You don't love him at all. You don't care about anyone." Mrs. Elliott had not taken Andy by January 15, but she let Howard know that she might do so anyway any time now. In fact, her notes sounded more and more like a spokesman for Andy if he wanted to complain about life at home but didn't have the courage to say so consciously and openly. On January 18, Mrs. Elliott decided she wasn't going to take the boy after all. She had promised several times before that she would not come back any longer and that her appearance was the last one. But she always broke this pledge.

By now any orthodox psychologist or even parapsychologist would assume that the young man was materially involved not only in the composition of the notes but in actually writing them. I don't like to jump to conclusions needlessly, especially not when a prejudice concerning the method of communication would clearly be involved in assuming that the young man did the actual writing. But I decided to continue examining each and every word and to see whether the letters or the words themselves gave me any clue as to what human hand had actually written them, if any. It appeared clear to me by now that some if not all of the notes purporting to be the work of Mrs. Elliott were in the hand of Mrs. Beaird. But it was not a very good copy of her handwriting. Rather did it seem to me that someone had attempted to write in Mrs. Beaird's hand who wasn't actually Mrs. Beaird. As for the other notes, those signed by Henry Anglin, Hiram Quinn and those unsigned but seemingly the work of Mrs. Beaird herself, they had certain common denominators amongst them. I had asked Mr. Beaird to supply me with adequate examples of the handwriting of both Andy and Mrs. Beaird. That is to say, handwritten notes not connected in any way with the psychic phenomena at the house. I then studied these examples and compared them with the notes which allegedly came from nowhere or which materialized by falling from the ceiling in front of a very astonished Mr. Beaird.

I singled out the following letters as being characteristic of the writer, whoever he or she may be. The capital letter T, the lower case e, lower case p, g, y, r, and capital B, C, L, and the figure 9. All of these appeared in a number of notes. They also appear in the sample of Andy's handwriting, in this case a list of song titles which he liked and which he was apparently going to learn on his guitar. There is no doubt in my mind that the letters in the psychic notes and the letters on Andy's song list are identical. That is to say that they were written by the same hand. By that I do not mean to say, necessarily, that Andy wrote the notes. I do say, however, that the hand used to create the psychic notes is the same hand used consciously by Andy Beaird when writing notes of his own. I am less sure, but suspect, that even the notes seemingly in the handwriting of his mother are also done in the same fashion and also traceable to Andy Beaird.

On December 7, 1965, one of the few drawings in the stack of notes appeared. It showed a man in a barber chair and read, among other annotations, "Aren't the barbers sweet, ha ha." It should be remembered that Andy's great ambition in life was to be a barber. In fact, when I met and interviewed him he was going to barber school.

What then is the meaning of all this? Let us not jump to conclusions and say Andy Beaird wrote the notes somehow unobserved, smuggled them into Mr. Beaird's room somehow unnoticed, and made them fall from the ceiling seemingly by their own volition, somehow without Mr. Beaird noticing this. In a number of reported instances this is a possibility, but in the majority of cases it simply couldn't have happened in this manner, not unless Howard Beaird was not a rational individual and was, in fact, telling me lies. I have no doubt that Mr. Beaird is telling me the truth and that he is a keen and rational observer. Consequently the burden of truth for the validity of the phenomena does not rest on his gift of observation, but on the possibility of producing such paranormal occurrences despite their seeming improbability yet reconciling this with the ominous fact that they show strong indications of being Andy Beaird's handwriting.

We must recognize the tension existing for many years in the Beaird household, the unhappy condition in which young Andy found himself as he grew up, and the fact that for a number of years he was an introspected and suppressed human being unable to relate properly to the outside world and forced to find stimulation where he could. Under such conditions certain forces within a young person can be exteriorized and become almost independent of the person himself. Since these forces are part of the unconscious in the person and therefore not subject to the logical controls of the conscious mind, they are, in fact, childish and frequently irrational. They are easily angered and easily appeased and, in general, behave in an infantile fashion. By the same token these split-off parts of personality are capable of performing physical feats, moving objects, materializing things out of nowhere and, in general, contravening the ordinary laws of science. This we know already because cases of poltergeists have occurred with reasonable frequency in many parts of the world. In the case of the Beaird family, however, we have two other circumstances which must be taken into account. The first is the presence in the house of not one but two emotionally unstable individuals. Mrs. Beaird's increasing divorce from reality, leading to a state of schizophrenia, must have freed some powerful forces within her. Her seemingly unconscious preoccupation with some aspects of sex indicates a degree of frustration on her part yet an inability to do anything about it at the conscious level. We have long recognized that the power supply used to perform psychic phenomena is the same power inherent in the life force or the sexual drive in man, and when this force is not used in the ordinary way it can be diverted to the supernormal expression, which in this case took the form of poltergeist phenomena. We have, therefore, in the Beaird case, a tremendous reservoir of untapped psychic energy subject to very little conscious control on the part of the two individuals in whose bodies these energies were stored and developed.

Were the entities purporting to use these facilities to express themselves beyond the grave actually the people who had once lived and died in the community? Were they, in fact, who they claimed to be, or were they simply being re-enacted unconsciously perhaps by the split-off part of the personalities of both Andy and Mrs. Beaird? Since Howard Beaird has examined the signature of one of those entities, at least, and found it to be closely similar, if not identical, with the signature of the person while alive, and since, in that particular case, access to the signature was not possible to either Andy or Mrs. Beaird, I'm inclined to believe that actual nonphysical entities were, in fact, using the untapped energies of these two unfortunate individuals to express themselves in the physical world. Additional evidence, I think, would be the fact that in several cases the names and certain details concerning the personalities of several individuals whom Howard Beaird knew in their former residence in Grand Saline were not known or accessible to either his wife or the young man. I am not fully satisfied that there could not have been some form of collusion between Andy and these so-called spirit entities in creating the phenomena, but if there was such collusion it was on the unconscious level. It is my view that Andy's unexpressed frustrations and desires were picked up by some of these discarnate entities and mingled with their own desire to continue involving themselves in earth conditions and thus became the driving force in making the manifestations possible.

What about the fact that Andy Beaird's handwriting appears in the majority of the notes? If Andy did not write these notes physically himself, could they have been produced in some other manner? There is no doubt in my mind that in at least a large percentage of the notes Andy could not have written them physically and dropped them in front of his father without Mr. Beaird noticing it. Yet, these very same notes also bear unmistakable signs that they are the work of Andy Beaird's hand. Therefore the only plausible solution is to assume that a spiritual part of Andy's body was used to create the notes in the same way in which seemingly solid objects have, at times, been materialized and dematerialized. This is known as a "physical" phenomenon and it is not entirely restricted to poltergeist cases but has, on occasion, been observed with solid objects which were moved from one place to another, or which appeared at a place seemingly out of nowhere, or disappeared from a place without leaving any trace. The phenomenon is not unique nor particularly new. What is unique, or nearly so in the case of the Beaird family of Tyler, Texas, is the fact that here the obvious is not the most likely explanation. I do not think Andy Beaird wrote those notes consciously. I do believe that his writing ability was used by the entities expressing themselves through him. I believe that Andy was telling the truth when he said he was surprised by the appearance of the notes and at no time did he have knowledge of their contents except when one of the other spirit entities informed him about them. The same applies, of course, to Mrs. Beaird. In the phenomenon known as automatic writing, the hand of a living person, normally a fully rational and conscious individual, is used to express the views, memories and frequently the style of writing of a dead individual. The notes which fluttered down from the ceiling at the Beaird home are not of the same kind. Here the paper had first to be taken from one place and impressed with pencil writing in the hand of another person before the note itself could be materialized in plain view of witnesses. This is far more complex than merely impressing the muscular apparatus of a human being to write certain words in a certain way.

Why then did the phenomena cease when the Beairds moved from one house to another if the entities expressing themselves through Andy and Mrs. Beaird had not found satisfaction? There was no need for them to simply leave off just because the Beairds moved from one house to the other. There must have been something in the atmosphere of the first house that in combination with the untapped psychic energies of Andy and Mrs. Beaird provided a fertile ground for the phenomena.

Apparently some disturbances have continued in the former Beaird home, while none have been reported by them in their new house. The current owners of the old Beaird home, however, refused to discuss such matters as psychic phenomena in the house. They are fully convinced that their fundamentalist religion will allow them to take care of these occurrences. To them psychic phenomena are all the work of the devil.

And so the devil in Tyler, Texas, may yet erupt once again to engulf a family, if not an entire community, with the strange and frightening goings-on which, for three years, have plagued the Beaird family to the point of emotional and physical exhaustion. The Beairds themselves are out of danger. Andy has grown up and his untapped powers will unquestionably be used in more constructive channels as the years go by. Mrs. Beaird has assumed her rightful position in her husband's house and has closed the door on her unhappy past. Howard Beaird, the main victim of all the terrible goings on between 1965 and 1968, is satisfied that they are nothing now but memories. He has no desire to bring them back. His sole interest in my publishing an account of these incredible happenings was to inform the public and to help those who might have similar experiences.

Midwest

Oklahoma

I am indebted to a young lady by the name of Lori Buzza for the verified account of a friend who has been psychic from her early years onward. The girl's name is Penny McDaniel. Today she has come to terms with her ESP faculty and is no longer frightened by it. She is able to foretell when a telephone might ring and has, on occasion, done trance work in which personalities of the deceased have come through her. But in 1965 when she was in her early teens something happened that really frightened her, when she visited her grandmother in an area of Oklahoma that was Indian territory. Part of the present-day house is built over a spot where there was once an old log cabin. One of the rooms of the house is in fact built on the exact foundations of that non-existent cabin.

There were other guests besides her parents and Penny, so the question of where each was to sleep came up and caused some problems. The grandmother tried to fix the young girl a cot in the living room, but Penny insisted that that was perfectly ridiculous since there seemed to be a very nice bedroom not being used by anyone. After an embarrassing silence her grandmother explained that the bedroom Penny was referring to would not be available to her either. Why not, Penny wanted to know. Because, explained her grandmother, somewhat uneasily, people had been hearing strange noises and seeing inexplicable things in that room and it had been finally closed off and no one had entered it for years. Nonsense, Penny decided. She was not afraid of such things as haunted rooms. There was no such thing as ghosts and if the others were too scared to sleep in the closed-off room, she certainly wasn't. Finally her grandmother shrugged and gave her the key to the room. No one wanted to come along with her to help her make up the bed, so Penny went on her own. When she stuck the key into the lock and opened the door she was greeted by musty air. Evidently the room had not been aired out or entered for many years. Everything was covered with thick dust, but the hour was late and Penny was not in the mood to clean up. All she did was make up the bed and go to sleep, not touching anything else.

It must have been the middle of the night when she awoke with a jolt. She had a feeling of a presence in the room. She looked around and at the foot of her bed stood a woman dressed in pioneer clothes. Her figure was completely white and as Penny looked at her she seemed to fade away slowly. Penny decided she was dreaming and started to turn over and go back to sleep. A moment later when she was still not fully asleep she heard sounds by the side of her bed. It sounded as if some animal were passing by. She turned and to her horror saw the perfect imprints of a dog's forepaws on the side of the bed. At this point she screamed. Her mother came rushing in and turned on the lights. At the side of the bed there were paw prints in the dust on the floor and not far away from the paw prints, at the foot of the bed, were a set of woman's footprints.

After this Penny did not sleep for the rest of the night. She sat up in the living room waiting for daybreak. Her mother had in the meantime gone back to sleep, assuming that Penny would be all right away from the haunted room. It was around six o'clock in the morning when Penny had a strong impulse to get up and walk out of the house. As if driven by an unseen force she found herself walking in the yard, turning around the back of the house and directing her steps to a spot directly under the windows of the very bedroom she had slept in earlier that night. As she looked down on the ground she discovered the skeleton of a hand and a foot and scraps of scalp placed there in a perfect triangle. Looking at what she instantly knew were human remains, she screamed for her mother and then passed out. It was not until three days later that she came to in a local hospital. As soon as she had recovered her wits, Penny, her brother Tom, and Mrs. McDaniel, the mother, joined forces to investigate the occurrence. Digging into local historical records, they discovered that there had been ample reason for the frightening event to take place.

Back during pioneer days a log cabin had stood on the spot where the haunted room was later built. In it lived a family consisting of a husband, a wife, and a sheepdog. There were no neighbors directly nearby so no one is sure exactly when the tragedy happened. One day the nearest neighbors, some distance away, saw smoke rising from the homestead and decided to investigate. On approaching the house they discovered that the cabin had been burned by Indians and all the family killed, including the dog. The bodies were all burned except the woman's. It was already late in the day and the neighbors decided not to brave the Indians they assumed were still lurking around the area and returned to their own homes. The next morning they returned to bury the family. It was then that they discovered that the Indians had apparently returned during the night and had cut off the woman's right hand and foot and had also scalped her. As they were searching through the rubble of the cabin they discovered the missing hand and foot and scalp placed in a triangle beneath where two windows of the log cabin had been in back of the house. They had been placed there in some sort of ritual.

Arkansas

Hollygrove is only a small town in eastern Arkansas, but to Sharon Inebnit it is the center of her world. She lives there with her farmer husband in quiet rural Arkansas far from metropolitan centers. Little Rock is a long way off and not a place one is likely to visit often. Her mother lives in Helena close to the Mississippi state line. Traveling east on Highway 86 and then on 49 Sharon has gone back and forth a few times in her young life. She knows the area well. It is not an area of particular merit but it has one advantage: it's very quiet. About halfway between Hollygrove and Helena stands an old house that attracted Sharon every time she passed it. There was no reason for it, and yet whenever she passed the old house something within her wondered what the house's secret was.

Sharon is now in her early twenties. She has lived with an extraordinary gift of ESP since infancy. That is a subject one doesn't discuss freely in her part of the world. People either ridicule you or, worse, think you're in league with the devil. So Sharon managed to keep her powers to herself even though at times she couldn't help surprising people. She would often hear voices of people who weren't even within sight. If she wanted someone to call her, all she had to do was visualize the person and, presto, the person would ring her. Whenever the telephone rings she knows exactly who is calling. Frequently she has heard her neighbors talking 500 yards from her house, yet she is so sensitive she cannot stand the television when it is turned on too loud.

Her husband, a farmer of Swiss extraction, is somewhat skeptical of her powers. He is less skeptical now than he was when he first met her. Back in the summer of 1963 when she and her present husband first kept company she was already somewhat of a puzzle to him. One day, the fifteen-year-old girl insisted they drive into Helena, which was about five miles from where they were then. Her boyfriend wanted to know why. She insisted that there was a baseball game going on and that a private swimming party was in progress at the municipal pool. She had no reason to make this statement, however, nor any proof that it was correct, but they were both very much interested in baseball games, so her boyfriend humored her and decided to drive on to Helena. When they arrived at Helena they found that a baseball game was indeed going on and that a private swimming party was in progress at the municipal pool just as Sharon had said. Helena has a population of over 10,000 people. Sharon lives 25 miles away. How could she have known this?

In March of 1964 her maternal grandmother passed away. She had been close to her but for some reason was unable to see her in her last moments. Thus the death hit her hard and she felt great remorse at not having seen her grandmother prior to her passing. On the day of the funeral she was compelled to look up, and there before her appeared her late grandmother. Smiling at her, she nodded and then vanished. But in the brief moment when she had become visible to Sharon the girl understood what her grandmother wanted her to know. The message was brief. Her grandmother understood why she had not been able to see her in her last hours and wanted to forgive her.

In April of 1964 when she was just sixteen years old she married her present husband. They went to Memphis, Tennessee, for four days. All during their honeymoon Sharon insisted on returning home. She felt something was wrong at home, even though she couldn't pinpoint it. Though it wasn't a hot period of the year she felt extremely warm and very uncomfortable. Eventually her husband gave in to her urgings and returned home with her. Assuming that her psychic feelings concerned an accident they might have on the road, she insisted that they drive very carefully and slowly. There was no accident. However, when they entered the driveway of her home she found out what it was she felt all that distance away. A large fertilizer truck had hit a gasoline truck in front of her mother's house. A tremendous fire had ensued, almost setting her mother's house on fire. The blaze could be seen clearly in towns over 5 miles away. Both trucks burned up completely. It was the heat from the fire she had felt all the way to Memphis, Tennessee.

The house outside of Hollygrove, however, kept on calling her and somehow she didn't forget. Whenever she had a chance to drive by it she took it, looking at the house and wondering what its secret was. On one such occasion it seemed to her that she heard *someone play a piano inside the vacant house.* But that couldn't very well be; she knew that there was no one living inside. Perhaps there were mice jumping up and down the keyboard, if indeed there was a piano inside the house. She shook her head, dismissing the matter. Perhaps she had only imagined it. But somehow the sound of songs being played on an old piano kept on reverberating in her mind. She decided to do some research on the house.

Tom Kameron runs an antique shop in Hollygrove, and since the old house was likely to be filled with antiques he would be the man to question about it. That at least was Sharon's opinion. She entered the shop pretending to browse around for antiques. A lady clerk came over and pointed at an old lamp. "I want to show you something that you'll be interested in," she said. "This came from the old Mulls house here." Sharon was thunderstruck. The Mulls house was the house she was interested in. She began to question the clerk about the antiques in the Mulls house. Apparently a lot of them had been stolen or had disappeared during the last few years. Since then a caretaker had been appointed who guarded the house. At this point the owner of the shop,

Tom Kameron, joined the conversation. From him Sharon learned that the house had belonged to Tom Mulls, who had passed away, but Mrs. Mulls, although very aged, was still alive and living in a sanitarium in Little Rock. Kameron himself had been a friend of the late owners for many years.

The house had been built by a Captain Mulls who had passed away around 1935. It was originally built in St. Augustine, Florida, and was later moved to Hollygrove.

The captain wasn't married, yet there was a woman with him in the house when it stood in Hollygrove. This was an Indian girl he had befriended and who lived with him until her death. The man who later inherited the house, Tom Mulls, was an adopted son. Apparently Captain Mulls was very much in love with his Indian lady. After her death he had her body embalmed and placed in a glass casket which he kept in a room in the house. It stayed there until he died, and when Tom took over the house he buried the casket in the cemetery not far away. Her grave still exists in that cemetery. There were many Indian relics and papers dealing with Indian folklore in the house during her lifetime, but they have all disappeared since. The Indian girl played the piano very well indeed, and it was for her that the captain had bought a very fine piano. Many times he would sit listening to her as she played song after song for his entertainment.

The house has been vacant for many years but people can't help visiting it even though it is locked. They go up to the front steps and peer in the windows. Sharon was relieved to hear that she was not the only one strangely attracted to the old house. Others have also been "called" by the house as if someone inside were beckoning to them. Over the years strangers who have passed by the house have come to Mr. Kameron with strange tales of music emanating from the empty house. What people have heard wasn't the rustling of mice scurrying over a ruined piano keyboard but definite tunes, song after song played by skilled hands. Eventually the house will pass into the hands of the state since Mrs. Mulls has no heirs. But Sharon doubts that the ghost will move out just because the house changes hands again. She feels her presence, very much alive and wholly content to live on in the old house. True, she now plays to a different kind of audience than she did when Captain Mulls was still alive, but then it is just possible that the captain has decided to stay behind also if only to listen to the songs his Indian lady continues to play for his entertainment.

Call of the Midwest

Somehow the idea of ghosts and haunted houses in the prosaic Middle West does not quite fit. Ghosts, one thinks, belong in English castles and, at best, New England mansions. But the Midwest—really!

Nevertheless, there was and is a steady stream of letters, phone calls, even visitors, from the golden wheat belt known as the heart of the country.

Corn has nothing to do with it, either. People who have psychic experiences in Dubuque and Oshkosh are not necessarily what New Yorkers so ungallantly refer to as "hicks." Possessors of some of the finest and most perceptive minds were born and raised in the middle portions of our country.

After my Art Linkletter appearance, a veritable avalanche of reports reached me. People who wanted my book, and many others who just wanted to tell me of *their* ghosts.

A girl named Joyce Soule wrote me from Jackson, Michigan, that she frequently felt an unseen presence and heard strange noises; a lady by the name of Mrs. Josephine Younker once lived in a haunted house in Salt Lake City where she saw the apparition of a man who had been killed in the very room she was in; Mrs. Sandra Stover of Wichita, Kansas, told me of her mother whose ghost she had encountered on more than one occasion; some of the letters are genuinely moving and have about them the touch of sincerity and genuineness. Naturally, I investigate each case thoroughly before coming to any final conclusions.

There were also letters of little value, or cases of troubled souls more in need of a good psychiatrist than a parapsychologist. But these were surprisingly few. Then, too, there are letters of almost comical simplicity.

Anthony Klimas of Chicago, Illinois, complained that he had "rapping in my house and pounding at ceiling, knocking at door, calling by name."

Perhaps most typical of most of the letters I received was the almost subdued way in which Mrs. Mathilda Alter, of Decatur, Illinois, wrote of *her* haunted house:

> When I was a child, my mother and five of us children moved to Missouri, just nine miles from Lamar, Missouri, President Truman's home town. Right in Lamar there was a house where no one could lock the doors shut to stay or windows closed. People were afraid of this house and nobody would even move in it.
>
> The house we moved into was claimed to be a haunted house. One evening we were all sitting in the kitchen by the fire of our coal-range, at twilight and no lamps lighted to give any light other than twilight. A "window" came on the wall on the same side of the house as at the front, where it could not be anyone walking by with a lantern.
>
> This shadow went around and appeared on all the four walls of our kitchen. Our big brothers went outside to see what it was and there was nothing to see. Then we slept upstairs and many nights there would be a rustling noise of heatherbloom petticoats go by our beds from the boys' room through our room to the head of the stairways and then the noise would fade away.
>
> Never did know what that was all about. Then one afternoon my older sister and my mother were in the kitchen sewing

and some great big noise hit the floor of the boys' room over the kitchen and sounded like something fell over like a dresser or wardrobe. My mother and sister hurried upstairs to see what the noise could be and everything was in place. Nothing out of the way.

Then one night my oldest brother went up to bed early in the evening and after he had been in bed around an hour, a sound came through to the kitchen from the floor of his bedroom, sounding like someone scooting a kitchen chair back and forth across the bedroom floor. Well, there was no chair in his room, and there also was a carpet from wall to wall on the floor, so we knew it wasn't my brother up in his sleep, but mother checked by going up to see if she could see anything.

Nothing to be seen.

Then when school began my youngest brother and I used to study at the kitchen table and my mother and sister went to the corn crib to shell corn for the chickens' next morning breakfast. While they were down there, my brother and I heard a noise in the stairway like someone coming downstairs using a cane to help him walk.

I picked up the lamp and my brother and I went to the turn in the stairs and there stood the image of an old long-whiskered man with a cane in his hand which very muchly scared us, for I was eight and my brother was eleven years old, and the old man looking at us!

We hurriedly ran back down our few steps and ran to the corn crib to tell Mom and my sister, screaming as we went. My mother hurried to the house to see what the old man looked like, but he had vanished away.

Mother told our neighbor who had told us to expect these things and they told mother and my older brothers that an old peddler had been murdered in the room that my older brothers slept in and his body was put in the attic and his peddler pack was found by the creek that was back of our place, and some of his clothes, too.

We lived there two years but we finally gave up and moved away from there shortly after the last episode.

P.S. I meant to tell you also that a large blood stain was on the floor of the bedroom that was as much as three feet in diameter either way, which was the spot where the murder was performed. We never did find out what happened to the people who did the thing, that lived in this house, but we put a rag carpet down wall to wall on the floor to cover the stain and *that is* where these strange noises started from all the time.

I hope I have not bored you with my story but I am telling you the truth of things that happened there.

No, she had not bored me at all. Giving precise and unemotional testimony, she had told a story which has many parallels in many parts of the world.

Mrs. Harold Schulte of Elkader, Iowa, writes:

I have had several experiences of this nature. I saw the apparition of a woman as I drove up to a junction stop sign on a pitch-black night at 3:00 o'clock in the morning. She was walking along the highway shoulder directly opposite a country cemetery, and I knew at once what it was.

I drove on to another junction about 200 feet and turned my car around and drove back and she still walked on, not seeing me at all. I saw her twice in the full glare of the headlights of my car. This was the most striking experience I've had, although I have had others. All of which makes me wonder if I could be psychic, too, as some others are.

Mrs. Schulte need not wonder. Only a mediumistic person could have seen a ghost. Although, contrary to popular superstition, cemeteries are usually bare of ghosts, there is always the possibility that a person confused by death might find herself in a grave for which she had not been ready, and her first and strongest thought would be to "walk away" from it immediately.

The interest in things psychic is deeply rooted in the American population, far more deeply than one might suspect on the surface.

From Independence, Missouri, comes this cheerful note:

We have decided to write to you. There is three of us. We started with a meditation group. One day while sitting at the table, two of us saw a spirit of a man; we saw enough to know it was the full form of a man, about 6 feet tall. We could distinguish some features but not all of them.

At another time we saw the spirit of a woman about 5 feet tall. We could distinguish her features also. Both times these spirits vanished without speaking. We have felt cool breezes and smelled strange odors. We have seen streaks of silver light in a darkened room.

We are three housewives and know very little about this. Mrs. Donna Johnson, Mrs. Edith Tate, Mrs. Marie Worth.

Thanks to Gene Lundholm of California, a student of the occult, I heard of a haunted house in Superior, Wisconsin. The witness is a professional nurse of high standing in the community. Here is her statement:

We moved into this house in the year 1909. We were renting from the church, which had used it as a parsonage. We noticed that upstairs, in the back storeroom, there was a peculiar odor. Dad took up the floor thinking there might be dead mice or rats under the floor. My sister had scrubbed the floor with hylex, etc., thinking something might have been spilled.

We found nothing and could never explain the phenomena.

One night, when Mother was in bed in the room next to it, a man entered and stood at the foot of the bed staring at her. She was very frightened. The minister's wife had told Mama that it was a "bad house," but did not tell why. Mother never told us about this until we were grown. A man named William Penn had once lived in it. His daughter was supposed to have looked exactly like me. Mother said that the apparition had just disappeared into thin air after a while.

One night when we kids were sitting at the kitchen table, we heard someone coming down the stairs, slowly. The doorknob turned and the door started to open. We ran out of the house and down the street and met the folks who had been at church.

Later on, after we moved, the house was sold to the hospital for a nurse's training home. I happened to tell one of the girls who trained there that we had lived there. She said she had been expelled from the school of nursing because the authorities said she had been drunk when she reported having seen a man in this particular room when she came home.

Frequently we heard footsteps on all the stairways: from upstairs down and down the basement. Tappings on the windows were explained by Mother as being branches blowing against the window. However, the trees were not close enough to touch the house.

Hildur Lundholm.

Mrs. Charles E. Wofford, of St. Louis, Missouri, has a great deal of American Indian blood.

My grandmother (who raised me) was Cherokee Indian and Irish, and she used to call it "Second Sight." I loved her, but must admit she was a bit overwhelming to live with. We'd had a silly quarrel. She died and I'd not had a chance to make my apology. The night after the funeral I was awakened to see her standing at the foot of my bed. I said "Mama, what are you doing here?—you are dead!" She smiled. I wept. "Oh, I am so sorry. I didn't mean what I said. I loved you so much."

"I know you did, honey, now don't grieve about it any longer. I loved you, too." And with that, she was gone. To this day I believe I truly saw her, but who can prove it was no more than an unusually clear and vivid dream? I think a part of her still remains in that house. Now and then one could hear sounds of footsteps going back and forth upstairs and the sound of furniture being moved about. But no one ever heard it but my mother, me, and mother's two dogs who would simply have fits about it.

Mrs. Wofford has had many bouts with the psychic, ranging all the way from apparitions to premonitions. On nine separate occasions, she foretold when someone was about to die or had died.

I did know that my stepfather was going to die in an accident. I was talking to his wife on the phone. The thought went through my head, "Pop is going to die in an accident." I glanced at the clock. It was 5:15 P.M. At 5:20 P.M., my phone went completely haywire and was out of service until 9:00 P.M. It rang at nine—it was one of Pop's friends. . . .

"I have bad news for you, Dot."

"Pop was killed in an accident at five fifteen, wasn't he?"

"Yes! How in the name of God did you know?"

"I don't know how I knew. . . . I just did."

"Did someone tell you?"

"No. The thought came to me at that time. I'd been sitting here all evening waiting for your call."

The people who write to me of their psychic experiences are by no means spinsters and old people vaguely remembering bygone days. Candy Bosselmann of Fort Wayne, Indiana, is seventeen. She writes:

I have a natural gift, but it's not completely developed yet. Our family has always had this. My mother is very psychic and hears knocks on the door or tapping at the window as if done by nails before someone's death. I received a premonition when my grandmother passed away. I heard her scream when she was halfway across town, and smelled flowers in the house three days after she was buried. Every once in a while, someone follows me downstairs. . . .

Clifford Steele of Indianapolis, Indiana, is even younger. Now sixteen years of age, this bright, almost precocious youngster came to see me with his mother on my last visit to Indianapolis.

"I knew of my father's death at the time it happened some five miles away in our family car," he said by way of introduction. "Mrs. Ruby Wann, who was present, can attest to this."

Evidently, young Clifford has various forms of psychic abilities. "When President Kennedy was elected to office," he said quietly, "I told mother he'd be assassinated in office." Mrs. Steele nodded agreement. This was in 1960, she added, and horrified her no end. When Clifford was only four years old, he complained of seeing a "white shape" no one else was able to observe.

In 1962, the family lived at Belmont, Ohio, in a house that had been the property and home of one John Frawley for many years. Against the oldster's will, he was removed from his Third Street house by his family and placed in a nursing home, where he eventually died. That he was most unhappy there can be seen from the fact that despite his advanced age and poor condition he once walked away from the home.

Soon after Mrs. Steele and her young son had moved into the house, they noticed a "presence." Bric-a-brac was found crushed when no one was in the house who could have done it, and doors opened at night from the inside. Mr. Frawley had never really left, it would appear.

At another house the Steeles occupied after that, in Indianapolis proper, footsteps coming down the hall were clearly heard by them. They once found the door blocked from the inside and had to crawl in through the basement, although there was nobody in the house at the time who could have done this. The elevator shaft was blocked off, and footsteps always stopped short at the shaft. Clifford thinks the former owner of the house fell into the shaft and died there.

Mrs. Edith O'Brien of Akron, Ohio, had her own brush with the Unknown, which of course isn't quite so unknown to me after hearing of it thousands of times in more or less the same pattern. She writes:

> Several years ago, I had rooms in the home of an old family friend who was almost blind. Every night, I made a habit of reading a chapter from the Bible to Mr. Henry before he went to bed. This particular evening as we were sitting in the living room and I was reading the usual chapter, heavy footsteps started from the kitchen door and stopped just at the living-room door.

Needless to say, I was terrified for I had securely locked all the doors hours before, and there was no one in the house but me and Mr. Henry.

I couldn't speak, but Mr. Henry looked at me and said, "Edith, I thought we were alone in the house." I called the police who came and examined the house carefully, but found nothing disturbed and no one but us in the house—no door that had not been locked. The very next night, a heavy oak table which was in Mr. Henry's room was lying across his bed when he went to retire. Since Mr. Henry was nearly blind, I always opened his bed for him before he went to his room and everything had been in order—the heavy table in its usual place. After this happened, Mr. Henry said, "It won't be long until something happens in this house. These same footsteps were heard walking in the same way, and a mirror shattered from top to bottom just before Mother died."

Within a few days, Mr. Henry was dead.

Mildred Eastman lives at Willoughby, Ohio, a far cry from glamorous British castles where ghosts are supposed to abound. Apparitions of the dead or dying are nothing new to her.

I have had what might be called "visitations" from the other world since I was eighteen years old. I was playing the piano in a sitting room back of the old parlor, when my attention was drawn to the wide-open doorway. I continued to play, but looked around and saw a short woman standing there with a bouffant dress, hands crossed on the fullness of the gown, her dark hair parted in the middle.

I then noticed that I could see the Christmas tree through her, and I became concerned, and the vision vanished. Three days later my aunt was found dead, and in her possessions was an old daguerreotype and it was the little lady in every respect that I had seen in my vision. She was my aunt's mother.

Again, when my mother was very ill at the hospital, I awoke at 7:30 A.M., sat up in bed, and was amazed to see a milk-white oblong coming onto the bedroom door which was closed. In it, my mother appeared. She had on clothes that I remembered; she pulled her skirt out and touched her hat as much as to say I am on my way, I am leaving. I watched this for some time, then I said out loud, "Yes, Mother, you have left this earth, I am sure, and want to tell me so."

They called me an hour later to tell me that this was the time she actually passed on.

Mrs. H. J. Weidmann lives in Duquesne, Pennsylvania. Her family has had "ESP" all their lives and they take it as completely normal and part of their daily lives.

One night Dad and I were up late, when we saw the figure of Bill Schmidt, a friend of ours, at 4:00 A.M., against the kitchen door. Dad said, "Bill Schmidt just died," and at exactly 4:00 A.M., Bill died in a hospital about two miles away from our home. We knew then something was "different" with us. Dad died a year ago, but he has visited our home many times since then. Our lamps go on and off, doors open and close; our dog, who loved Dad, will suddenly sit up and wag his tail as he used to do when Dad would come into the house. My sons, Thad and Christie, and a neighbor boy, Mike, have been here when all of this happened.

Dad took such an interest in all our boys that we feel he's still doing so.

Ghosts are part of the everyday scene to some people who take their supernatural gifts without panic or worry. Of course, they are careful about the persons to whom they tell their experiences. Too many people like to scoff at that which they fail to understand, or don't wish to accept as true under any circumstances if their philosophy of life involves a firm disbelief in any form of a "hereafter."

Jane Dempsey of Pittsburgh, Pennsylvania, has lived with the psychic world all her life.

In 1947 I had a very serious operation. Before my operation, my aunt, who was dead for several years, appeared to me and said, "Jane, you're going to have a very serious operation. I am going to be with you for a while, while they are operating, but I can't stay too long. You are going to suffer terribly, and all the doctors will think you're dying, but you won't die." The operation lasted nine hours. It happened just as she said it would.

In 1953 my father appeared to me. In October, 1963, my brother-in-law appeared to me when my sister was laid out, and said he came to get my sister, who was his wife.

Several years ago I had a feeling I should get in touch with a girl friend I had not seen for years. Since I am deaf, I had my daughter call her. She died a few days later. I knew she had books that I wanted. I had my daughter get in touch with the people who were disposing of her things. My daughter said to the woman we had never met, "I would like to buy Mrs. Ralston's books." The woman said, "I'm sorry, but I can't do anything with her books. I have to find a person by the name of Jane Bednards." My daughter said, "That is my mother's maiden name." The woman said, "Take all these books, because

Mrs. Ralston has appeared to me and does not want anyone else to have them."

Thus Mrs. Dempsey got her books, and another case entered into the bulging annals of psychic research.

From West Elizabeth, Pennsylvania, comes a note from Mrs. Helen Tosi, who, as she says, has "a problem" about a ghost.

> We have all seen him in the house, several years ago, a man who lived in the house and who met with an accident in the mines. My two sisters were in bed one night when they woke up and saw him sitting on the cedar chest, and all of a sudden, he disappeared into the hall, and vanished. We have been hearing loud noises in the basement at night and in the kitchen, when we are in bed. I don't know what will happen next.
>
> The man was killed some forty years ago, right after he went to work. His name was Mr. Friday. I still hear footsteps even now.

And so it goes. English manor houses may be more historical than Pennsylvania coal mines, but the ghosts walk on. In the nether world all boundaries are hazy.

But the Call of the Midwest has other aspects, too. There is a vigorous interest in psychic matters in some quarters where it matters. People like John J. Strader, for instance, whose ancestors helped found the city of Cincinnati and who is still one of the leading and most solid citizens of that river city. Jack Strader gladly discusses his interest in Sixth Sense phenomena with anyone intelligent who will listen.

He is not ashamed of it as so many people of substance still are. I remember the time my wife and I were in Cincinnati as the guests of the Straders. At a dinner party the president of the local university engaged me in a bit of scrutinizing conversation. Mr. Strader, of course, had maneuvered him across the table from me, and for an hour and a half we talked of nothing else but the scientific evidence for survival. I cannot for the life of me tell you what I had for dessert that evening, but I do remember that Dr. Langsam was impressed.

Our first meeting with the Straders was under the most unusual conditions. I had been asked to appear on the Ruth Lyons television show on the Crosley Broadcasting stations, having just returned from California, where I had appeared at length on the Art Linkletter and Steve Allen programs, among many others. I was shocked, however, to receive a letter from Ruth Lyons on January 17, in which the astute TV personality reneged on our meeting:

> I sincerely regret that I do not believe that I can do an interview without inviting a great deal of controversy. I am certain that you are entirely sincere in what you believe, but I am afraid I would receive a great deal of mail, both pro and con on the subject of "parapsychology" which would be very difficult for many of our viewers to understand.

I must confess I wrote Miss Lyons a rather tart letter in which I told her, among many other things, not to underestimate the intelligence of her audience.

When Jack Strader heard of the Lyons incident, he was so incensed that he personally arranged for a visit to Cincinnati for my wife and myself, with full television, radio and press coverage far in excess of what I would have had originally.

Moreover, in meeting Jack and Joan Strader, and their daughter, Jackie, we found ourselves in a group of deeply sympathetic but also sensibly critical people who had already demonstrated such psychic talents as automatic writing and psychic photography.

The family homestead of the Straders was not free of the occult. The room upstairs in which Mr. Strader's mother passed her last painful moments in the physical state, has on occasion been the scene of some unexplained noises, such as knocks and footsteps, especially in the early hours of the morning. On one occasion in January of 1964, the Straders had been working a modern and improved version of the planchette, with the important addition of direct psychic impressions received by Mrs. Strader, who is mediumistic. Their daughter was out for the evening, and the Straders, as was their wont, were waiting for her return.

At about 12:30, the doorbell rang announcing the fact that our daughter was safely home from a party, along with her escort. I went to answer the summons and just as the two young people closed the door behind them, the fireplace tongs were seen to rise from their normal position and fling themselves upon the floor, some three feet distant from the regular resting spot.

Of course, Jacqueline knew that some psychic force had to be the answer, so with a gleam in her eyes, she approached the next room where we had been gathered and said, "Better slow it down, things are humming tonight!" The young gentleman never got an explanation . . . and he hasn't been back either.

I believe that excess energy . . . is what partly made it possible for the fire tongs to be lifted and tossed through the air. I further believe that the reason for the "show" was a kind of rebellion on the part of our unseen friends at having our excellent contact disturbed, or broken into. It's just my theory however.

I shall have the tongs firmly lashed down for your visit—just in case!

Well, the tongs did not take off for me, but they did appear in a photograph I took of Jack Strader in the next room playing the organ, on which he is an expert. The point is that the tongs and container are several yards away from the organ and could not possibly have been in the picture I took. Yet, they are superimposed on the organ. My camera is completely double-exposure proof. The Unseen Friends were indeed greeting me in style.

The Ghostly Maid

I received a curious letter from a Mrs. Stewart of Chicago, Illinois, explaining that she was living with a ghost and didn't mind, except that she had lost two children at birth and this ghost was following not only her but also her little girl. This she didn't like, so could I please come and look into the situation?

I could and did. On July 4, I celebrated Independence Day by trying to free a hung-up lady ghost on Chicago's South Side. The house itself was an old one, built around the late 1800s, and not exactly a monument of architectural beauty. But its functional sturdiness suited its present purpose—to house a number of young couples and their children, people who found the house both convenient and economical.

In its heyday, it had been a wealthy home, complete with servants and backstairs for them to go up and down on. The three stories are even now connected by an elaborate buzzer system, which, however, hasn't worked for years.

I did not wish to discuss the phenomena at the house with Mrs. Stewart until after Sybil Leek, who was with me, had had a chance to explore the situation. My good friend Carl Subak, a stamp dealer, had come along to see how I worked. He and I had known each other thirty years ago when we were both students, and because of that he had overcome his own skepticism and come along. Immediately on arrival, Sybil ascended the stairs to the second floor as if she knew where to go. Of course she didn't; I had not discussed the matter with her at all. But despite this promising beginning, she drew a complete blank when we arrived in the apartment upstairs. "I feel absolutely nothing," she confided and looked at me doubtfully. Had I made a mistake? On a hot July day, had we come all the way to the South Side of Chicago on a wild ghost chase?

We gathered in a bedroom where there was a comfortable chair and windows on both sides that gave onto an old-fashioned garden; there was a porch on one side and a parkway on the other. The furniture, in keeping with the modest economic circumstances of the owners, was old and worn, but it was functional and they did not seem to mind.

In a moment, Sybil Leek had slipped into trance. But instead of a ghost's personality, the next voice we heard was Sybil's own, although it sounded strange. Sybil was "out" of her own body, but able to observe the place and report back to us while still in trance.

The first thing she saw were maps, in a large round building somehow connected with the house we were in.

"Is there anyone around?" I asked.

"Yes," Sybil intoned, "James Dugan."

"What does he do here?"

"Come back to live."

"When was that?"

"1912."

"Is there anyone with him?"

"There is another man. McCloud."

"Anyone else?"

"Lots of people."

"Do they live in this house?"

"Three, four people . . . McCloud . . . maps . . ."

"All men?"

"No . . . girl . . . Judith . . . maidservant . . ."

"Is there an unhappy presence here?"

"Judith . . . she had no one here, no family . . . that man went away

. . . Dugan went away . . ."

"How is she connected with this Dugan?"

"Loved him."

"Were they married?"

"No. Lovers."

"Did they have any children?"

There was a momentary silence, then Sybil continued in a drab, monotonous voice.

"The baby's dead."

"Does she know the baby's dead?"

"*She cries . . . baby cries . . .* neglected . . . by Judith . . . guilty . . ."

"Does Judith know this?"

"Yes."

"How old was the baby when it died?"

"A few weeks old."

Strange, I thought, that Mrs. Stewart had fears for her own child from this source. She, too, had lost children at a tender age.

"What happened to the baby?"

"She put it down the steps."

"What happened to the body then?"

"I don't know."

"Is Judith still here?"

"She's here."

"Where?"

"This room . . . and up and down the steps. She's sorry for her baby."

"Can you talk to her?"

"No. She cannot leave here until she finds—You see if she could get Dugan . . ."

"Where is Dugan?"

"With the maps."

"What is Dugan's work?"

"Has to do with roads."

"Is he dead?"

"Yes. She wants him here, but he is not here."

"How did she die?"

"She ran away to the water . . . died by the water . . . but is here where she lived . . . baby died on the steps . . . downstairs . . ."

"What is she doing here, I mean how does she let people know she is around?"

"She pulls things . . . *she cries* . . ."

"And her Christian name?"

"Judith Vincent, I think. Twenty-one. Darkish, not white. From an island."

"And the man? Is he white?"

"Yes."

"Can you see her?"

"Yes."

"Speak to her?"

"She doesn't want to, but perhaps . . ."

"What year does she think this is?"

"1913."

"Tell her this is the year 1965."

Sybil informed the spirit in a low voice that this was 1965 and she need not stay here any longer. Dugan is dead, too.

"She has to find him," Sybil explained and I directed her to explain that she need only call out for her lover in order to be reunited with him "Over There."

"She's gone . . ." Sybil finally said, and breathed deeply.

A moment later she woke up and looked with astonishment at the strange room, having completely forgotten how we got here, or where we were.

There was no time for explanations now, as I still wanted to check out some of this material. The first one to sit down with me was the owner of the flat, Mrs. Alexandra Stewart. A graduate of the University of Iowa, twenty-five years old, Alexandra Stewart works as a personnel director. She had witnessed the trance session and seemed visibly shaken. There was a good reason for this. Mrs. Stewart, you see, had met the ghost Sybil had described.

The Stewarts had moved into the second floor apartment in the winter of 1964. The room we were now sitting in had been hers. Shortly after they moved in, Mrs. Stewart happened to be glancing up toward the French doors, when she saw a woman looking at her. The figure was about five feet three or four, and wore a blue-gray dress with a shawl, and a hood over her head, for which reason Mrs. Stewart could not make out the woman's features. The head seemed strangely bowed to her, almost as if the woman were doing penance.

I questioned Mrs. Stewart on the woman's color in view of Sybil's description of Judith. But Mrs. Stewart could not be sure; the woman could have been white or black. At the time, Mrs. Stewart had assumed it to be a reflection from the mirror, but when she glanced at the mirror, she did not see the figure in it. When she turned her attention back to the figure, it had disappeared. It was toward evening and Mrs. Stewart was a little tired, yet the figure was very real to her. Her doubts were completely dispelled when the ghost returned about a month later. In the meantime she had had the dresser that formerly stood in the line of sight moved farther down, so that any reflection as explanation would simply not hold water. Again the figure appeared at the French doors. She looked very unhappy to Mrs. Stewart, who felt herself strangely drawn to the woman, almost as if she should help her in some way as yet unknown.

But the visual visitations were not all that disturbed the Stewarts. Soon they were hearing strange noises, too. Above all there was the crying of a baby, which seemed to come from the second-floor rear bedroom. It could also be heard in the kitchen, though less loud, and it seemed to come from the walls. Several people had heard it and there was no natural cause to account for it. Then there were the footsteps. It sounded like someone walking down the backstairs, the servants' stairs, step by step, hesitatingly, and not returning, but just fading away!

They dubbed their ghostly guest "Elizabeth," for want of a better name. Mrs. Stewart did not consider herself psychic, nor did she have any interest in such matters. But occasionally things had happened to her that defied natural explanations, such as the time just after she had lost a baby. She awoke from a heavy sleep with the intangible feeling of a presence in her room. She looked up and there, in the rocking chair across the room, she saw a woman, now dead, who had taken care of her when she herself was a child. Rocking gently in the chair, as if to reassure her, the Nanny held Mrs. Stewart's baby in her arms. In a moment the vision was gone, but it had left Alexandra Stewart with a sense of peace. She knew her little one was well looked after.

The phenomena continued, however, and soon they were no longer restricted to the upstairs. On the first floor in the living room, Mrs. Stewart heard the noise of someone breathing close to her. This had happened only recently, again in the presence of her husband and a friend. She asked them to hold their breath for a moment, and still she heard the strange breathing continue as before. Neither of the men could hear it, or so they said. But the following day the guest came back with another man. He wanted to be sure of his observation before admitting that he too had heard the invisible person breathing close to him.

The corner of the living room where the breathing had been heard was also the focal point for strange knockings that faulty pipes could not explain. On one occasion they heard the breaking of glass, and yet there was no evidence that any glass had been broken. There was a feeling that someone other than the visible people was present at times in their living room, and it made them a little nervous even though they did not fear their "Elizabeth."

Alexandra's young husband grew up in the building trade, and now works as a photographer. He too has heard the footsteps on many occasions, and he knows the difference between them and a house settling or timbers creaking—these were definitely human noises.

Mrs. Martha Vaughn is a bookkeeper who had been living in the building for two years. Hers is the apartment in the rear portion of the second floor, and it includes the back porch. Around Christmas of 1964, she heard a baby crying on the porch. It was a particularly cold night, so she went to investigate immediately. It was a weird, unearthly sound—to her it seemed right near the porch, but there was nobody around. The yard was deserted. The sound to her was the crying of a small child, not a baby, but perhaps a child of from one to three years of age. The various families shared the downstairs living room "like a kibbutz," as Mrs. Stewart put it, so it was not out of the ordinary for several people to be in the downstairs area. On one such occasion Mrs. Vaughn also heard the breaking of the *invisible* glass.

Richard Vaughn is a laboratory technician. He too has heard the baby cry and the invisible glass break; he has heard pounding on the wall, as have the others. A skeptic at first, he tried to blame these noises on the steam pipes that heat the house. But when he listened to the pipes when they were acting up, he realized at once that the noises he had heard before were completely different.

"What about a man named Dugan? Or someone having to do with maps?" I asked.

"Well," Vaughn said, and thought back, "I used to get mail here for people who once lived here, and of course I sent it all back to the post office. But I don't recall the name Dugan. What I do recall was some mail from a Washington Bureau. You see, this house belongs to the

University of Chicago and a lot of professors used to live here."

"Professors?" I said with renewed interest.

Was Dugan one of them?

Several other people who lived in the house experienced strange phenomena. Barbara Madonna used to live there too. But in May of that year she moved out. She works three days a week as a secretary and moved into the house in November of the previous year. She and her husband much admired the back porch when they first moved in, and had visions of sitting out there drinking a beer on warm evenings. But soon their hopes were dashed by the uncanny feeling that they were not alone, that another presence was in their apartment, especially around the porch. Soon, instead of using the porch, they studiously avoided it, even if it meant walking downstairs to shake out a mop. Theirs was the third-floor apartment, directly above the Stewart apartment.

A girl by the name of Lolita Krol also had heard the baby crying. She lived in the building for a time and bitterly complained about the strange noises on the porch.

Douglas McConnor is a magazine editor, and he and his wife moved into the building in November of the year Barbara Madonna moved out, first to the second floor and later to the third. From the very first, when McConnor was still alone—his wife joined him in the flat after their marriage a little later—he felt extremely uncomfortable in the place. Doors and windows would fly open by themselves when there wasn't any strong wind.

When he moved upstairs to the next floor, things were much quieter, except for one thing: always on Sunday nights, noisy activities would greatly increase toward midnight. Footsteps, the sounds of people rushing about, and of doors opening and closing would disturb Mr. McConnor's rest. The stairs were particularly noisy. But when he checked, he found that everybody was accounted for, and that no living person had caused the commotion.

It got to be so bad he started to hate Sunday nights.

I recounted Sybil's trance to Mr. McConnor and the fact that a woman named Judith had been the central figure of it.

"Strange," he observed, "but the story also fits my ex-wife, who deserted her children. She is of course very much alive now. Her name is Judith."

Had Sybil intermingled the impression a dead maidservant with the imprint left behind by an unfit mother? Or were there two Judiths? An any rate the Stewarts did not complain further about uncanny noises, and the girl in the blue-gray dress never came back.

On the way to the airport, Carl Subak seemed unusually silent as he drove us out to the field. What he had witnessed seemed to have left an impression on him and his philosophy of life.

"What I find so particularly upsetting," he finally said, "is Sybil's talking about a woman and a dead baby—all of it borne out afterwards by the people in the house. But Sybil did not know this. She couldn't have."

No, she couldn't.

In September, three years later, a group consisting of a local television reporter, a would-be psychic student, and an assortment of clairvoyants descended on the building in search of psychic excitement. All they got out of it were more mechanical difficulties with their cameras. The ghosts were long gone.

The Ghost Husband

People all over the world have moved into houses that seemed ordinary and pleasant, and spent years without ever encountering anything out of the ordinary. Then, one day, something happens to disturb their tranquility: a ghost appears, strange noises are heard, and a psychic presence makes itself known.

Why is it that phenomena occur at times long after someone moves into an affected house? Of course, there are just as many cases where the ominous presence is felt the very moment one steps across the threshold. But in cases where ghosts make their presence manifest long after the new tenants have moved in, certain conditions have not been right for such manifestations to take place at the beginning. For instance, it may involve the presence of youngsters in the household who furnish the energy for ghosts to appear. Or it may be that the shadowy entities remaining behind in the house are dimly aware of the new tenants, but wish to find out more about them before manifesting to them. Either way, once manifestations begin, the owner of the house has the choice of either ignoring them, fighting them—or coming to terms with them.

In the majority of cases, unfortunately, people simply think that by ignoring the phenomena or trying hard to explain them by so-called natural causes, the matter can be solved. Ignoring problems never helps, in any area of life. When it comes to psychic phenomena, the phenomena may become worse, because even the most benighted ghost, barely aware of its predicament, will become more powerful, more restless, by being ignored.

Take Mrs. A.M.B., for instance. She lives in central Illinois and is by training and profession a practical nurse, engaged in psychiatric work. If anything, she can distinguish psychosis from psychic activity. She has had ESP abilities ever since she can remember. When she was twelve years old, she was playing in front of her house when she met what to her was an old man, inquiring about a certain widow living in the next block of the village. Mrs. B. knew very well that the lady had become a widow when her husband was killed while working as a crossing guard during a blizzard the previous winter. She remembered the man well, but the stranger did not resemble the deceased at all, so she assumed he was a relative inquiring about the dead man.

The stranger wanted to know where the widow had moved to. Mrs. B. explained that the lady had gone to visit a sister somewhere in Missouri, due to the fact, of course, that her husband had been killed in an accident. At that, the stranger nodded; he knew of the accident, he said. "Come," Mrs. B. said to the stranger, "I'll show you where another sister of the widow lives, not more than two blocks away from here. Perhaps they can tell you what town in Missouri she is visiting." The stranger obliged her, and the two were walking along the front porch, toward the steps leading down into the street, still in conversation. At that moment, her mother appeared at the front door in back of her and demanded to know what she was talking about. The girl was surprised, and explained that the gentleman was merely asking where Mrs. C. had gone, and added, "I told him she went to Missouri." But the mother replied, in a surprised tone of voice, "What are you talking about? I don't see anyone." The little girl immediately pointed at the visitor, who by that time had had enough time to get to the steps, for the front porch was rather large.

But—to her shock—she saw no one there! Immediately the girl and her mother walked into the yard, looking about everywhere without finding any trace of the strange visitor. He had simply vanished the moment the little girl had turned around to answer her mother.

Lizzy's Ghost

Mrs. Carolyn K. lived in Chicago, Illinois, with her husband and four children. She had for years been interested in ESP experiences, unlike her husband, who held no belief of this kind. The family moved into its present home some years ago. Mrs. K. does not recall any unusual experiences for the first six years, but toward the end of April, six years after they moved in, something odd happened. She and her husband had just gone to bed and her husband fell asleep almost immediately. Mrs. K., however, felt ill at ease and was unable to fall asleep, since she felt a presence in the bedroom.

Within a few minutes she saw, in great detail, a female figure standing beside the bed. The woman seemed about thirty years old, had fair skin and hair, a trim figure, and was rather attractive. Her dress indicated good taste and a degree of wealth, and belonged to the 1870s or 1880s. The young woman just stood there and looked at Mrs. K., and vice versa. She seemed animated enough, but made no sound. Despite this, Mrs. K. had the distinct impression that the ghost wanted her to know something specific. The encounter lasted for ten or fifteen minutes, then the figure slowly disintegrated.

The experience left Mrs. K. frightened and worried. Immediately she reported it to her husband, but he brushed the incident aside with a good deal of skepticism. In the following two weeks, Mrs. K. felt an unseen presence all about the house, without, however, seeing her mysterious visitor again. It seemed that the woman was watching her as she did her daily chores. Mrs. K. had no idea who the ghost might be, but she knew that their house was no more than fifty years old and that there had been swamp land on the spot before that. Could the ghost have some connection with the land itself, or perhaps with some of the antiques Mrs. K. treasured?

About two weeks after the initial experience, Mr. K. was studying in the kitchen, which is located at the far eastern end of the house, while Mrs. K. was watching television in the living room at the other end of the house. Twice she felt the need to go into the kitchen and warn her husband that she felt the ghost moving about the living room, but he insisted it was merely her imagination. So she returned to the living room and curled up in an easy chair to continue watching television. Fifteen minutes later, she heard a loud noise reverberating throughout the house. It made her freeze with fright in the chair, when her husband ran into the living room to ask what the noise had been.

Upon investigation, he noticed a broken string on an antique zither hanging on the dining room wall. It was unlikely that the string could have broken by itself, and if it had, how could it have reverberated so strongly? To test such a possibility, they broke several other strings of the same zither in an effort to duplicate the sound, but without success. A few weeks went by, and the ghost's presence persisted. By now Mrs. K. had the distinct impression that the ghost was annoyed at being ignored. Suddenly, a hurricane lamp hanging from a nail on the wall fell to the floor and shattered. It could not have moved of its own volition.

Again some time passed, and the ghost was almost forgotten. Mrs. K's older daughter, then six years old, asked her mother early one morning who the company was the previous evening. Informed that there had been no guests at the house, she insisted that a lady had entered her bedroom, sat on her bed and looked at her, and then departed. In order to calm the child, Mrs. K. told her she had probably dreamt the whole thing. But the little girl insisted that she had not, and furthermore, she described the visitor in every detail including the "funny" clothes she had worn. Appalled, Mrs. K. realized that her daughter had seen the same ghostly woman. Apparently, the ghost felt greater urgency to communicate now, for a few days later, after going to bed, the apparition returned to Mrs. K.'s bedroom. This time she wore a different dress than on the first meeting, but it was still from the 1880s. She was wiping her hands on an apron, stayed only for a little while, then slowly disintegrated again. During the following year, her presence was felt only occasionally, but gradually Mrs. K. managed to snatch a few fleeting impressions about her. From this she put together the story of her ghost. She was quite unhappy about a child, and one evening the following winter, when Mrs. K. felt the ghost wandering about in their basement, she actually heard her crying pitifully for two hours. Obviously, the distraught ghost wanted attention, and was determined to get it at all costs.

One day the following summer, when Mrs. K. was alone with the children after her husband had left for work, one of the children complained that the door to the bathroom was locked. Since the door can be locked only from the inside, and since all four children were accounted for, Mrs. K. assumed that her ghost lady was at it again. When the bathroom door remained locked for half an hour and the children's needs became more urgent, Mrs. K. went to the door and demanded in a loud tone of voice that the ghost open the door. There was anger in her voice and it brought quick results. Clearly the click of a lock being turned was heard inside the bathroom and, after a moment, Mrs. K. opened the bathroom door easily. There was no one inside the bathroom, of course. Who, then, had turned the lock—the only way the door could be opened?

For awhile things went smoothly. A few weeks later, Mrs. K. again felt the ghost near her. One of her daughters was sitting at the kitchen table with her while she was cutting out a dress pattern on the counter. Mrs. K. stepped back to search for something in the refrigerator a few feet away, when all of a sudden she and her daughter saw her box of dressmaking pins rise slightly off the counter and fall to the floor. Neither one of them had been near it, and it took them almost an hour to retrieve all the pins scattered on the floor.

A little later, they clearly heard the basement door connecting the dining room and kitchen fly open and slam shut by itself, as if someone in great anger was trying to call attention to her presence. Immediately they closed the door, and made sure there was no draft from any windows.

An instant later, it flew open again by itself. Now they attached the chain to the latch—but that didn't seem to stop the ghost from fooling around with the door. With enormous force, it flew open again as far as the chain allowed, as if someone were straining at it. Quickly Mrs. K. called a neighbor to come over and watch the strange behavior of the door but the minute the neighbor arrived, the door behaved normally, just as before. The ghost was not about to perform for strangers.

One evening in the summer some years later, Mr. K. was driving some dinner guests home and Mrs. K. was alone in the house with the children. All of a sudden, she felt her ghost following her as she went through her chores of emptying ashtrays and taking empty glasses into the kitchen. Mrs. K. tried bravely to ignore her, although she was frightened and she knew that her ghost knew it, which made it all the more difficult to carry on.

Not much later, the K. family had guests again. One of the arriving guests pointed out to Mrs. K. that their basement light was on. Mrs. K. explained that it was unlikely, since the bulb had burned out the day before. She even recalled being slightly annoyed with her husband for having neglected to replace the bulb. But the guest insisted, and so the K's opened the basement door only to find the light off. A moment later another guest arrived. He wanted to know who was working in the basement at such a late hour, since he had seen the basement light on.

Moreover, he saw a figure standing at the basement window looking out. Once more, the entire party went downstairs with a flashlight, only to find the light off and no one about.

That was the last the K's saw or heard of their ghost. Why had she so suddenly left them? Perhaps it had to do with a Chicago newspaperwoman's call. Having heard of the disturbances, she had telephoned the K's to offer her services and that of celebrated psychic Irene Hughes to investigate the house. Although the K's did not want any attention because of the children, Mrs. K. told the reporter what had transpired at the house. To her surprise, the reporter informed her that parallel experiences had been reported at another house not more than seven miles away. In the other case, the mother and one of her children had observed a ghostly figure, and an investigation had taken place with the help of Irene Hughes and various equipment, the result of which was that a presence named Lizzy was ascertained.

From this Mrs. K. concluded that they were sharing a ghost with a neighbor seven miles away, and she, too, began to call the ghostly visitor Lizzy. Now if Lizzy had two homes and was shuttling back and forth between them, it might account for the long stretches of no activity at the K. home. On the other hand, if the ghost at the K's was not named Lizzy, she would naturally not want to be confused with some other unknown ghost seven miles away. Be this as it may, Mrs. K. wishes her well, wherever she is.

Little Girl Lost

Mrs. J. P. lived in central Illinois, in an old three-story house with a basement. Prior to her acquiring it, it had stood empty for six months. As soon as she had moved in, she heard some neighborhood gossip that the house was presumed haunted. Although Mrs. P. is not a skeptic, she is level-headed enough not to take rumors at face value.

She looked the house over carefully. It seemed about eighty years old, and was badly in need of repair. Since they had bought it at a bargain price, they did not mind, but as time went on, they wondered how cheap the house had really been. It became obvious to her and her husband that the price had been low for other reasons. Nevertheless, the house was theirs, and together they set out to repaint and remodel it as best they could. For the first two weeks, they were too busy to notice anything out of the ordinary. About three weeks after moving in, however, Mr. and Mrs. P. began hearing things such as doors shutting by themselves, cupboards opening, and particularly, a little girl persistently calling, "Mama, Mama" with a great deal of alarm. As yet, Mr. and Mrs. P. tried to ignore the phenomena.

One evening, however, they were having a family spat over something of little consequence. All of a sudden a frying pan standing on the stove lifted off by itself, hung suspended in midair for a moment, and then was flung back on the stove with full force. Their twelve-year-old son flew into hysterics, Mr. P. turned white, and Mrs. P. was just plain angry. How dare someone invade their privacy? The following week, the ten-year-old daughter was watching television downstairs in what had been turned into Mrs. P.'s office, while Mr. P. and their son were upstairs also watching television. Suddenly, a glass of milk standing on the desk in the office rose up by itself and dashed itself to the floor with full force. The child ran screaming from the room, and it took a long time for her father to calm her down.

As a result of these happenings, the children implored their mother to move from the house, but Mrs. P. would have none of it. She liked the house fine, and was not about to let some unknown ghost displace her. The more she thought about it, the angrier she got. She decided to go from floor to floor, cursing the ghost and telling him or her to get out of the house, even if he or she used to own it.

But that is how it is with Stay-Behinds: they don't care if you paid for the house. After all, they can't use the money where they are, and would rather stay on in a place they are familiar with.

The Seminary Ghost

Maryknoll College of Glen Ellyn, Illinois, a Roman Catholic seminary, closed its doors in June 1972, due to a dwindling interest in what it had to offer. In the fall a few years before, a seminarian named Gary M. was working in the darkroom of the college. This was part of his regular assignments, and photography had been a regular activity for some years, participated in by both faculty and students.

On this particular occasion, Mr. M. felt as though he were being watched while in the darkroom. Chalking it up to an active imagination, he dismissed the matter from his mind. But in the spring a few years later, Mr. M. was going through some old chemicals when he received the strongest impression of a psychic presence. He was loading some film at the time, and as he did so, he had the uncanny feeling that he was not alone in the room. The chemicals he had just handled were once the property of a priest who had died three years before. The following day, while developing film in an open tank, he suddenly felt as though a cold hand had gone down his back. He also realized that the chemicals felt colder than before. After he had turned the lights back on, he took the temperature of the developer. At the start it had been 70°F., while at the end it was down to 64°F. Since the room temperature was 68°F, there was a truly unaccountable decrease in temperature.

The phenomena made him wonder, and he discussed his experiences with other seminarians. It was then learned that a colleague of his had also had experiences in the same place. Someone, a man, had appeared to him, and he had felt the warm touch of a hand at his cheek.

Since he was not alone at the time, but in a group of five students, he immediately reported the incident to them. The description of the apparition was detailed and definite. Mr. M. quickly went into past files, and came up with several pictures, so that his fellow student, who had a similar experience, could pick out that of the ghostly apparition he had seen. Without the slightest hesitation, he identified the dead priest as the man he had seen. This was not too surprising; the students were using what was once the priest's own equipment and chemicals, and perhaps he still felt obliged to teach them their proper use.

The Suicide Ghost

In Springfield, Illinois, lived a couple named Gertrude and Russell Meyers. He worked as a stereotyper on the local newspaper, and she was a high-school teacher. Both of them were in their late twenties and couldn't care less about such things as ghosts.

At the time of their marriage, they had rented a five-room cottage that had stood empty for some time. It had no particular distinction but a modest price, and was located in Bloomington where the Meyerses then lived.

Gertrude Meyers came from a farm background and had studied at Illinois Wesleyan as well as the University of Chicago. For a while she worked as a newspaperwoman in Detroit, later taught school, and as a sideline wrote a number of children's books. Her husband Russell, also of farm background, attended Illinois State Normal University at Normal, Illinois, and later took his apprenticeship at the Bloomington Pantograph.

The house they had rented in Bloomington was exactly like the house next to it, and the current owners had converted what was formerly one large house into two separate units, laying a driveway between them.

In the summer, after they had moved into their house, they went about the business of settling down to a routine. Since her husband worked the night shift on the newspaper, Mrs. Meyers was often left alone in the house. At first it did not bother her at all. Sounds from the street penetrated into the house and gave her a feeling of people nearby. But when the chills of autumn set in and the windows had to be closed to keep it out, she became gradually aware that she was not really alone on those lonely nights.

One particular night early in their occupancy of the house, she had gone to bed leaving her bedroom door ajar. It was ten-thirty and she was just about ready to go to sleep when she heard rapid, firm footsteps starting at the front door, inside the house, and coming through the living room, the dining room, and finally approaching her bedroom door down the hall leading to it.

She leapt out of bed and locked the bedroom door. Then she went back into bed and sat there, wondering with sheer terror what the intruder would do. But nobody came.

More to calm herself than because she really believed it, Mrs. Meyers convinced herself that she must have been mistaken about those footsteps. It was probably someone in the street. With this reassuring thought on her mind, she managed to fall asleep.

The next morning, she did not tell her new husband about the nocturnal event. After all, she did not want him to think he had married a strange woman! But the footsteps returned, night after night, always at the same time and always stopping abruptly at her bedroom door, which, needless to say, she kept locked.

Rather than facing her husband with the allegation that they had rented a haunted house, she bravely decided to face the intruder and find out what this was all about. One night she deliberately waited for the now familiar brisk footfalls. The clock struck ten, then ten-thirty. In the quiet of the night, she could hear her heart pound in her chest.

Then the footsteps came, closer and closer, until they got to her bedroom door. At this moment, Mrs. Meyers jumped out of bed, snapped on the light, and tore the door wide open.

There was nobody there, and no retreating footsteps could be heard.

She tried it again and again, but the invisible intruder never showed himself once the door was opened.

The winter was bitterly cold, and it was Russell's habit of building up a fire in the furnace in the basement when he came home from work at three-thirty A.M. Mrs. Meyers always heard him come in, but did not get up. One night he left the basement, came into the bedroom and said, "Why are you walking around this freezing house in the middle of the night?"

Of course she had not been out of bed all night, and told him as much. Then they discovered that he, too, had heard footsteps, but had thought it was his wife walking restlessly about the house. Meyers had heard the steps whenever he was fixing the furnace in the basement, and by the time he got upstairs they had ceased.

When Mrs. Meyers had to get up early to go to her classes, her husband would stay in the house sleeping late. On many days he would hear someone walking about the house and investigate, only to find himself quite alone. He would wake up in the middle of the night thinking his wife had gotten up, but immediately reassured himself that she was sleeping peacefully next to him. Yet there was *someone* out there in the empty house!

Since everything was securely locked, and countless attempts to trap the ghost had failed, the Meyerses shrugged and learned to live with their peculiar boarder. Gradually the steps became part of the atmosphere of the old house, and the terror began to fade into the darkness of night.

In May of the following year, they decided to work in the garden and, as they did so, they met their next-door neighbors for the first time. Since they lived in identical houses, they had something in common, and conversation between them and the neighbors—a young man of twenty-five and his grandmother—sprang up.

Eventually the discussion got around to the footsteps. It seemed that they, too, kept hearing them. After they had compared notes on their experiences, the Meyerses asked more questions. They were told that before the house was divided, it belonged to a single owner who had committed suicide in the house. No wonder he liked to walk in both halves of what was once his home!

The Phantom Dog

There are reports of wild animals appearing after their deaths, but the majority of animal-related psychic incidents concern domestic animals, especially dogs and cats. Perhaps it is because our pets take on part of our human personality and thus rise above the status of "dumb animals," or perhaps because the bond of love is so strong between master and pet.

Mrs. Elwood Kruse is a housewife in Burlington, Iowa. Her husband is an electrical engineer and neither of them is a student of occult matters, although Mrs. Kruse has a history of premonitions and similar ESP experiences. She has learned to live with it and, if anything, it has made her even more cautious in accepting unorthodox happenings than if she had no such abilities. She has always loved animals and, having been raised in the country, has always been surrounded by dogs, cats, birds, or fish. Her husband at first had some reservations about having animals in a home, but eventually he gave in and allowed her to get a puppy for their daughters.

It was Christmas, 1964 when she bought an Irish setter puppy and named him Fiaca. The children were elated, and even Mr. Kruse, not overly fond of dogs, came to like the animal.

On December 18, 1965, her husband had to telephone Mrs. Kruse to tell her the sad news. Their dog had been run over by a car and killed instantly. Mrs. Kruse was terribly upset. The Christmas season was at hand and memories of Fiaca's arrival a year before would sadden the holidays. But they tried to bear up under their loss.

On the day before Christmas, exactly one year to the day after the dog's arrival at the Kruse home, Mrs. Kruse was in the kitchen when suddenly she heard a strange noise at the front door. It sounded like a dog scratching to be let in. At once she thought, oh, Fiaca wants to get into the house—then the chilling thought came to her that this could not very well be since he was dead. So she went to the front door and peeked through the glass, but there was nothing outside that could have made the noise. She returned to her kitchen explaining her experience as due to her missing the dog at this time of year.

The incident slipped her mind until a few days after the holiday. She heard the sound very clearly again and knew it was not her imagination playing tricks. Again she looked out the door and saw nothing special. The house was new; the storm door was made of aluminum, and the noise was that of animal claws raking up and down on the metal, just as Fiaca used to do. There was no tree close enough to have caused the noise with branches scraping against the door. She told her husband about the second experience but he would not believe her.

The sounds kept coming back, usually in the afternoon. Then one night in the second week of January 1966, it happened again. This time she was not alone but was playing bridge in the living room with her husband and their friends Mr. and Mrs. Marvin Turl. Mr. Turl is a psychology student with an interest in parapsychology.

Mr. Kruse and Susan Turl kept playing, evidently not hearing anything. But Marvin Turl looked up. He too had heard the scratching. He knew nothing at that time of Mrs. Kruse's earlier experiences. But he confirmed that the noise sounded to him like a dog scratching on the door to be let in. Mrs. Kruse and Mr. Turl went to the door and flipped the porch light on. There was no dog outside. Nothing.

The next day Mrs. Kruse confided the strange happenings to her mother and found her receptive to the idea of a psychic phenomenon involving their dog. She suggested that Mrs. Kruse acknowledge her dog's presence verbally the next time the scratching occurred, and open the door as if the dog were actually present.

Two days went by with Mrs. Kruse hoping the ghostly scratching would return. On the third day, in the afternoon, she heard the familiar scratching again. Quickly she went to the door, opened it wide, and said, "Come on in, Fiaca." She felt terribly silly doing this, but after she had done it, the depression over the dog's untimely death seemed somehow to have left her and she felt better about the whole matter. She returned to the kitchen and continued her work.

A little later she found herself in the living room. Imagine her surprise when she found the carpet near the front door covered by a whitish substance, similar to fine dust. The substance trailed into the dining room, where it disappeared for a stretch, only to reappear near the door leading from the kitchen to the living room. She found more of the white substance in the hall, most of it at the end where Fiaca used to curl up on the carpet and sleep. From that spot he could observe all three bedrooms, and it was his favorite spot.

Although Mrs. Kruse had no knowledge of the nature of ectoplasm or materializations, it struck her at once that the white substance marked exactly the way Fiaca used to go about the house: from the front door into the dining room, then a mad dash through the kitchen, and then down the hall to check the bedrooms.

She looked at the white stuff but did not touch it. A little later, her father passed by it and observed it too. But by nightfall it had somehow dissolved. The scratching at the front door was never heard again after that day.

Perhaps, Mrs. Kruse thinks, the dog wanted to come home one more time to make sure everything was all right. The Kruses are glad he took the trouble, for they know that Fiaca is all right too, in his new place.

The Fraternity Ghost

Several years ago, a tragic event took place at a major university campus in Kansas. A member of one of the smaller fraternities, TKE, was killed in a head-on automobile accident on September 21. His sudden death at so young an age—he was an undergraduate—brought home a sense of tragedy to the other members of the fraternity, and it was decided that they would attend his funeral in New York en masse.

Not quite a year after the tragic accident, several members of the fraternity were at their headquarters. Eventually one of the brothers and his date were left behind alone, studying in the basement of the house. Upon completion of their schoolwork, they left. When they had reached the outside, the girl remembered she had left her purse in the basement and returned to get it. When she entered the basement, she noticed a man sitting at the poker table, playing with chips. She said something to him, explaining herself, then grabbed her purse and returned upstairs. There she asked her date who the man in the basement was, since she hadn't noticed him before. He laughed and said that no one had been down there but the two of them. At that point, one of the other brothers went into the basement and was surprised to see a man get up from his chair and walk away. That man was none other than the young man who had been killed in the automobile crash a year before.

One of the other members of the fraternity had also been in the same accident, but had only been injured, and survived. Several days after the incident in the fraternity house basement, this young man saw the dead boy walking up the steps to the second floor of the house. By now the fraternity realized that their dead brother was still very much with them, drawn back to what was to him his true home—and so they accepted him as one of the crowd, even if he was invisible at times.

The Ghost and the Puppy

Alice H. lived in a five-room bungalow flat in the Middle West. She worked part-time as a saleswoman, but lived alone. Throughout her long life she never had any real interest in psychic phenomena. She even went to a spiritualist meeting with a friend and was not impressed one way or another. She was sixty-two when she had her first personal encounter with the unknown.

One night she went to bed and awoke because something was pressing against her back. Since she knew herself to be alone in the apartment, it frightened her. Nevertheless, she turned around to look—and to her horror she saw the upper part of her late husband's body. As she stared at him, he glided over the bed, turned to look at her once more with a mischievous look in his eye, and disappeared on the other side of the bed. Mrs. H. could not figure out why he had appeared to her, because she had not been thinking of him at that time. But evidently he was to instigate her further psychic experiences.

Not much later, she had another manifestation that shook her up a great deal. She had been sound asleep when she was awakened by the whimpering of her puppy. The dog was sleeping on top of the bed covers. Mrs. H. was fully awake now and looked over her shoulder where stood a young girl of about ten years, in the most beautiful blue tailored pajamas. She was looking at the dog. As Mrs. H. looked closer, she noticed that the child had neither face nor hands nor feet showing. Shaken, she jumped out of bed and went toward the spirit. The little girl moved back toward the wall, and Mrs. H. followed her. As the little girl in the blue pajamas neared the wall, it somehow changed into a beautiful flower garden with a wide path! She walked down the path in a mechanical sort of way, with the wide cuffs of her pajamas showing, but still with no feet. Nevertheless, it was a happy walk, then it all disappeared.

The experience bothered Mrs. H. so she moved into another room. But her little dog stayed on in the room where the experience had taken place, sleeping on the floor under the bed. That first experience took place on a Sunday in October, at four A.M. The following Sunday, again at four o'clock, Mrs. H. heard the dog whimper, as if he were conscious of a presence. By the time she reached the other room, however, she could not see anything. These experiences continued for some time, always on Sunday at four in the morning. It then became clear to Mrs. H. that the little girl hadn't come for her in particular—but only to visit her little dog.

Conversation with a Ghost

David H. lives in Michigan. When he was eight he had his first encounter with a ghost. The house his parents lived in was more than a hundred years old, and rather on the large side. David slept in one of two main rooms on the upper floor of the house; the room next to it was unfurnished. One night he was lying in bed when he had a sudden urge to sit up, and as he did so he looked down the hall. All of a sudden he noticed a small, shadowlike man jump down from the attic and run toward him. But instead of coming into his room, he turned down the stairs. David could see that he wore a small derby hat but what was even more fascinating was the fact that the figure walked about two inches above the floor! After the figure had disappeared, David thought it was all his imagination. A particularly bright eight-year-old, he was not easily taken in by fantasies or daydreams.

But the strange figure reappeared several times more, and eventually David came to the conclusion that it was real. He asked his parents whether he could swap rooms with them and they agreed to let him sleep downstairs. It was about that time that his mother told him that she had heard the old piano playing at night downstairs. She had thought that it was the cat climbing up on the keys, but one night the piano played in plain view of herself and one of her daughters, without even a trace of the cat in the room. There was also the sound of pages in a book being turned in the same area, although nobody had a book or turned any pages.

David settled down in his room on the lower floor and finally forgot all about his ghostly experiences. Shortly after, he heard a crunching noise on the stairs, as if someone were walking on them. He assumed it was his mother coming down the stairs to tell him to turn off his radio, but no one came.

As he grew older, he moved back upstairs, since the room on the ground floor had become too small for him. This proved to be somewhat of a strain for him: many times he would be lying in bed when someone would call his name. But there was never anyone there. Exasperated, the youngster spoke up, challenging the ghost to give some sign of his presence so that there could be communication between them. "If you can hear me, make a noise," David said to his ghost. At that very moment, the door to his room began to rattle without apparent cause. Still unconvinced, since the door had rattled before because of natural causes, David continued his monologue with, "If you are there, show yourself," and at that moment he heard a strange noise behind him. The door to his closet, which had been closed, was slowly opening. This wasn't very reassuring, even though it might represent some kind of dialogue with the ghost.

Shortly thereafter, and in broad daylight, just as he had gotten home from school, David heard a very loud noise in the upper portion of the house: it sounded as if all their cats were tearing each other to pieces, and the sound of a lot of coat hangers falling down augmented the bedlam. Quickly, David ran up the stairs—only to find neither cats nor fallen coat hangers. And to this day, David doesn't know who the strange visitor was.

The Electrocuted Ghost

Mrs. Jane Eidson was a housewife in suburban Minneapolis. She was middle-aged and her five children ranged in age from nine to twenty. Her husband, Bill, traveled four days each week. For eight years they had lived in a cottage-type brick house that was twenty-eight years old.

The first time the Eidsons noticed that there was something odd about their otherwise ordinary-looking home was after they had been in the house for a short time. Mrs. Eidson was in the basement sewing, when all of a sudden she felt that she was not alone and wanted to run upstairs. She suppressed this strong urge but felt very uncomfortable. Another evening, her husband was down there practicing a speech when he had the same feeling of another presence. His self-control was not as strong as hers, and he came upstairs.

In discussing their strange feelings with their next-door neighbor, they discovered that the previous tenant also had complained about the basement. Their daughter Rita had never wanted to go to the basement by herself and, when pressed for a reason, finally admitted that there was a man down there. She described him as dark-haired and wearing a plaid shirt. Sometimes he would stand by her bed at night and she would become frightened, but the moment she thought of calling her mother, the image disappeared. Another spot where she felt his presence was the little playhouse at the other end of their yard.

The following spring, Mrs. Eidson noticed a bouncing light at the top of the stairs as she was about to go to bed in an upstairs room that she occupied while convalescing from surgery. The light followed her to her room as if it had a mind of its own. When she entered her room the light left, but the room felt icy. She was disturbed by this, but nevertheless went to bed and soon had forgotten all about it as sleep came to her. Suddenly, in the middle of the night, she woke and sat up in bed. Something had awakened her. At the head of her bed she saw a man who was "beige-colored," as she put it. As she stared at the apparition it went away, again leaving the room very chilly.

About that same time, the Eidsons noticed that their electric appliances were playing tricks on them. There was the time at five A.M. when their washing machine went on by itself, as did the television set in the basement, which could only be turned on by plugging it into the wall socket. When they had gone to bed, the set was off and there was no one around to plug it in.

Who was so fond of electrical gadgets as to turn them on in the small hours of the morning?

Finally Mrs. Eidson found out. In May 1949, a young man who was just out of the service had occupied the house. His hobby was electrical wiring, it seems, for he had put in a strand of heavy wires from the basement underground through the yard to the other end of the property. When he attempted to hook them up with the utility pole belonging to the electric company, he was killed instantly. It happened near the place where Mrs. Eidson's girl had seen the apparition. Since the wires are still in her garden, Mrs. Eidson is not at all surprised that the dead man likes to hang around.

And what better way for an electronics buff to manifest as a ghost than by appearing as a bright, bouncy light? As of this writing, the dead electrician is still playing tricks in the Eidson home, and Mrs. Eidson is looking for a new home—one a little less unusual than their present one.

The Ghost and the Golf Cap

Lana T., one of seven children from eastern Missouri, has ESP to a considerable extent. Three of her sisters also have this ability, so perhaps it runs in the family. She and her husband lived in a big city in central Missouri. Clairvoyant dreams and other verified incidents of ESP led to an interest in the much-maligned Ouija board, and she and her three sisters, Jean, Judy, and Tony, became veritable addicts of this little gadget. A close friend and her husband moved into a nearby house in the same community, without realizing that the house had become available due to the suicide of the previous owner.

Mrs. T.'s friend had come from another state, so the local facts were not too well known to her. When the new owner discovered that her neighbor, Lana T., had psychic gifts and an interest in occult matters, she confided freely in her. It appeared that one of the bathrooms was always cold, regardless of the weather outside or the temperature in the rest of the house; a certain closet door would simply not stay closed; and the heat register was bound to rattle of its own volition. Objects would move from one place to another, without anyone having touched them. Footsteps were heard going up and down the hall, as if someone were pacing up and down. Once the new owner saw a whitish mist that dissolved immediately when she spoke to it.

Her husband, publisher of a local newspaper, would not even discuss the matter, considering it foolish. But one night he woke up and informed her that he had just been touched by a cold, clammy hand. This was enough to drive the new owner to consult with her neighbor.

Lana T. offered to try and find out who the disturbing ghost was. Together with one of her sisters, she sat herself down with her trusty Ouija board and asked it to identify the disturbing entity in the house. Ouija board communication is slow and sometimes boring, but, in this instance, the instrument rapidly identified the communicator as a certain Ted. A chill went down Mrs. T.'s spine, for Ted was the man who had committed suicide in her friend's house.

From then on, a veritable conversation ensued between Mrs. T. and the ghost, in which he explained that he was angry because the new owner had burned something of his. Mrs. T. asked what the new owner could do to satisfy him, and the angry ghost replied that she should destroy something of her own to make up for his loss—something white.

When Mrs. T. described her conversation with the ghost to the new owner of the house, the lady was mystified. She could not recall having burned anything belonging to the former owner. Back to the Ouija board went Mrs. T. When she demanded that the ghost describe the item in question more fully, he replied, somewhat impatiently, that it had been white with green trim and had the letters SFCC on it. Mrs. T. returned to her neighbor with this additional information. This time she struck paydirt: shortly after the couple from out of state had moved into the house, the lady of the house had discovered an old golf cap in the top drawer of one of her closets, white with green trim and the initials of the country club, SFCC, on it! The cap had somehow bothered her, so she had tossed it into the trash can and the contents of the can were later burned.

The ghost had told the truth. But how could she satisfy his strange whim in return? At that time she and her husband had considered buying a small, expensive white marble statue. They decided to forego this pleasure. Perhaps their sacrifice of this "white" item would make up for the lost golf cap? Evidently it did—for the house has been quiet ever since!

The Girls' School Ghost

In one of the quietest and most elegant sections of old Cincinnati, where ghosts and hauntings are rarely whispered about, stands a lovely Victorian mansion built around 1850 in what was then a wealthy suburb of the city.

The house was brought to my attention some years ago by John Strader of Clifton, a descendant of one of the early Dutch families who settled Cincinnati, and himself a student of the paranormal. The owners at that time were the Stenton family, or rather, of one of the apartments in the mansion, for it had long been subdivided into a number of apartments lived in by various people.

Soon after they had taken up residence in the old house, the Stentons were startled by noises, as if someone were walking in the hall, and when they checked, there was never anyone about who could have caused the walking. Then, two weeks after they had moved in, and always at exactly the same time—2:10 A.M.—they would hear the noise of a heavy object hitting the marble floor; of course there was nothing that could have caused it.

Shortly thereafter, while Mrs. Stenton and her father were doing some research work in the flat, someone softly called out her name, Marilyn. Both heard it. What really upset them was the sound of arguing voices coming from the area of the ceiling in their bedroom: Mrs. Stenton had the impression that there were a group of young girls up there.

But the most dramatic event was to transpire a couple of weeks later. Someone had entered the bedroom, and as she knew she was alone, her family being in other parts of the house, she was frightened, especially when she saw what appeared to be a misty figure. As soon as she had made eye contact with it, the figure shot out of the room, through the French doors leading to a studio, managing to knock the Venetian blinds on the doors, causing them to sway back and forth.

Shortly before I visited Cincinnati to deal with this case, Mrs. Stenton had another eerie experience. It was winter and had been snowing the night before. When Mrs. Stenton stepped out onto their front porch, she immediately noticed a fresh set of footprints on the porch, heading *away* from the house.

The house was originally built in 1850 as a large private home; later it became a girls' school, and much later an apartment house of sorts. The Stenton's apartment is the largest in the house, encompassing seven rooms.

When I looked into the case I discovered some additional details. In 1880 a young man of the Henry family had committed suicide in the house by shooting himself, and after the family moved the house could not be sold for a long time. It became known as being haunted and was boarded up. Finally a girls' school, the Ealy School, bought it in 1900.

Other tenants had also encountered unusual phenomena ranging from "presences" to noises of objects hitting floors, and footsteps following one around when no one was, in fact, doing so. Even the dog owned by one of the tenants would under no condition enter the area of the disturbances and would put up a fearsome howl.

But the item most likely to have an answer to the goings-on came to me by talking to some of the oldsters in the area: one of the young girls in the school was said to have hanged herself upstairs, above the Stenton's apartment. Was it her ghost or that of young Henry who could not leave well enough alone?

The Burning Ghost

I treat each case reported to me on an individual basis. Some I reject on the face of the report, and others only after I have been through a long and careful investigation. But other reports have the ring of truth about them and are worthy of belief, even though some of them are no longer capable of verification because witnesses have died or sites have been destroyed.

A good example is the case reported to me by Mrs. Edward Needs, Jr., of Canton, Ohio. In a small town by the name of Homeworth, there is a stretch of land near the highway that is today nothing more than a neglected farm with a boarded-up old barn still standing. The spot is actually on a dirt road, and the nearest house is half a mile away, with wooded territory in between. This is important, you see, for the spot is isolated and a man might die before help could arrive. On rainy days, the dirt road is impassable. Mrs. Needs has passed the spot a number of times, and does not particularly care to go there. Somehow it always gives her an uneasy feeling. Once, their car got stuck in the mud on a rainy day, and they had to drive through open fields to get out.

It was on that adventure-filled ride that Mr. Needs confided for the first time what had happened to him at that spot on prior occasions. It was the year when Edward Needs and a friend were on a joy ride after dark. At that time Needs had not yet married his present wife, and the two men had been drinking a little, but were far from drunk. It was then that they discovered the dirt road for the first time.

On the spur of the moment, they followed it. A moment later they came to the old barn. But just as they were approaching it, a man jumped out of nowhere in front of them. What was even more sobering was the condition this man was in: engulfed in flames from head to toe! Quickly Needs put his bright headlights on the scene, to see better. The man then ran into the woods across the road and just disappeared.

Two men never became cold sober more quickly. They turned around and went back to the main highway fast. But the first chance they had, they returned with two carloads full of other fellows. They were equipped with strong lights, guns, and absolutely no whiskey. When the first of the cars was within twenty feet of the spot where Needs had seen the apparition, they all saw the same thing: there before them was the horrible spectacle of a human being blazing from top to bottom, and evidently suffering terribly as he tried to run away from his doom. Needs emptied his gun at the figure: it never moved or acknowledged that it had been hit by the bullets. A few seconds later, the figure ran into the woods—exactly as it had when Needs had first encountered it.

Now the ghost posse went into the barn, which they found abandoned although not in very bad condition. The only strange thing was spots showing evidence of fire: evidently someone or something had burned inside the barn without, however, setting fire to the barn as a whole. Or had the fiery man run outside to save his barn from the fire?

The Ghost of the Murdered Child

O n January 7, Mr. and Mrs. S. moved into an older house on South Fourth Street, a rented, fully-furnished two-bedroom house in a medium-sized city in Oklahoma. Mrs. S.'s husband was a career service man in the Army, stationed at a nearby Army camp. They had a small boy, and looked forward to a pleasant stay in which the boy could play with neighborhood kids, while Mrs. S. tried to make friends in what to her was a new environment.

She was not easily frightened off by anything she cannot explain, and the occult was the last thing on her mind. They had lived in the house for about two weeks when she noticed light footsteps walking in the hall at night. When she checked on them, there was no one there. Her ten-year-old son was sleeping across the hall, and she wondered if perhaps he was walking in his sleep. But each time she heard the footsteps and would check on him, she found him sound asleep. The footsteps continued on and off for a period of four months.

Then one Sunday afternoon at about two o'clock, when her husband was at his post and her son in the backyard playing, she found herself in the kitchen. Suddenly she heard a child crying very softly, as if afraid to cry aloud. At once she ran into the backyard to see if her son was hurt. There was nothing wrong with him, and she found him playing happily with a neighborhood boy. It then dawned on her that she could not hear the child crying outside the house, but immediately upon reentering the house, the faint sobs were clearly audible again.

She traced the sound to her bedroom, and when she entered the room, it ceased to be noticeable. This puzzled her to no end, since she had no idea what could cause the sounds. Added to this were strange thumping sounds, which frequently awakened her in the middle of the night. It sounded as if someone had fallen out of bed.

On these occasions, she would get out of bed quickly and rush into her son's room, only to find him fast asleep. A thorough check of the entire house revealed no source for the strange noises. But Mrs. S. noticed that their Siamese cat, who slept at the foot of her bed when these things happened, also reacted to them: his hair would bristle, his ears would fly back, and he would growl and stare into space at something or someone she could not see.

About that time, her mother decided to visit them. Since her mother was an invalid, Mrs. S. decided not to tell her about the strange phenomena in order to avoid upsetting her. She stayed at the house for three days, when one morning she wanted to know why Mrs. S. was up at two o'clock in the morning making coffee. Since the house had only two bedrooms, they had put a half-bed into the kitchen for her mother, especially as the kitchen was very large and she could see the television from where she was sleeping. Her mother insisted she had heard footsteps coming down the hall into the kitchen. She called out to what she assumed was her daughter, and when there was no answer, she assumed that her daughter and her son-in-law had had some sort of disagreement and she had gotten up to make some coffee.

From her bed she could not reach the light switch, but she could see the time by the illuminated clock and realized it was two o'clock in the morning. Someone came down the hall, entered the kitchen, put water into the coffee pot, plugged it in, and then walked out of the kitchen and down the hall. She could hear the sound of coffee perking and could actually smell it. However, when she didn't hear anyone coming back, she assumed that her daughter and son-in-law had made up and gone back to sleep.

She did likewise, and decided to question her daughter about it in the morning. Mrs. S. immediately checked the kitchen, but there was no trace of the coffee to be found, which did not help her state of mind. A little later she heard some commotion outside the house, and on stepping outside noticed that the dogcatcher was trying to take a neighbor's dog with him. She decided to try and talk him out of it, and the conversation led to her husband being in the service, a statement that seemed to provoke a negative reaction on the part of the dogcatcher. He informed Mrs. S. that the last GI to live in the house was a murderer. When she wanted to know more about it, he clammed up immediately. But Mrs. S. became highly agitated. She called the local newspaper and asked for any and all information concerning her house. It was then that she learned the bitter truth.

In October two years before, a soldier stationed at the same base as her husband had beaten his two-year-old daughter to death. The murder took place in what had now become Mrs. S.'s bedroom. Mrs. S., shocked by the news, sent up a silent prayer, hoping that the restless soul of the child might find peace and not have to haunt a house where she had suffered nothing but unhappiness in her short life.

The Ghost of the Henpecked Husband

Mike L. lives in Tennessee, where his family has been in residence for several generations. Ever since he can remember, he has had psychic ability. At the time when a favorite uncle was in the hospital, he was awakened in the middle of the night to see his uncle standing by his bed. "Goodbye, Michael," the uncle said, and then the image faded away. At that instant, Mike knew that his uncle had passed away, so he went back to sleep. The following morning, his mother awoke him to tell him that his uncle had passed away during the night.

In April, he and his wife moved to a residential section in one of the large cities of Tennessee. They bought a house from a lady well in her seventies who had the reputation of being somewhat cranky. She was not too well liked in the neighborhood.

Shortly after they had settled down in the house, they noticed footsteps in the rafters over their bedroom. Regardless of the hour, these footsteps would come across the ceiling from one side of the room to the other. Whenever they checked, there was no one there who could have caused the footsteps.

While they were still puzzled about the matter, though not shocked, and since they had had psychic presences in other houses, something still more remarkable occurred. There were two floor lamps in the living room, on opposite sides of the room. One night, Mr. L. awoke and noticed one of the floor lamps lit. Since he clearly remembered having turned it off on going to bed, he was puzzled, but got out of bed and switched it off again. As if to complement this incident, the other floor lamp came on by itself a few nights later, even though it had been turned off by hand a short time before.

This was the beginning of an entire series of lights being turned on in various parts of the house, seemingly by unseen hands. Since it was their practice not to leave any lights on except for a small night light in their daughter's room, there was no way in which this could be explained by negligence or on rational grounds. The house has a basement, including a small space below the wooden front porch. As a result of this hollow space, if anyone were walking on the porch, the steps would reverberate that much more audibly. The L.'s frequently heard someone come up the porch, approach the door, and stop there. Whenever they looked out, they saw no one about. Not much later, they were awakened by the noise of a large number of dishes crashing to the floor of the kitchen, at least so they thought. When they checked, everything was in order; no dish had been disturbed.

They were still wondering about this when they caught the movement of something—or someone—out of the corner of their eye in the living room. When they looked closer, there was no one there. Then the dresser in the bedroom *seemed* to be moving across the floor, or so it sounded. By the time they got to the room, nothing had been changed.

One night, just after retiring, Mr. L. was shocked by a great deal of noise in the basement. It sounded as if someone were wrecking his shop. He jumped out of bed, grabbed a gun, opened the basement door, and turned on the light. There was an audible scurrying sound, as if someone were moving about, followed by silence.

Immediately Mr. L. thought he had a burglar, but realized he would be unable to go downstairs undetected. Under the circumstances, he called for his wife to telephone the police while he stood at the head of the stairs guarding the basement exit. As soon as he heard the police arrive, he locked the only door to the basement and joined them on the outside of the house. Together they investigated, only to find no one about, no evidence of foul play. Even more inexplicable, nothing in the shop had been touched. About that time, Mr. L. noticed a tendency of the basement door to unlock itself seemingly of its own volition, even though it was Mr. L.'s custom to lock it both at night and when leaving the house. During the daytime, Mrs. L. frequently heard footsteps overhead when she was in the basement, even though she was fully aware of the fact that there was no one in the house but her.

By now, Mr. and Mrs. L. realized that someone was trying to get their attention. They became aware of an unseen presence staring at them in the dining room, or bothering Mrs. L. in one of the other rooms of the house. Finally, Mike L. remembered that a Rosicrucian friend had given them a so-called Hermetic Cross when they had encountered ghostly troubles in another house. He brought the cross to the dining room and nailed it to the wall. This seemed to relieve the pressure somewhat, until they found a calendar hung in front of the cross, as if to downgrade its power.

Mr. L. made some further inquiries in the neighborhood to find out who the unseen intruder might be. Eventually he managed to piece the story together. The woman from whom they had bought the house had been a widow of about nine years when they had met her. The husband had been extremely unhappy in the house; he was not permitted to smoke, for instance, and had to hide his cigarettes in a neighbor's basement. Nothing he did in his own house met with his wife's approval, it appeared, and he died a very unhappy man. Could it not be that his restless spirit, once freed from the shackles of the body, finally enjoyed his unobstructed power to roam the house and do whatever he pleased? Or perhaps he could now even enjoy the vicarious thrill of frightening the later owners, and for the first time in his long life, become the stronger party in the house.

West

The Whaley House Ghosts

I first heard about the ghosts at San Diego's Whaley House through an article in *Cosmic Star*, Merle Gould's psychic newspaper, back in 1963. The account was not too specific about the people who had experienced something unusual at the house, but it did mention mysterious footsteps, cold drafts, unseen presences staring over one's shoulder and the scent of perfume where no such odor could logically be—the gamut of uncanny phenomena, in short. My appetite was whetted. Evidently the curators, Mr. and Mrs. James Redding, were making some alterations in the building when the haunting began.

I marked the case as a possibility when in the area, and turned to other matters. Then fate took a hand in bringing me closer to San Diego.

I had appeared on Regis Philbin's network television show and a close friendship had developed between us. When Regis moved to San Diego and started his own program there, he asked me to be his guest.

We had already talked of a house he knew in San Diego that he wanted me to investigate with him; it turned out to be the same Whaley House. Finally we agreed on June 25th as the night we would go to the haunted house and film a trance session with Sybil Leek, then talk about it the following day on Regis' show.

Sybil Leek came over from England a few years ago, after a successful career as a producer and writer of television documentaries and author of a number of books on animal life and antiques. At one time she ran an antique shop in her beloved New Forest area of southern

England, but her name came to the attention of Americans primarily because of her religious convictions: she happened to be a witch. Not a Hallowe'en type witch, to be sure, but a follower of "the Old Religion," the pre-Christian Druidic cult which is still being practiced in many parts of the world. Her personal involvement with witchcraft was of less interest to me than her great abilities as a trance medium. I tested her and found her capable of total "dissociation of personality," which is the necessary requirement for good trance work. She can get "out of her own body" under my prodding, and lend it to whatever personality might be present in the atmosphere of our quest. Afterwards, she will remember nothing and merely continue pleasantly where we left off in conversation prior to trance—even if it is two hours later! Sybil Leek lends her ESP powers exclusively to my research and confines her "normal" activities to a career in writing and business.

We arrived in sunny San Diego ahead of Regis Philbin, and spent the day loafing at the Half Moon Inn, a romantic luxury motel on a peninsula stretching out into San Diego harbor. Regis could not have picked a better place for us—it was almost like being in Hawaii. We dined with Kay Sterner, president and chief sensitive of the local California Parapsychology Foundation, a charming and knowledgeable woman who had been to the haunted Whaley House, but of course she did not talk about it in Sybil's presence. In deference to my policy, she waited until Sybil left us. Then she told me of her forays into Whaley House, where she had felt several presences. I thanked her and decided to do my own investigating from scratch.

My first step was to contact June Reading, who was not only the director of the house but also its historian. She asked me to treat confidentially whatever I might find in the house through psychic means. This I could not promise, but I offered to treat the material with respect and without undue sensationalism, and I trust I have not disappointed Mrs. Reading too much. My readers are entitled to all the facts as I find them.

Mrs. Reading herself is the author of a booklet about the historic house, and a brief summary of its development also appears in a brochure given to visitors, who keep coming all week long from every part of the country. I quote from the brochure.

"The Whaley House, in the heart of Old Town, San Diego—restored, refurnished and opened for public viewing—represents one of the finest examples extant of early California buildings.

"Original construction of the two-story mansion was begun on May 6, 1856, by Thomas Whaley, San Diego pioneer. The building was completed on May 10, 1857. Bricks used in the structure came from a clay-bed and kiln—the first brick-yard in San Diego—which Thomas Whaley established 300 yards to the southwest of his projected home.

"Much of 'Old San Diego's' social life centered around this impressive home. Later the house was used as a theater for a traveling company, 'The Tanner Troupe,' and at one time served as the San Diego County Court House.

"The Whaley House was erected on what is now the corner of San Diego Avenue and Harney Street, on a 150-by-217-foot lot, which was part of an 8 1/2-acre parcel purchased by Whaley on September 25, 1855. The North room originally was a granary without flooring, but was remodeled when it became the County Court House on August 12,1869.

"Downstairs rooms include a tastefully furnished parlor, a music room, a library and the annex, which served as the County Court House. There are four bedrooms upstairs, two of which were leased to 'The Tanner Troupe' for theatricals.

"Perhaps the most significant historical event involving the Whaley House was the surreptitious transfer of the county court records from it to 'New Town,' present site of downtown San Diego, on the night of March 31, 1871.

"Despite threats to forcibly prevent even legal transfer of the court house to 'New Town,' Col. Chalmers Scott, then county clerk and recorder, and his henchmen removed the county records under cover of darkness and transported them to a 'New Town' building at 6th and G Streets.

"The Whaley House would be gone today but for a group of San Diegans who prevented its demolition in 1956 by forming the Historical Shrine Foundation of San Diego County and buying the land and the building.

"Later, the group convinced the County of San Diego that the house should be preserved as an historical museum, and restored to its early-day splendor. This was done under the supervision and guidance of an advisory committee including members of the Foundation, which today maintains the Whaley House as an historical museum.

"Most of the furnishings, authenticated as in use in Whaley's time, are from other early-day San Diego County homes and were donated by interested citizens.

"The last Whaley to live in the house was Corinne Lillian Whaley, youngest of Whaley's six children. She died at the age of 89 in 1953. Whaley himself died December 14, 1890, at the age of 67. He is buried in San Diego in Mount Hope Cemetery, as is his wife, Anna, who lived until February 24, 1913."

When it became apparent that a thorough investigation of the haunting would be made, and that all of San Diego would be able to learn of it through television and newspapers, excitement mounted to a high pitch.

Mrs. Reading kept in close touch with Regis Philbin and me, because ghosts have a way of "sensing" an impending attempt to oust them—and this was not long in coming. On May 24th the "activities" inside the house had already increased to a marked degree; they were of the same general nature as previously noticed sounds.

Was the ghost getting restless?

I had asked Mrs. Reading to prepare an exact account of all occurrences within the house, from the very first moment on, and to assemble as many of the witnesses as possible for further interrogation.

Most of these people had worked part time as guides in the house during the five years since its restoration. The phenomena thus far had occurred, or at any rate been observed, mainly between 10 <H>a.m. and 5:30 pm, when the house closes to visitors. There is no one there at night, but an effective burglar alarm system is in operation to prevent flesh-and-blood intruders from breaking in unnoticed. Ineffective with the ghostly kind, as we were soon to learn!

I shall now quote the director's own report. It vouches for the accuracy and calibre of witnesses.

Phenomena Observed at Whaley House
By Visitors

Oct. 9, 1960—Dr. & Mrs. Kirbey, of New Westminster, B.C., Canada. 1:30-2:30 pm (He was then Director of the Medical Association of New Westminster.)

While Dr. Kirbey and his wife were in the house, he became interested in an exhibit in one of the display cases and she asked if she might go through by herself, because she was familiar with the Victorian era, and felt very much at home in these surroundings. Accordingly, I remained downstairs with the Doctor, discussing early physicians and medical practices.

When Mrs. Kirbey returned to the display room, she asked me in hesitating fashion if I had ever noticed anything unusual about the upstairs. I asked her what she had noticed. She reported that when she started upstairs, she felt a breeze over her head, and though she saw nothing, realized a pressure against her, seemed to make it hard to go up. When she looked into the rooms, had the feeling that someone was standing behind her, in fact so close to her that she turned around several times to look. Said she expected someone would tap her on the shoulder. When she joined us downstairs, we all walked toward the courtroom. As we entered, again Mrs. Kirbey turned to me and asked if I knew that someone inhabited the courtroom. She pointed to the bailiff's table, saying as she did, "Right over there." I asked her if the person was clear enough for her to describe, and she said:

"I see a small figure of a woman who has a swarthy complexion. She is wearing a long full skirt, reaching to the floor. The skirt appears to be a calico or gingham, small print. She has a kind of cap on her head, dark hair and eyes and she is wearing gold hoops in her pierced ears. She seems to stay in this room, lives here, I gather, and I get the impression we are sort of invading her privacy."

Mrs. Kirbey finished her description by asking me if any of the Whaley family were swarthy, to which I replied, "No."

This was, to my knowledge, the only description given of an apparition by a visitor, and Mrs. Kirbey the only person who brought up the fact in connection with the courtroom. Many of the visitors have commented upon the atmosphere in this room, however, and some people attempting to work in the room comment upon the difficulty they have in trying to concentrate here.

By Persons Employed at Whaley House
April, 1960
10:00 a.m. By myself, June A. Reading, 3447 Kite St. Sound of Footsteps—in the Upstairs

This sound of someone walking across the floor, I first heard in the morning, a week before the museum opened to the public. County workmen were still painting some shelving in the hall, and during this week often arrived before I did, so it was not unusual to find them already at work when I arrived.

This morning, however, I was planning to furnish the downstairs rooms, and so hurried in and down the hall to open the back door awaiting the arrival of the trucks with the furnishings. Two men followed me down the hall; they were going to help with the furniture arrangement. As I reached up to unbolt the back door, I heard the sound of what seemed to be someone walking across the bedroom floor. I paid no attention, thinking it was one of the workmen. But the men, who heard the sounds at the time I did, insisted I go upstairs and find out who was in the house. So, calling out, I started to mount the stairs. Halfway up, I could see no lights, and that the outside shutters to the windows were still closed. I made some comment to the men who had followed me, and turned around to descend the stairs. One of the men joked with me about the spirits coming in to look things over, and we promptly forgot the matter.

However, the sound of walking continued. And for the next six months I found myself going upstairs to see if someone was actually upstairs. This would happen during the day, sometimes when visitors were in other parts of the house, other times when I was busy at my desk trying to catch up on correspondence or bookwork. At times it would sound as though someone were descending the stairs, but would fade away before reaching the first floor. In September, 1962, the house was the subject of a news article in the *San Diego Evening Tribune,* and this same story was reprinted in the September 1962 issue of *Fate* magazine.

Oct. & Nov. 1962. We began to have windows in the upper part of the house open unaccountably. We installed horizontal bolts on three windows in the front bedroom, thinking this would end the matter. However, the really disturbing part of this came when it set off our burglar alarm in the night, and we were called by the Police and San Diego Burglar Alarm Co. to come down and see if the house had been broken into. Usually, we would find nothing disturbed. (One exception to this was when the house was broken into by vandals, about 1963, and items from the kitchen display stolen.)

In the fall of 1962, early October, while engaged in giving a talk to some school children, class of 25 pupils, I heard a sound of someone walking, which seemed to come from the roof. One of the children interrupted me, asking what that noise was, and excusing myself from them, I went outside the building, down on the street to see if workmen from the County were repairing the roof. Satisfied that there was no one on the roof of the building, I went in and resumed the tour.

Residents of Old Town are familiar with this sound, and tell me that it has been evident for years. Miss Whaley, who lived in the house for 85 years, was aware of it. She passed away in 1953.

Mrs. Grace Bourquin, 2938 Beech St.
Sat. Dec. 14, 1963, noon—Was seated in the hall downstairs having lunch, when she heard walking sound in upstairs.

Sat. Jan. 10, 1964, 1:30 P.M. Walked down the hall and looked up the staircase. On the upper landing she saw an apparition—the figure of a man, clad in frock coat and pantaloons, the face turned away from her, so she could not make it out. Suddenly it faded away.

Lawrence Riveroll, resides on Jefferson St., Old Town.
Jan. 5, 1963, 12:30 noon

Was alone in the house. No visitors present at the time. While seated at the desk in the front hail, heard sounds of music and singing, described as a woman's voice. Song "Home Again." Lasted about 30 seconds.

Jan. 7, 1963, 1:30 P.M.

Visitors in upstairs. Downstairs, he heard organ music, which seemed to come from the courtroom, where there is an organ. Walked into the room to see if someone was attempting to play it. Cover on organ was closed. He saw no one in the room.

Jan. 19, 1963, 5:15 P.M.

Museum was closed for the day. Engaged in closing shutters downstairs. Heard footsteps in upper part of house in the same area as described. Went up to check, saw nothing.

Sept. 10-12, 1964—at dusk, about 5:15 P.M.

Engaged in closing house, together with another worker. Finally went into the music room, began playing the piano. Suddenly felt a distinct pressure on his hands, as though someone had their hands on his. He turned to look toward the front hall, in the direction of the desk, hoping to get the attention of the person seated there, when he saw the apparition of a slight woman dressed in a hoop skirt. In the dim light was unable to see clearly the face. Suddenly the figure vanished.

J. Milton Keller, 4114 Middlesex Dr.

Sept. 22, 1964, 2:00 P.M.

Engaged in tour with visitors at the parlor, when suddenly he, together with people assembled at balustrade, noticed crystal drops hanging from lamp on parlor table begin to swing back and forth. This occurred only on one side of the lamp. The other drops did not move. This continued about two minutes.

Dec. 15, 1964, 5:15 P.M.

Engaged in closing house along with others. Returned from securing restrooms, walked down hall, turned to me with the key, while I stepped into the hall closet to reach for the master switch which turns off all lights. I pulled the switch, started to turn around to step out, when he said, "Stop, don't move, you'll step on the dog!" He put his hands out, in a gesture for me to stay still. Meantime, I turned just in time to see what resembled a flash of light between us, and what appeared to be the back of a dog, scurry down the hall and turn into the dining room. I decided to resume a normal attitude, so I kidded him a little about trying to scare me. Other people were present in the front hall at the time, waiting for us at the door, so he turned to them and said in a rather hurt voice that I did not believe him. I realized then that he had witnessed an apparition, so I asked him to see if he could describe it. *He said he saw a spotted dog, like a fox terrier, that ran with his ears flapping, down the hall and into the dining room.*

May 29,1965, 2:30 P.M.

Escorting visitors through house, upstairs. Called to me, asking me to come up. Upon going up, he, I and visitors all witnessed a black rocking chair, moving back and forth as if occupied by a person. It had started moving unaccountably, went on about three minutes. Caused quite a stir among visitors.

Dec. 27, 1964, 5:00 P.M.

Late afternoon, prior to closing, *saw the apparition of a woman dressed in a green plaid gingham dress.* She had long dark hair, coiled up in a bun at neck, was seated on a settee in bedroom.

Feb. 1965, 2:00 P.M.

Engaged in giving a tour with visitors, when two elderly ladies called and asked him to come upstairs, and step over to the door of the nursery. These ladies, visitors, called his attention to a sound that was like the cry of a baby, about 16 months old. All three reported the sound.

March 24, 1965, 1:00 P.M.

He, together with Mrs. Bourquin and his parents, Mr. & Mrs. Keller, engaged in touring the visitors, when for some reason his attention was directed to the foot of the staircase. He walked back to it, and heard the sound of someone in the upper part of the house whistling. No one was in the upstairs at the time.

Mrs. Suzanne Pere, 106 Albatross, El Cajon.
April 8, 1963, 4:30 P.M.

Was engaged in typing in courtroom, working on manuscript. Suddenly she called to me, calling my attention to a noise in the upstairs. We both stopped work, walked up the stairs together, to see if anyone could possibly be there. As it was near closing time, we decided to secure the windows. Mrs. Pere kept noticing a chilly breeze at the back of her head, had the distinct feeling that someone, though invisible, was present and kept following her from one window to another.

Oct. 14, 21; Nov. 18, 1964

During the morning and afternoon on these days, called my attention to the smell of cigar smoke, and the fragrance of perfume or cologne. This occurred in the parlor, hall, upstairs bedroom. In another bedroom she called my attention to something resembling dusting powder.

Nov. 28, 1963, 2:30 P.M.

Reported seeing an apparition in the study. A group of men there, dressed in frock coats, some with plain vests, others figured material. One of this group had a large gold watch chain across vest. Seemed to be a kind of meeting; all figures were animated, some pacing the floor, others conversing; all serious and agitated, but oblivious to everything else. One figure in this group seemed to be an official, and stood off by himself. This person was of medium stocky build, light brown hair, and mustache which was quite full and long. He had very piercing light blue eyes, penetrating gaze. Mrs. Pere sensed that he was some kind of official, a person of importance. He seemed about to speak. Mrs. Pere seemed quite exhausted by her experience witnessing this scene, yet was quite curious about the man with the penetrating gaze. I remember her asking me if I knew of anyone answering this description, because it remained with her for some time.

Oct. 7., 1963, 10:30 A.M.

Reported unaccountable sounds issuing from kitchen, as though someone were at work there. Same day, she reported smelling the odor of something baking.

Nov. 27, 1964, 10:15 A.M.

Heard a distinct noise from kitchen area, as though something had dropped to the floor. I was present when this occurred. She called to me and asked what I was doing there, thinking I had been rearranging exhibit. At this time I was at work in courtroom, laying out work. Both of us reached the kitchen, to find one of the utensils on the shelf rack had disengaged itself, fallen to the floor, and had struck a copper boiler directly below. No one else was in the house at the time, and we were at a loss to explain this.

Mrs. T.R. Allen, 3447 Kite Street

Was present *Jan. 7, 1963, 1:30 P.M.* Heard organ music issue from courtroom, when Lawrence Riveroll heard the same (see his statement).

Was present *Sept. 10-12, 1964,* at dusk, with Lawrence Riveroll, when he witnessed apparition. Mrs. Allen went upstairs to close shutters, and as she ascended them, described a chill breeze that seemed to come over her head. Upstairs, she walked into the bedroom and toward the windows. Suddenly she heard a sound behind her, as though something had dropped to the floor. She turned to look, saw nothing, but again experienced the feeling of having someone, invisible, hovering near her. She had a feeling of fear. Completed her task as quickly as possible, and left the upstairs hastily. Upon my return, both persons seemed anxious to leave the house.

May, 1965 (the last Friday), 1:30 P.M.

Was seated in downstairs front hall, when she heard the sound of footsteps.

Regis Philbin himself had been to the house before. With him on that occasion was Mrs. Philbin, who is highly sensitive to psychic emanations, and a teacher-friend of theirs considered an amateur medium.

They observed, during their vigil, what appeared to be a white figure of a person, but when Regis challenged it, unfortunately with his flashlight, it disappeared immediately. Mrs. Philbin felt extremely uncomfortable on that occasion and had no desire to return to the house.

By now I knew that the house had three ghosts, a man, a woman and a baby—and a spotted dog. The scene observed in one of the rooms sounded more like a psychic impression of a past event to me than a bona fide ghost.

I later discovered that still another part-time guide at the house, William H. Richardson, of 470 Silvery Lane, El Cajon, had not only experienced something out of the ordinary at the house, but had taken part in a kind of seance with interesting results. Here is his statement, given to me in September of 1965, several months *after* our own trance session had taken place.

In the summer of 1963 I worked in Whaley House as a guide.

One morning before the house was open to the public, several of us employees were seated in the music room downstairs, and the sound of someone in heavy boots walking across the upstairs was heard by us all. When we went to investigate the noise, we found all the windows locked and shuttered, and the only door to the outside from upstairs was locked. This experience first sparked my interest in ghosts.

I asked June Reading, the director, to allow several of my friends from Starlight Opera, a local summer musical theatre, to spend the night in the house.

At midnight, on Friday, August 13, we met at the house. Carolyn Whyte, a member of the parapsychology group in San Diego and a member of the Starlight Chorus, gave an introductory talk on what to expect, and we all went into the parlor to wait for something to happen.

The first experience was that of a cool breeze blowing through the room, which was felt by several of us despite the fact that all doors and windows were locked and shuttered.

The next thing that happened was that a light appeared over a boy's head. This traveled from his head across the wall, where it disappeared. Upon later investigation it was found to have disappeared at the portrait of Thomas Whaley, the original owner of the house. Footsteps were also heard several times in the room upstairs.

At this point we broke into groups and dispersed to different parts of the house. One group went into the study which is adjacent to the parlor, and there witnessed a shadow on the wall surrounded by a pale light which moved up and down the wall and changed shape as it did so. There was no source of light into the room and one could pass in front of the shadow without disturbing it.

Another group was upstairs when their attention was directed simultaneously to the chandelier which began to swing around as if someone were holding the bottom and twisting the sides. One boy was tapped on the leg several times by some unseen force while seated there.

Meanwhile, downstairs in the parlor, an old-fashioned lamp with prisms hanging on the edges began to act strangely. As we watched, several prisms began to swing by themselves. These would stop and others would start, but they never swung simultaneously. There was no breeze in the room.

At this time we all met in the courtroom. Carolyn then suggested that we try to lift the large table in the room.

We sat around the table and placed our fingertips on it. A short while later it began to creak and then slid across the floor approximately eight inches, and finally lifted completely off the floor on the corner where I was seated.

Later on we brought a small table from the music room into the courtroom and tried to get it to tip, which it did. With just our fingertips on it, it tilted until it was approximately one inch from the floor, then fell. We righted the table and put our fingertips back on it, and almost immediately it began to rock. Since we knew the code for yes, no, and doubtful, we began to converse with the table. Incidentally, while this was going on, a chain across the doorway in the courtroom was almost continually swinging back and forth and then up and down.

Through the system of knocking, we discovered that the ghost was that of a little girl, seven years old. She did not tell us her name, but she did tell us that she had red hair, freckles, and hazel eyes. She also related that there were four other ghosts in the house besides herself, including that of a baby boy. We conversed with her spirit for nearly an hour.

At one time the table stopped rocking and started moving across the floor of the courtroom, into the dining room, through the pantry, and into the kitchen. This led us to believe that the kitchen was her usual abode. The table then stopped and several antique kitchen utensils on the wall began to swing violently. Incidentally, the kitchen utensils swung for the rest of the evening at different intervals.

The table then retraced its path back to the courtroom and answered more questions.

At 5:00 A.M. we decided to call it a night—a most interesting night. When we arrived our group of 15 had had in it a couple of real believers, several who half believed, and quite a few who didn't believe at all. After the phenomena we had experienced, there was not one among us who was even very doubtful in the belief of some form of existence after life.

It was Friday evening, and time to meet the ghosts. Sybil Leek knew nothing whatever about the house, and when Regis Philbin picked us up the conversation remained polite and non-ghostly.

When we arrived at the house, word of mouth had preceded us despite the fact that our plans had not been announced publicly; certainly it had not been advertised that we would attempt a séance that evening. Nevertheless, a sizable crowd had assembled at the house and only Regis' polite insistence that their presence might harm whatever results we could obtain made them move on.

It was quite dark now, and I followed Sybil into the house, allowing her to get her clairvoyant bearings first, prior to the trance session we were to do with the cameras rolling. My wife Catherine trailed right behind me carrying the tape equipment. Mrs. Reading received us cordially. The witnesses had assembled but were temporarily out of reach, so that Sybil could not gather any sensory impressions from them. They patiently waited through our clairvoyant tour. All in all, about a dozen people awaited us. The house was lit throughout and the excitement in the atmosphere was bound to stir up any ghost present!

And so it was that on June 25, 1965, the Ghost Hunter came to close quarters with the spectres at Whaley House, San Diego. While Sybil meandered about the house by herself, I quickly went over to the Court House part of the house and went over their experiences with the witnesses. Although I already had their statements, I wanted to make sure no detail had escaped me.

From June Reading I learned, for instance, that the Court House section of the building, erected around 1855, had originally served as a granary, later becoming a town hall and Court House in turn. It was the only two-story brick house in the entire area at the time.

Not only did Mrs. Reading hear what sounded to her like human voices, but on one occasion, when she was tape recording some music in this room, the tape also contained some human voices—sounds she had not herself heard while playing the music!

"When was the last time you yourself heard anything unusual?" I asked Mrs. Reading.

"As recently as a week ago," the pert curator replied, "during the day I heard the definite sound of someone opening the front door. Because we have had many visitors here recently, we are very much alerted to this. I happened to be in the Court Room with one of the people from the Historical Society engaged in research in the Whaley papers, and we both heard it. I went to check to see who had come in, and there was no one there, nor was there any sound of footsteps on the porch outside. The woman who works here also heard it and was just as puzzled about it as I was."

I discovered that the Mrs. Allen in the curator's report to me of uncanny experiences at the house was Lillian Allen, her own mother, a lively lady who remembered her brush with the uncanny only too vividly.

"I've heard the noises overhead," she recalled. "Someone in heavy boots seemed to be walking across, turning to come down the stairway—and when I first came out here they would tell me these things and I would not believe them—but I was sitting at the desk one night, downstairs, waiting for my daughter to lock up in the back. I heard this noise overhead and I was rushing to see if we were locking someone in the house, and as I got to almost the top, a big rush of wind blew over my head and made my hair stand up. I thought the windows had blown open but I looked all around and everything was secured.

"Just how did this wind feel?" I asked. Tales of cold winds are standard with traditional hauntings, but here we had a precise witness to testify.

"It was cold and I was chilly all over. And another thing, when I lock the shutters upstairs at night, I feel like someone is breathing down the back of my neck, like they're going to touch me—at the shoulder—that happened often. Why, only a month ago."

A Mrs. Frederick Bear now stepped forward. I could not find her name in Mrs. Reading's brief report. Evidently she was an additional witness to the uncanny goings-on at this house.

"One evening I came here—it was after five o'clock; another lady was here also—and June Reading was coming down the stairs, and we were talking. I distinctly heard something move upstairs, as if someone were moving a table. There was no one there—we checked. That only happened a month ago."

Grace Bourquin, another volunteer worker at the house, had been touched upon in Mrs. Reading's report. She emphasized that the sounds were those of a heavy man wearing boots—no mistake about it. When I questioned her about the apparition of a man she had seen, about six weeks ago, wearing a frock coat, she insisted that he had looked like a real person to her, standing at the top of the stairs one moment, and completely gone the next.

"He did not move. I saw him clearly, then turned my head for a second to call out to Mrs. Reading, and when I looked again, he had disappeared."

I had been fascinated by Mrs. Suzanne Pere's account of her experiences, which seemed to indicate a large degree of mediumship in her makeup. I questioned her about anything she had not yet told us.

"On one occasion June Reading and I were in on the study and working with the table. We had our hands on the table to see if we could get any reaction."

"You mean you were trying to do some table-tipping."

"Yes. At this point I had only had some feeling in the house, and smelled some cologne. This was about a year ago, and we were working with some papers concerning the Indian uprising in San Diego, and all of a sudden the table started to rock violently! All of the pulses in my body became throbbing, and in my mind's eye the room was filled with men, all of them extremely excited, and though I could not hear any sound, I knew they were talking, and one gentleman was striding up and down the center of the room, puffing on his cigar, and from my description of him June Reading later identified him as Sheriff McCoy, who was here in the 1850's. When it was finished I could not talk for a few minutes. I was completely disturbed for a moment."

McCoy, I found, was the leader of one of the factions during the "battle" between Old Town and New Town San Diego for the county seat.

Evidently, Mrs. Bourquin had psychically relived that emotion-laden event which did indeed transpire in the very room she saw it in!

"Was the Court House ever used to execute anyone?" I interjected.

Mrs. Reading was not sure; the records were all there but the Historical Society had not gone over them as yet for lack of staff. The Court functioned in this house for two years, however, and sentences certainly were meted out in it. The prison itself was a bit farther up the street.

A lady in a red coat caught my attention. She identified herself as Bernice Kennedy.

"I'm a guide here Sundays," the lady began, "and one Sunday recently, I was alone in the house and sitting in the dining room reading, and I heard the front door open and close. There was no one there. I went back to continue my reading. Then I heard it the second time. Again I checked, and there was absolutely no one there. I heard it a third time and this time I took my book and sat outside at the desk. From then onward, people started to come in and I had no further unusual experience. But one other Sunday, there was a young woman upstairs who came down suddenly very pale, and she said the little rocking chair upstairs was rocking. I followed the visitor up and I could not see the chair move, but there was a clicking sound, very rhythmic, and I haven't heard it before or since."

The chair, it came out, once belonged to a family related to the Whaleys.

"I'm Charles Keller, father of Milton Keller," a booming voice said behind me, and an imposing gentleman in his middle years stepped forward.

"I once conducted a tour through the Whaley House. I noticed a lady who had never been here act as if she were being pushed out of one of the bedrooms!"

"Did you see it?" I said, somewhat taken aback.

"Yes," Mr. Keller nodded, "I saw her move, as if someone were pushing her out of thc room."

"Did you interrogate her about it?"

"Yes, I did. It was only in the first bedroom, where we started the tour, that it happened. Not in any of the other rooms. We went back to that room and again I saw her being pushed out of it!"

Mrs. Keller then spoke to me about the ice-cold draft she felt, and just before that, three knocks at the back door! Her son, whose testimony Mrs. Reading had already obtained for me, then went to the back door and found no one there who could have knocked. This had happened only six months before our visit.

I then turned to James Reading, the head of the Association responsible for the upkeep of the museum and house, and asked for his own encounters with the ghosts. Mr. Reading, in a cautious tone, explained that he did not really cotton to ghosts, but—

"The house was opened to the public in April 1960. In the fall of that year, October or November, the police called me at two o'clock in the morning, and asked me to please go down and shut off the burglar alarm, because they were being flooded with complaints, it was waking up everybody in the neighborhood. I came down and found two officers waiting for me. I shut off the alarm. They had meantime checked the house and every door and shutter was tight."

"How could the alarm have gone off by itself then?"

"I don't know. I unlocked the door, and we searched the entire house. When we finally got upstairs, we found one of the upstairs front bedroom windows open. We closed and bolted the window, and came down and tested the alarm. It was in order again. No one could have gotten in or out. The shutters outside that window were closed and hooked on the inside. The opening of the window had set off the alarm, but it would have been impossible for anyone to open that window and get either into or out of the house. Impossible. This happened *four times*. The second time, about four months later, again at two in the morning, again that same window was standing open. The other two times it was always that same window."

"What did you finally do about it?"

"After the fourth incident we added a second bolt at right angles to the first one, and that seemed to help. There were no further calls."

Was the ghost getting tired of pushing *two* bolts out of the way?

I had been so fascinated with all this additional testimony that I had let my attention wander away from my favorite medium, Sybil Leek. But now I started to look for her and found to my amazement that she had seated herself in one of the old chairs in what used to be the kitchen, downstairs in back of the living room. When I entered the room she seemed deep in thought, although not in trance by any means, and yet it took me a while to make her realize where we were.

Had anything unusual transpired while I was in the Court Room interviewing?

"I was standing in the entrance hall, looking at the postcards," Sybil recollected, "when I felt I just had to go to the kitchen, but I didn't go there at first, but went halfway up the stairs, and a child came down the stairs and into the kitchen and I followed her."

"A child?" I asked. I was quite sure there were no children among our party.

"I thought it was Regis' little girl and the next thing I recall I was in the rocking chair and you were saying something to me."

Needless to say, Regis Philbin's daughter had *not* been on the stairs. I asked for a detailed description of the child.

"It was a long-haired girl," Sybil said. "She was very quick, you know, in a longish dress. She went to the table in this room and I went to the chair. That's all I remember."

I decided to continue to question Sybil about any psychic impressions she might now gather in the house.

"There is a great deal of confusion in this house," she began. "Some of it is associated with another room upstairs, which has been structurally altered. There are two centers of activity."

Sybil, of course, could not have known that the house consisted of two separate units.

"Any ghosts in the house?"

"Several," Sybil assured me. "At least four!"

Had not William Richardson's group made contact with a little girl ghost who had claimed that she knew of four other ghosts in the house? The report of that séance did not reach me until September, several months after our visit, so Sybil could not possibly have "read our minds" about it, since our minds had no such knowledge at that time.

"This room where you found me sitting," Sybil continued, "I found myself drawn to it; the impressions are very strong here. Especially that child—she died young."

We went about the house now, seeking further contacts.

"I have a date now," Sybil suddenly said, "1872."

The Readings exchanged significant glances. It was just after the greatest bitterness of the struggle between Old Town and New Town, when the removal of the Court records from Whaley House by force occurred.

"There are two sides to the house," Sybil continued. "One side I like, but not the other."

Rather than have Sybil use up her energies in clairvoyance, I felt it best to try for a trance in the Court Room itself. This was arranged for quickly, with candles taking the place of electric lights except for what light was necessary for the motion picture cameras in the rear of the large room.

Regis Philbin and I sat at Sybil's sides as she slumped forward in a chair that may well have held a merciless judge in bygone years.

But the first communicator was neither the little girl nor the man in the frock coat. A feeble, plaintive voice was suddenly heard from Sybil's lips, quite unlike her own, a voice evidently parched with thirst.

"Bad . . . fever . . . everybody had the fever . . ."

"What year is this?"

"Forty-six."

I suggested that the fever had passed, and generally calmed the personality who did not respond to my request for identification.

"Send me . . . some water. . . ." Sybil was still in trance, but herself now. Immediately she complained about there being a lot of confusion.

"This isn't the room where we're needed . . . the child . . . she is the one. . . ."

"What is her name?"

"Anna . . . Bell . . . she died very suddenly with something, when she was thirteen . . . chest. . . ."

"Are her parents here too?"

"They come . . . the lady comes."

"What is this house used for?"

"Trade . . . selling things, buying and selling."

"Is there anyone other than the child in this house?"

"Child is the main one, because she doesn't understand anything at all. But there is something more vicious. Child would not hurt anyone. There's someone else. A man. He knows something about this house . . . about thirty-two, unusual name, C . . . Calstrop . . . five feet ten, wearing a green coat, darkish, mustache and side whiskers, he goes up to the bedroom on the left. He has business here. His business is with things that come from the sea. But it is the papers that worry him."

"What papers?" I demanded.

"The papers . . . 1872. About the house. Dividing the house was wrong. Two owners, he says."

"What is the house being used for, now, in 1872?"

"To live in. Two places . . . I get confused for I go one place and then I have to go to another."

"Did this man you see die here?"

"He died here. Unhappy because of the place . . . about the other place. Two buildings. Some people quarrelled about the spot. He is laughing. He wants all this house for himself."

"Does he know he is dead?" I asked the question that often brings forth much resistance to my quest for facts from those who cannot conceive of their status as "ghosts."

Sybil listened for a moment.

"He does as he wants in this house because he is going to live here," she finally said. *"It's his house."*

"Why is he laughing?"

A laughing ghost, indeed!

"He laughs because of people coming here thinking it's *their* house! When he knows the truth."

"What is his name?" I asked again.

"Cal . . . Caltrop . . . very difficult as he does not speak very clearly . . . he writes and writes . . . he makes a noise . . . he says he will make even more noise unless you go away."

"Let him," I said, cheerfully hoping I could tape-record the ghost's outbursts.

"Tell him he has passed over and the matter is no longer important," I told Sybil.

"He is upstairs."

I asked that he walk upstairs so we could all hear him. There was nobody upstairs at this moment—everybody was watching the proceedings in the Court Room downstairs.

We kept our breath, waiting for the manifestations, but our ghost wouldn't play the game. I continued with my questions.

"What does he want?"

"He is just walking around, he can do as he likes," Sybil said. "He does not like new things . . . he does not like any noise . . . except when he makes it. . . ."

"Who plays the organ in this house?"

"He says his mother plays."

"What is her name?"

"Ann Lassay . . . that's wrong, it's Lann—he speaks so badly . . . Lannay . . . his throat is bad or something. . . ."

I later was able to check on this unusual name. Anna Lannay was Thomas Whaley's wife!

At the moment, however, I was not aware of this fact and pressed on with my interrogation. How did the ghost die? How long ago?

"'89 . . . he does not want to speak; he only wants to roam around."

Actually, Whaley died in 1890. Had the long interval confused his sense of time? So many ghosts cannot recall exact dates but will remember circumstances and emotional experiences well.

"He worries about the house . . . he wants the whole house . . . for himself . . . he says he will leave them . . . papers . . . hide the papers . . . he wants the other papers about the house . . . they're four miles from here . . . several people have these papers and you'll have to get them back or he'll never settle . . . never . . . and if he doesn't get the whole house back, he will be much worse . . . and then, the police will come . . . he will make the lights come and the noise . . . and the bell . . . make the police come and see him, the master . . . of the house, he hears bells upstairs . . . he doesn't know what it is . . . he goes upstairs and opens the windows, wooden windows . . . and looks out . . . and then he pulls the . . . no, it's not a bell . . . he'll do it again . . . when he wants someone to know that he really is the master of the house . . . people today come and say he is not, but he is!"

I was surprised. Sybil had no knowledge of the disturbances, the alarm bell, the footsteps, the open window . . . and yet it was all perfectly true. Surely, her communicator was our man!

"When did he do this the last time?" I inquired.

"This year . . . not long. . . ."

"Has he done anything else in this house?"

"He said he moved the lights. In the parlor."

Later I thought of the Richardson séance and the lights they had observed, but of course I had no idea of this when we were at the house ourselves.

"What about the front door?"

"If people come, he goes into the garden . . . walks around . . . because he meets mother there."

"What is in the kitchen?"

"Child goes to the kitchen. I have to leave him, and he doesn't want to be left . . . it was an injustice, anyway, don't like it . . . the child is twelve . . . chest trouble . . . something from the kitchen . . . bad affair. . . ."

"Anyone's fault?"

"Yes. Not chest . . . from the cupboard, took something . . . it was an acid like salt, and she ate it . . . she did not know . . . there is something strange about this child, someone had control of her, you see, she was in the way . . . family . . . one girl . . . those boys were not too good . . . the other boys who came down . . . she is like two people . . . someone controlled her . . . made her do strange things and then . . . could she do that. . . ."

"Was she the daughter of the man?"

"Strange man, he doesn't care so much about the girl as he does about the house. He is disturbed."

"Is there a woman in this house?"

"Of course. There is a woman in the garden."

"Who is she?"

"Mother. Grandmother of the girl."

"Is he aware of the fact he has no physical body?"

"No."

"Doesn't he see all the people who come here?"

"They have to be fought off, sent away."

"Tell him it is now seventy years later."

"He says seventy years when the house was built."

"Another seventy years have gone by," I insisted.

"Only part of you is in the house."

"No, part of the house . . . you're making the mistake," he replied.

I tried hard to convince him of the real circumstances. Finally, I assured him that the entire house was, in effect, his.

Would this help?

"He is vicious," Sybil explains. "He will have his revenge on the house."

I explained that his enemies were all dead.

"He says it was an injustice, and the Court was wrong and you have to tell everyone this is his house and land and home."

I promised to do so and intoned the usual formula for the release of earthbound people who have passed over and don't realize it. Then I recalled Sybil to her own self, and within a few moments she was indeed in full control.

I then turned to the director of the museum, Mrs. Reading, and asked for her comments on the truth of the material just heard.

"There was a litigation," she said. "The injustice could perhaps refer to the County's occupancy of this portion of the house from 1869 to 1871. Whaley's contract, which we have, shows that this portion of the house was leased to the County, and he was to supply the furniture and set it up as a Court Room. He also put in the two windows to provide light. It was a valid agreement. They adhered to the contract as long as the Court continued to function here, but when Alonzo Horton came and developed New Town, a hot contest began between the two communities for the possession of the county seat. When the records were forcefully removed from here, Whaley felt it was quite an injustice, and we have letters he addressed to the Board of Supervisors, referring to the fact that his lease had been broken. The Clerk notified him that they were no longer responsible for the use of this house—after all the work he had put in to remodel it for their use. He would bring the matter up periodically with the Board of Supervisors, but it was tabled by them each time it came up."

"In other words, this is the injustice referred to by the ghost?"

"In 1872 he was bitterly engaged in asking redress from the County over this matter, which troubled him some since he did not believe a government official would act in this manner. It was never settled, however, and Whaley was left holding the bag."

"Was there a child in the room upstairs?"

"In the nursery? There were several children there. One child died here. But this was a boy."

Again, later, I saw that the Richardson séance spoke of a boy ghost in the house.

At the very beginning of trance, before I began taping the utterances from Sybil's lips, I took some handwritten notes. The personality, I now saw, who had died of a bad fever had given the faintly pronounced name of Fedor and spoke of a mill where he worked. Was there any sense to this?

"Yes," Mrs. Reading confirmed, "this room we are in now served as a granary at one time. About 1855 to 1867."

"Were there ever any Russians in this area?"

"There was a considerable otter trade here prior to the American occupation of the area. We have found evidence that the Russians established wells in this area. They came into these waters then to trade otters."

"Amazing," I conceded. How could Sybil, even if she wanted to, have known of such an obscure fact?

"This would have been in the 1800's," Mrs. Reading continued. "Before then there were Spaniards here, of course."

"Anything else you wish to comment upon in the trance session you have just witnessed?" I asked.

Mrs. Reading expressed what we all felt.

"The references to the windows opening upstairs, and the ringing of these bells. . . ."

How could Sybil have known all that? Nobody told her and she had not had a chance to acquaint herself with the details of the disturbances.

What remained were the puzzling statements about "the other house." They, too, were soon to be explained. We were walking through the garden now and inspected the rear portion of the Whaley house. In back of it, we discovered to our surprise still another wooden house standing in the garden. I questioned Mrs. Reading about this second house.

"The Pendington House, in order to save it, had to be moved out of the path of the freeway . . . it never belonged to the Whaleys although Thomas Whaley once tried to rent it. But it was always rented to someone else."

No wonder the ghost was angry about "the other house." It had been moved and put on *his* land . . . without his consent!

The name *Cal* . . . *trop* still did not fall into place. It was too far removed from Whaley and yet everything else that had come through Sybil clearly fitted Thomas Whaley. Then the light began to dawn, thanks to Mrs. Reading's detailed knowledge of the house.

"It was interesting to hear Mrs. Leek say there was a store here once . . ." she explained. "This is correct, there was a store here at one time, but it was not Mr. Whaley's."

"Whose was it?"

"It belonged to a man named Wallack . . . Hal Wallack . . . that was in the seventies."

Close enough to Sybil's tentative pronunciation of a name she caught connected with the house.

"He rented it to Wallack for six months, then Wallack sold out," Mrs. Reading explained.

I also discovered, in discussing the case with Mrs. Reading, that the disturbances really began after the second house had been placed on the grounds. Was that the straw that broke the ghost's patience?

Later, we followed Sybil to a wall adjoining the garden, a wall, I should add, where there was no visible door. But Sybil insisted there had been a French window there, and indeed there was at one time. In a straight line from this spot, we wound up at a huge tree. It was here, Sybil explained, that Whaley and his mother often met—or are meeting, as the case may be.

I was not sure that Mr. Whaley had taken my advice to heart and moved out of what was, after all, his house. Why should he? The County had not seen fit to undo an old wrong.

We left the next morning, hoping that at the very least we had let the restless one know someone cared.

A week later Regis Philbin checked with the folks at Whaley House. Everything was lively—chandelier swinging, rocker rocking; and June Reading herself brought me up to date on July 27th, 1965, with a brief report on activities—other than flesh-and-blood—at the house.

Evidently the child ghost was also still around, for utensils in the kitchen had moved that week, especially a cleaver which swings back and forth on its own. Surely that must be the playful little girl, for what would so important a man as Thomas Whaley have to do in the kitchen? Surely he was much too preoccupied with the larger aspects of his realm, the ancient wrong done him, and the many intrusions from the world of reality. For the Whaley House is a busy place, ghosts or not.

On replaying my tapes, I noticed a curious confusion between the initial appearance of a ghost who called himself Fedor in my notes, and a man who said he had a bad fever. It was just that the man with the fever did not have a foreign accent, but I distinctly recalled "fedor" as sounding odd.

Were they perhaps two separate entities?

My suspicions were confirmed when a letter written May 23, 1966—almost a year later—reached me. A Mrs. Carol DeJuhasz wanted me to know about a ghost at Whaley House . . . no, not Thomas Whaley or a twelve-year-old girl with long hair. Mrs. DeJuhasz was concerned with an historical play written by a friend of hers, dealing with the unjust execution of a man who tried to steal a harbor boat in the 1800's and was caught. Make no mistake about it, nobody had observed this ghost at Whaley House. Mrs. DeJuhasz merely thought he ought to be there, having been hanged in the backyard of the house.

Many people tell me of tragic spots where men have died unhappily but rarely do I discover ghosts on such spots just because of it. I was therefore not too interested in Mrs. DeJuhasz' account of a possible ghost. But she thought that there ought to be present at Whaley House the ghost of this man, called Yankee Jim Robinson. When captured, he fought a sabre duel and received a critical wound in the head. Although alive, he became delirious and was tried without representation, *sick of the fever.* Sentenced to death, he was subsequently hanged in the yard behind the Court House.

Was his the ghostly voice that spoke through Sybil, complaining of the fever and then quickly fading away? Again it was William Richardson who was able to provide a further clue or set of clues to this puzzle. In December of 1966 he contacted me again to report some further experiences at the Whaley House.

"This series of events began in March of this year. Our group was helping to restore an historic old house which had been moved onto the Whaley property to save it from destruction. During our lunch break one Saturday, several of us were in Whaley House. I was downstairs when Jim Stein, one of the group, rushed down the stairs to tell me that the cradle in the nursery was rocking by itself. I hurried upstairs but it wasn't rocking. I was just about to chide Jim for having an overactive imagination when it began again and rocked a little longer before it stopped. The cradle is at least ten feet from the doorway, and a metal barricade is across it to prevent tourists from entering the room. No amount of walking or jumping had any effect on the cradle. While it rocked, I remembered that it had made no sound. Going into the room, I rocked the cradle. I was surprised that it made quite a bit of noise. The old floorboards are somewhat uneven and this in combination with the wooden rockers on the cradle made a very audible sound.

"As a matter of fact, when the Whaleys were furnishing carpeting for the house, the entire upstairs portion was carpeted. This might explain the absence of the noise.

"In June, Whaley House became the setting for an historical play. The play concerned the trial and hanging of a local bad man named Yankee Jim Robinson. It was presented in the Court Room and on the grounds of the mansion. The actual trial and execution had taken place in August of 1852. This was five years before Whaley House was built, but the execution took place on the grounds.

"Yankee Jim was hanged from a scaffold which stood approximately between the present music room and front parlor.

"Soon after the play went into rehearsal, things began to happen. I was involved with the production as an actor and therefore had the opportunity to spend many hours in the house between June and August. The usual footsteps kept up and they were heard by most of the members of the cast at one time or another. There was a group of us within the cast who were especially interested in the phenomenon: myself, Barry Bunker, George Carroll, and his fiancée Toni Manista. As we were all dressed in period costumes most of the time, the ghosts should have felt right at home. Toni was playing the part of Anna, Thomas Whaley's wife. She said she often felt as if she were being followed around the house (as did we all).

"I was sitting in the kitchen with my back to the wall one night, when I felt a hand run through my hair. I quickly turned around but there was nothing to be seen. I have always felt that it was Anna Whaley who touched me. It was my first such experience and I felt honored that she had chosen me to touch. There is a chair in the kitchen which is made of rawhide and wood. The seat is made of thin strips of rawhide crisscrossed on the wooden frame. When someone sits on it, it sounds like the leather in a saddle. On the same night I was touched, the chair made sounds as if someone were sitting in it, not once but several times. There always seems to be a change in the temperature of a room when a presence enters. The kitchen is no exception. It really got cold in there!

"Later in the run of the show, the apparitions began to appear. The cast had purchased a chair which had belonged to Thomas Whaley and placed it in the front parlor. Soon after, a mist was occasionally seen in the chair or near it. In other parts of the house, especially upstairs, inexplicable shadows and mists began to appear. George Carroll swears that he saw a man standing at the top of the stairs. He walked up the stairs and through the man. The man was still there when George turned around but faded and disappeared almost immediately.

"During the summer, we often smelled cigar smoke when we opened the house in the morning or at times when no one was around. Whaley was very fond of cigars and was seldom without them.

"The footsteps became varied. The heavy steps of the man continued as usual, but the click-click of high heels was heard on occasion.

Once, the sound of a small child running in the upstairs hall was heard. Another time, I was alone with the woman who took ticket reservations for *Yankee Jim*. We had locked the doors and decided to check the upstairs before we left. We had no sooner gotten up the stairs than we both heard footfalls in the hall below. We listened for a moment and then went back down the stairs and looked. No one. We searched the entire house, not really expecting to find anyone. We didn't. Not a living soul.

"Well, this just about brings you up to date. I've been back a number of times since September but there's nothing to report except the usual footfalls, creaks, etc.

"I think that the play had much to do with the summer's phenomena. Costumes, characters, and situations which were known to the Whaleys were reenacted nightly. Yankee Jim Robinson certainly has reason enough to haunt. Many people, myself included, think that he got a bad deal. He was wounded during his capture and was unconscious during most of the trial. To top it off, the judge was a drunk and the jury and townspeople wanted blood. Jim was just unlucky enough to bear their combined wrath.

"His crime? He had borrowed (?) a boat. Hardly a hanging offense. He was found guilty and condemned. He was unprepared to die and thought it was a joke up to the minute they pulled the wagon out from under him. The scaffold wasn't high enough and the fall didn't break his neck. Instead, he slowly strangled for more than fifteen minutes before he died. I think I'd haunt under the same circumstances myself.

"Two other points: another of the guides heard a voice directly in front of her as she walked down the hall. It said, 'Hello, hello.' There was no one else in the house at the time. A dog fitting the description of one of the Whaley dogs has been seen to run into the house, but it can never be found."

Usually, ghosts of different periods do not "run into" one another, unless they are tied together by a mutual problem or common tragedy. The executed man, the proud owner, the little girl, the lady of the house—they form a lively ghost population even for so roomy a house as the Whaley House is.

Mrs. Reading doesn't mind. Except that it does get confusing now and again when you see someone walking about the house and aren't sure if he has bought an admission ticket.

Surely, Thomas Whaley wouldn't dream of buying one. And he is not likely to leave unless and until some action is taken publicly to rectify the ancient wrong. If the County were to reopen the matter and acknowledge the mistake made way back, I am sure the ghostly Mr. Whaley would be pleased and let matters rest. The little girl ghost has been told by Sybil Leek what has happened to her, and the lady goes where Mr. Whaley goes. Which brings us down to Jim, who would have to be tried again and found innocent of stealing the boat.

There is that splendid courtroom there at the house to do it in. Maybe some ghost-conscious county administration will see fit to do just that.

I'll be glad to serve as counsel for the accused, at no charge.

The Millbrae Poltergeist Case

One wouldn't think a spanking, modern home perched on a hill at Millbrae, a sunny little town outside San Francisco, could harbor a poltergeist case, one of those sinister disturbances, usually Germanic, involving a teenager or otherwise emotionally unabsorbed person in the household of the living. *Poltergeist* only means "noisy ghost," and a ghost it is—the youngster is not playing any pranks; the youngster is being used to play them with, by a disturbed person no longer in possession of a physical body.

I heard of the Millbrae case from a young girl who used to live in that house before she decided she was old enough to have a place of her own and consequently moved out to a nearby town called Burlingame. At 20, Jean Grasso had a high school education and a big curiosity about things she cannot explain. Such as ESP.

In 1964, she had an experience that particularly upset her because it did not fit in with the usual experiences of life she had been taught in school.

She was in bed at the time, just before falling asleep, or, as she puts it so poetically, "just before the void of sleep engulfs you." Miss Grasso is not at a loss for words, and is as bright a young girl as you want to meet. Her world is very real to her and has little or no room for fantasies.

Still, there it was. Something prevented her from giving in to sleep. Before she knew what she was doing, she saw her own bare feet moving across the floor of her bedroom; she grabbed the telephone receiver and blurted into it—"Jeannie, what's wrong? Did you get hurt?" The telephone had *not* rung. Yet her best friend, who was almost like a sister to her, was on the line. She had been in an automobile accident in which she had been run off the road and collided with a steel pole, but except for being shook up, she was all right.

What made Jean Grasso jump out of a warm bed to answer a phone that had not yet rung, to speak by name to someone who had not yet said "hello," and to inquire about an accident that no one had told her about as yet?

The dark-haired girl is of Italian and Greek background and works as the local representative of a milk company. She is neither brooding nor particularly emotional, it seemed to me, and far from hysterical. The uncanny things that happened in her life intrigued her more in an intellectual way than in an emotional, fearful way.

When she was sixteen, she and five other girls were playing the popular parlor game of the ouija board in one of the bedrooms. Jean and Michele di Giovanni, one of the girls, were working the board when it started to move as if pushed by some force stronger than themselves.

Still very skeptical about ouija boards, Jean demanded some sign or proof of a spiritual presence. She got a quick reply: four loud knocks on the wall. There was nobody in back of the walls who could have caused them. Suddenly, the room got very cold, and they panicked and called the "séance" off then and there.

Ever since, she has heard uncanny noises in her parents' house. These have ranged from footsteps to crashing sounds as if someone or something were thrown against a wall or onto the floor. There never was a rational explanation for these sounds.

After Jean moved out to her own place in Burlingame, she returned home for occasional weekends to be with her mother. Her mother sleeps in the living-dining room area upstairs, to save her the trouble of walking up and down the stairs to the bedroom level, since she has a heart condition.

On the occasions when Jean spent a weekend at home, she would sleep in her mother's former bedroom, situated directly underneath the one fixed for her on the upper level.

One night, as Jean lay awake in bed, she heard footsteps overhead. They walked across the ceiling, "as if they had no place to go."

Thinking that her mother had breathing difficulties, she raced upstairs, but found her mother fast asleep in bed. Moreover, when questioned about the footsteps the next morning, she assured her daughter she had heard nothing.

"Were they a man's footsteps or a woman's?" I asked Jean Grasso when we discussed this after the investigation was over.

"A man's," she replied without hesitation.

Once in a while when she is in the dining area upstairs, she will see something out of the corner of an eye—a flash—something or somebody moving about—and as soon as she concentrates on it, it is not there. She has chalked all that up to her imagination, of course.

"When I'm coming down the steps, in the hall, I get a chill up my spine," the girl said, "as if I didn't want to continue on. My mother gets the same feelings there, too, I recently discovered."

That was the spot where my psychic photograph was taken, I later realized. Did these two psychic people, mother and daughter, act like living cameras?

"Do you ever have a feeling of a presence with you when you are all alone?"

"Yes, in my mother's bedroom, I feel someone is watching me and I turn but there's no one there."

I questioned her about the garden and the area around the basement. Jean confessed she did not go there often since the garden gave her an uneasy feeling. She avoided it whenever she could for no reason she could logically explain.

One night when she spent the weekend at her parents' house and was just falling asleep a little after midnight, she was awakened by the sound of distant voices. The murmur of the voices was clear enough but when she sat up to listen further, they went away. She went back to sleep, blaming her imagination for the incident. But a week later, to the day, her incipient sleep was again interrupted by the sound of a human voice. This time it was a little girl's or a woman's voice crying out, *"Help . . . help me!"*

She jumped up so fast she could hear her heart beat in her ears. Surely, her mother had called her. Then she remembered that her mother had gone to Santa Cruz. There was nobody in the house who could have called for help. She looked outside. It was way after midnight and the surrounding houses were all dark. But the voice she had just heard had not come from the outside. It was there, right in the haunted room with her!

I decided to interview Jean's mother, Mrs. Adriana Grasso, a calm pleasant woman whose skepticism in psychic matters has always been pretty strong.

"We've had this house since 1957," she explained, "but it was already five years old when we bought it. The previous owners were named Stovell and they were about to lose it when we bought it. I know nothing about them beyond that."

The very first night she went to bed in the house, something tried to prevent her from doing so. Something kept pushing her back up. On the first landing of the stairs leading down to the bedroom level, something kept her from continuing on down. She decided to fight it out. Every time after that first experience she had the same impression— that she really *shouldn't* be coming downstairs!

"I hear footsteps upstairs when I'm downstairs and I hear footsteps downstairs when I'm upstairs, and there never is anyone there causing them," she complained.

On several occasions, she awoke screaming, which brought her daughter running in anxiously. To calm her, she assured her she had had a nightmare. But it was not true. On several different occasions, she felt something grabbing her and trying to crush her bones. Something held her arms pinned down. Finally, she had to sleep with the lights on, and it seemed to help.

A big crash also made the family wonder what was wrong with their house. Mrs. Grasso heard it *upstairs* and her son Allen, upstairs at the same time, thought it was *downstairs*—only to discover that it was neither here nor there!

"Many times the doorbell would ring and there was no one outside," Mrs. Grasso added, "but I always assumed it was the children of the neighborhood, playing tricks on us."

Loud noises as if a heavy object had fallen brought her into the garage to investigate, but nothing had fallen, nothing was out of place. The garage was locked and so was the front door. Nobody had gotten in. And yet the noises continued; only three days before our arrival, Mrs. Grasso awoke around one in the morning to the sound of "someone opening a can in the bathroom," a metal container. In addition, there was thumping. She thought, why is my son working on his movies at this hour of the night? She assumed the can-opening noises referred to motion picture film cans, of which her son has many. But he had done nothing of the sort.

Soon even Allen and Mr. Grasso heard the loud crashes, although they were unwilling to concede that it represented anything uncanny. But the family that hears ghosts together, also finds solutions together—and the Grassos were not particularly panicky about the whole thing. Just curious.

It was at this point that I decided to investigate the case and I so advised Jean Grasso, who greeted us at the door of her parents' house on a very warm day in October 1966. In addition to Sybil and my wife

Catherine, two friends, Lori Cierf and Bill Wynn, were with us. We had Lori's car and Bill was doing the driving.

We entered the house and immediately I asked Sybil for her psychic impressions. She had not had a chance to orient herself nor did I allow her to meet the Grassos officially. Whatever she might "get" now would therefore not be colored by any rational impressions of the people she met or the house she was in.

"There is something peculiar about the lower portion of the house," Sybil began, referring to the bedroom floor. The house *was* built in a most peculiar manner. Because the lot was sloping toward a ravine, the top floor reached to street level on the front side of the house only. It was here that the house had its living room and entrance hall. On the floor below were the bedrooms, and finally, a garage and adjoining work room. Underneath was a basement, which, however, led to ground level in the rear, where it touched the bottom of the ravine.

At this point, however, Sybil and I did not even know if there was a lower portion to the house, but Jean Grasso assured us there was. We immediately descended the stairs into the section Sybil had felt invaded by psychic influences.

We stopped at the northeast corner of the bedroom floor where a rear entrance to the house was also situated, leading to a closed-in porch whence one could descend to the ground level outside by wooden stairs.

"What do you feel here, Sybil?" I asked, for I noticed she was getting on to something.

"Whatever I feel is below this spot," she commented. "It must have come from the old foundations, from the land."

Never let it be said that a ghost hunter shies away from dusty basements. Down we went, with Catherine carrying the tape recorder and one of the cameras. In the basement we could not stand entirely upright—at least I couldn't.

"That goes underneath the corridor, doesn't it?" Sybil said as if she knew.

"That's right," Jean Grasso confirmed.

"Somebody was chased here," Sybil commented now, "two men . . . an accident that should never have happened . . . someone died here . . . *a case of mistaken identity.*"

"Can you get more?" I urged her.

"There is a lingering feeling of a man," Sybil intoned. "He is the victim. He was not the person concerned. He was running from the water's edge to a higher part of land. He was a fugitive."

Anyone coming from the San Francisco waterfront would be coming up here to higher ground.

"Whom was he running from?"

"The Law . . . I feel uniforms. There is an element of supposed justice in it, but . . ."

"How long ago was he killed?"

"1884."

"His name?"

"Wasserman . . . that's how I get it. I feel the influence of his last moments here, but not his body. He wants us to know he was Wasserman but not the Wasserman wanted by the man."

"What does he look like to you?"

"Ruddy face, peculiarly deep eyes . . . he's here but not particularly cooperative."

"Does he know he is *dead?*" I asked.

"I don't think he knows that. But he notices *me.*"

I asked Sybil to convey the message that we knew he was innocent.

"Two names I have to get," Sybil insisted and started to spell, "Pottrene . . . P-o-t-t-r-e-n-e . . . Wasserman tells me these names . . . P-o-v-e-y . . . Povey . . . he says to find them . . . these people are the men who killed him."

"How was he killed?"

"They *had* to kill him. They thought that he was someone else."

"What was the other one wanted for?"

"He doesn't know. He was unfortunate to have been here."

"What is his first name?"

"Jan. J-a-n."

Upon my prodding, Sybil elicited also the information that this Jan Wasserman was a native of San Francisco, that his father's name was Johan or John, and he lived at 324 Emil Street.

I proceeded then to exorcise the ghost in my usual manner, speaking gently of the "other side" and what awaited him there.

Sybil conveyed my wishes to the restless one and reported that he understood his situation now.

"He's no trouble," Sybil murmured. She's very sympathetic to ghosts.

With that we left the basement and went back up the stairs into the haunted bedroom, where I took some photographs; then I moved into the living room area upstairs and took some more—all in all about a dozen black and white photographs, including some of the garage and stairs.

Imagine my pleased reaction when I discovered a week later, when the film came back from the laboratory, that two of the photographs had psychic material on them. One, taken of the stairs leading from the bedroom floor to the top floor, shows a whitish substance like a dense fog filling the front right half of my picture. The other remarkable photograph taken of Mrs. Grasso leaning against the wall in the adjoining room shows a similar substance with mirror effect, covering the front third of the area of the picture.

There is a reflection of a head and shoulders of a figure which at first glance I took to be Mrs. Grasso's. On close inspection, however, it is quite dissimilar and shows rather a heavy head of hair whereas Mrs.

Grasso's hairdo is close to the head. Mrs. Grasso wears a dark house-coat over a light dress but the image shows a woman or girl wearing a dark dress or sweater over a white blouse.

I asked Jean Grasso to report to me any changes in the house after our visit.

On November 21, 1966, I heard from her again. The footsteps were gone all right, but there was still something strange going on in the house. Could there have been *two* ghosts?

Loud crashing noises, the slamming of doors, noises similar to the thumping of ash cans when no sensible reason exists for the noises have been observed not only by Jean Grasso and her mother since we were there, but also by her brother and his fiancée and even the non-believing father. No part of the house seems to be immune from the disturbance.

To test things, Jean Grasso slept at her mother's house soon after we left. At 11 P.M., the thumping started. About the same time Mrs. Grasso was awakened by three knocks under her pillow. These were followed almost immediately by the sound of thumping downstairs and movements of a heavy metallic can.

Before I could answer Jean, I had another report from her. Things were far from quiet at the house in Millbrae. Her brother's fiancée, Ellen, was washing clothes in the washing machine. She had closed and secured the door so that the noise would not disturb her intended, who was asleep in the bedroom situated next to the laundry room.

Suddenly she distinctly heard someone trying to get into the room by force, and then she felt a "presence" with her which caused her to run upstairs in panic.

About the same time, Jean and her mother had heard a strange noise from the bathroom below the floor they were then on. Jean went downstairs and found a brush on the tile floor of the bathroom. Nobody had been downstairs at the time. The brush had fallen by itself . . . into the middle of the floor.

When a picture in brother Allen's room lost its customary place on the wall, the thumb tack holding it up disappeared, and the picture itself somehow got to the other side of his bookcase. The frame is pretty heavy, and had the picture just fallen off it would have landed on the floor behind the bookcase; instead it was neatly leaning against the wall on top of it. This unnerved the young man somewhat, as he had not really accepted the possibility of the uncanny up to this point, even though he had witnessed some pretty unusual things himself.

Meanwhile, Jean Grasso managed to plow through the microfilm files at the San Mateo County library in Belmont. There was nothing of interest in the newspapers for 1884, but the files were far from complete.

However, in another newspaper of the area, the *Redwood City Gazette,* there was an entry that Jean Grasso thought worth passing on for my opinion. A Captain Watterman is mentioned in a brief piece, and the fact the townspeople are glad that his bill had died and they could be well rid of it.

The possibility that Sybil heard Wasserman when the name was actually Watterman was not to be dismissed—at least not until a Jan Wasserman could be identified from the records somewhere.

Since the year 1884 had been mentioned by the ghost, I looked up that year in H.H. Bancroft's *History of California,* an imposing record of that state's history published in 1890 in San Francisco.

In Volume VII, on pages 434 and 435, I learned that there had been great irregularities during the election of 1884 and political conditions bordered on anarchy. The man who had been first Lieutenant Governor and later Governor of the state was named R.W. Waterman!

This, of course, may only be conjecture and not correct. Perhaps she really did mean Wasserman with two "S's." But my search in the San Francisco Directory (Langley's) for 1882 and 1884 did not yield any Jan Wasserman. The 1881 Langley did, however, list an Ernst

Wassermann, a partner in Wassermann brothers. He was located at 24th Street and *Potrero Avenue.*

Sybil reported that Wasserman had been killed by a certain Pottrene and a certain Povey. Pottrene as a name does not appear anywhere. Could she have meant Potrero? The name Povey, equally unusual, does, however, appear in the 1902 Langley on page 1416.

A Francis J. Povey was a foreman at Kast & Company and lived at 1 Beideman Street. It seems rather amazing that Sybil Leek would come up with such an unusual name as Povey, even if this is not the right Povey in our case. Wasserman claimed to have lived on Emil Street. There was no such street in San Francisco. There was, however, an Emma Street, listed by Langley in 1884 (page 118).

The city directories available to me are in shambles and plowing through them is a costly and difficult task. There are other works that might yield clues to the identity of our man. It is perhaps unfortunate that my setup does not allow for capable research assistants to help with so monumental a task, and that the occasional exact corroboration of ghostly statements is due more to good luck than to complete coverage of all cases brought to me.

Fortunately, the liberated ghosts do not really care. They know the truth already.

But I was destined to hear further from the Grasso residence.

On January 24th, 1967, all was well. Except for one thing, and that really happened back on Christmas Eve.

Jean's sister-in-law was sleeping on the couch upstairs in the living room. It was around two in the morning, and she could not drop off to sleep, because she had taken too much coffee. While she was lying there, wide awake, she suddenly noticed the tall, muscular figure of a man, somewhat shadowy, coming over from the top of the stairs to the Christmas tree as if to inspect the gifts placed near it. At first she thought it was Jean's brother, but as she focused on the figure, she began to realize it was nobody of flesh-and-blood. She noticed his face now, and that it was bearded. When it dawned on her what she was seeing, and she began to react, the stranger just vanished from the spot where he had been standing a moment before. Had he come to say goodbye and had the Christmas tree evoked a long-ago Christmas holiday of his own?

Before the sister-in-law, Ellen, could tell Jean Grasso about her uncanny experience, Jean herself asked if she had heard the footsteps that kept *her* awake overhead that night. They compared the time, and it appeared that the footsteps and the apparition occurred in about the same time period.

For a few days all was quiet, as if the ghost were thinking it over. But then the pacing resumed, more furiously now, perhaps because something within him had been aroused and he was beginning to understand his position.

At this point everybody in the family heard the attention-getting noises. Mrs. Grasso decided to address the intruder and to tell him that I would correct the record of his death—that I would tell the world that he was not, after all, a bad fellow, but a case of mistaken identity.

It must have pleased the unseen visitor, for things began to quiet down again, and as of February 6, at least, the house had settled down to an ordinary suburban existence on the outskirts of bustling San Francisco.

But until this book is in print, the Grassos won't breathe with complete ease. There is always that chance that the ghost decides I am not telling the world fast enough. But that would seem patently unreasonable. After all, he had to wait an awfully long time before we took notice of him. And I've jumped several ghosts to get him into print as an emergency case. So be it: Mr. Wasserman of Millbrae is not *the* Mr. Wasserman they were looking for, whoever they were. They just had themselves a wild ghost chase for nothing.

Who Killed Carol?

O ne would think that in a well arranged society such as ours the chances of murder occurring should be reasonably slim. Unfortunately, every day brings new crimes of violence, many of which are never solved. A police force hampered by inadequate funds, manpower, and frequently lacking in imagination, has become immune to the emotional aspects of so many unsolved murders. Some years ago I was able to supply the New York Police with material obtained through psychic sources pertaining to the unsolved murder of financier Serge Rubinstein. Despite the fact that the authorities acknowledged the cooperation of myself and medium Ethel Johnson Meyers, despite their recognizing some of the names and situations as valid in the case, no culprit was ever brought into Court or to justice in that bizarre case. Perhaps the public did not care, either, for Rubinstein was a brilliant sharpshooter whose career was spotty and often barely within the limits of legality. But law enforcement agencies all over the world accept the cooperation of investigators like myself, if not openly, then at least tacitly, for they often find themselves in the unpleasant position of having no place to turn for further clues.

The case which follows involves a murder which shook the world at the time it happened, because of the youth and prominence of its victim. As I write these lines, the culprit is still free. I have therefore changed the names somewhat, not to protect the innocent, but to avoid tipping off the guilty. Even though I have changed a few names, I have reported the case exactly as it happened.

It was a chilly day in November, 1963 when the police discovered the nude body of a young girl whom I shall call Carol, in her apartment on one of the quieter streets of Hollywood. Only 22 years old, she was the daughter of a prominent businessman in the Midwest, and had come to California to seek fame and fortune as they say.

Working as an actress when jobs were available, and as an occasional photographers' model, she lived alone in one of those two-story bungalows that make up the majority of Hollywood apartment houses. The rent was within her means, and her family back home occasionally sent her some money. She was the apple of her father and mother's eyes and their only daughter. The search for a glamorous career had been Carol's idea; the family was against it. But Carol was strong-willed and went to Hollywood over her parents' objections. They visited her frequently, and eventually the family assumed she would be all right. Carol's roles were getting larger and Carol became known as a pretty, young ingénue. Her friends in those days were many, but she introduced few of them to her parents. The world she had known at home and her new world in Hollywood were miles apart. As her career left her enough free time, she circulated widely among the young set of actors, photographers, camera men and others who are either just within or on the fringe of the television and motion picture business in California.

She and her mother had always been very close, so Carol did confide in her when affairs of the heart came up. At one of the parties she met a young actor named Artie, with whom she was being seen more and more around town. He was then only an unknown bent on making it big; today he is a rising young actor with credits known around the casting agencies.

But there were complications. Artie had an entanglement with another girl at the time he met Carol. Although he had told her he would break off his relationship with the girl, he never did so entirely during the time he and Carol went together. This worried Carol and she often wrote to her mother about it. Artie was the boy she wanted to marry, and on one occasion she introduced him to her parents.

As time went on, Carol's relationship with Artie was an "off again, on again" courtship punctuated by jealousy and occasional arguments. But neither broke off entirely with the other. Ultimately, Artie assured Carol he loved her and their relationship sailed into smoother waters. But nothing was said about marriage.

There the matter stood when the girl's body was found dead of a heavy fall or blow. Her murder electrified the movie colony, for Carol's many friends feared they would be called in by the police to testify. They were right. Dozens upon dozens of people were questioned, released, questioned, and released again. Everybody had the proper answers and alibis.

The only thing the police could establish with certainty was that Carol had had several visitors that fateful evening. Among her callers was Artie, a natural suspect, but he had left early in the evening. The doctors had fixed the time of death at around 2 A.M. Artie's alibi for that period was firm. The police had to look elsewhere for their culprit. Was it an unexpected visitor? An intruder? Or did one of her several earlier callers return later?

The investigation continued for several months, but gradually tapered off, despite the anguished demands of the parents not to let up and despite promises of a reward for any information leading to the arrest of the murderer. To be sure, the police never gave up. But they had run out of leads. Having followed up every one, and having checked out everyone Carol had known in Hollywood, they had arrived at a blank wall.

At this point the parents looked to psychic sources for help. In 1964, they brought a celebrated Dutch psychic to the scene of the crime with the full blessing of the police. The results, however, were disappointing. Carol's mother then made the rounds of assorted mediums, always hopeful that one of them might turn up a useful clue. While some of them 'saw' the tragedy clairvoyantly, nothing strong enough to be of value emerged.

We corresponded, and I made certain suggestions that Carol's mother try to adjust her own thinking to the inevitable reality of the situation.

Finally, I invited the parents to come to New York. We would try to have a go at the mystery with the late Betty Ritter, a medium whose accuracy I had learned to appreciate over the years. Only after Carol's parents had actually arrived in New York, did I call Betty to set the time for our experiment, which took place on January 13, 1964 at my house.

I doubted that Betty would have recognized the names of either parents or of the girl, for she did not read newspapers regularly. But to dispel all doubts, I arranged for them to arrive fifteen minutes before Betty, and then introduced them by another name.

Betty had no way of "guessing" that these people were from out of town, or that a murder was involved, or that they had a daughter. To her, they looked like any nice, respectable middle-aged couple, friends of mine, interested in a "psychic reading."

We took our places around the dining room table and as is always the rule with my investigations, no discussion or questions of any kind were allowed.

Within a minute after we had sat down, Betty became very agitated. She remarked that she saw the spirit of a crying woman, who was not supposed "to go so soon," as she put it, and that something had happened out West that wasn't supposed to have happened. With that, she took a ring proffered her by the mother, a ring that had once belonged to the murdered girl.

"This spirit has her arms around you, sir," Betty said now, pointing to the father, "and she is crying and very upset. I see a musical clef, or something to do with entertainment." The room fell silent now with expectation.

"You are seeking a clue," Betty continued, "about the death of a woman who hasn't been gone long." The father's face remained immobile; he wasn't going to help. His wife however was quite emotional now; she realized that Betty had made some kind of contact. Clutching a pin that had once belonged to Carol, Betty, her eyes half closed, said, "It happened so fast . . . Stanley . . . I don't know what they wanted from me . . . He grabbed me by the neck . . . two men . . . bothering me . . . down the street. It was a man who whistled a lot . . . I was afraid to tell anybody . . . extort . . . someone was trying to take something from me . . . I was alone in the house, key into door. And there they were."

There were also names and initials—but I can't disclose them. All this made little, if any, sense to me at the time, but evidently the parents recognized it as valid.

The description of the attack had been graphic enough and needed no explanation, but the initials needed some placing: those named by Betty were two men on the list of potential suspects; they lived together in a house on *Stanley* Hill!

"You've come a long way, she says, and I've travelled with you on this trip," Betty continued. How could she know that the parents were not local people?

She then described the girl as a beautiful brunette, with a good figure, and *wearing a velvet dress.* At this point, the mother suppressed a little outcry.

"There are parties down the street," Betty said, "and the two men came from there. Some man made a comment. Two fish together."

Later I discovered that Carol had recently worn a *velvet dress* to a costume party, a dress she was particularly fond of. Carol's birth sign was Pisces.

The police had made a list of potential culprits, and since Carol was

498

a popular girl, the list was not short. Without my questioning her, Betty Ritter now mentioned some of the men Carol might have known, not necessarily her murderers.

"Heart and S . . . cross him out . . . ring with W or M . . . cross it off, too . . . S. and W. grabbed her . . . but don't forget A., he was one of them, too! Down the street, third house, woman knows, photographer W., lady at house L. She was a hanger-on. J. drops in once in a while. Photographer is bearded."

Later she explained these initials. By "cross him off," Betty had meant the person was bad medicine, not necessarily guilty or innocent. I discovered there was a man initialed S., another named W.M., and Carol's landlady "living down the street" was indeed initialled L.; her husband was and is a bearded photographer! J. was the initial of the superintendent. How could Betty Ritter have "guessed" all these details and connected them with the murdered girl?

"Something had happened she was afraid to talk about, but she didn't think it would lead to this," Betty explained. "There was no breaking in, *he had a key,* and she trusted this person. She knew him, went to the kitchen while he was there. Arthur . . . was to have gotten married."

Carol and Artie had indeed planned to marry, but sometime before her untimely death, the engagement was broken by Artie, although Carol did not accept this as final and continued to see him.

"Keep your chin up, *Mommie,*" the spirit communicator made Betty say now, "I don't want you to grieve. I'm happy here, though I'm missing music and nice things . . ." Nobody present had indicated at any time that the lady with me was the mother. Her daughter had always referred to her as Mommie, not Mother. "She's showing me some kind of toy animal," Betty added.

Later on the mother acknowledged this. "The toy animal still exists—it used to be her favorite knickknack."

I thanked Betty when I noticed she was getting tired, and sent her home.

A copy of the transcript was forwarded to the police, but no action could be taken. Something much more specific was needed. Still, the local police were impressed with the results and the methods I had used, and I was asked to continue, if I could, and advise them of any further findings.

In February of 1964 the parents went to California to go over the files in search of new clues. It was not easy for them to do this, for their agony was still fresh.

"Everyone and no one seems guilty," Carol's mother wrote to me afterwards. The puzzle remained. Unfortunately, there had been a time lapse of three days between the murder and the discovery of the body. The parents then offered a monetary reward for a limited time to anyone coming forward with vital information about the murder. The reward was never collected.

With some difficulty, the parents contacted another famous Dutch seer, and brought him to the house. "It was not a stranger," the psychic said. Then he examined a photograph of Carol and Artie together. Feeling the boy's face with his fingertips, he suggested, "This boy is *capable* of murder." But he would not commit himself beyond that.

My contact with Carol's parents resumed the week before Christmas, when they paid a hurried visit to New York. On that occasion I asked for Carol's ring, so that my good friend Sybil Leek could have a go at it. I introduced them to Sybil, but Mrs. Leek preferred to work on the ring at a quieter moment. Needless to say, I did not tell Sybil anything about a murder. I only told her the couple had a daughter who was dead, and that the ring had once belonged to her.

A week after Christmas Sybil had sufficiently calmed down from the hectic holiday activities that I could finally hand her the ring for a reading.

"I have the impression of a young man wearing a pinkish shirt," she began immediately, and described this person as having longish hair, with a peculiarity of the position of the eyes in relation to the rest of his face, that is, the distance between the eyes is wider than it should be. She saw him with a camera slung over the shoulder and felt he had something to do with photography. Then she got the impression of a name and started to spell it. I asked Sybil to concentrate on this man.

"This man flies a lot, brings drugged cigarettes in the bottom of his camera," Sybil said. "The girl has her picture taken by him. He is very angry, because she wants to go and he doesn't want her to go."

Then she described in horrifying, chilling detail how he placed his arm around the girl's neck and killed her, leaving her body on the floor near a fireplace. It was *not premeditated* murder, she explained, but the outcome of an argument between them.

I asked if the man had been alone.

"Yes," she said, her eyes closed and thoughts concentrated on the ring in her fist, "there were people there, but they went; he stayed." I asked for a description of the room in which the tragedy had occurred.

"There's a small house and you turn left when you go in. I only see one room but there are doors. A few steps up, then a little step and into the room. A music rack on the side of the fireplace."

What about the young man, what did he do after the murder?

"He walked around a little road and got into a car, then went south. His own place is not far from the girl's."

Sybil also mentioned the fact that the girl was not too cooperative, and did not wish to have the man punished for personal, sentimental reasons. This of course made things twice as difficult for me.

Then on January 9, 1968, Carol's mother came to New York again. I had offered earlier to take her to a good psychometrist if she would bring along a couple of objects that had belonged to her daughter.

I telephoned Ethel Johnson Meyers and asked if she could see me and "a friend." On January 11, we went to her apartment on the West

Side. I introduced the mother by a fictitious name, then handed Ethel Carol's ring. Immediately, Mrs. Meyers "picked up" the person of the owner. "Large eyes, a good-looking individual, interested in *experiences* and seeking them, but something extraordinarily tragic about this. . . ." And suddenly the medium grimaced with pain, complaining about being "crushed in," and exhibiting all the details of a death struggle. "I've wanted an experience, but this isn't what I wanted," Ethel said now, quoting the girl. "Five minutes before or later, it could have been avoided."

I asked for clarification of this cryptic remark. Ethel began to shiver as if in terror. Heavy breathing and inarticulate cries followed. Only gradually did the words make sense. "No, no, no . . . no!" She was evidently resisting an unseen but recognized attacker. "Don't—No!"

"Mommie . . . help . . ." Carol was now in control of the medium, "Tell us who was with you . . . tell us who did it," I urged.

Evidently the answer involved emotional conflicts, for the medium almost choked, trying to reply. "Momma . . . Momma . . ." I asked the mother to speak up. As a result the girl (through Ethel) broke into a series of near-hysterical laughs. Again it took some time to calm her down. No actress could have produced the utter devastation the medium now exhibited. "Where am I?" she finally said. The mother then handed Ethel a bracelet which had once been worn by her daughter. The reaction was instantaneous. "L. . . . L. . . ." she said, repeating it several times, then adding, "Allan . . . Al . . . don't want to . . . no . . ." "Allan" had been to the house that night but she had not let him in: he had *pushed* his way in. She had met him before, with Jim. The superintendent of the apartment house, Jim, liked to give parties. Was she referring to him? "What time is it, what time is it?" she kept asking, still in partial shock. She had bit the attacker in the lip. She didn't know what he did for a living. She had met him before and he lived in the same complex of buildings. But this was the first time he had ever *entered* her apartment. "Still there," she said, insisting he had not moved from the house after her death. She was expecting "someone" that night—but it all happened too fast. The attacker had been white, but dark complexioned, with black hair; there was something wrong with his lip; he was about forty years old.

"I hurt so . . . I can't think . . ." she exclaimed, "five minutes more . . . I would have had the phone off the hook . . ." Apparently, she had been talking to someone on the phone, and if the intruder had come five minutes before, perhaps this would have stopped him. I had rarely seen Ethel so overcome with confusion and emotional turmoil. It was very difficult to make head or tail from the testimony.

"Cover me up," she now mumbled. Ethel could not know that the girl's body was found nude. "Don't let go of me, Momma," she pleaded. "I'm sorry, forgive me."

After a few moments, the spirit left and Ethel "returned" to her old self, a little more shaken than usual. I gave a complete report to the Homicide Squad, stressing the points made by my psychic friends and their unseen "helpers."

Shortly after I had sent a detailed transcript of my various psychic investigations to the police department, I received an annotated appraisal of the same. Paragraph for paragraph, name for name, was carefully weighed by the investigating officers and evaluated as to the possible accuracy. There was no attempt to play down my contribution to a possible solution of the case nor indeed the entire field of extrasensory perception research. Nevertheless, the overall impression was one of disappointment on the part of the police that nothing more tangible had resulted from my work thus far. It should be made clear here that those named by my various psychics are not necessarily the murderer or murderers or guilty of anything illegal. It is in the nature of psychometry and other forms of mediumship to pick up names and situations from the immediate surroundings of a person, regardless of the importance of such names. Thus it may very well be that some of the individuals named by psychics may have been on the side of the angels, even good friends trying to help the murdered girl. Any inference that those names in these pages are necessarily guilty of anything would be wrong. In fact, there were so many *potential* suspects in this case that in the end the police were unable to pinpoint anyone sufficiently to even make a temporary arrest. Two of the more prominent individuals questioned had to be left alone eventually, since they had been completely cooperative with the authorities, even submitting to lie detector tests which remained negative.

The case never left the dock of the police department nor indeed my own files. On November 30, 1969 I let medium Shawn Robbins hold an envelope pertaining to the case. Immediately Shawn tuned in on the situation. She described a girl, aged twenty-three—the exact age Carol was at the time of her death. "The person you are looking for has short black hair. He is tall, slim and his hair is cut country style." On October 9, 1971 I consulted Gar Osten, a rising young astrologer whom I had met through Shawn Robbins and who worked closely with her in many instances. He and Shawn, together, decided to cast the horoscope of the late Carol and see whether in so doing they might come up with some clues as to the murderer. Osten remarked that "the planet Mercury indicates the last relationship, which was also the murderer. This was an on again, off again affair. The actor-musician is indicated." Gar and Shawn's interpretation of his chart brought up a number of interesting points. Neither knew much about Carol, except that she had been an actress and had been murdered.

"She had a subtle, versatile and changeful nature, inconstant and imitative. She was much affected by surroundings and those with whom she came in contact. A basic lack of security, lack of confidence and a feeling of unworthiness troubled her. She did not face issues squarely and had to be helped herself, although she was receptive to the needs of others. There was a great need for self expression which could have taken the direction of a creative talent. She was weak when it came to knowing when to stop which included drinking, socializing, spending, believing the promises of others. She was attracted to the underdog and had friends among those who were weak or afflicted with emotional and physical difficulties. There was danger of being deceived by others or she suffered disillusion and the danger of scandal. She found pleasure in secret affairs of the heart. She had an eccentric tendency in regard to the use of money: She might have been generous to the wrong persons and turn away from the deserving.

"I believe this girl had four love attachments in her lifetime. The first did not turn out well and was secret in nature. Perhaps a change in schools or a move of the home of some kind ended it. The second attachment began in the last half of 1961 into early 1962. He was in a responsible position and could have been an employer or father figure. He definitely did not come from the environment where she was born. The desire was for marriage but this relationship did not work out and shortly after she entered another one. The third relationship began early in 1962. This man is shown to have been connected with the arts, music or acting. He was systematic, not reliable, and able to sense an advantage. The deception was self-inflicted on her part and from the first it was not destined to work out. There was an aspect about this man that she found difficult to deal with which frustrated her. *The fourth attachment I believe to be the murderer.* This lover is shown to be young, with intellectual leanings, possibly a student and restless and watery in nature. Theirs was an attraction through weakness rather than strength. They both had problems and they found comfort together. He seems to have had artistic leanings, musical interests or perhaps films. Their meeting might have occurred through the career. I believe they met for the first time in August 1962. It was self-deception and the relationship seems to have been broken off about December 14, 1962, but resumed again in mid-May, 1963.

"The murder itself was set into motion by a solar eclipse on July 20, 1963." However, Shawn felt that the murderer was not a young man with whom Carol had had a long relationship. "I am sure suspicion is cast on him, I am sure the mother knows," she added, "He has been to Carol's house maybe once and she went out with him maybe three times." "Do the police suspect him?" I asked. Shawn shook her head "No. He has been interviewed, but has a perfect alibi. Also he would not have had any reason to murder her. Except of course that I don't think he is well."

A Miss W., resident of Hollywood who did not know either Carol nor anyone else connected with the case but who has had psychic dreams for a number of years, communicated one particularly strong dream impression to me. She had this dream shortly after the murder had taken place. In this dream she saw a man who allegedly had been attracted to Carol at a studio where he was very important. No one knew she was seeing him and he was a challenge to her. The night he came to kill her she was very happy since he told her that they could be together always from now on. As they were making love he was kissing her and then strangled her.

Fourteen years after the murder, the police, the parents, and Carol's friends know that there are two men who could have committed the crime. But did they? Then too, did the murderer arrive, evil intent in his heart, or did he merely come to pay a social call and wound up in the midst of a heated argument with Carol? Did he seize her body and in the heat of the discussion, cause her death? From a psychic research point of view, it seems obvious that Carol is shielding someone she loves very much. That man is Artie. Oddly enough, she may be protecting him without need to. Is it possible that Carol knew her neighbor had killed her but thought at the same time that the crime would somehow be pinned on Artie, the man she very much wanted to marry.

In protecting Artie, she was therefore not protecting a suspect, but merely a lover to whom she felt greater loyalty than he had shown towards her.

Is This You, Jean Harlow?

If any movie actress deserved the name of "the vamp," it certainly was Jean Harlow. The blonde actress personified the ideal of the 1930s—slim and sultry, moving her body in a provocative manner, yet dressing in the rather elegant, seemingly casual style of that period. Slinky dresses, sweaters and colorful accessories made Jean Harlow one of the outstanding glamor girls of the American screen. The public was never let in on any of her personal secrets or, for that matter, her personal tragedies. Her life story was carefully edited to present only those aspects of her personality that fitted in with the preconceived notion of what a glamorous movie star should be like. In a way, Jean Harlow was the prototype of all later blonde glamor girls of the screen, culminating with the late Marilyn Monroe. There is a striking parallel, too, in the tragic lives and sometimes ends of these blonde movie queens. Quite possibly the image they projected on the screen, or were forced to project, was at variance with their own private achievements and helped pave the way to their tragic downfalls.

To me, Jean Harlow will always stand out as the glamorous goddess of such motion pictures as *Red Dust,* which I saw as a little boy. The idea that she could have had an earthbound life after death seems to be very far from the image the actress portrayed during her lifetime. Thus it was with some doubt that I followed up a lead supplied by an English newspaper, which said the former home of the screen star was haunted.

The house in question is a handsome white stucco one-family house set back somewhat from a quiet residential street in Westwood, a section of Los Angeles near the University generally considered quiet and upper middle class. The house itself belongs to a professional man and his wife who share it with their two daughters and two poodles. It is a two-story building with an elegant staircase winding from the rear of the ground floor to the upper story. The downstairs portion contains a rather large oblong living room which leads into a dining room. There are a kitchen and bathroom adjacent to that area and a stairway leading to the upper floor. Upstairs are two bedrooms and a bathroom.

When I first spoke on the telephone to Mrs. H., the present occupant of the house, asking permission to visit, she responded rather cordially. A little later I called back to make a definite appointment and found that her husband was far from pleased with my impending visit. Although he himself had experienced some of the unusual phenomena in the house, as a professional, and I suppose as a man, he was worried that publicity might hurt his career. I assured him that I was not interested in disclosing his name or address, and with that assurance I was again welcomed. It was a sunny afternoon when I picked up my tape recorder and camera, left my taxicab in front of the white house in Westwood, and rang the bell.

Mrs. H. was already expecting me. She turned out to be a petite, dark-blonde lady of around thirty, very much given to conversation and more than somewhat interested in the occult. As a matter of fact, she had read one of my earlier books. With her was a woman friend; whether the friend had been asked out of curiosity or security I do not know. At any rate the three of us sat down in the living room and I started to ask Mrs. H. the kind of questions I always ask when I come to an allegedly haunted house.

"Mrs. H., how long have you lived in this house?"

"Approximately four years."

"When you bought it, did you make any inquiries as to the previous owner?"

"I did not. I didn't really care. I walked into the house and I liked it and that was that."

"Did you just tell your husband to buy it?"

"Yes. I told him, 'This is our house.' I had the realtor go ahead and draw up the papers before he saw it because I knew he would feel as I did."

"Where did you live before?"

"All over—Brentwood, West Los Angeles, Beverly Hills. I was born in Canada."

"How many years have you been married?"

"Seventeen."

"You have children?"

"I have two daughters, nine and twelve."

"Did the real-estate man tell you anything about the house?"

"He did not."

"After you moved in and got settled, did you make some changes in it?"

"Yes; it was in kind of sad shape. It needed somebody to love it."

"Did you make any structural changes?"

"No. When we found out the history of the house we decided we would leave it as it was."

"So at the time you moved in, you just fixed it?"

"Yes."

"When was the first time that you had any *unusual* feelings about the house?"

"The day before we moved in I came over to direct the men who were laying the carpet. I walked upstairs and I had an experience at that time."

"What happened?"

"My two dogs ran barking and growling into the upstairs bedrooms; I went up, and I thought I heard something *whisper in my ear*. It scared me."

"That was in one of the upstairs bedrooms?"

"No, in the hallway just before the master bedroom. The dogs ran in barking and growling as if they were going to get somebody, and then when they got in there they looked around and there was nobody there."

"What did you hear?"

"I could swear I heard somebody say, *'Please help me!'* It was a soft whisper, sort of hushed."

"What did you do?"

"I talked to myself for a few minutes to get my bearings. I had never experienced anything *like that,* and I figured, 'Well, if it's there, fine.' I've had *other* ESP experiences before, so I just went about my business."

"Those other experiences you've had—were they before you came to this house?"

"Yes. I have heard my name being called."

"In this house or in another?"

"In other homes."

"Anyone you could recognize?"

"No, just female voices."

"Did you *see* anything unusual at any time?"

"I saw what I assume to be ectoplasm. . . . It was like cigarette smoke. It moved, and my dogs whined, tucked their tails between their legs, and fled from the room."

"Did you tell your husband about the whisper?"

"I did not. My husband is skeptical. I saw no reason to tell him."

"When was the next time you had any feeling of a presence here?"

"The night we moved in, my husband and I were lying in bed. Suddenly, it was as if the bed were hit by a very strong object three times. My husband said 'My God, I'm getting out of here. This place is haunted.' I replied, 'Oh, shush. It's all right if someone is trying to communicate. It's not going to hurt.' And to the ghost I said, 'You're welcome—how do you do; but we've got to get some sleep—we're very, very tired—so please let us be.'"

"And did it help?"

"Yes."

"How long did the peace last?"

"Well, the jerking of the bed never happened again. But other things happened. There is a light switch on my oven in the kitchen. For a long time after we moved in, the switch would go on every so often—by itself."

"Would it take anyone to turn it physically, to turn on the light?"

"Yes, you'd have to flip it up."

"Was there anybody else in the house who could have done it?"

"No, because I would be sitting here and I'd hear the click and I would go there and it would be *on*. It's happened ten or fifteen times, but recently it has stopped."

"Any other phenomena?"

"Something new one time, at dusk. I was walking from one room to the other. I was coming through the dining room, and for some reason I looked up at the ceiling. There it was, this light—"

"Did it have any particular shape?"

"No. It moved at the edges, but it really didn't have a form. It wasn't a solid mass, more like an outline. It was floating above me."

"Did you hear anything?"

"Not at that time. I have on one occasion. I was sitting right in the chair I am in now. My Aunt Mary was in that chair, and we both heard *sobs*. Terrible, sad, wrenching sobs coming from the corner over there by the mailbox. It was very upsetting, to say the least."

"Were these a woman's sobs?"

"Definitely."

"Did you see anything at the time?"

"No. I just felt terribly sad, and the hair stood up on my arms. Also, in this house there are *winds* at times, when there is no window open."

"Are there any cold spots that cannot be explained rationally?"

"Very frequently. Downstairs, usually here or in the upstairs bedroom, sometimes also in the kitchen."

"At the time your Aunt Mary was sitting here and you heard the sobs, did she also hear them?"

"Oh, she did, and I had to give her a drink."

"Have you heard any other sounds?"

"Footsteps. Up and down the stairs when nobody was walking up or down."

"Male or female?"

"I would say female, because they are light. I have also felt things brush by my face, touching my cheek."

"Since you came to this home, have you had any unusual dreams?"

"Definitely. One very important one. I was in bed and just dozing off, when I had a vision. I saw very vividly a picture of the upstairs bathroom. I saw a hand reaching out of a bathtub full of water, going up to the light switch, the socket where you turn power on and off. It then turned into a vision of wires, and brisk voltage struck the hand; the hand withered and died. It upset me terribly. The next morning my husband said, 'You know, I had the strangest dream last night.' He had had the *identical dream!*"

"Identical?"

"Practically. In his version, the hand didn't wither, but he saw the sparks coming out of it. I went into the bathroom and decided to call in an electrician. He took out the outdated switch. He said, 'Did you know this is outlawed? If anybody had been in the tub and reached up and touched the switch, he would have been electrocuted!' We moved the switch so the only way you can turn the switch on is *before* you go into the bathroom. You can no longer reach it from the tub. Whoever helped me with this—I'm terribly grateful to her."

"Is there anything else of this kind you would care to tell me?"

"I have smelled perfume in the upstairs children's bedroom, a very strong perfume. I walked into the room. My little daughter who sleeps there doesn't have perfume. That's the only place I smell it, my little girl's bedroom."

"Has any visitor ever come to this house without knowledge of the phenomena and complained about anything unusual?"

"A friend named Betty sat in the kitchen and said, 'My gosh, I wish you'd close the windows. There's such a draft in here.' But everything was shut tight."

"Has your husband observed anything unusual except for the dream?"

"One evening in the bedroom he said, 'Boy, there's a draft in here!' I said there couldn't be. All the windows were closed."

"What about the children?"

"My youngest daughter, Jenny, has complained she hears a party in her upstairs closet. She says that people are having a party in it. She can hear them."

"When was the house built?"

"I believe in 1929."

"Was it built to order for anyone?"

"No. It was just built like many houses in this area, and then put up for sale."

"Who was the first tenant here?"

"It was during the Depression. There were several successive tenants."

"How did Jean Harlow get involved with the house?"

"She was living in a small home, but the studio told her she should live in a better area. She rented this house in the early '30s and moved into it with her parents."

"How long did she live here?"

"About four years. She paid the rent on it longer, however, because after she married, her folks stayed in this house. I believe she married her agent."

"How did she die?"

"She died, I understand, as the result of a beating given to her by her husband which damaged her kidneys. The story goes that on the second night, after their honeymoon, he beat her. She came back to this house, took her mother into the bathroom and showed her what he had done to her. She was covered with bruises. She tried to make up with him, but to no avail. The night he killed himself, she was in this house. There was a rumor that he was impotent or a latent homosexual. He shot himself. When she heard the news, she was in her upstairs bedroom. She tried to commit suicide, because she thought she was the reason. She took an overdose of sleeping pills."

"Did she succeed?"

"She did not. Her parents put pressure on her to move out of this house. She built another one and subsequently died of a kidney disease."

"Not immediately after the beating?"

"No—a few years later. Her parents were Christian Scientists, and she didn't have ordinary medical help at the time."

"Then what took place in this house, emotionally speaking? The marriage to Paul Bern, the news of his suicide, and her own attempt to commit suicide upstairs. Which rooms were particularly connected with these events?"

"The living room. She was married there. And the bathroom upstairs. I left it as it was."

"Do you have any feelings about it?"

"I have a feeling about the bathroom. I know she's been in that bathroom many times. I don't know if she tried to commit suicide in the bathroom or if she took the pills in the bedroom."

"Where did the actual beating take place?"

"They say it was in the bathroom downstairs."

"Which is the bathroom you have such a weird feeling in, the downstairs or the upstairs?"

"Downstairs."

"Anything pertaining to the front or the outside of the house?"

"There are knocks at our front door when there is nobody there; visitors would say, 'There's someone at your door,' and there wasn't. . . . It happens all the time."

"Are you sure other people hear the knocks too?"

"Yes."

"Somebody couldn't have done it and run away in a hurry?"

"No. It's a funny knock. Kind of gentle. It isn't like a 'let-me-in' type knock. Flesh-and-blood people wouldn't knock on a door that way."

"When was the last time you had any feeling of a presence in this house?"

"Maybe two or three months ago."

"Do you feel she's still around?"

"Yes. Also, I feel she was very upset at the way she was portrayed as a kind of loose woman without morals. Her biography presents her as something she was not."

"Do you think she's trying to express herself through you?"

"No, but I think it's terrible what they've done to her reputation. They had no right to do that."

"Do you feel that she's trying to set the record straight?"

"I would imagine. I can only put myself in her place. If I were to cross over under those circumstances, I would be very unhappy. I hope someday somebody will write another book about Harlow and go into it with a sensitive, loving attitude instead of sensationalism as a way to make a fast buck."

I thanked Mrs. H. and prepared to leave the house that had once been Jean Harlow's. Perhaps the lady of the house was merely reliving the more emotional aspects of the late screen star's life, the way an old film is rerun from time to time on television. Was she picking up these vibrations from the past through psychometry? Or was there perhaps something of the *substance* of Jean Harlow still present in the atmosphere of this house? As I walked out the front door into the still-warm late afternoon, I looked back at Mrs. H., who stood in the doorway waving me good-bye. Her blonde hair was framed by the shadow cast by the door itself. For a fleeting moment, some of the blonde glamor of the late Jean Harlow seemed to have impressed itself upon her face. Perhaps it was only my imagination, but all of a sudden I felt that Jean Harlow hadn't really left the house where so much of her emotional life had taken place.

A Visit With Carole Lombard, Thanks To Julie Parrish

I was in San Diego, California, doing a local television show to discuss one of my books. A fellow guest was an attractive young lady who had had some psychic experiences, so the producer thought that putting us together on this show was a stroke of genius. It turned out to be more than that: it was the hand of fate. A close friendship of many years' standing and many exciting adventures into the supernatural, so called, were the result of this "chance" meeting. I was asked to interview the young lady on the show, and I did. We hit it off right away. That is how I met Julie Parrish for the first time.

Julie was then appearing in a daytime serial called *Good Morning, World*. She had done numerous stints on television shows and appeared in several motion pictures. In retrospect I find it ironical that she appeared in *Harlow* for Paramount. But the subject that intrigued Julie most at that time was not so much how to get a good role in another movie as how to understand herself and her strange psychic abilities. In the five years that I have known Julie she has come a long way. She has been a professional astrologer whose predictions I have quoted liberally in a book called *The Prophets Speak,* and she has been a psychic whose extraordinary sensitivity was recorded by Jess Stearn in one of his earlier works. She is one of the stars of the revived series *Peyton Place* and leads a very busy life that doesn't permit her so much psychic activity as she might like. It was all there in her "chart" several years ago, so she is quite content to let fate take a hand in her life and simply wait to see what happens.

Julie Parrish is five feet five, has dark-blonde hair which from time to time turns brown, hazel eyes and a slim figure. At that time she looked about twenty-two, and now, five years later, she looks about twenty-three. This is due not to any miracle but to her deep understanding of Yoga, her diet of health foods, and her observance of the rhythm of proper living, all of which allow her to replenish her depleted energies even after doing one television show a day, five days a week, year in and year out. Julie is an advanced soul in the esoteric sense. She has read a great deal and met many people in the esoteric field who have taught her some of the fundamentals of balancing body, mind and spirit in daily living. All this has not materially advanced her career, but it has made her into a very strong person, able to cope with the stress of a Hollywood career under conditions which might make weaker individuals falter.

In 1961 Julie was living in Toledo, Ohio, sharing an apartment on Collingwood Boulevard with two roommates. It was a very well preserved old house; the girls' apartment was a huge one which took up the entire top floor. On this particular day she found herself all alone recuperating from a cold. As she lay in bed she gradually slipped into that state between wakefulness and sleep in which psychic experiences frequently occur. As she did so, she became aware of a lady all dressed in black, wearing a mourning veil and hat, standing in the doorway. Julie could not see her face well, but the woman looked at her and then slowly crossed to the closet on her right and looked inside. Petrified, Julie watched her without moving. She tried to scream, but no sound came. The woman then turned and walked toward the bed. In panic, Julie closed her eyes. The woman moved closer and bent down to her, and Julie could actually feel her breath on her face. It was as though she were taking her breath away. With all the strength Julie could muster, she burst out of the trance state, and as she did, the woman disappeared.

After Julie had moved to Los Angeles, she lived in an old house built in the thirties by the late Wilfred Orme of the Warner Brothers art department. There she spent four and a half years. During that time she had many psychic experiences—people running around and slamming doors, loud footsteps, inaudible conversations. Whenever she checked she would find that no one was there. These manifestations always took place during the daytime, when she could have seen plainly whether there was really anyone there or not. Strangely, they took place only when Julie was in that state between wakefulness and sleep where physical responses are low yet attention is still riveted on anything unusual around oneself. The large number of these psychic experiences so unnerved her that she put aluminum foil on her bedroom windows, so that whenever she rested, no light would come in through the windows and send her into the astral state.

Several times Julie felt that someone unseen was trying to smother her. Each time the experience threw her into a panic. Eventually she investigated the background of the house and discovered that a man had killed himself in it. The only redeeming feature of her experiences in the house was that when she was in the psychic state she could hear the radio playing beside her bed even though it was not turned on. When in her normal state of wakefulness she turned the radio on, she would discover that it was broadcasting the music she had heard in her head while in the psychic state.

In the late sixties she went to Las Vegas on business. It was a dark afternoon in November when she registered at the Sands Hotel and checked into room 1888. Tired from the trip and from a long evening the night before, she went to bed, hoping to sleep late the next day. Thus it was already well into that day when she awoke. What broke her sleep was not the lateness of the hour, however, but the laughing and the loud conversation of three men and two women sitting and standing in various positions around a table at the foot of her bed. Julie immediately sensed that they were not exactly "nice people." They stared at her, and she felt embarrassed, since she wasn't wearing much because of the warmth of the room. A man on the right turned to the others and said, "What should we do with her?"

This abruptly brought her back to her conscious state. She realized then that she had seen the ghosts of five people who had been killed in the immediate vicinity and who had for some reason chosen her room to go over old memories.

Late in 1969 Julie moved to New York for a while and decided to work with me in perfecting her control over the psychic talent she so amply possessed. We used hypnosis to widen her psychic perception, and eventually I tested her in various ways to determine how much her psychometry had grown as a result of our working together. Among other things, I tested her with letters written by various people whom I knew but of whom Julie knew nothing. She was quite remarkable with a note from the late Bishop James Pike and with another letter written by a late friend of mine, Dr. Thomas Mabbott, professor of English at Hunter College. In each case she characterized the writer quite accurately, even though she could not have deduced anything from the writing itself or the contents. But it was in October of the following year, in Hollywood, that Julie and I worked on our most interesting case together.

In 1967 I first heard of a haunted house where the late Carole Lombard had lived. During a séance in Greenwich Village, I heard of a Mexican-born lady named Adriana de Sola who had been to the Village flat and had seen a ghost in it, and I became interested in meeting her. Some time later I did meet her in Hollywood. Miss de Sola was by vocation a poet and writer, but she made her living in various ways, usually as a housekeeper. In the late forties she had been engaged as such by a motion picture producer of some renown. She supervised the staff, a job she performed very well indeed, being an excellent organizer. Carefully inspecting the house before agreeing to take the position, she had found it one of those quiet, elegant houses in the best part of Hollywood that could harbor nothing but good. Confidently, Adriana had taken the job.

A day or two after her arrival, she was fast asleep in her room when she found herself aroused in the middle of the night by someone shaking her. Fully awake, she realized that she was being shaken by the shoulder. She sat up in bed, but there was no one to be seen. Even though she could not with her ordinary sight distinguish any human being in the room, her psychic sense told her immediately that there was someone standing next to her bed. Relaxing for a moment and closing her eyes, Adriana tried to tune in on the unseen entity. Immediately she saw, standing next to her bed, a tall, slim woman with blonde hair down to her shoulders. What made the apparition or psychic impression the more upsetting to Adriana was the fact that the woman was bathed in blood and quite obviously suffering.

Adriana realized that she had been contacted by a ghostly entity but could not get herself to accept the reality of the phenomenon, and hopefully ascribed it to an upset stomach, or to the new surroundings and the upsets of having just moved in. At the same time, she prayed for the restless one. But six or seven days later the same thing happened again. This time Adriana was able to see the ghost more clearly. She was impressed with the great beauty of the woman she saw and decided to talk about her experience with her employers in the morning. The producer's wife listened very quietly to the description of the ghostly visitor, then nodded. When Adriana mentioned that the apparition had been wearing a light suit covered with blood, the lady of the house drew back in surprise. It was only then that Adriana learned that the house had once been Carole Lombard's and that the late movie star had lived in it very happily with Clark Gable. Carole Lombard had died tragically in an airplane accident, when her plane, en route to the East where she was going to do some USO shows, hit a mountain during a storm. At the time, she was wearing a light-colored suit.

Miss de Sola was pleased, in a way, that her psychic ability had been proved correct. At the same time, she realized that the two visits by the restless one were not going to be the only ones, and she was not prepared to open herself up to further visitations. Two days later she regretfully informed her employers that she could not stay on after all.

Many years later Julie Parrish asked me to look into a case of some interest brought to her attention by a doctor friend of hers named Doris August. The doctor had a house in Hollywood where some disturbances of a psychic nature had occurred. Would I follow through?

The house, an older wooden structure set back a bit from the street in a quiet section of Hollywood, turned out to be the former home of the motion picture producer who had tried to employ Miss De Sola. Since then several owners had come and gone in rapid succession. The doctor felt quite comfortable in it, and the feeling of a presence had not in the least disturbed her, especially as she was convinced of the reality of psychic phenomena. We did not discuss anything about the house at first, but I asked that Julie move about the two stories to see whether she could pick up anything unusual, in a psychic sense, and also to feel out the house for any actual presences that might have remained in the atmosphere. After a while she stretched out on a couch in the living room and I placed her into light trance. We lowered the lights, closed the windows and the door and waited quietly for what might come through Julie's lips, or for that matter what might happen to us. The only other person present was Dr. August.

For the first five or six minutes there was absolutely nothing. I decided to start by addressing myself to the unseen entity or entities present. I realized, of course, that Julie knew that the house had once belonged to Carole Lombard, as did I. Beyond this fact, however, no details were known to either of us. Anything Dr. August might tell us would have to be discussed after the attempt to make contact with the entity in the house.

The traffic on Sunset Boulevard, a few yards away, seemed strangely muted at this moment, and I had the distinct feeling that we were back in the thirties. The atmosphere of the house felt musty and contained, as if time had stood still and we had stepped into a time lock of sorts. I looked toward the handsome bar in the corner of the room, for no particular reason, and then addressed myself to parties unknown.

"If there is anyone present who wishes to communicate with us, let him speak through Julie. We have come as friends, to set things right, to help if we can. Julie, do you see anyone present in this atmosphere?"

"There's a woman here, but she's laughing at you. She doesn't understand what it is you're doing and why."

"What does she look like?"

"She has on a *red dress,* and she's a blonde. She doesn't know what you're doing here."

"I'm here to help her make contact. Does she seem young or old?"

"She's young."

"Is she hurt in any way?"

"She seems fine, but *I* don't feel well."

"What do you feel?"

"I feel very hot; my head is hurting, and my throat hurts. I think this is something that she's showing me *she* feels."

"Ask her to identify herself by name."

"What is your name? . . . Her name is Carole."

"Is this her house?"

"Yes."

"Does she remember passing over? Dying?"

"She doesn't know that she's dead."

"Does she remember a plane ride she took many years ago?"

"Yes, she does."

"Does she remember being in that airplane?"

"She seems confused."

"Is there anyone she wants to find?"

"She's looking for Clark. She came back and he didn't recognize her; she tried to talk to him and he couldn't talk to her; he couldn't see her. And now she can't find him. She wants very much to find him because she wants to tell him that she's sorry, that she loves him very much. But he couldn't hear her."

"Where did she try to talk to him?"

"I don't know. She's feeling these things."

"All right, we will help her. Ask her to listen very carefully."

(In a whisper) "Okay."

"Carole, you were in a plane accident. The plane crashed. You were killed. Your spirit survived. You came back to your house, but no one could see or hear you because you were a spirit and they were not psychic enough to understand this. Does she understand?"

"She's very quiet."

"You have passed over into the next stage of life. You are very much alive, but out of the physical body. You are a spirit. But this must not upset you. Clark has been over some years too. You are both on the same side, and you could get together if you wished. Does she wish to find Clark?"

"Yes."

"She must call out to him. First she must understand that she has passed over and is no longer in the physical world. Does she understand that?"

"She's trying to."

"Tell her she must not hold onto this house which is *not* of the spirit world; the moment she relinquishes her attachment to this house, she will be free to find him."

"She says it's her house, but things have changed."

"Does she wish to join Clark? I will tell her what she must do."

"She hears you."

"Call for Clark to take you away from this house, to *his* house, and he will come for you. That is all that is necessary. But she must do it of her own volition. Is she doing it?"

"Well, she hesitates."

"Why is she hesitating?"

"Is there a—a Mrs.—Reade—R-e-d-e—"

"Who is Mrs. Rede?"

"A dressmaker!"

"What about her?"

"She has—the jewelry. She has the earrings."

"What does she want done with them?"

"She just wants to tell you. She left it there. She took it off and threw it there."

"Is it all right with her that Mrs. Rede has her jewelry?"

"It's not there anymore; she only wanted you to know where it was, at the time. People were looking."

"Does she remember the accident?"

"She was very frightened."

"Tell her she's fine now, and fully alive. Tell her to begin by calling for Clark."

"She's using her mind."

"I ask that this entity be helped across, to relinquish all ties with this house and earth, and to be taken in hand by the one she seeks. I ask that my friends on the other side actively assist her in crossing. Carole, go from this place; do not look back upon it; keep it in your memories, but go on to better things, and above all, go on to join your loved one. He awaits you."

"Yes. She understands."

"I send you away from this house, Carole, into the next stage of life where you will find Clark if you desire. I send you away from the earth plane. Go now."

"She's not here anymore."

A moment later Julie Parrish was back to herself. Shaking off the sleeplike trance, she sat up and spoke to me about the experience of the last few minutes. She remembered most of it, although not everything. Since the trance had been a light one, that was to be expected. Immediately I questioned Julie about her conscious memories of the encounter with the entity in this house, before she could forget it or before discussion could add details which were not originally in her mind. What exactly did she recall?

"I saw a blonde lady."

"What kind of a dress did she wear?"

"Red. She was slim, very pretty, and had blue eyes."

"Hair?"

"Short, kind of curly."

"Anything else about her?"

"She seemed confused. As if she were in limbo."

"How do you yourself feel?"

"Fine."

I now turned to the owner of the house. "Dr. August, how long have you been in this house?"

"Twenty years."

"Have you ever experienced anything unusual?"

"No."

"Has anyone else?"

"They say they have. Kenny Kingston, the psychic, came here six months ago. He and a number of friends wanted to have a séance."

"But did anyone have any experiences prior to that?"

"No, but they knew it was Carole Lombard's house and they wanted to try."

"What happened during the séance?"

"They said they saw her. She came into the room with flowers and seemed very happy."

"How was she described?"

"Very slender; had her hair kind of loose, and she was wearing a *red dress.*"

"How many people saw her?"

"The whole group—there were about thirty—said that they did."

"Dr. August, do you have any comments on the material we have just obtained with Julie?"

"Only this: On the night Kenny Kingston was here with his group, he told us there had been a big fight between Clark and Carole, just before she left on her fatal journey."

The entranced Julie had spoken of a tearful Carole asking forgiveness from her Clark. Julie had no way of knowing either about the quarrel just prior to Carole Lombard's last flight or that she had been seen by others in the house prior to her visit wearing the identical red dress Julie had seen her in. Perhaps a lover's quarrel and a red dress aren't much in the way of psychic evidence; as evidence goes. But psychic researchers must attach comparatively great importance to minor details, because only thus are they able to come to any kind of conclusion when dealing with the ghosts of well-known personalities. The press may have published much about the major aspects of Carole Lombard's life, but I doubt that they printed any report of a lover's quarrel just before her departure for New York, or mentioned anything about a red dress.

Word From Marilyn Monroe

T welve years after Marilyn Monroe died mysteriously at the age of thirty-six, she still makes headlines. Norman Mailer has written a book about her; a photographic exhibit of her life and times drew capacity crowds in Los Angeles; and a national magazine printed some of her unpublished poems as reported by Norman Rosten, a writer who knew her well. Magazines often run cover stories on the late screen star, and her name is still a household word for sex appeal.

This is not the place to discuss the merits or lack of same surrounding the work of Marilyn Monroe. Others have written of her work as an actress and of her tragic life as a human being, and it is common knowledge that toward the end of her life she was miserable and confused. That she may have taken her life through an overdose of sleeping pills is generally accepted and rarely questioned. Legend has it that she took the pills after losing a role in a comeback film. Other rumors attributed her suicide to a lover's rejection of her. Since the lover was a prominent figure, married at the time, the matter was hushed up in order to keep the breath of scandal away from him.

The coroner's verdict was "probable suicide." There was no evidence that her death was due to either murder or accident, and since an overdose of sleeping pills is generally under the control of the one taking them, the logical conclusion was suicide. With that, the matter was closed.

During the last years of her life, when Marilyn lived as Arthur Miller's wife on New York's East Side, she was befriended by the late

John Myers, the English dentist turned medium of whom I have written in many of my books. John Myers was both a psychic healer and an amateur painter. His apartment on Sutton place was only a short walk from Marilyn Monroe's apartment, and they saw each other on several occasions. Myers suggested that he paint her as the modern Mona Lisa; the screen star, flattered, agreed. (The painting later won a prize at a UNICEF exhibition at the United Nations.) During the times over the years when I worked with Myers, he spoke glowingly of Marilyn Monroe. It was almost as if he had taken her under his wing, to protect her from harm to come. On several occasions he had warned her against sleeping pills. The healing he gave her for her state of neurotic anxiety seemed to relax her for a while. After the news of her sudden passing, Myers placed his portrait of the late screen star in his special healing room.

The room is perhaps the quietest part of his apartment, semi-dark because of drapes covering the windows. It is here that he does his psychic work. It was in this room that Myers produced, under test conditions, psychic photographs of a late aunt of mine of whom he knew nothing, and of others who were recognized by those present. Among those witnessing the demonstration of psychic photography by Myers were a renowned newspaper columnist and a reporter from one of the wire services.

Shortly after Myers had placed his portrait of Marilyn in his special room, strange things began to happen. Although he was in the habit of turning off the light switch whenever he left the room, he found it turned on again, seemingly of its own volition, on several occasions when he knew that no one else had entered the room. On one occasion he found a personal note in his room which he knew he had not written, nor was there any way in which such a note might have entered the locked room. Unfortunately Myers never disclosed the contents of this note, explaining only that it was a private matter.

Shortly after the incidents with the light switch, Marilyn appeared to the medium. She explained that there had been an accident and that she had had no intention of doing away with herself. As Marilyn explained it to Dr. Myers, she was alone in her home when she received word of being dismissed from the picture she was then making. She tried to find sleep but it wouldn't come. Used to the crutch provided by sleeping pills, she took one after another, forlornly staring out the window. As she drifted into a state of semi-consciousness, she was no longer aware of her motions or the number of pills she had actually taken. Her senses became dulled, and even if she had wanted to stop or ring for help, she was unable to do so. In one of the accounts dealing with the life of John Myers, *He Walks in Two Worlds*, by Maurice Barbanell, Myers is quoted as reporting that Marilyn had said to him, "I did not understand that I was poisoning myself, but it was then too late." After this incident, Marilyn reappeared several times to Myers.

In 1969 I published a number of psychic photographs taken by Myers in a work entitled *Psychic Photography, Threshold of a New Science*. One of the most controversial pictures in this book is a psychic photograph on which at least two dozen portraits appeared. Among the celebrities bunched together in this amazing photograph is Marilyn Monroe, dressed in one of her most glamorous gowns and holding a tablet across her body on which are written the words "Mistake—Not Suicide." The tablet appears to be a piece of paper upon which these words have been typed. That, however, does not necessarily brand this photograph a fake. Since Myers has produced similar photographs under my control and in my presence, I have no reason to consider this photograph anything but authentic.

It would seem, then, that Marilyn was still searching for recognition of the truth of her passing several years after the event itself. This is not unusual in cases where people die tragically or violently before their time. It would appear that Marilyn's most compelling need in the afterlife was to explain to the world that she had not taken her own life but had died as the result of a simple accident.

Susan Cabot is a petite, dark-haired young woman who gained early fame in a number of motion pictures and on the stage. Her singing voice reaches to three octaves, and for a while she was considered one of the most promising new stars on the Hollywood horizon. Shortly after the birth of her first child she withdrew from her career in order to devote herself to the care of her little boy, who had a strange afflic-tion seemingly beyond the capabilities of the medical profession. During the past year Susan Cabot has again reached out for the lime-light. She is returning to the screen, stage, and television, because she has found new truths in meditation and in her involvement with the psychic world.

In April of 1972 we sat in her comfortable living room discussing both Susan's own experiences with the shadowy world of ESP and her remembrances of Marilyn Monroe. The house is one of the older resi-dences in Beverly Hills, quiet, well-built in the Spanish style so promi-nent in the area, and pleasantly cluttered with the momentoes of a busy screen star's life—from photographs to framed letters to books and gifts from admirers.

"When did you first meet Marilyn Monroe?"

"I was called to Columbia to do a film. Freddy in the music depart-ment introduced us. She came to practice her singing. She loved music, and she was singing 'Those Little White Lies.' We shared some music lessons."

"Did you meet her socially afterwards?"

"Yes. When we first met, we went together everywhere, including some parties, because I was terrified of dating. I had just come from New York. There was such a strong bond between us—"

"You mean like telepathy?"

"Yes. She would start a sentence and I'd finish it for her."

"Did you ever discuss psychic phenomena? Was there an interest in that?"

"No, because I had only the most intellectual contact with everybody. The main thing was that we were both born to be serious artists and not just sex symbols, and we didn't want to just date and be thrown about, and so we found safety in dating together."

"What happened when you heard of her death?"

"I didn't believe she had commited suicide."

"Was there any contact between her and you after her death?"

"Yes."

"What sort of thing?"

"It was as if she were saying, 'Do you remember when I said this?' That was the first time. This feeling . . . I can't call it an apparition. I can't say I heard anything. I can't say I saw anything. But I felt the presence of Marilyn at my shoulders. It was as if, when this presence was felt, she reminded me of the last time I saw her. At the time, we hadn't seen each other for a long period. I felt that she didn't remember me any longer. She was surrounded by a lot of people. Now, standing next to me, she was reminding me of this incident. She looked at me for a split second, and suddenly I felt oblivious of who *I* was. She narrowed her eyes and said, 'What am I doing here?' Then she said, 'I didn't mean to do this, you know I didn't mean to do this,' and she began to cry, and I was crying, too."

"She didn't mean to do it? How did it happen then?"

"She was in terrible pain."

"So she took these pills?"

"She couldn't stand it. She took the pills to go to sleep."

"Did she ever indicate to you that she would want somebody to know about this?"

"I don't know. I just know she was pleading for understanding. It wasn't just a message."

"Do you think she is troubled?"

"She's still confused."

"Do you think she is aware of her own death?"

"I see her hunched over, begging." Susan shrugged.

Susan Cabot is no stranger to psychic phenomena herself. When she lived in New York she had one of the most harrowing experiences with the world beyond the flesh. She was living at the time in one of those little apartments consisting of one room and an alcove for the bed. This particular apartment was on top of a French restaurant and there was an electric sign on the outside of the building. The windows were barred both in the living room and in the alcove above it, because there was a roof extending over the alcove where people might conceivably try to enter the apartments below. That particular night Susan couldn't sleep. She was tossing in bed wondering about her future. Suddenly she became aware of a presence in her room. It looked like a light flashing on and off, coming to her from the ceiling. There was no rational explanation for such a light, so at first she thought it was her vivid imagination. Imagine her horror when she suddenly saw the light turn into a figure of what looked like a musketeer from another age! His grim face with a slightly hooked nose stared at her in the most unfriendly manner. In his hand he had a dagger which he now raised as if to strike at her. During this time there was no sound whatsoever.

A musketeer in a Fifty-sixth Street apartment in New York City? Was Susan's motion picture imagination perhaps running away with her? I immediately questioned her about the apparition.

"Did he look three-dimensional?"

"Absolutely."

"What did you do?"

"I wanted to scream, but I couldn't. I was frightened, and I pleaded with him silently—'Don't kill me, please don't kill me.' I was looking at him while saying this. I didn't dare move. I was trapped. I knew if I moved, it would be the end of me."

"How did it end?"

"He listened and turned around. He lowered his dagger."

"Did he speak?"

"No. But I didn't feel his hatred as much."

"How did he disappear?"

"Through the wall."

"Walking?"

"I saw his cape vanish into the darkness."

"Did you hear anything?"

"The swish of the cape."

"Did he ever come back?"

"Yes. The next night."

"Did he look the same?"

"No. He was smiling."

"Did he have the dagger?"

"No. But his hand lay on his belt."

"Was he still filled with hatred?"

"No. It was as though he had had his victims. It was like the smile of victory."

"Did he return after that?"

"There were three more times. He was there right by my side. He didn't enter from anywhere—he was just there."

"How did he leave?"

"He disappeared. I didn't hear anything. I didn't even see him go, as I did the first time. Years later he appeared again when I had my baby. I then lived across town in a penthouse."

"What did you see?"

"I was facing west and there was this enormous window and the balcony. I didn't see anything, but I felt him."

"How did you know that is was *him*?"

"I knew. At the same time, I physically saw someone trying to get into the room. He tried to get to the baby. But the musketeer came as if to help me."

"Was this the last time you have seen or felt him?"

"Once or twice I felt a presence, but I'm not sure it was him."

"But who is he? Is he trying to protect you? What is the reason for his contact?"

"I don't know."

Recently Susan has been able to help various friends through her ESP ability. She gets flashes about future events and passes them on freely, in the hope that she can help people avert problems or tragedy. She doesn't consider herself a professional psychic by any means but wants to develop her innate talent in this respect. To her it is all a great surprise. Somehow she feels she has lived before, and that some of the people who have come to her in this life have shared experiences with her in another existence. She wants very much to know who she was, because it will help her understand better who she is now. Susan, with all her beauty and talents, has much in common with the late Marilyn Monroe. She too is forever searching for her sense of identity and mission.

Rudolph Valentino Is Very Much Alive

Not only the great of the historical world or the political scene reach out to further express themselves through living individuals, stars of the stage and screen who are in a way rulers of their own firmament also have that desire at times.

About twenty years ago Miss L., a young lady from New England of excellent educational and social background, found herself increasingly interested in extrasensory perception and psychic research. As a result, she sought out certain study groups which might further her interest in the areas of the occult in general and of astrology. Through one of these circles she was eventually invited to a séance. At first she thought the whole idea of a séance more of a lark but was fascinated by the possibilities of discovering hitherto unknown horizons. There was nothing in Miss L.'s character that was either abnormal or particularly conducive to being taken over by another entity. She had many interests in life, and this was merely still another way of finding out things in the world she lived in. The séance was attended by half a dozen professional people from New York City and the surrounding areas. There was a medium present. This lady managed to make contact with a number of deceased entities and the proceedings were only intermittently interesting. After awhile the communications would cease and everybody would go home. Toward the end of the evening, however, as entity, who claimed to be the late Rudolph Valentino, manifested. At this point the professional medium present ceased to be the intermediary and Miss L. was taken over by the entity, lapsing into a sudden trance state. After she came out of it, she remembered absolutely nothing. But during the time she was under the influence of the alleged Valentino entity, she spoke with his voice and expressed some of his views. Among these views were a desire to continue a relationship with his fans on the earth plane, and an expression of regret that he was no longer able to be with them in the flesh. The matter was dismissed as an interesting experience and was not further thought of by those who took part in this particular meeting.

But for Miss L., it was by no means over. As soon as she had returned to her home and found a moment of quiet, Valentino returned and spoke to her. From that moment on, he was her steady companion. By no means hostile or in any way threatening, his overpowering presence nevertheless constituted a major shift in Miss L.'s personality development. From her many conversations with the unseen visitor, she became familiar with his life on earth, far more extensively than she could have been from reading books about the celebrated screen star. She decided she wanted to visit the places where he grew up and went to Italy to the village where he was born, to the cemetery where he lay buried, and she even tried to find people who knew him when he was still alive. This development took several years, to be sure, during which time Valentino was constantly "with her." What had appeared at first as a doubtful identification became a certainty, as he disclosed to her things from his private life only he could have known. As time went on, she changed her outer appearance to look more Italian for him. She even changed the name she gave to people whom she met for the first time, and she called herself by another name vaguely resembling Valentino's. All that time her parents had no idea of what she was going through. They noticed, however, that she seemed to shun the company of flesh-and-blood companions more and more and that she made no attempt to get married. Unfortunately, there never was a truly close relationship between herself and her parents, so she could not confide in them even so unorthodox a matter as her relationship with the deceased Valentino. Perhaps if she had, there would have been a better understanding, and perhaps her future would have been guided in different directions. But she kept her secret well and spoke of it only to those who were familiar with psychic matters, and to those who knew her from the very beginning of her discovery that Rudolph Valentino wanted to talk to her.

At this point what had started as a gentle possession turned into an obsession. She bought up old Valentino films in order to look at them time and again with the help of friends who had movie projectors. She collected photographs and other memorabilia of Valentino's life. She learned all there was to be learned about him from the books written about him, but added to this knowledge generously from the material she said she received first-hand from the departed.

On the anniversary of Valentino's death she would go to pieces emotionally. Yet she would tell those few of her friends who understood and were compassionate enough to listen to her that he lived on because of her. The love relationship between Miss L. and the late screen star blossomed into full bloom as time went on. At one point she confided openly to me that she wanted to join her beloved one as soon as possible. Since I heard ominous overtones of possible suicide in her statements, I decided it was time to do something about it. After I reasoned with her fruitlessly that such a joining before her appointed time was contrary to cosmic law—at any rate, it would only keep her and Valentino further apart according to my own information, I turned my attention to the departed one directly.

In a séance arranged for that purpose and without Miss L.'s presence, I managed with the help of the original medium who had "brought" him in, to make contact with Valentino again. I earnestly pleaded with him not to create a difficulty for both himself in his world and Miss L. in hers, by allowing her to cross the threshold from physi-

cal life into spirit life before her time and in a violent fashion. I anticipated a great struggle, but to my surprise, Valentino agreed. Quite some
time had passed, of course, since his original appearance; the relationship between himself and Miss L., such as it was, had now gone on for
a number of years. Perhaps he was tiring of it, or perhaps he really
became convinced by my arguments. At any rate he promised to speak
to her in the same sense I had pleaded with him.

Even though Miss L. did not know of my conversation with her
astral lover, her attitude changed from that moment on. She did not
break off her relationship, but it appeared to me, on the few occasions
when I saw her, that she considered her relationship with Valentino
now more a matter of friendship, and she somehow realized she could
not join him until it was so ordained. But her life was still not her own.
Her interests still did not lie in the mundane sphere, as they would with
any normal, beautiful, young woman. There was something terribly sad
and confused about her, and had I had more opportunity to speak to
her, perhaps I could have done something about her premature death.
As it was it came as a complete shock to me, although I had always felt
that Miss L.'s life would not be either happy or very long. While she
was living in the West, she passed on accidentally through a combination of medicines she had taken for legitimate reasons. Unknown to her,
she had an allergy to certain chemicals, and as a result of that allergy
she died. One might say that fate had taken a hand in the matter and
brought her to her beloved Valentino after all. But in the several subsequent communications I have had from her through reliable psychics,
there does not seem to be any mention of that relationship at all. I have
no reason to doubt the genuineness of these messages, since much private and personal detail was given during the communications that
could be known only to Miss L. or to myself. Perhaps Valentino felt the
excitement of working through a living person was one thing, while a
deep, romantic, lasting love relationship with someone in his own world

another. At any rate, Miss L. seems as well adjusted to the new life she now lives "over there" as she was prior to that certain séance when Rudolph Valentino had come into her life. But for a period of some ten years she lived as if she were part and parcel of Valentino's own personality, merely an extension of his own being into the physical world. She had not sought this relationship at the outset, but once it had occurred, she had eagerly nurtured it and encouraged his hold upon her. Both possession and obsession existed between them, and perhaps it even brought a degree of happiness to both while it lasted.

Elvis Presley: Death Is Not The End!

Elvis lives!

Not just in our memories, but in another dimension from which he has communicated with me and my associates for the past six months. He has given overwhelming proof of his identity, and he has given us a message for the world he left over two years ago.

"I am whole, I am well, I am here!"

With those shattering words Elvis Presley's spirit reached across the gulf that separates his world from ours, to communicate with his former bodyguard and step-brother David Stanley and Stanley's mother Dee Presley in a spine-tingling two-hour séance arranged by me just a few days after the King of Rock died in his Memphis, Tennesee home.

As the startled relatives looked on, wondering whether this was truly a contact, Elvis' spirit spoke with uncanny accuracy about intimate conversations the family had had before his death, secrets they had known but not publicized, places they had been together and experiences they had shared.

"I talked to Elvis, it was unbelievable," declared a shaken David Stanley, the 23-year-old intimate of The King who came of age touring on the road with him. Stanley was at Graceland, Elvis' home, the day the star passed on.

"The medium used the exact words Elvis told me two days before he died—*I'll be around*, I'll take care of you.' As a demonstration of psychic ability, the séance was authentic. It impressed me."

To which Dee Presley added, "Oh yes, he was here, I know. It was a definite psychic contact."

This dramatic confrontation, in a séance I had arranged after I had become convinced that the contact was genuine, was the climax of several months of communications with Elvis Presley which I have conducted in the privacy of my study through a timid, soft-spoken housewife and mother named Dorothy Sherry.

It is my profession to investigate unusual claims in parapsychology, and sift the genuine from the false or doubtful: but three months of investigation and the most painstaking tests have now convinced me that Elvis Presley has indeed been in continual contact with Dorothy Sherry, whose role as the psychic go-between was neither chosen nor desired. It was an acute source of embarrassment and fear for her until she began to work with me, and to understand what was taking place.

Dorothy Sherry never met Elvis Presley. She has not been to any concerts of his, does not collect his records or consider herself a fan of his. I've talked to a friend of hers and to her mother and verified these circumstances. But because the Presley communication came to her spontaneously, as a surprise and in a sense, unwanted (though she has since accepted it) I consider Dorothy's case one of the most evidential instances of spirit communication in my twenty-five years as a practicing parapsychologist and researcher.

I also know why Presley picked this unlikely intermediary to be his spokeswoman in the world of flesh: her very lack of interest in his career and fame, her status as a simple housewife horrified by any thoughts of publicity or public acclaim, was ideally suited to make his attempt to communicate the more believable and the evidence that much stronger.

At first, I was extremely doubtful about the whole matter. Any scientific investigator is bound to be, especially when dealing with a well known personality about whom much has been printed, published and broadcast. Although I haven't the slightest doubt that Dorothy never read any books about Presley, nor any newspaper stories concerning him, the fact that these sources exist must be taken into account when evaluating the evidence obtained through her entranced lips. But so many intimate details of Elvis' life, either unpublished or unknown to the public at large, have come to light in the course of my investigation that I cannot possibly doubt the authenticity of this contact from the beyond. Hours of in-depth investigative interviews, actual trance experiments and other professional tests have proven to me time and again, just as the final séance convinced the family—that Elvis Presley is still very much "alive" and able to communicate with our world.

With breathtaking accuracy, Elvis revealed details of his life and family, his home and his personality, that are simply too rich in detail and possessed of the human mood and flavor of Elvis to be derived from research. At the final séance, conducted in a New York Hotel suite, Elvis' surprised relatives confessed they saw him pace the room, heard his laughter, and were struck time and again by the mannerisms and pecularities of mood changes so characteristic of the Elvis they had known in life. The range of emotions displayed during the séance drained all of us just by being there, while it left Dorothy, our medium, shaken and crying as she passed on the words of the star.

The atmosphere was electric with anticipation as a candle was lit in front of a simple photograph of Elvis. Shortly after Dorothy had relaxed sufficiently to allow the spirit of Elvis to impress her, the séance got underway.

Within moments, the tense expression on the family's faces turned to shocked surprise, as the medium established direct contact with the singer. It was obvious that he recognized them, even though Dorothy had no idea who Dee or David were. Through the medium, however, Elvis made it clear he understood the historic significance of this confrontation; to prove his true identity from the beyond and to get his messages across. As I watched the usually placid face of Dorothy Sherry change to a near-likeness of Elvis, who now controlled her, statements came from Elvis in rapid succession which left no doubt about his identity and actual presence in our midst.

He told of a private conversation he had had with his stepbrother David Stanley just a few days before his death. "I'll take care of you, even if I'm not here," Elvis told the young man who had grown up in his home and who had travelled with Elvis, charged with protecting the singer.

He revealed intricate details of the Las Vegas Hilton Hotel, where he often performed. Dorothy Sherry has never been to Las Vegas.

He spoke of David's career goals, his love for cameras and his desire to be an actor. Since Dorothy never met David Stanley before the séance, and had no idea who he was when she entered the room, there was no way she could have acquired such intimate knowledge.

He mentioned the nights they had spent singing gospel songs in hotel rooms, and how they alternated between high-pressured worries and mad laughter during those cross-country tours. None of this is public knowledge, and all of it is quite true.

He revealed to Dee Presley his concern over past, unpublicized death threats to his daughter, and expressed his deep feelings of guilt again and again over neglecting her while in the body.

He directed a message to Dee Presley concerning the last phone call that she had anxiously made after a traumatic argument in a previous call strained their relationship. It was a call made the day Elvis died, and nobody but Dee Presley could have known of it.

He admitted to having been a psychic healer, and that on one occasion he had healed the injured leg of a friend. The incident proved to be authentic, according to David Stanley, but of course neither it nor Presley's healing power were ever known publicly.

He revealed at the séance that he was in a state of total paranoia just before his passing, deeply concerned about his security and threats against his life—a fact only Stanley and a handful of intimates knew.

He used the exact words he had said to bodyguard Stanley two days before he died, "I'll take care of you, I'll be around," thus proving his identity beyond any doubt.

He displayed an intimate knowledge of Stanley's career goals, including his thoughts of being a photographer and frantic desire to be as famous as his idolized stepbrother, facts readily admitted afterwards by the young man.

As tears streamed down the medium's face, Elvis spoke of his fears and anxieties, his great concern at being alone after his mother's death. It was a side of the star never shown in public and known only to his closest relatives and friends.

Practically before Dorothy was entranced, Elvis asked for Charley, being very concerned over his well-being. Charley Hodge is a musician and close friend of the singer's, whose depression over Elvis' death had worried David Stanley so much that he was in almost daily contact with him the week before the séance.

He referred to his interest in reincarnation and the many conversations he and David had had on this subject.

He described his palatial home, Graceland, in much detail, mentioned his grandmother and two favorite pieces of jewelry, all of the information corresponding to known facts.

He spoke of his mother, now with him in the world of spirit, and her weakness while in the flesh concerning alcohol, a fact which has never been publicized for obvious reasons, but which according to the family, is nevertheless entirely accurate.

The relatives came away from the séance convinced that Elvis had indeed been present. David Stanley confessed he 'heard his laughter' the way only Elvis would laugh; Dee Presley felt his anger rising like a physical force, precisely the way it was when the singer was still alive in this world. At the same time, the medium complained of being practically burned with searing heat and trembling with anger, but unable to understand why. Dee Presley, however, understood.

My involvement with Dorothy Sherry began when a friend of many years telephoned me to ask a favor. The favor consisted of seeing a certain friend whose daughter had a peculiar problem she couldn't handle: unwanted spirit communication, her husband's disapproval, and fears that she was going mad because nobody would believe her. I was in no hurry to see the young woman, fully convinced that the whole thing was nothing more than self-delusion.

Eventually, however, Dorothy came to see me at my study in Manhattan. Haltingly, she explained that she had on occasion been psychic, such as the time when she "saw" a vision of an extremely fat man with a cigar in his mouth, a very red face and wearing a hat on the back of his head. When she mentioned it to her mother, her mother took out the family album and showed her, for the first time, a picture of her long-dead uncle Nat.

But the thing that really shook her happened one day early in January of this year—she didn't know the exact date because she hadn't bothered to keep notes. The whole thing seemed much too preposterous to her at the time. Suddenly, the name of Elvis Presley burst into her mind, and at the same instant, he appeared to her.

"I was fully awake at the time," Dorothy explained, "sitting on my couch, with all the lights on. He wore a white shirt open at the neck, with folded-up cuffs, and he held out his hand to me, saying, 'You can come with me now.'"

Dorothy obeyed and held out her hand, only it wasn't her physical hand, which stayed with her body on the couch. Elvis was taking her on an astral flight, what parapsychologists call an out-of-the-body experience, the first of many such flights she was to undertake in the months to come.

When I realized who the spirit communicator was, I began to question Dorothy severely. I spoke to her mother, I spoke to our mutual friend: she was telling the truth. She had never shown an unusual interest in either Presley or rock and roll music. The contact had come spontaneously, out of the blue, as it were!

"It was around eleven o'clock at night, my husband was already asleep. I took Elvis' hand, and as I turned around I looked back at myself sitting on the couch. Then we went through a sort of tube or tunnel, with bright lights at the other end. Next, we ended up in a field covered with grass and beautiful flowers."

"Didn't it seem strange that a famous singer like Elvis Presley should choose to make contact with you?" I inquired.

"As a matter of fact that was the first thing I asked him. How come *me*? We talked for over four hours that night. He said he had known me in a previous life, and that I had been his wife. I said I found that extremely hard to believe. But he assured me it was so. Then he talked about his daughter, his ex-wife and some of the things he had done for which he was now sorry, especially the way he died."

"How did you get back?"

"He walked me back, kissed me on the cheek, and the next thing I knew, I was back on my couch."

Elvis met her again the night after and this time his mother was with him. Evidently the mother disapproved of Dorothy. Dorothy got scared, and Elvis didn't return for two weeks. Dorothy still couldn't get used to the idea that it was really him, and she began to worry about her sanity. Her mother had read some of my books and was wondering how she could get in touch with me for advice. Meanwhile, Dorothy went astral travelling with Elvis practically night after night. Apparently, he took her to visit places that had meant something to him in his life.

"I've been taken to Las Vegas, to his dressing room at the Hilton Hotel, to the penthouse, and even on the stage. I've been to the house he had when he died, and we go to another place, a long, beautiful ranch house, and he seems to be looking for something when we get there."

"Can you actually feel him?"

"Oh yes, I can feel his shirt, his face, and his hands . . . they're callused and he bites his fingernails."

Dorothy, though calmer now, still couldn't believe that she was taking astral flights with the late Elvis Presley. Why was he communicating with a simple housewife with two kids? Again and again, Presley talked of their previous lives together and his realization that he would be with her again in a future lifetime.

Elvis, according to Dorothy, explained he was happy to be reunited with his mother, dead many years. Though he seemed upset concerning his daughter on earth, he felt serene in his new environment.

"If it seems brighter here, it is because God is all around us. The higher you go, the brighter it gets as you get closer to God," Dorothy quotes Elvis as telling her.

But Dorothy still couldn't accept the situation, so on one astral flight, Elvis arranged for Dorothy's dead grandmother to speak to her.

"I didn't expect to see her," Dorothy explained. "I was with Elvis, and we were walking down this dirt road, over there, and suddenly there she was. 'How is he treating you?' my grandmother asked, and, me, well, I like to kid, so I said, 'He's doing all right.' With that she turns on him and screams, 'You got special permission for this, you're supposed to help my grandaughter! I'm not there anymore and I'm depending on you!"

"How did you feel about this?"

"I began to tell myself, well, this must be happening, I couldn't make it all up! I don't have that kind of imagination."

Dorothy couldn't be more right. She is a pleasant, average housewife, in her early thirties, with two growing kids, a husband who won't have any truck with "the supernatural." She is not the sort of person who would go out of her way to get attention or make waves. Dorothy decided she would confide in her mother, who immediately suggested that I be contacted. Her mother understood, for she, too had had occasional ESP experiences and took Dorothy at her word. On several occasions she was with her daughter when Elvis appeared. To Dorothy, he was a three-dimensional man, but to her mother "a shadow." Then "the shadow" spoke, and Dorothy's mother clearly heard him say to her, 'Don't worry, I'm not taking your girl away with me.'

About that time, Elvis made her do automatic writing. This is a recognized form of mediumship in which an alleged spirit communicates by forcing the hand of a psychic individual to write, usually very rapidly and in the spirits own style and handwriting rather than the living partner's. Dorothy showed me some samples, which were pretty rough scribbles. Still, I could clearly make out a line reading, *Not to be afraid . . . love her . . . need her . . . ask Holzer . . . teach you about the Other Side . . .*

There was no holding Dorothy back now. Her mother recalled an old friend who had sometimes mentioned me, and the contact was made.

Dorothy came to see me once a week, and in between she was to keep notes of her encounters with Elvis. If anything unusual happened, she was to telephone me long distance. Her astral flights with Elvis continued meanwhile, and this time she took careful notes of their conversations. Elvis kept impressing on her one thing in particular. He didn't like people to impersonate him, using his name 'as a ladder.' Dorothy assured him there was nothing she could do about it. Who would listen to *her*?

Then he took her on an astral flight to his home, Graceland, in Memphis, Tennessee. "We were out behind the house and I walked right into the wrought iron furniture and I bruised my knee," Dorothy said and showed me the physical bruise she had as a result. "It was a low table, with a glass top, and I smacked right into it, and it sure hurt. This happened June first."

I later established that the wrought iron table does in fact exist, exactly where Dorothy had bumped into in the astral: but of course she could not have known this, since the garden furniture is not widely publicized in any way.

Their journeys always started out the same way, up from the couch, out of Dorothy's physical body, and through the tunnel. She would then find herself crossing a bridge and gliding into a room with large, white columns. Then there was a smaller bridge, and they would be in a beautiful park. There were other people there, too, but Dorothy did not know them. Some wore clothes of an earlier period, others were in robes. There was a diffused kind of light around them. Then all of a sudden, she would go through another tunnel with Elvis, and would find herself in the driveway of his home. When they went around to the back of the house Dorothy bumped into the garden furniture.

All this material is similar to what Dr. Ramond Moody discovered when researching his best-selling book *Life After Life*, stories of people who were temporarily (but clinically) dead and who managed to return and be revived despite incredible odds against their survival. Accounts of going through tunnels with bright lights have also been told to me by many people with bona fide experiences involving visits to what we usually call "the world beyond." There are several dozen such verified accounts in my book, *Beyond This Life*. One can argue that Dorothy Sherry *may* have read these books, but did she? I think not. She came to me to be reassured that her visitations from Elvis were not hallucinatory, not to gain notoriety or profit. Bumping into the wrought iron table in Elvis' backyard brought Dorothy back into her body instantly and left her with a terrific headache as well as a bruised leg.

How do they get back into Dorothy's world, I wanted to know.

"We come back through a tunnel. It takes longer coming back than going out, and he helps me down, then I open my eyes and I can still see him, and he'll wave and say, 'I'll see you tomorrow night' and then he just walks away . . . into nothing. I always feel exhausted afterwards."

I asked Dorothy what else Elvis had told her about himself.

"They called him The King and he felt he was, in his own home, and so he sometimes was rough on people, would scream and rant and have his own way. Now he is sorry he acted that way. He took a lot of drugs, but he didn't kill himself, he says. Only, he got himself on a tack where instead of taking two pills, he would take six. Subconsciously, he wanted to die. He was very unhappy, very lonely. But he says it may have been through his own fault, his moods."

Now I pressed for some detail about his private life that could not be known to Dorothy, or for that matter to me or anyone in the outside world. Dorothy hemmed and hawed and finally said, yes, there was something he did as a little boy. He peed on the wall! Later, I discovered that he had been reprimanded as a child for smearing peanut butter on the wall. Could she have misunderstood the word?

On June 9th, Elvis came to Dorothy in my study. After some preliminaries, I asked if he had a message for anyone.

"He says he sends his apologies to Sonny West, Red's cousin . . . if they feel hurt in any way, he didn't mean it."

The names meant nothing to me, but I have since realized they are two of the authors of a recent book about Elvis.

I asked what Elvis was doing on the Other Side, when he wasn't taking Dorothy on astral visits. Working on some of his songs, still trying to improve them, Dorothy replied. They do give concerts over there, but of course they don't have records. When I asked who was in charge Elvis replied that they are called "the teachers" and that above them was "The All-Knowing."

"Elvis says he has always known there was a God, and there is. He doesn't know though if God is a person. He still feels ignorant and he is going to school over there."

I asked if Elvis' mother was with him all the time, but it appears she is on a higher level of consciousness while Elvis is still on the first. I then wondered if Elvis had gotten through to anyone else except Dorothy since his passing. After all, I've received several claims from self-styled psychics that they had received messages from The King. Not one of them proved worthy of belief.

"He's gotten through to his father, in the dream state, and told him to stop the counterfeit Elvis Presleys, and to keep an eye on his daughter. This was in January of this year. Only one psychic has had contact with him, someone named Wright. But he says, 'I wouldn't pay attention to her, sir.' He means you."

I thought this was good a time as any to ask for the essence of Elvis' message to the world.

"*Please make people aware of The Other Side, that we are not dead.* Life goes on. This is only a bus stop. There are so many over here who want to communicate, but people don't understand . . . *death is not the end!*" And then he added, "Try to make Dorothy understand about reincarnation. At times, there are mistakes. But I will wait for her. The bond between us is very strong."

I then examined some of Dorothy's notes, taken at her own home immediately on awaking from one of her astral excursions with Elvis. On June 11 she remarked that he talked about his ability with karate and showed her some of his kicks. I discovered much later that David, his stepbrother, had learned karate with him. "Elvis is concerned about his father's health. Taking care of his affairs may be too much for him. And tell The Colonel he is glad he is making money, but isn't enough, enough?"

In an earlier entry, May 26th, Dorothy visited Elvis' home again. "I saw a red sectional couch and a very massive kitchen; outside somewhere on the grounds is a big fountain with colored lights."

The next day she discovered that Elvis had his cologne "specially mixed" and on May 29th Elvis even decided to watch Ella Fitzgerald on the Johnny Carson show with Dorothy! He liked her gospel songs, and as I was later to learn, he sang gospel songs himself. "I found it amusing," Dorothy wrote, "that he stood and watched television. As we turned to leave, the room got suddenly bright, like the sun coming from behind a cloud. As we crossed over, it got brighter and brighter. I asked Elvis what it was and he only said that it was 'His essence.' We walked for a while and saw other couples which Elvis told me were couples like ourselves who had made contact."

On June 14th, Elvis came through as soon as Dorothy had sat down on the couch in my study. According to her, he was wearing a black cashmere sweater this time. When I asked him to tell me exactly what he wanted done about his affairs, Dorothy was quick to reply.

"He's concerned about his father. Heart trouble, and there is also something wrong with his circulatory system. He says there's been enough sideshow activities and souvenirs. 'I'm a private man. I want them off my property, all these people. They are traipsing up and down my property. There's plenty outside for them to buy. I don't want them walking around my mama's grave. This is like a sideshow, a zoo. They have to realize I was a person and not some kind of god."

Dorothy was now less concerned about her sanity, as I had long since convinced her that hers was an apparently genuine case of spirit communication. But now she worried lest the world would not believe her, and by implication, she would be letting Elvis down. I understood her concern, knowing full well that the will to disbelieve is very strong when people are afraid to alter their basic philosophies. I encouraged her to request additional bits and pieces of personal information that would help us make the identification of Elvis Presley even stronger than it already was.

During the last week of June, Dorothy came up with some additional information jotted down the morning after an astral flight with Elvis.

"Fay Harris was a friend of his mother's in Tupelo . . . and his aunt's name is Tressie and she's living . . . and his uncle Vestor married his aunt Clitis, they were his father's brother and his mother's sister. Oh, and his car caught fire once when he just started on his way to a show in a small town. And he's met Bill Black, a bass player who had started out with him . . . and his mother once tore up a pair of very dirty sneakers when he was in his early teens . . ."

This material was not the sort of thing one finds in books about a celebrity. I asked Dorothy if she could recall a particular place in detail, other than Graceland.

"The Hilton Hotel in Las Vegas," she replied without a moment's hesitation. "He took me backstage to his dressing room. It had in it a couch, a large mirror over a table, and there's an elevator which runs behind it, off the hallway, so he can get on stage without being seen by the crowds. Oh, and something funny: the parking lot is in front of the hotel—not behind, not below, but actually in front." It wasn't until the final séance on July 13, that these data were all confirmed as correct by David Stanley, who had been there, after all. But as for Dorothy, she has never been to Las Vegas in her life.

When we finally met with the family for that final séance on July 13, Dorothy was a bundle of nerves. Just like Elvis, she is a very private person. I assured her that nobody was interested in anything but the truth, and she did not have to perform like a trained circus elephant. After all, Dorothy is not a publicity-hungry professional clairvoyant with an eye toward headline-making, but a simple housewife and mother who just happens to be psychic and somehow fell into this bizarre situation very much against her will. But since she seemed a little nervous, I gave her light suggestion—not deep hypnosis but merely a form of relaxation therapy which I often use with tense individuals.

Within minutes after Dee and David had joined Danny Schwarz of the *National Enquirer* staff and myself in the suite, Dorothy became conscious of Elvis' presence in the room. At the same time I noticed that her face seemed to take on another person's characteristics as she became more relaxed and as the communication proceeded. Here, then, is the way it went.

Séance Transcript, July 12, 1978, 12:30 p.m. Present: Dr. Hans Holzer, Dee Presley, David Stanley, Dan Schwartz.

After I had admonished everyone to be relaxed, uncross their legs and create an expectant, calm, atmosphere, I placed Dorothy into a state of light trance, in order or remove resident fears and tension at being in the presence of strangers. Dorothy is a very shy, private person not accustomed to being displayed in public. I next called on Elvis Presley to communicate with us—any one of us, if he so chose. Within moments, Dorothy announced that Elvis was present, accompanied by his mother.

"She's short, and wears a kind of housedress with a belt. Elvis is laughing!"

"Why is he laughing?" I asked.

"He wants to know if the Colonel has Ok'd this interview."

I said, "There are three other people here. I hope he's satisfied with their coming."

"He says he hopes they are satisfied with *his* coming. . . . He wants to know, where's Charley? And did his father see a doctor?"

After some remarks about the family, I asked Elvis to describe his after-life conditions.

"They go to school, everybody has a job to do. He is watching over me. We were married before."

"How does he feel about reincarnation?"

"He says you can certainly believe it, and this is the whole point of this meeting. If people would just believe it, it would change the world and mankind wouldn't be so damn stupid."

"Has he discussed reincarnation with anybody while in the physical state?"

"Oh, yes, many times; with his father and his friends."

I asked Elvis to identify "the gentleman sitting opposite Dorothy."

"I'm getting . . . a half-brother . . . did someone use a camera on stage during one of the last concerts? Someone wrote a poem later . . . he says, 'Hell, they know I'm here.' He's standing alongside this gentleman now. He loves him . . . he's standing there laughing his fool head off . . . he wants it to come across that he wants people to believe that they exist, that they are well, and that they are alive . . . and want to communicate with loved ones. This was the whole purpose, he says."

I asked Dorothy to describe what she saw at Elvis' house.

"In back of the house . . . it looked like a handball court but it's played with a racquet and I saw a chain-link fence and there is wrought iron furniture directly behind the yard."

There had been some mention of Elvis' fear of being hurt in an earlier session. I asked, Was he ever harmed by a fan?

"In Texas. He was practically mauled. He was afraid . . . there were threats. Threats against his daughter. There were phone calls, some kind of communications with his father . . . somebody jumped on stage and Elvis thought he was being threatened, went into a total panic. But his friends quickly pushed, knocked him off stage."

"Who were these friends?"

"Doesn't want to talk about them. They wrote a book that he hopes his father is doing something, about, or the Colonel. He thought they were his friends and that they were loyal to him; he's been hurt."

"By whom?"

"Red, Sonny, Dave. They turned against me, they twisted everything and blew it up. Why would they want to talk about me like that."

"How does he feel about impersonators?"

"He worked hard getting where he was and he started from nothing. Why should they use his name? He wants them to stop. He says they stink. 'If I ever looked like that, I'd never walk on a stage again.'"

"Did he have the power of psychic healing?"

"He believed he did . . . discussed it with friends . . . there was something with a leg and he healed it. Somebody's son, skiing, he says, forget it."

"What about his hands?"

"Bites his nails and the ends of his fingers are extremely rough, and the sides of his hands are extremely rough."

"How is that so?"

"Karate . . . he used to work out with Dave, Sonny, those guys we talked about before."

I asked Elvis if there were something he was complaining about. "He's not complaining about anything, but there's one thing he couldn't understand, it's that book. 'From the first page to the last, they hurt me by writing this book. They made me sound that I should be in a home, that I was crazy. I was a little crazy, we're all a little crazy. You know that. They wrote lies, they turned on me. . . . I trusted them, I trusted them with my life, Red, Sonny and Dave . . .'"

"Would you like someone else to write a book that would rectify matters?"

"My family . . . tell the Colonel he should finally write that book."

I then asked that he identify some personal jewelry, in order to deepen his proof of identity.

"There's a diamond cross . . . there's a bracelet that Ginger was supposed to give to Lisa. She hasn't given it to Lisa. It's a promise."

As I was still asking for additional data on jewelry, Dorothy said, "He's turning from one mood to another, he does that often . . ." (looking directly at David) "'Give my daddy a kiss . . . a hug and a kiss. Watch after him.'"

Dorothy became restless now, intimating that Elvis was making her upset. I appealed to him to restrain his emotions, so we could continue.

"He has touched this lady, his hand is on her shoulder . . ."

"What about the lady?" (referring to Dee Presley).

. . . a phone call. He called her."

"Is the phone call important?"

"Yes. . . . I'm starting to burn. . . . I can't hear."

At this point, the contact was abruptly interrupted, but I managed to restore it by calming both Elvis, with firm words, and Dorothy, by taking her hands for a moment. Evidently the business about that telephone call was so emotionally upsetting it had blown our psychic fuse!

Then Elvis was back.

"He says he loves these people, he's not angry, he's sorry. Because he's very hot-tempered. He's coming back, I can see him."

"Is there something we ought to know that you haven't told us?"

"He wants people to acknowledge that he is here, he is whole, he is well, he is here with his Momma. She is well, but she is not quite as happy . . . she blames herself for his early death . . . she failed him . . . overpowered . . . she drank, she drank . . . she's very sorry."

Apparently, the emotions and memories brought back were too much for Elvis, for Dorothy suddenly said. "He's leaving. . . . I'm losing him, but he's still touching me . . ."

"I don't want him to leave upset."

"He's hurting my shoulder, he's got very big hands . . ."

"Why is he upset?"

"'There's been enough written about me. I have no privacy, at least let me have some. Please!'"

I explained carefully the need for information that would clearly establish his identity, and that we were not prying. Suddenly, his mood seemed to soften, an abrupt change from searing anger of only moments before.

"He wants to know if they can remember singing the gospel songs all night long. At home, in hotels, anywhere. His Momma loved the gospel songs."

Was there any other request, something we had not touched upon?

"He wants the people off his property, he wants them to stop throwing garbage about his Momma's grave. They're like wolves. Get them off his property. He wants his daughter looked after. He wants his father to have some say with Lisa. The only thing he regrets is he wanted his daughter to have a home life. He's afraid she's going to grow up wrong. He's crying, my God, he's crying! He's always been alone, and his daughter is always going to be alone . . . look after his little girl, his baby, his wife . . . don't let Pris hurt her, her mother, he doesn't want her in a boarding school. He wants her to have love."

At this point, Dorothy's hands were shaking visibly, tears were streaming down her face and she still felt "like burning up." I decided the emotions displayed and transferred to the medium were so strong that I had to release her. Elvis understood, and that he was free to return to Dorothy anytime. And so he went in peace, and Dorothy became herself once again.

When the séance ended, Dorothy, still in a state of great agitation which she herself could not understand, asked for a glass of water. She felt hot and shaky, a state she had never been in before. As soon as her equilibrium was restored, I escorted her to the elevator and then returned to the suite.

David Stanley, who had initially been negative toward the entire encounter, was now a changed man. He readily confirmed many of the things that had been said through Dorothy's mediumship, and added that he himself had actually realized that Elvis was pacing up and down behind him, just as Dorothy had claimed. As for Dee Presley, her strict religious outlook made it difficult for her to accept spirit communication outside the religious establishment, and she was frank in admitting she did not "believe in" reincarnation, a cardinal point in Elvis' message and continued existence on the Other Side. Despite this, she was visibly impressed with what had just transpired in her presence.

"That phone call," she kept saying to us, "if she could only get more about that telephone call—when it was made, and under what circumstances."

I promised Dee I would ask Dorothy to convey this request to Elvis if he should come to her that night.

"The following morning, July 15, Dorothy called me in great agitation. "I've got your answer," she said, explaining that Elvis was pleased with our séance, but at the same time frank in admitting he had been extremely agitated by the presence of two family members: his stepbrother David, his close friend and bodyguard with whom he had shared so much of his life, and his stepmother who knew so much of his personal dilemma. But, Dorothy told me on the telephone, there had been a lot of anger and fighting between Elvis and Dee—he had resented his father's marriage at first, feeling it had come too soon after his mother died.

But what about the telephone call, I pressed. Under what circumstances was it made?

"It's connected with a doctor . . . an ambulance . . . the house," Dorothy replied.

The truth of the matter is this: there were two telephone calls on that last day of Elvis' life on earth. The first one was a consuming, heated argument between himself and his stepmother. The second one, moments before his passing, had tried to smooth things over again between them. Only Dee knew this, and of course, Elvis.

When David Stanley left the séance, he shook my hand and said, "Elvis would have liked you. He was interested in many of the things you do."

I wish I had known. But it's never too late. Because spirit communication isn't wishful thinking, deliberate fraud or a hoax: though it can be, at times, when used by unscrupulous persons. But when it is real, as it is between Elvis Presley and Dorothy Sherry, it should be told to the world. Every little bit of *truth* helps.

James Dean, And Lesser Hollywood Ghosts

North Beachwood Drive in Hollywood is an average street. Most of the houses on this particular block are two- or four-family houses divided up into apartments. Farther up the street is one of the major motion picture studios, but the block in question is rather quiet and not at all ghostly in appearance. The C. family moved into apartment No. 4 in one of the houses on the 1200 block in 1963. Mr. C. is an artist, and they had a four-year-old daughter at the time. The apartment was the only one at the top of a stairway, and anyone coming up those stairs would be a member of the C. family or someone paying them a visit.

Shortly after the C.'s had moved into their new apartment, they noticed some rather unusual things. After they had settled in the new place and started paying attention to the surroundings, they became aware of a strange phenomenon occurring every night between eight and nine P.M. *Someone was walking up their stairs.* At first only Mrs. C. paid attention to it. Clearly those were the footsteps of a very old person having difficulty ascending the stairs. The footsteps were deliberate and loud, slowing down and then picking up speed again. After a while they stopped, but no one was heard coming *down* the stairs again. This went on for several evenings in succession.

Mrs. C. realized that there was no one actually coming up the stairs, and she wondered if she was hallucinating. She therefore did not mention it to her husband. A few days passed. One evening, again at the same hour, her husband suddenly looked at her and said, "Quiet, I hear something." Both C.'s then clearly heard the same slow footsteps coming up their stairway. This time, however, they jumped up and tore the door open. There was no one there. Mr. C. immediately ran down the stairs as quickly as he could and looked around the corner and up and down the block, but there was no one to be seen. Mrs. C. then confessed that she had heard the same noises several nights in a row.

They decided to lie in wait the following night. Sure enough, between eight and nine pm someone unseen tried to come up their stairs, and when they ran out to look, there was no one about. They were puzzling as to what to do about this phenomenon when their neighbor, Peggy V., decided to spend a night with them. Her daughter and the C.'s daughter were playmates. That night, everyone was fast asleep—Mrs. V. on the couch in the living room and the C.'s in their bedroom—when an uproar woke them between two and three A.M. What woke Mrs. C. was an incessant scream coming from Mrs. V. As soon as she could be calmed down somewhat, Mrs. V. explained that she had been awakened by the sound of someone brushing his teeth and gargling in the bathroom. Puzzled as to who it might be, Mrs. V. had sat up on the couch. To her horror she clearly heard the dining room chairs in the dark apartment being pulled from the table, people sitting down on them, glasses being used and silverware tinkling, and muffled conversation. Since she knew very well that there was no one but herself and the C.'s in the apartment at the time, she screamed in absolute horror, unable to understand what was happening.

In conversation the following morning, Mrs. C. discovered that her neighbor had some occult interest in the past and was apparently "mediumistic." The C.'s themselves were not hostile to the idea of ghosts. Both of them were slightly interested in the occult and had a few books on the subject in their library. Mr. C. had always felt that ghosts were indeed possible, although he had never thought of having some of his own in the place where he lived.

The next day Mrs. C. went to see the owner of the building. After some hesitation, the landlady, Mrs. S., admitted that the previous tenant of their apartment had committed suicide in it—as a matter of fact, in the very bed in which the C.'s were now sleeping. That was quite enough for the C.'s. They decided to move from the apartment. When Mrs. S. was told of their determination to live elsewhere, she gave them an argument. "The old lady was a wonderful person," she exclaimed. "It is not a shame to commit suicide." Tactfully Mrs. C. explained about the phenomena they had witnessed.

Mrs. C. had had no ESP experiences either before or after living in the apartment on Beachwood. Nor had she any desire to again experience anything like it. One ghost was quite enough for her.

Polly Blaize is a lady in her early fifties, filled with the joy of life and spilling over with the excitement of many experiences with the world of spirits. She comes from a distinguished old New England family; many of her ancestors were either passengers on the *Mayflower* or early colonial dignitaries, and she counts two American presidents, Franklin Pierce and John Tyler, among her near relatives. Of Scottish background, she left New England at an early age to come to Hollywood, where she worked briefly for Warner Brothers. An early marriage proved a failure but left her with two small children. After a succession of various administrative jobs, she eventually remarried in 1965. Her husband is a design engineer working for NASA. Polly—or as she is more formally known, Pauline—lives with her husband in one of the beach communities south of Los Angeles now, but the experiences I am about to relate happened to her when she lived in and around Hollywood.

In 1924, not long after she had moved to California with her parents, Polly became friendly with a young boy named Billy Bennett. They were teenagers together when their families lived across from each other on Highland Avenue in Hollywood. Billy lived in an apartment that was part of a row of one-story apartments of the court type. The apartments have long since been leveled. His mother was then a famous screen star by the name of Belle Bennett, best known for her starring role in the 1925 version of *Stella Dallas*.

Time passed, and Pauline was married. Her marriage did not last very long, and she found herself at age twenty with the responsibility for two small children, a one-year-old daughter and a two-year-old son. One night she was in bed, fully awake, when she heard the shrieking sounds of what seemed to her like a flock of birds. The window was open and she heard the birds coming through it, hovering around her with the sound of beating wings. The sound was so loud she could bare- ly hear the human voice in the midst of this flock of birds. There was nothing to be seen, but the voice was that of Billy Bennett. "Beware of people who can hurt you, I still love you; I am ever near to protect you," the voice said, over and over. All this time she could see absolutely nothing but the darkness of the room.

Only a few days before the incident, Billy had died suddenly at the Presbyterian Hospital in Hollywood. His warning proved to be accurate indeed. For many years Mrs. Blaize lived almost as a recluse, until she met her second husband and married again, this time with happier results.

But the incident that has etched itself most deeply into her memo- ry took place in 1935 when her daughter was five years old. They had just moved into a one-bedroom apartment on Cheremoya Avenue in Hollywood. It consisted of a living room and a bedroom, and between the two was a dressing room large enough to contain a chest of draw- ers, a counter, and a large dressing mirror. About a week after they had moved into this apartment, Polly was suddenly awakened by the sound of what seemed to her like a heavy thud. It sounded as if a human body had dropped, followed by what sounded like a body pulling itself across the living room floor, from the dressing room area halfway to the kitchen, which was located on the other side of the living room. At first Polly paid no attention to these odd sounds, but when they repeated themselves exactly in the same manner at exactly the same time night after night, she became alarmed. Much later, she learned that her little girl was just as much aware of these sounds as she was.

Polly decided to make some inquiries of the landlady. The latter, named Beatrice Scriver, listened to the account of the nightly disturbances and then turned white. Since everyone in the building, which contained eight apartments, seemed to be familiar with the story, there was nothing for Mrs. Scriver to do but to let Polly in on the secret.

Prior to Polly's moving into the apartment, the place had belonged to a woman and her nineteen-year-old son. The young man was a successful athlete and had high hopes for a professional career. Suddenly he was informed that he would have to lose one of his legs because of severe illness. After he had been given this verdict by his doctors, the young man returned home and in front of his dressing room mirror shot himself to death. He fell to the floor, his body hitting it near the dressing-room door. Not quite dead, he pulled himself into the living room, pushed himself up on one elbow, then dropped again to the floor, only to try to pull himself up again. He did this several times in an effort to reach his mother, who was then in the kitchen. Because she had the water running, she had not heard the shot through the closed door.

Polly shuddered. Mrs. Scriver had described the exact sounds she had heard night after night in her apartment. But there was still another sound she wanted an explanation for. It sounded to her as if a basket were being pulled along the floor. The landlady nodded grimly. The young man's body had been taken out of the apartment in a basket, down the back stairs and to the morgue.

But that was not the end of the story by any means. Being spiritually attuned, Polly realized she had to help release the young man from his sufferings. Quite obviously, she argued, he did not realize what had happened to him. (In the intervening time, the young man's mother had also passed away.)

Polly thanked the landlady for the information and went back to her apartment. Her eyes fixed themselves on the dark rug on her living room floor. Turning the carpet back, she noticed a large brown stain and realized that it was made by the young man's blood. That was all the proof she needed. That night she waited until the sounds started up again. Speaking in a soft voice, she then called him by name.

"Your mother has gone ahead of you and is waiting for you; do not keep her waiting any longer," she said, pleading with the unseen presence. There was only silence.

Several nights in a row she spoke the same words, and finally there was a sound in answer to her pleading. She was seated in a chair near the spot where he had died when she suddenly heard a long, drawn-out voice as if called to her from far away, saying, "Mama—help me." The voice sounded hollow, as if it were coming from some distant place, but she heard it clearly and responded. For a while the sounds continued. Polly did not give up; she kept repeating her plea, asking the young man to reach out to his mother so that he could be free from the unhappy surroundings where he had died. Ultimately the message got through to him, and just as suddenly as the phenomena had entered Polly's life, they stopped. With a sigh of relief Polly Blaize realized that she had successfully freed the ghostly young athlete.

Lise Caron and her husband Leo moved to Los Angeles in 1965. The family had originally lived in Paris, but the two older daughters, named Liliane and Nicole, had decided to strike out on their own and go to the United States. They liked it so much they induced their parents to follow them. Thus Mr. and Mrs. Caron and the third daughter joined the two girls in Los Angeles in a house at El Centro Avenue in the 1200 North block. A cluster of houses in the Spanish style is arranged around a narrow courtyard, open on one side toward the street. The landlord occupies the house at the bottom of this cluster of houses, and the apartment that was to be the home of the Carons is the first one on the right.

Liliane had been married a short time before her parents' arrival in Los Angeles and had moved out, leaving Nicole the sole occupant of the apartment. Nicole had decided that the place was too small for three additional people and had therefore rented a single apartment close by, intending to leave her former apartment to her parents and their youngest daughter.

When Lise Caron arrived at the house, she had a good impression of it. The street was quiet, the house, though old, seemed in good condition, and she felt that they would be happy in it. The apartment itself consisted of a good-sized living room separated from the dining room by a folding door.

At the time of their arrival, the dining room had been transformed into a bedroom for Martine, the youngest daughter. Between the dining room and a short hallway stood a chest of drawers. On top of the chest a candle was burning. Surprised, Mrs. Caron turned to her daughters, asking why they were burning a candle. The answer was an evasive one, but Lise was too tired from the long journey to pay much attention to it. Thus, when Nicole implored her mother to leave the candle in its place, she nodded and went on to other things. To the right side of the hallway was a bedroom in which stood two beds separated by a night table with a lamp on it. To the left of the hallway was the bathroom, and in front of the dining room door was the kitchen door. This kitchen door would swing with a particular noise as it went from one side to the other. In every room there were flowers and green plants helping to create a happy impression. The Carons were so happy to be together again after the long separation that they lingered over their dinner. It was late when they decided to go to bed.

Mr. and Mrs. Caron went to their bedroom, while Martine closed the folding door between bedroom and living room. She then went to bed in her makeshift bedroom in the living room.

Almost as soon as Mr. Caron lay down he was asleep. Mrs. Caron was still in the bathroom when she suddenly received the impression that there was someone observing her. Turning around, she saw no one. She continued with her chores, but again received the distinct impression that someone was standing at the bathroom door staring at her. Turning around again, she said, "Is that you, Leo?" But a look into the bedroom convinced her that her husband was fast asleep. She decided to see whether Martine might have gotten up and come in to see her.

Martine was still up, and when her mother came over to her she seemed to have a strange look on her face. "What is wrong?" Mrs. Caron asked her daughter.

"I don't feel comfortable here," the girl said, and explained that she had a strange feeling of a presence. Mrs. Caron did not wish to upset her youngest daughter, so she made light of this, at the same time opening the folding door to change the atmosphere of the room. The only light came now from the flickering candle, and that too helped to create somewhat spooky impression. But since everyone was tired, she did not want to make an issue of it and decided to find out about the candle later. Then she returned to bed. As soon as she had lain down, she again had the feeling of another presence.

But the next few days were too exciting to leave room for worry about the impressions of that first night, and in the end she ascribed her strange feelings to the need for adjustment to new surroundings.

Unfortunately, the impressions continued night after night. A few days after their arrival she woke up to the noise of the kitchen door swinging. She thought that her husband had gone to the kitchen to get a drink. But a glance at his bed showed her he had not. A little later, she awoke again to see someone standing between their two beds. She thought her husband had gotten up, but to her surprise saw that he was fast asleep. In fact, she could see right through the strange person standing between the two beds. She sat bolt upright, her heart pounding, looking straight ahead at the apparition. At that moment, the stranger vanished into thin air.

She awakened her husband and told him what had happened. Quickly he put on his coat and ran around to the outside of the house, thinking an intruder had somehow gotten into the apartment. But there was no one about.

The next morning she decided to talk about this with her older daughters. It was then that she received an explanation for the strange goings-on and the flickering candle on the dresser. When the two girls had first rented the apartment, they too had the feeling of a presence with them. At first they had been rather scared by it, but after some time they ignored the unusual impressions, preferring to live with whatever it was that was disturbing in the atmosphere rather an to look for a new apartment. This had gone on for some time, when one night they were aroused by the noise of the kitchen door opening. Both girls woke up simultaneously fastening their eyes upon the darkness of their bedroom. There between the two beds stood a man. Their first thought was that a burglar had gotten into the house. As they jumped from their beds the apparition vanished. A quick check of doors and windows disclosed that none of them was open, nor was there anyone outside. Several days later Liliane heard the same noise again. Bravely she opened her eyes and saw a white apparition close to Nicole's bed. Again she sat up in bed, and the apparition vanished. She was not sure, but the second apparition might have been that of a woman. After that the two girls decided they needed the help of a medium and went to see famed clairvoyant Brenda Crenshaw. Mrs. Crenshaw, wife of newspaper writer James Crenshaw, has been a practicing medium in the Hollywood area for many years and has an impeccable reputation for honesty and accu-racy. After a few minutes the two girls were told that the medium saw the problem surrounding them quite clearly.

It appeared that a young couple had committed suicide in the apartment some time before. On checking this they found the infor-mation to be correct. From that moment on they decided to place a candle in the apartment and to pray for the unfortunate ones every day, in the hope that they might find peace. With their daily prayer becom-ing part of the routine, they managed to continue living in the haunted apartment.

Mrs. Caron wasn't exactly ecstatic about the idea of continuing to live with the ghostly couple. On the other hand, she thought that per-haps she might release them. She promised herself to stay calm should anything further occur. Her opportunity came a few nights after her conversation with her daughters. She woke up again to the sound of the kitchen door opening by itself. Slowly Mrs. Caron looked up and saw a young man standing between the two beds, close enough to be touched. He was standing near her husband's feet. Mrs. Caron could see him very clearly. He was a short man, with curly hair, but since his back was turned toward her she could not see his face. She estimated that he was between thirty and thirty-five years old. He stood there without mov-ing, as if transfixed. Mrs. Caron hoped that he would turn around so she could see his face, but he did not. After a while the apparition start-ed slowly to vanish, until it was completely gone. He never returned to the apartment visually, but his influence could still be felt for a long time after this incident.

Continuing their prayers for the release of the unhappy couple, the Carons nevertheless felt that their apartment was not exactly a happy one and decided to move just as soon as they could find another place.

I spoke to Mrs. Caron in 1970 and found that all was well in their new place. She had no idea as to what had happened to the apartment on El Centro Avenue but readily supplied me with additional information about the landlord. In October of 1972 I drove to the house on El Centro Avenue in the company of Paula Davidson and her brother.

Walking about in front of the apartment, Paula felt nothing in particular. As for me, I felt rather depressed at the sight of this cluster of houses, which somehow reminded me of something out of Hollywood's past, but that may have been due to my knowledge of the incidents just described. Bravely I rang the doorbell. A dark-haired middle-aged lady opened the door, peering out at me, wondering what I wanted. I explained that I was writing a book about Hollywood; not saying that I meant *haunted* Hollywood. I asked the lady whether she knew anything about the background of her apartment.

"I am sorry I can't help you," she replied politely. "I have been living here only two years."

"Is there anything special that you might have observed during those years?" I asked.

The lady shook her head and smiled rather wryly. "Nothing really. Except that I've been very unhappy here. I've had nothing but bad luck ever since I moved into this apartment. I haven't the vaguest idea why."

Anyone who thinks that such experiences are rare and happen only to the imaginative or perhaps those who are "believers" just doesn't know his facts. I have hundreds upon hundreds of parallel cases in my files, all of them reported by sane, sensible and rational people from every social and economic level. These incidents occur in new houses as well as in old ones. Take the case of Mrs. Barbara McDuffa, a lady who now lives in West Los Angeles. She had gone through a harrowing and, to her, inexplicable experience which preyed on her mind until she could find some sort of explanation for it. She needed a "rational" explanation, because otherwise there was the suggestion that she had perhaps imagined the whole thing or that there was something wrong with her powers of perception. Eventually she heard of my work and telephoned me while I was on the Gil Henry radio program in the area. We talked about the matter, and I assured Mrs. McDuffa that there was nothing wrong with her mind, her eyes or her hearing. It just happened that she had moved into a haunted apartment.

In the late sixties, Mrs. McDuffa, her mother, and her son David moved into a brand-new, never before-lived-in apartment on Roscoe Boulevard in Panorama City, a community at the end of Van Nuys, which in turn borders on North Hollywood. At that time Mrs. McDuffa scoffed at the supernatural or the notion that there might be ghosts or haunted apartments. If anyone had mentioned such possibilities to her, she would have thought him insane or jesting.

The first night after they had moved into the new apartment, they went to bed fairly early, because there remained much work to be done in the morning. It was a warm night and Mrs. McDuffa couldn't sleep. She decided to get up and open the bedroom window. As she started for the window, she suddenly perceived a tall figure of a man, wearing an overcoat and hat, standing in the closet doorway at the foot of the bed. Mrs. McDuffa had left the closet door open, but there wasn't anything in it as yet since they hadn't unpacked their things. When she saw the figure she rushed for the light switch. As soon as the light went on the figure disappeared. For a moment Mrs. McDuffa was stunned, but then she assumed that she had had an hallucination and went back to bed.

The following night she was awakened from a deep sleep by the sound of footsteps on the carpet. As she was trying to get her bearings, she noticed that her mother had been awakened by the same noises. It sounded as if someone were walking on the carpet, shuffling his feet, yet there was no one to be seen. The two women exchanged experiences but eventually put them out of their minds, since there was a great deal of work to be done in the apartment, and no one had much time to think about such matters as the supernatural.

The footsteps, however, continued for several nights. They were now joined by a tapping sound on the window of the bedroom. Since there weren't any shutters or trees or bushes or anything else near the window that could have caused this noise, they were puzzled. Worried that the unseen phenomena might upset the little boy, the ladies then put the boy's bed into their room and shut the door of the other room at night. Still thinking that it might be a prowler or some other physical force, they pulled a dresser up in front of the door so that no one could enter. The door of the bedroom opened into a little corridor. There was no direct access to either the windows or the entrance door of the apartment. That night, as if in response to their new security measures, the closed bedroom door started to rattle. The door-knob moved as if someone were trying to get in. The force rattling the door was so strong that only a wind of hurricane force could have caused it. Nevertheless, it was totally quiet outside the house; none of the windows were open, and there was no natural explanation for the rattling sound or the movement of the door-knob. The women had to conclude that they had been "blessed" by a ghost.

One day Mrs. McDuffa was combing her hair in her bedroom. Suddenly she felt a pressure on her shoulder and then felt something brushing her cheek as if an unseen person had passed very close by her. She turned around, but again there was no one to be seen. Shortly after this experience she heard the noise of a glass being put down as if someone had taken a drink of water in the kitchen. There was no one in the kitchen at the time. Several days after this experience, Mrs. McDuffa, now fully aware that there was something strange going on in their apartment, went to bed, turning on the bedside lamp in order to read. The moment she had turned it on, the lamp went out by itself. Three times Mrs. McDuffa turned it on, only to see it go out of its own volition. She checked the bulb, but it worked perfectly in other lamps. The next day she called in an electrician and had the switch examined as well as the lamp. He could find nothing wrong with either. That night she turned the lamp on again and nothing went wrong with it. Apparently her unseen visitor had decided to leave things well enough alone for that night.

Several days after this experience, Mrs. McDuffa was getting ready to go to work. It was a dark, rainy morning, and as she shut the door she looked back toward the apartment. A bright light shone across the living room as if the sun were shining in. Both her mother and her son saw the same thing and looked at her in amazement. There was no way such a light could have appeared in her living room.

One evening everyone had gone to bed; the hall light was left on and the door between the two bedrooms stood open. Mrs. McDuffa was looking toward the open bedroom door when she suddenly became aware of two roundish shapes made of a white, cloud-like substance. It seemed to her to resemble in a vague way the outlines of a human figure, but no details could be seen. As she observed this apparition in a state of shock mingled with fascination, the whitish shape slowly drifted into the second bedroom and disappeared.

But that was the end of the trail as far as Mrs. McDuffa was concerned. The following day she made arrangements to move. They had lived at the apartment for less than three months. Since she had lived in many places before without encountering anything unusual, Mrs. McDuffa became convinced that she had somehow stumbled upon a very haunted apartment. She has no idea who the apparition might be, nor did she make any inquiries with the landlord. All she wanted was to get out of the place, and fast.

John K. is twenty-six years old, lives in Hollywood and works as a freight cashier at a steamship company. "I don't quite know where to begin," he said when he contacted me in May of 1971. He explained that he felt he was being harassed by reincarnation memories or by someone he thought was in some mysterious way connected with his personality. Since I am always on the lookout for "evidential" reincarnation cases, I was naturally interested. In October of the same year we met at the Continental Hotel in Hollywood. Mr. K. turned out to be a slight, quiet-spoken young man far from hysterical and not particularly involved with the occult. Gradually I pieced his amazing story together and discovered what lay at the base of his strange and terrifying experiences.

John K. was born in a small town in the Ozarks with a population of only forty-two people. The house he was born and raised in was quite old, built before the Civil War. His family lived there until he reached the age of twelve, when they moved to another small town in southwestern Arizona. There his father was employed by the government on a nearby Army base. At the age of twenty, Mr. K. dropped out of college after his junior year and headed straight for Los Angeles, where he has lived ever since.

His first twelve years in the Ozarks were spent on a farm with five brothers and two sisters. The family lived a very primitive life. There was no indoor plumbing; heat was provided by a coal stove, and each Saturday night the entire family would take turns bathing in the same tub of water. At first there was no electricity in the house. For the first three grades, Mr. K. went to a one-room schoolhouse. "Our teacher was very young and had not yet finished her college education but was permitted to teach us anyway."

Mr. K. explained, "The reason I am relating all of my earlier surroundings to you is to point out the fact that the first twelve years of my life I lived a very isolated existence." Until he reached the age of ten, Mr. K. had not seen a television set; entertainment in his family consisted mainly of playing cards and talking. He attended the local Southern Baptist Church, into which he was duly baptized; however, after the family left the farm they dropped out of organized religion.

From an early age John K. received the impression of a presence which no one else could see. None of his immediate family had ever been out of the country, yet he was aware of the presence of a French lady whose name, he came to know, as Jacqueline. When he mentioned the presence of this woman to his family he was laughed at and told he had a fantastic imagination, so he stopped talking about it. At an early age he also developed the ability to dream of events that later happened *exactly* as seen in his dreams. These prophetic dreams did not forecast great events but concerned themselves with everyday matters. Nevertheless, they were upsetting to the boy. He never remembered his dreams, but when the event became objective reality he started to shiver and realized he had seen it all before. This, of course, is called *déjà vu* and is a fairly common ESP phenomenon. He could not discuss his dreams with his family, since psychic experiences were not the kind of thing one could talk about in the Ozarks in the early fifties. But he hated to stay in the house alone; he had a terrible fear of darkness and of the house itself.

One afternoon when he was ten years old, he happened to be in the house alone, upstairs in the back bedroom. All of a sudden he knew there was a presence there, and the most horrifying fear swept through him, as if he were being chocked to death. The walls seemed to vibrate, and he heard a loud sound for which there did not seem to be any natural explanation. Eventually he was able to break out of his terror and flee down the stairs.

There was something else that seemed strange about John K. from an early age on. He could never relate to men and felt completely at ease only with women—his grandmother, his mother, and his older sister. When he was very young, he began playing with his older sister, six years his senior, and enjoyed playing girls' games tremendously. He would never join his brothers in boys' games. He loved wearing long flowing dresses, fashions of an earlier time that he had found in the attic. Whenever he wore these dresses, he felt completely at ease and seemed to have a rather sophisticated air about him. The strange thing was that he insisted on wearing only those dresses of an earlier period of history; the shorter dresses of the current era interested him not at all. At those times he felt as though he were another person.

It was during those early childhood days that he first became aware of Jacqueline. Especially when he played with his sister, he felt that he was sexually just like her. He continued to wear dresses around the house until the time he started to school. Often when he came home from school he would go upstairs and put on his dresses. Finally, his father became aware of the boy's tendency and threatened to send him to school wearing a dress if he didn't stop, so John stopped. However, the impression of a female life inside him and the desire to wear long dresses persisted.

"Needless to say," he explained in complete frankness, "I was not the average run-of-the-mill boy, and I turned out to be very effeminate and was teased constantly by my schoolmates." Rejected by the other boys, he began to turn within himself and did not bother to explain his ideas to others. Although he had never traveled outside the four southern states surrounding his native village, he began to feel very emotional about France, particularly Paris. "I somehow seemed to have fond memories of a life of many human pleasures, a life of a woman who was very aware and felt a need to express herself totally," John K. explained, adding that he knew by that time that Jacqueline, whoever she might have been, had led the life of a prostitute. He thus had a sense of heavy religious condemnation, of being a wicked sinner with the threat of hell hanging over him.

When the family finally moved to Arizona, he thought that perhaps some of his agonies would subside. But the conflict between his present surroundings and the world of Jacqueline increased almost daily. At the age of fourteen he felt that since he could not belong to this world he might as well kill himself and return to where he really belonged. He wrote a farewell note to his mother, the only one to whom he could relate at the time, his sister having married and his grandmother having grown old and feeble. In the note he told his mother that he was going to return to where he belonged, that he felt he had come from another planet and it was time for him to go back. He then ran a rope over one of the rafters in his room, put a chair under it, and placed the noose around his neck, ready to jump. Then fate intervened in the person of one of his mother's friends who had stopped by unexpectedly. Since his mother was asleep, John had to answer the door. The visit lasted a long time, and by the time the lady had left he was no longer in the mood to take his own life.

From then on he did rather well in school, although most people thought him too shy and introverted. He never dated girls, since he felt himself female. But he did make friends with one particular boy and remained close friends with him for ten years. Later, the boy moved to Los Angeles. When John K. dropped out of school in his junior year of college, he came to Los Angeles and moved in with his friend. At the time he was twenty years old. He still felt like a female and was still continually aware of Jacqueline.

It was then that John became involved in the homosexual world and had the first sexual experience of his life. Whenever he had sexual relations, he felt strongly that he was fulfilling the part of the woman.

About six months after he came to Los Angeles, he started to have terrible dreams. One night when he was totally awake he suddenly saw a woman standing at the foot of his bed. She was wearing a long nightgown and had long hair and was smiling at him. She seemed to float just above the floor. At first John thought that it was his imagination and passed it off as a silly dream. The next night the same thing happened. He realized the apparition wanted to tell him something.

Strangely enough, he wasn't particularly frightened. The third night the apparition returned, and her smile had turned into a frown of deep sorrow. She returned the following night, and this time her face showed utter terror. Deep veins stood out on her face, her eyes were bloodshot, and her mouth grinned hideously.

She returned once again the following night, and this time her entire head had been torn off, and blood was spilled all over her beautiful flowing gown. John was fully aware of the utter torment of her soul. That same night something grabbed hold of his arm and forcibly yanked him out of bed and onto the floor. He screamed for help from his roommate, who was in the next room, but the young man had no compassion for his condition and yelled out for John to shut up or he would have him committed. After this incident John thought he was going mad and wondered to whom he could turn for advice.

A few months passed. He was still living in Hollywood with the same roommate but by this time was a prostitute himself. He had gone to college and found himself a good job, but he had had a strong urge to become a prostitute, and so followed it. Whenever he engaged in these activities he felt a very deep satisfaction. Also at this time he resumed wearing female clothes, and since his roommate was a make-up artist by profession, he would do the make-up for him. John would never go into the streets in this array; he would wear these clothes only at home. His friends began to call him Jackie, for Jacqueline.

Whenever he put on the clothes, John became another person. The first time he saw himself in complete make-up and female clothing he felt that Jacqueline had won at last. He now felt that she had taken total possession of him and that he was cursed for life.

"It was not a simple case of transvestitism or going in female drag," John explained, "It was a complete soul satisfaction on my part, and when Jacqueline came out she controlled me completely. She was very strong and I was very weak."

It finally reached the point that when John came home at night he would dress up in female clothing and spend the entire evening in this manner. He even slept in evening gowns. He removed all the hair from his body and delighted in taking baths and dousing himself with perfumes. This went on for two years, until John felt that something had to be done about it. He realized something was wrong with him.

About that time another friend introduced him to Buddhism. For three years he practiced the Buddhist religion, and through it was able to find many answers for himself that had eluded him before. Because of his devotion to Buddhism, Jacqueline finally left, never to return again. A new male image began to emerge slowly but surely as a result of his Buddhist practices, and once again he was able to relate to the environment around him and find a reason for living.

Through a friend, John received my address. He contacted me in the hope I might hypnotize him and regress him to an earlier life in which he might encounter Jacqueline. John was firmly convinced that his predicament had been due to an unfulfilled reincarnation problem, and that perhaps through hypnosis I might put him further on the road to recovery.

"I never felt fulfillment during my pre-Buddhist sexual contacts while portraying Jacqueline," he told me, "but it did satisfy my Jacqueline personality completely. But she is totally gone now and a new John is emerging—one who is not afraid of the dark anymore and who can live alone and stand on his own two feet, and who will someday marry a girl and have a family. I am very optimistic about the future."

Although neither John nor his immediate family had had any interest in or knowledge of occult practices, this was not entirely true of others in his background. An Aunt Mary had been a practicing witch, had owned many books dealing with witchcraft of the fifteenth and sixteenth centuries, and had been a sore subject in the family. Nobody dared talk about her. But she had died before John was born, and all knowledge John had of his Aunt Mary was necessarily secondhand. Nevertheless, there had been ESP talents in the family on his father's side, mainly messages from dead relatives, though John was never able to obtain any details. In his family the occult was something not suitable for family conversation.

After Jacqueline had left John, he kept having ESP experiences unrelated to his ordeal. They were not world-shaking experiences, but they did convince him that his ESP faculty had remained unimpaired by the hold Jacqueline had exercised upon him for so many years. A short time before our meeting there had been a steamship strike and he was laid off. He was wondering if he should get another job outside the steamship industry when he had a strange dream. In the dream he saw his boss at the steamship company coming out of his office and saying to someone, "Call John K. back to work." At the same time he saw the number 7 flash through the dream. Upon awakening he remembered every detail. On September 7 his boss came out of his office and told an aide, "Call John K. back to work," and, as foreseen in the dream, he returned to his former position.

I was rather interested in his continuing ESP experiences since I had begun to wonder whether Jacqueline was indeed a reincarnation memory or perhaps something else. We proceeded to begin hypnotic regression. I first took John K. down to age twenty, when he remembered every detail of his life. He even remembered the names of his best friends and what was on his desk at the time. I then took him back to age twelve and his life in Missouri. In each case he even knew his exact height at the time. He knew the names of the nearest neighbors, how many children they had and even the name of their dog. Satisfied that he was deeply in the third stage of hypnotic regression, I then took him back beyond the threshold of birth into an alleged earlier life. I worked very hard and very gradually to see whether we could locate some other personality that had been John K. in a previous lifetime, but he saw nothing. I then asked him to look specifically for Jacqueline.

"Do you know who she is?" I asked.

"She is someone who doesn't like me."

"Is she a real person?"

"Yes."

"Have you ever lived in France?"

"No."

I then took him as far back as the Middle Ages, fifty years at a time, in case there were other incarnations. When we got to the year 1350, he said he felt very strange and put his hands upon his chest in a gesture I interpreted as religious. But there was no recognition of another person. I then took him, step by step, back into the present, finally awakening him, and then inquiring how he felt. Since John was a good hypnotic subject, he remembered absolutely nothing of what he had said during hypnosis.

"Do you feel different from the way you felt fifteen minutes ago?" I inquired.

"Well, I had a headache before I came; I don't have a headache now."

He felt well-rested and satisfied with himself. Jacqueline had not put in an appearance, as she would have if she had been part of John K. I then explained to the young man that his ordeal had not been caused by reincarnation memories or an unfulfilled earlier lifetime. To the contrary, he had been victimized by an independent entity, not related to him in any way, who had somehow sought him out to serve as her medium of expression in the physical world. Jacqueline, the French prostitute, whose choice of clothes indicated that she had lived in the nineteenth century, wanted to live in this century through another body. For reasons of her own she had chosen a male body for her experiment.

If there was any reincarnation connection between the two, it remained obscure. There is, of course, the possibility that John K. had been in another life someone close to Jacqueline, in her time, and had since reincarnated while Jacqueline had not, and that the woman attached herself to John K. just as soon as she could after his birth into the present life. I myself tend to favor this theory. It is unfortunate that this earlier John K. could not be rediscovered either consciously or in hypnosis. But if this earlier incarnation had led a fully satisfactory life, the need to retain traces of memory would not be there.

In the case of Jacqueline, her inner conflict between what she was doing and the religious pressure exerted upon her must have been the compelling factor in keeping her in a time slot, or, rather, suspended in time, preventing her from reincarnating herself. In her predicament and frustration she needed to express herself through someone in the present, since she could not herself go on and be someone else. Deprived of her medium, Jacqueline perhaps will have found an avenue of escape into the next stage of existence and hopefully will not be heard from again.

When it comes to seeing the ghosts of celebrities, all sorts of people are likely to imagine they are in touch with their favorite movie star, when in fact they are merely expressing a wish fulfillment. In such cases, however, there exists a real attachment, an admiration for the personality involved. Frequently the people who have such fantasies are fans who have never met the star in question but wish they had.

Not so with attractive Doris Danielson, a Texas divorcee whom I met in Houston, after she had requested my help in clearing up the mystery of her psychic experiences. Now in her thirties, she works as a secretary.

"Miss Danielson, have you ever had any interest in psychic phenomena since you have grown up?" I began my questioning.

"No, I haven't."

"Have you had any experiences whatever that you might classify as psychic besides the one we are about to discuss?"

"No."

"When did this phenomenon take place?"

"It was in March of 1957. I was about to be discharged from the Air Force and was staying with a friend, Roger Smith, overnight. His house was in Trenton, New Jersey. I had been a stewardess, and I was planning to leave for New York to try to get into modeling. This happened the night before I left.

"I woke up for some reason in the middle of the night and crawled to the edge of the bed on my hands and knees. I asked myself, why did I wake up? I couldn't think of any reason. Then I looked at the door—it appeared to be getting brighter! Then a circle formed in the middle of the door. It was red. The circle started coming toward me. And inside the circle was *James Dean's head.*"

"Had you seen his face before?"

"I'd seen him in the movies, but I had no particular interest in James Dean; I simply thought he was a good actor. But I never thought about him. The only parallel in my life was that my boyfriend at the time resembled James Dean somewhat in his likes and dislikes, such as motorcycles, speed, and all that."

"Did he *look* like him?"

"Not really."

"How long did the image last?"

"I don't know, but I kept thinking if I stared at it long enough it might disappear. I did, but instead it floated across the room, and only then did it disappear. It came from the door and floated toward me as I was sitting on the bed. Just a head in a circle."

"Did it speak?"

"No."

"Was there any form of movement?"

"I can't remember any form of movement. His hair was very curly. Suddenly, it was gone. I sat there and pinched myself to make sure I was awake. When it was gone I really became scared, and I prayed."

"Have you had any similar experiences before or after?"

"No. The only other experience I had was after I had moved to Houston. I was married then, and my husband had gone on guard duty and was to be away for two weeks. Two days after he was gone, this happened. I had just turned out all the lights and gone to bed. I heard somebody come down the hallway. I thought it was my husband coming back, although I wasn't expecting him. He was the only one who had a key. I said, 'Bob, is that you?' But there was no answer. Then I felt someone come right into the bedroom and stand by my bed. The springs of the bed creaked as if someone were sitting on it. I shot out of the bed on the other side and ran to the bathroom, where I turned on the lights. There was nobody in the bedroom."

"Was the house in any way connected with a tragedy?"

"No. It was a brand-new house when we moved in."

"Did the footsteps sound like a man's or a woman's?"

"I had thought it was my husband coming home, but I don't know how I *could* have heard footsteps, because there was a rug on the floor."

"Have you seen any James Dean movies since the first incident?"

"No."

One can only surmise that the late actor recognized Doris as a potential communicator, but somehow never got his message across the veil.

The Two Lives Of Gaye Spiegelman, Topless Mother Of Eight

In the spring of 1966 I happened to be in San Francisco, doing the rounds of various television shows in connection with the book I was then promoting. I was invited to be a guest on Bill Gordon's interview program, which was telecast from a local nightclub. One of the fellow guests on this particular program was an exotic dancer by the name of Gaye Spiegelman, who was then appearing at the club. When Mr. Gordon told me before the program that I would share the spotlight with Gaye, who billed herself as the topless mother of eight, I was somewhat taken aback. Not that the atmosphere of striptease is exactly alien to me. As a theatrical columnist for twelve years I have visited such emporiums many times in a professional capacity and have made a number of friends among exotic dancers and others employed in this particular border area of showbusiness. I have no prejudices against anyone earning an honest living, whether or not the method by which he or she earns his keep is orthodox or accepted by society. But I was surprised by the choice of what appeared to be a striptease headliner as a fellow guest on a program devoted largely to the exploration of extrasensory perception. I could not understand why Bill Gordon had chosen Mrs. Spiegelman, of all people, to be on the show. But I had a book to promote, and I resigned myself to trying to get along with whoever was on the show, whether or not they were perfect debating mates on the subject.

Imagine my pleasant surprise when I met Mrs. Spiegelman for the first time. Instead of the showbusiness-hardened, flip, bleached blonde that I had expected, I met a smart-looking, dark eyed and dark-haired young woman of about thirty, conservatively dressed—at least on this occasion—who was both modest and friendly. Five minutes after our meeting we were friends. Ten minutes later I had learned of her lifelong interest in psychic phenomena and her own abilities in that respect. Now I realized why the shrewd Bill Gordon had brought us together on his program. As it turned out, we had a lively and fascinating discussion concerning the reality of psychic phenomena, with an occasional plug for my book and her night club thrown in for good measure. Before we parted she promised to send me some notes about her own psychic experiences, and I in turn promised to interview her backstage at the El Cid night club the next time I came to San Francisco.

True to my promise, my wife and I went to Gaye's show when we were next in San Francisco. Gaye put on an entertaining, humorous night club act consisting of comedy numbers interspersed with straight dancing that showed her professional dance training to good advantage. It was clear from the beginning that she was a trained entertainer. After the show we spent an hour or so with her backstage. I had already fortified myself with some background material about her career, so I was aware of the fact that she was a rising new star on the exotic firmament. This was at the time when topless dancing had just come into fashion and people were still somewhat shocked by the idea of women entirely exposing their breasts. As a matter of fact, Gaye's routine was quite tame and decorous, but in 1966 it seemed rather far out even for San Francisco, because her act showed what had happened to her in real life. Bored by the routines of a housewife and mother, she had taken flight and wound up on the stage as an exotic dancer. Since her dance made the latter profession look far more glamorous than her earlier one, it was likely to entice other housewives in the audience to try the same.

Unfortunately, very few of them had the basic equipment nature had given Gaye. As Gaye pointedly assured her admirers in publicity releases, her figure was all hers, without benefit of silicone. She billed herself as the topless mother of eight children, which indeed she was.

As is often the case, Gaye's background contained the germs of her later psychic experiences in that both her grandparents were also psychic. The earliest incident she remembers concerns her grandfather, a native of Bucharest, Rumania, who was then living in Berkeley, California. A letter had arrived from Gaye's mother saying that she was feeling fine, but her grandfather, on reading this, insisted that they leave immediately, for he felt that Gaye's mother was terribly ill at that very moment. They arrived at the house of Gaye's parents barely in time to save her mother's life. She had hurt herself and was bleeding profusely.

Shortly after her marriage Gaye was visiting her parents in Santa Rosa, California. Her grandmother lay ill in the local hospital. At one o'clock in the morning their dog started to howl in a way she had never done before, and Gaye felt "strange" at that moment. It turned out to be the precise moment when her grandmother died.

Gaye married a local furniture dealer and they had one child. She found it difficult to conceive another time, even though she wanted desperately to have more children. She went from doctor to doctor without results. One afternoon she was resting when the doorbell rang; she got up from the couch and went downstairs to see who was at the door. It turned out to be her aunt, who told her that her grandmother was present. Gaye heard herself say, "Well, ask her to come in." Then her grandmother, *who had passed away some time before,* walked in and up the stairs without saying a single word. Gaye put her arms around her and knelt, telling her grandmother of the problem she was having conceiving another child. Without saying a word her grandmother nodded yes. At that precise moment the telephone rang. Gaye picked it up and heard the operator say, "There is a party from Berkeley trying to reach you, but she has left the line." Gaye quickly replied, "Thank you, operator, but I just received that call," and hung up. Gaye did not know anyone in Berkeley except her late grandmother. Neither before that time nor after did she receive any call from anyone from Berkeley.

Exactly nine months after this incident she had a baby boy.

Gaye's ability to connect telepathically with people some distance away proved itself long before she became what I consider my most amazing case of possession. She had a friend by the name of Vinio. It was their friendship that first aroused her interest in psychic research. On one occasion she knew he was aboard a President Lines ship crossing the ocean somewhere in the middle of the Pacific. She had just been operated on, and as she came out of the anesthetic she suddenly had a vision of this man in the Ambassador Hotel in San Francisco. As soon as she could she put through a person-to-person call to him at the hotel in San Francisco. The hotel had him paged, and, sure enough, he was there. Apparently he had decided to leave the ship in Los Angeles and on the spur of the moment had come to San Francisco. At the time when Gaye telephoned, he had just checked in.

With eight children to take care of, including one set of twins and an adopted child, Gaye's considerable salary was not enough to cover expenses. Thus she was always economy-minded and appreciated a bargain when she saw one. Once she needed some jackets for her children and looked all over for a set for her twins. Most of the jackets she saw were priced at about ten dollars each, which was more than she could afford. Suddenly she had a vision in which she saw two pink jackets priced at $2.98 in Woolworth's in downtown San Francisco. She immediately rushed to the store and demanded those two pink jackets. She was told that they did not have them in pink, only in other colors. But, Gaye, who is a very persistent person, requested that they check again. The saleslady shook her head but complied. A moment later she returned from the storage with two pink jackets priced at exactly $2.98.

They had been at the bottom of a box that had been earmarked to be put away. Even the salespeople did not know about them.

On at least one occasion her thoughts reached out to another person, someone whom she did not know and yet came to know as a result of her telepathic powers. For a long time Gaye had wanted to learn Tahitian dancing in earnest. She was doing some of it in her night club act at El Cid but knew she was faking it, even though it came across as professional. She wanted to study with a good Tahitian choreographer to improve her style, but there was no way she could go to Tahiti; because of her schedule and lack of money, such a trip was out of the question. Yet for several weeks she kept having dreams of going to Tahiti, and saw herself doing Tahitian dancing in those dreams.

That summer she received a letter at the night club from a professor of physiology who had seen a sign announcing her act but had never actually seen her perform or tried to make contact before. His letter was not an attempt to initiate a relationship, but the result of several dream visions he had had of Gaye Spiegelman and himself with her eight children walking barefoot along the white sands of Tahiti. He was quite sure the beach was in Tahiti. The professor concluded the letter by saying he felt rather foolish about it all, and apologized for contacting her.

To his surprise Gaye wrote him a serious reply, explaining that apparently she and he were on the same wavelength psychically and that she too had visions of going to Tahiti. From this correspondence a friendship resulted, and a short time later the professor came to San Francisco to meet her for the first time. He arrived at the El Cid at one-thirty in the morning, and after a brief chat they had coffee together. Unexpectedly they decided to spend the weekend in Honolulu. That was all the time either of them had to spare. In Honolulu she spent the entire time taking a crash course with a Tahitian choreographer. There was nothing romantic about her association with the professor, and while they had not wound up on Tahiti, dancing with a Tahitian was close enough for Gaye.

Even Gaye's fame and career were partly the result of a vision. The wife of a prominent businessman, she was living the comparatively quiet life of a housewife with a brood of children in Santa Rosa, active in the social life of the city. One day she had a vision of a certain night club called The Squirrel Cage in downtown Santa Rosa. It wasn't the kind of place she would normally go to, but in this vision she not only saw the place but also saw herself doing a go-go dance in it. She tried to dismiss the vision as ridiculous, but it was so strong she decided to test it. She called up the place and immediately asked the manager if he was looking for a go-go dancer. To her surprise he answered, "Yes, how did you know?" Still thinking that the whole thing was nothing more than a gag, she identified herself to him. Astonishingly, he knew of her and asked her to come down so that he could give her the job. The interesting part of this vision was that The Squirrel Cage had not yet been turned into a go-go place at the time of her vision. The owner was rebuilding the place and had been thinking of turning it into a go-go place *in the future*. That very night Gaye danced on the stage of The Squirrel Cage.

Gaye's career took another turn in the following months. Go-go dancing was on the way out in California and topless dancing was in. But it was inconceivable for the socialite mother of eight to appear as a topless dancer in a night club. On the other hand, Gaye was in the mood to try it, but incognito. For several months she appeared as the mysterious "Miss Exodus" at a place called El Rancho Rafaele in Encino, California. One day the celebrated San Francisco columnist Herb Caen came in to watch her and discovered her real identity. From that moment on Gaye Spiegelman was in demand as a topless dancer. Evenutally she replaced the equally celebrated Carol Doda at El Cid, one of the major landmarks of San Francisco's North Beach amusement area.

Variously billed as "Mama Spiegelman" and "The Topless Mother of Eight," Gaye was a "freak attraction," but only on the surface. She used her incredible motherhood as a contrast to her obviously svelte appearance, but she never exploited her children in any way. As a matter of fact they were never permitted to come to the theater. Gaye kept her family life as private as she possibly could.

Gaye's early dreams of becoming a serious ballet dancer were obviously not being realized, and when she turned thirty it dawned upon her that perhaps fate wanted her to be a comedienne instead. And indeed she was funny in her performances at the club.

During all the time she was appearing at El Cid she was also writing songs and contacting producers of films and plays in an attempt to become an actress and singer. One of her songs, called "Mama Wants To be A Go-Go Girl," was recorded, and she was asked to help other performers write routines. But her main goal was to become a legitimate attraction in her own right.

Affluence had brought with it a certain freedom and mobility. She decided to let the difficulties with her husband go unresolved and moved her children to a San Francisco suburb closer to her work. She left her eight children in the care of babysitters. At this time—1966— her twin girls, Sylvia and Nancy, were two years old; Scott five; Jackie seven; Tracy eight; Steven ten, and the oldest, Mark, thirteen. Gaye sent them to the best schools, spent as much time with them as she possibly could when not working, and tried to get the most competent people to look after them when she was away. If she used the label "Mother of Eight" she could do so proudly, for she was indeed a good mother to all eight of them.

During this time she knew that her late grandmother was looking out for her. On one occasion her favorite red nightgown, which her mother had bought her when she was first married, had blown away. One night she had just hung the nightgown up when a sudden gust of wind blew it out the window. Rather than chase after it over the hills of San Francisco, Gaye shrugged off her loss. Several months later, she opened a drawer and there was the missing nightgown, neatly folded. It had not been there the night before. Gaye was sure her late grandmother had returned the missing gown to please her.

But a more chilling experience taught her that her grandmother was indeed a good influence in her life. With so many children to look after she could not always watch them all. One day she happened to be in the kitchen when she heard her one-and-a-half-year-old boy calling through the intercom, "Mommy, come quickly." Not realizing that the child couldn't even talk yet, she rushed to his room and found him turning blue. He had swallowed a nickel and it had gotten stuck in his throat. By pounding him on the back she managed to dislodge the object and same the boy's life. Who had called out to her to come into the room? Gaye was convinced it was her mother, who had also passed away, or her grandmother.

From that day on, her relationship with her departed relatives was a continuing, even informal, one. Gaye took it for granted that people continued to exist beyond physical death and that love outlasted the grave. To her, communications with the other world were as natural as those in the world of the flesh. Shortly before her mother died she told Gaye of a dream vision in which she saw a man in black standing at the foot of her bed. She interpreted the dream as a prophecy of her death. Gaye had to admit that she too had had a dream about her mother's imminent death. Her mother nodded acceptingly. Two days later she died.

From time to time I had brief notes or cards from Gaye telling me of her whereabouts and blossoming career. I wanted to interview her again in depth, because I felt that someone who had had so many psychic experiences was likely to have new ones all the time. But whenever I was in San Francisco she was somewhere else; appearing in a show in Las Vegas or perhaps Los Angeles.

The last time I heard from her was in November of 1968, when she was appearing in a legitimate production called "Her Virtue Shall Be Saved" at the Hollywood Center Theater. It was Gaye's legitimate debut, after a fashion, and also her swan song; but neither she nor I knew that when I received the program of her show in the mail. On a double bill with Gerald Gordon's "Hot Spots," Gaye received good notices from the local theater critics. On recollection I thought it curious, though perhaps not significant, that my first meeting with her was on Bill Gordon's program in San Francisco, and the last time I heard from her in this life was when she appeared in another Gordon show, Gerald Gordon's play in Hollywood. The reviews were good enough to have led to further legitimate jobs if she had pursued her career in that direction.

The next time I heard anything concerning Gaye was when I picked up the *Los Angeles Herald Examiner* of December 4, 1968. Down, in the corner of page 8, and far from the prominent position she always enjoyed in her interviews, was a brief notice reading as follows:

FUNERAL FOR "TOPLESS MOTHER." (Santa Rosa, AP) Funeral Services were held yesterday for Gaye Spiegelman and three of her eight children killed in an auto wreck last Friday. Mrs. Spiegelman, 36, was a Santa Rosa housewife before she joined showbusiness a few years ago, billing herself as the "Topless Mother of Eight." She and her three children—Mark 15, David 5, and an adopted daughter Sylvia, 5, were killed near Victorville.

That was the entire final notice Gaye received.

For several years before her untimely death Gaye Spiegelman had had the companionship and the close friendship of a young woman named Donna Lake, who was a combination babysitter, children's nurse and personal secretary to Gaye. The first time I heard from Donna Lake was on March 23, 1969. She had known of my correspondence with her late friend and employer and felt that enough time had elapsed since the accident to communicate with me. She wanted me to know how it all happened, since the newspapers had found the story of Gaye Spiegelman no longer so fascinating now that the leer had gone out of the copy.

Donna Lake was thirtyish and out of a job, at loose ends, yet determined to be of use to someone other than herself even if she could not make a niche of her own in life. She had gone to college in Kansas City, Missouri, where her parents still lived. After several jobs as a beautician, she was still not sure where her place in life was. Donna is tall and not ungainly, but possessed of a certain shyness and slightly out of step with the pressures of our times. Through her character runs a deep maternal streak, which she thought best to apply where really needed. She thus directed her attention to jobs where she could either replace or support a real mother.

One day she happened to be in Santa Barbara and picked up a newspaper. Reading the want ads, she came across Gaye's and immediately responded both logically and emotionally. Gaye was looking for a reliable person to take care of her children and act as secretary at the same time.

"We always believed that we got together through extrasensory perception," Donna explained to me, "because I picked up that particular paper just when she needed someone like me and I needed her."

As soon as the two women met, they established a relationship. Gaye asked for no references, trusting her inner knowledge that Donna was the companion she had been looking for all along. On her part, Donna, without worrying about the financial details, moved into Gaye's life and lived with Gaye and her children in Daly City from 1966 onward. "I stood by her through the trials and tragedies of her life, determined to help her all the way. There wasn't much money for a long time, and I stood by her even then. I would have given my life for her; she knew that. We planned the future together."

It was during that time that Donna had a premonitory dream. Gaye's late mother Sylvia appeared to her and asked her to take care of Gaye and had her promise that she would. The following morning she told her dream to Gaye, who took it as a matter of course. It did not occur to either woman that the dream had more than casual significance for the future.

Gaye meanwhile had obtained a divorce from her husband. More and more, her work took her to places like Hollywood and Las Vegas. She hated to be separated from her children, and whenever she had the chance she came up to northern California to be with them, if only for a weekend. When Mark, the oldest, had his bar mitzvah, the entire family was together for the occasion. That was in June of 1968, and it was the last time they were all together in this world.

On November 28, 1968, Gaye had to travel to Hollywood to fulfill an engagement. This time she was taking her entire family with her. Seven of the children—one boy was in Israel with his aunt at the time—Gaye, and a certain Marvin Brody would drive down in the car. Since there wasn't enough room for all of them in one car, Donna was to fly ahead and wait for them at the apartment. Brody was the author of the play Gaye was to appear in and had offered to help out by driving the car back from Las Vegas to Hollywood. At Victorville, California, a wheel came off the station wagon. Donna had been driving that same car for some time before and had noticed that there was some trouble with one of the rear wheels. She had had it looked at at a service station, but had been assured that the wheel was all right. But on that fateful day of November 29, the wheel came off as the car was being driven at considerable speed. Brody could not control it, and it went over the dividing line into traffic coming up on the other side of the road, hitting a trailer. A woman in the trailer was injured so severely that she died the following day. Gaye was thrown clear out of the car across a barbed wire fence and horribly mutilated. She lived for another two hours, suffering terribly. Apparently her face had been badly torn up, for she begged the highway patrolman to cover her so her children would not see her that way. Mark, Sylvia, and one of the twins were killed instantly. The other children had various injuries but survived the accident. The driver suffered a punctured lung but was saved from death by the steering wheel.

Donna had arrived a little earlier than she had anticipated and was taking a nap at the apartment when someone came to tell her that an accident had occurred. Donna was shattered. Gaye and her children had been all the family she had ever wanted, and now they were gone; she was at loose ends once again. She asked herself again and again, why did Gaye leave her here on earth; why was she sent by air away from the accident; why wasn't she permitted to die with her friend and employer?

The aftermath of the accident brought nothing but difficulties. There was no money. A few days before the accident Donna had borrowed on her own life insurance just to pay for things for the house. Gaye couldn't help but marvel at the thought that there was someone who cared that much to help out.

There were strange occurrences just prior to the tragedy. To begin with, Roger Barrett, who had been Gaye's romantic interest for a long time, had suddenly passed away nine days before she did. Gaye went to the funeral and suffered terribly. At the time she mumbled to Donna, "I just know something is going to happen." Was she perhaps unknowingly referring to her own death? Two weeks before her own passing, on November 13, Gaye wrote Donna a very emotional letter from Las Vegas in which she said: "Dear Donna, I cried on the plane all the way from Los Angeles. I tried not to break down in front of you and the children because you always seem to think of me as an unbending tower of strength." Donna had been worried about Gaye and had harbored uneasy feelings for her for some time. The letter continued, "I didn't want to leave you and the children. You all seem to need me and I also need all of you. My most beloved treasures are my children, and I've trusted their lives, their memories, their health, their learning all into your hands not only while I an away but even as I am at home. While you're out, the kids come rushing in, asking me, where's Donna? We depend on you for so much; how can we define how important you are to our everyday lives? I hope this letter gives you a little better understanding. Keep it, and when you feel unloved, unwanted and unneeded, try reading it again. I have no one to cry to; I must cry alone for the children I miss and pray for the day I can be a better mother to all of them. Take care; my love to all—Love, Gaye."

It was the last letter she wrote to Donna. After the funeral of Roger Barrett, Donna remarked that it would be a terrible thing for one of them to find the other dead. For several days she would go to Gaye's room to see if she was still alive. It was almost like a ritual. She did not know why she was doing it. In those final days of her life on earth, Gaye would assure Donna that she would always live with her, and that if she were to build a house, Donna's room would be right in the center of it.

Frequently Gaye would discuss funeral arrangements were she to die. She was very much concerned about how she would look in death. Since Donna had been a beautician for ten years, Gaye naturally trusted her to take good care of her appearance. When the time came it was Donna who helped the funeral home dress Gaye properly for her last ride. She was buried in her native Santa Rosa.

The night following the accident, Donna was so upset she couldn't sleep. Minor by comparison but nevertheless also upsetting was the fact that her own suitcase had been in the car and she needed some of her own things. Sometimes the two women would use the same clothes or makeup, so Donna decided to see if she could find two black bras among Gaye's things. The play had been cancelled immediately upon the news, but some of Gaye's things, which had been sent ahead, were still stored in her dressing room. Donna went to the theater and took them back to Gaye's apartment. But she was unable to find the bras. Exhausted from all that had happened, she decided to spend the night in what had been Gaye's room. Eventually sleep came to her, and *then she saw Gaye.* . . .

In this dream, Donna told me, Gaye looked exactly as she had always looked, but Donna could see mainly her face. "The first thing she told me was, you go and get everything out of that car and take it home. I want everything out of the car."

"Didn't she mention anything about the accident? Her death?" I asked.

"No, she didn't, but she told me that those bras I was looking for would be in the suitcase in the morning."

"Were they?"

"Yes, they were. How they got there I have no idea. They certainly weren't there the night before."

"What else did she tell you that first night of her contact with you after her death?"

"'I will be with you always. I will tell you all kinds of things. Don't worry about anything. First you have to get the stuff out of the car, then go to the funeral home and see how things are there.'"

The following morning Donna remembered every word of what Gaye had said. It didn't surprise her at all that her friend and former employer had come to her so soon after her passing. She had expected no less. The thought that their close relationship could end because of an accident had never entered her mind. It was merely a matter of time before contact would be re-established between them, and now that it had happened so quickly, Donna was pleased.

"What was the next time you had contact with Gaye?"

"At the funeral home. It seemed like she was standing next to me looking at the body. I was going over the details with the people at the funeral home and how she was to be made up in death. *Then I saw her standing next to me.* I didn't hear her speak but I sensed everything she wanted done, and I conveyed it to the funeral people."

"In other words, she arranged her own funeral."

"Yes, in a manner of speaking. Later she was present at the funeral also."

Afterward Donna went to the house in Santa Rosa, but Gaye did not appear to her there. That was not surprising, since it was her ex-husband's house and he was living in it with his second wife. There were no bad feelings between them, but the atmosphere evidently was not conducive to a close contact between Gaye and Donna.

After that first dream Gaye was in constant touch with Donna. She would communicate with her in her sleep, but Donna remembered everything upon awakening. It was as if Gaye were running things from the other side of life precisely as she had done while she was still in the body. In her sleep, Donna would see Gaye and speak to her as she had always done. Gaye had simply resumed her former position, and Donna was carrying out her orders and requests.

After the funeral, there remained the matter of properties and inheritance. Gaye's ex-husband announced he was going to Las Vegas where most of Gaye's belongings were. Neither Gaye nor Donna liked the idea, since their things had been intermingled and it would have been hard to decide which things belonged to Gaye and which to Donna.

When it appeared that Mr. Spiegelman was about to take possession of Gaye's belongings, Gaye instructed Donna, who was very naïve in such matters, to call an attorney to forestall Mr. Spiegelman's move. Eventually, under the prodding of the departed Gaye, Donna managed to keep the ex-husband from taking possession of her things. Gaye then told Donna exactly what she wanted her sister and brother-in-law to keep from among her personal belongings and what to sell.

Donna carried out each request from Gaye without questioning, without doubting that the order came directly from Gaye. The departed star even conducted a lawsuit from her perch in the next dimension, with Donna merely her mouthpiece. Nothing more was required of Donna except that she follow orders, and that she did explicitly and I might add, successfully—for every move Gaye told Donna to make was eventually crowned with success. The fatal accident had diminished none of Gaye's intellectual brilliance, nor sense of values. Her worldly involvement was as strong as ever—not so much for herself as to protect the interests of her children. There is no question that Gaye's motive in possessing Donna was of an unselfish kind, though possession it was.

It seemed perfectly natural of Donna that the welfare of the children should now be entrusted to her, though the determination as to what was to be done came from the deceased. All along the line she had felt that the children had two mothers, and now that one mother was removed from the scene the other had to take over. But Donna could not act without guidance. It also seemed to her that Gaye might see things from her vantage point much more clearly than Donna could on earth. Consequently she always assumed that Gaye's advice was right even when she, Donna, was unable to see or know why.

Apparently Gaye was able to reach Donna wherever she went. By no means a ghost or earthbound spirit, Gaye, who had known so much about the psychic world while in the body, knew how to travel in that world now that she was part of it.

About two months after Gaye's death, Donna went to visit a sick cousin in Texas. The first night Donna went to sleep in Texas, Gaye appeared to her and told her that her ex-husband was going to hurt her,

Donna. But Donna misunderstood, thinking she meant he was going to hurt her, Gaye, and she said she didn't see how he could possibly hurt her any longer. "No, no," Gaye replied, "It's not me but you he will try to hurt. Please be very careful."

The warning was more than timely. As soon as Gaye had left the scene her ex-husband did everything to discourage Donna's interest in the children. Creating a barrier between the children and Donna, their second mother, would indeed be hurting her terribly at a time when the surviving children were all she had left of her "family." During that time Gaye kept up a continuing barrage of orders. "Go back to San Francisco," she insisted, although she did not tell Donna how she was to accomplish this under the circumstances and with practically no financial means.

One night Gaye woke Donna from a sound sleep to tell her that she wanted her income tax returns straightened out and to go to a certain lawyer in Santa Rosa. She also instructed her on what to do about the life insurance. The need to look into this particular matter became clear to Donna in the days following the message. Gaye's ex-husband and her brother-in-law kept insisting that Donna send all papers and information concerning the insurance to them so they could attend to it. But that wasn't what Gaye wanted her to do. This left Donna in a quandary. She couldn't possibly tell Gaye's ex-husband that his dead wife was instructing her not to turn over the insurance policies.

Between the middle of February and the first week of April Gaye did not communicate with Donna directly, although Donna felt her presence almost constantly. A curious feeling came over her whenever she gave way to feelings of loneliness. Immediately she would feel the warm, surrounding personality of her friend as if to console her and make things easier for her.

Although she could hear Gaye's voice in her inner ear even while awake, no matter where she was, she could not actually see her except while asleep.

Evidently Gaye had definite plans for Donna's future without always telling her what they were. She began to interfere actively in Donna's career, although she could not arrange it so that her erstwhile companion was without financial worries. Donna reported to me, "Last night she told me I'm supposed to get a trunk and put all her things into it and then lock it up. But how am I to get such a trunk and how am I to pay for it?"

"How does she interfere with your career?" I asked.

"Well, she stopped me from getting several different jobs. On May 12, I went on an interview for a position with this lady, and I was ready to start, but something told me that it wouldn't work, that I shouldn't do it."

"Perhaps it had something to do with your wanting to look after the children?"

Donna shook her head. "No, that would be impossible because of the ex-husband. We just don't get along. He always resented me because I helped her."

"Did she ever tell you to contact *me*?"

"I'm sure she had something to do with my writing to you. It was a very strong, urgent feeling that I should. When she wants something done, she won't leave me in peace until it is taken care of. A few days ago she asked me to contact someone here in Hollywood about the songs she had written and to find out whether they had been copyrighted properly. Before her death she was unable to get hold of him, and now she wanted me to do it. Well, I called Don Costa Productions and asked for Warren Durkee just as she had instructed me, and sure enough they had those songs, but they had already been copyrighted."

"Was there anyone else who had contact with Gaye after her death?" I inquired. It had occurred to me that Gaye who knew so much about psychic communication might have found access to still another medium to carry out her wishes.

Donna nodded emphatically. "Yes, she had a friend and neighbor who lived right next door to us. This lady was very fond of Gaye, and after her death she placed some flowers once a week in front of the picture Gaye had given her when she was still alive. One day Gaye appeared to her and smiled. It really shook her up."

Donna and I agreed that we would try to have Gaye appear—to us both if possible or to Donna alone, but in my presence. After I had stated my desire to have contact with my departed friend, we both sat quietly for a moment, awaiting Gaye's arrival. It was my intention not only to investigate further the amazing after-death activities of "Mama" Spiegelman but, if possible, to ask her to consider Donna's *own* life and what her possession of Donna was doing to the free development of her friend's personality. I had had some misgivings that Donna was sacrificing her private life in order to carry out Gaye's wishes, but Donna assured me that Gaye was looking after her social life as well. She *wanted* her to go out and have a good time. It was Donna's own somewhat awkward personality, her shyness and her lack of experience which had brought about her isolation. Gaye had suggested that Donna write to an organization specializing in computerized introductions. She even gave her the name of that organization, Ellen's Circle, and predicted that Donna would meet a man through this contact. It later developed that she did meet such a man, and while he was not exactly Prince Charming about to rescue her from the doldrums of a dull existence, he was a social contact she enjoyed, and knowing him helped open up further contacts. Gaye had predicted all this, assuring her friend that "he'll remind you of my Roger." At the time I visited Donna, she hadn't yet met him. While she was looking forward to meeting him, she was terrified at the thought all the same.

"Don't you enjoy the company of men?" I asked.

"Not really."

"What about women?"

"Just her." While we were discussing this, Donna told me that Gaye was listening intently even though I could not see or hear her. "I've got this date for Sunday, you see," she continued, "and I really don't like to go out with men. I'm mortally frightened. But she told me to join Ellen's Circle, and to watch what I say to this man I will meet and watch what I write. 'Be careful what you write to him,' she said."

While Donna was telling me this she was reclining on one of the beds, while I leaned back in my confortable chair. I still did not sense the presence of Gaye. "Is she still here where you saw her before?" I asked.

"Yes," Donna replied. "Come and sit on the bed."

"Do you hear her outside of yourself or is it within you when she speaks to you?"

"Sometimes both ways. Sometimes she's so close to me that I could almost touch her, and at other times I feel like I'm *in* her. I mean, it is as if I could *feel* her body."

"You mean to say that you feel her spirit within your body?"

"Yes, that too. Sometimes she takes me places. It's like a dream, only it isn't a dream. Once I was in my room, but not in my room—I was in a different place I had never been to. It looked like an old-fashioned room. She was there. She looked like she looks now. We just talked as we always did, about just anything. This happened in the daytime. I had gone to sleep, and the next thing I knew, *there she was.* I didn't come out of it until about two in the afternoon."

"Tell her to come over to me and touch me," I suggested. Donna invited Gaye to touch me if she could. But even though Donna could clairvoyantly see her move about the room, I could not. I extended my hand and asked Gaye to touch it.

"She seems to pull back. What's the matter? Why is she this way? Why do I feel her that way?" Donna asked, puzzled.

"Do you still see her over here?"

"Now she is almost as if she were lying here with me on the bed. I feel her kind of inside me."

"Is she stronger when you're asleep?"

"Yes. The other day her son Mark was with her. That had never happened before. They're together now."

Despite coaxing and waiting, nothing psychical happened between my late friend Gaye and me during this session. Evidently she had not yet learned to materialize for anyone but Donna.

Ten days later, after I had returned to New York, I heard from Donna again. "When I left you at the hotel, Gaye began talking to me. She said, 'Now do you understand what I've been trying to tell you? You've been so upset over the accident and over being alone physically, without me, that there were times when I couldn't get through to you. I know you couldn't help it, and I'm really sorry I just couldn't tell you any other way. Those times you cried, all the time I was there, too. Remember what I told you the night of the accident, that I would always be with you to help and guide you. Now take care of yourself.'"

It appeared that my session with Donna had opened her up even further to Gaye's influence. Each day she received a list of things to do. First it was an order to take all of Gaye's poems and stories and to make copies of them. This was quite an effort, since Donna does not type well. But, Donna said, "I don't cry so much now. She's giving me things to do for her each day like she always did. I'm supposed to get two foot lockers, like the others we have, to store the important things we already have. She told me to write to certain people this week, and she said we must work together because no one else cares. I'm supposed to copy all the addresses into one address book and then to make an extra copy of the list. She tells me to call certain people on the telephone— for instance a man she wrote songs with. I did call him, though I didn't tell him she wanted Frank Sinatra to sing them. She wants me to get copies of the tapes she did. I can't do that now; it will have to wait. I don't have the station wagon to get things done. We buried Gaye's physical body in Santa Rosa, but her spiritual body is whole and shows no scars of the accident." At this point Donna was conducting her conversations with Gaye in a loud voice when she was alone in her room.

Meanwhile, Donna had met another man through the dating service. A fellow from Riverside had called her for a date. They had had coffee and then had walked along the beach. Donna could see Gaye watching them and smiling a few feet away.

But carrying out Gaye's orders was not enough to keep the blues away all the time. On June 19 Donna wrote me of her strong feelings about wanting to join Gaye. "I want to be with her. I try so hard to get so close to my loved one, to cross over and be with her. Sometimes I feel I am."

Far from merely settling her unfinished business, Gaye embarked on new ventures through Donna. She asked her to get certain songs for her, such as a copy of "Stranger on the Shore". She intended to write songs and stories through Donna's instrumentality. Donna already knew that Gaye was writing her letters since Donna's own style was far more simple and her grammar much weaker than what now emerged from her pen.

On June 24, I received another note from Donna. "Today I was about at the end of my rope, so to speak. Very nervous. Very upset. I said several things today out loud, pleading for her to please come to me: 'I can't do it without you. I don't want to be anywhere without you. You're the one I'm living for. I'm trying to do everything you've asked me to do. I love you, you know.'" Later that afternoon the pressure had left Donna. She was sure that her pleading had been heard by Gaye. A cousin had written to Donna warning her to watch out lest she cross the thin line dividing sanity from insanity. Donna was troubled by the letter but did not really understand what her cousin meant. But since the matter troubled Donna, Gaye decided to dictate a rejoinder to the cousin.

During all this time Gaye missed her surviving children terribly. She kept imagining there would be some way in which she could see them again. "'If I just could reach out and touch you and then for a moment we are very near.' I felt her touch and then I fell asleep," Donna wrote to me.

It was clear that the two personalities were merging more and more. What the end result would be was hard to determine at that point. I decided to keep a close watch on Donna. Soon she began to turn on Gaye's favorite television shows even though she herself had not the slightest interest in them. She continued Gaye's subscription to *Daily Variety* and looked for the names of people Gaye knew. Sometimes she would cut out an article that might have been of interest to Gaye in her performance. *More and more, Donna became an extension of Gaye Spiegelman.*

The weekend of June 28 brought still another experience for Donna. She seemed to have been asleep, or so she reported, and she felt she was with Gaye. She also saw the dead children Mark and David. She heard Mark say, as he often had in life, "You're pretty, Donna."

The following Saturday Gaye led Donna to a variety store for shopping purposes. Under Gaye's control Donna looked at various things such as pillows and shirts and then purchased what Gaye selected. A few days later Gaye asked her to have photographs of her and her dead children made and sent to me and Virginia D., the neighbor who had once seen her apparition. This was an expense Donna could not easily afford, and as soon as I found out about it I reimbursed her for them.

On July 31, Gaye dictated a letter to her oldest surviving son, Steven, whose birthday was coming up the following week. By this time the contact was continuous and close: "Sometimes we talk; sometimes we don't and just look at each other. Her beautiful dark eyes are soft and mostly she smiles at me. I have a strange feeling *she's alive in me.* Through me she will live forever. She knows this. We have this bond. We've had this bond for years. I even have her headaches where my whole head hurts, even my scalp. Sometimes it is almost unbearable. I am so happy *she* doesn't hurt anymore. I have really picked up many of her likes and dislikes, and sometimes I believe she just passed them on to me. *I know I'm living for her.*"

Part of Donna's devotion to Gaye involved setting her professional record straight. Donna felt that because of her early death Gaye had never been afforded the kind of fame she deserved. "I wonder what one has to have done to get into the wax museum in this area. I feel that Gaye belongs there, but how to manage this is beyond me at the moment. I want people to remember her. I don't want them to forget about a star, a very important star."

In early August Donna wrote, "This is the only thing that keeps me going, knowing she wants me to do something for her. During my sleep, or during the night, I am many places, usually with her, sometimes in the past, sometimes in the future. It is almost as if she is showing me the way to an unbelievable future. Like I am to meet a lover, like she did, who'll change my life. He'll be able to help me cope with all of this, including getting everything straightened out, like the insurance loan from her estate." Donna had loaned Gaye some money when things had been rough, borrowing on her own life insurance policy.

In 1967 Gaye had written a little book of funny sayings with illustrations. It was called *Happiness is Being the Topless Mother of Eight,* and it was harmless enough to be read by children, for whom it was primarily intended. Evidently Gaye was concerned about this book and wanted it to get a larger circulation. When she did not get results fast enough through Donna, she remembered the extreme devotion that her neighbor, Mrs. Virginia D., had shown toward her when she was still in the flesh. She appeared to her on August 13, 1969, and asked her to do something about the book. Virginia immediately got in touch with Donna to tell her what had happened. According to Virginia, Gaye had looked pretty much as she always had, but Virginia did notice that Gaye's hair had stood up on her head in a strange way. She was also wearing old, beat-up shoes.

On the first of October Gaye reminded Donna that some clothes of hers that had been put into hock when Gaye had urgently needed cash were about to be lost unless a payment was made. Donna verified this immediately and rushed down to save the clothes from being sold. "Sometimes I feel only half here," Donna wrote me. "My other half is with her, a part of her."

There was already some feeling of jealousy, even rivalry, between Donna and Virginia as to who was the true recipient of Gaye's favors. But Virginia's incipient heart disease made her a poor contender for that honor. Then, too, Gaye apparently made contact with Virginia only sporadically, whereas she was present with Donna all the time.

In February of 1970 I heard from Donna again. She sounded more composed and even happier now, perhaps because she had found a position she liked. She was working as a governess to two little girls in Woodland Hills. Meantime a friendship had sprung up between Donna and Debbie, Virginia's young daughter. Debbie, an aspiring actress, was also psychic, and both she and her teenage brother were given to astral travel.

"Gaye says Debbie and I will be together eventually, but it will take time and lots of patience," Donna wrote. "Debbie has begun to take Gaye's place with me. I didn't think there would ever be anyone to take Gaye's place, but it looks like Gaye has found Debbie for me. I hope everything turns out all right for both of us.

During the Decoration Day weekend of 1970 I managed to come to Hollywood and visit Donna. Donna said that Gaye kept telling her, "Wait for Debbie; she has the answers to all your problems." But Donna still had not escaped her financial troubles. Some of them were due to old debts incurred while she was still with Gaye that had never been properly cleared up. Others were simply due to the fact that she wasn't earning much. She was no longer working as a governess now but was entirely dependent on free-lance babysitting jobs, which were few. "Gaye is very plain in what she wants of me, but I wish she would get me help with my rent. If I don't get any babysitting jobs, what am I going to do?"

I helped Donna a little in her desperate plight, but her problem was more than merely financial. Donna had abdicated all her willpower, all her sense of reasoning to her dear friend on the other side of the curtain. Far from reassuming her autonomy and learning to govern her own affairs now that Gaye's hold seemed to be weakening somewhat, Donna was already planning to deliver herself to the nineteen-year-old Debbie, if that were possible. She wanted at all cost to avoid making decisions on her own. "Time will take care of it, Gaye says, but eventually I will have what I want and Debbie will be part of it."

By November Donna was working in a pet shop. It wasn't quite the same as babysitting, but in a manner of speaking it was similar. All this time I had tried to indicate to her, as delicately as possible, that she had to learn to stand on her own feet, and that in fact Gaye wanted the same thing for her if only she would interpret the messages correctly. Perhaps I took some license in telling her this, but I remembered Gaye Spiegelman vividly and knew that she would never knowingly exploit another human being, even for the purpose of expressing her own unfulfilled desires from the beyond. Since Gaye was not helping Donna by steering her toward material benefits, I reasoned, she must be trying to show Donna through hardship that she had to learn to make her own decisions and manage her own affairs.

In late November Donna acknowledged this line of thought. "I believe you are right. Gaye wants me to stand on my own feet and be independent. She has always wanted the best for me."

Donna's job in the pet shop ended abruptly, but in January of 1971 she managed to get a live-in position as a housekeeper for a recording engineer in Encino. Apparently her new situation helped calm her, for I didn't hear from her again until April.

"You will be real proud of me," she wrote. "I have been doing positive thinking. Have taken off some weight as well as doing other things. Debbie says I have a softer voice. I know I really feel different. There is a possibility that I may get back to helping someone in the entertainment field. If this all takes place in the near future, it will be because of Gaye Spiegelman. Oh, she came to me and wanted to know when you were going to put the story about her into one of your books as you promised you would."

After the accident Gaye had promised Donna that eventually her life would change for the better. The middle of May 1971 saw the fulfillment of that promise. Donna flew to Lincoln, Nebraska to start a new position as assistant to Ruth Colman, a singer and night club entertainer of some repute. I heard from Donna again on May 31, 1971. "My life is changing. Gaye is real proud of me."

Donna Lake had wanted to spend her life helping an entertainer, and when Gaye Spiegelman had died, that lifetime wish had been aborted. But Gaye Spiegelman realized that she owed Donna a great deal. Donna had been her companion, friend and employee, but she had never been paid a regular salary, and had even frequently been called upon to contribute her own meager savings to the family household. Providing Donna with an opportunity similar to the one she had lost through Gaye's death was not an easy task, and it took Gaye a year and a half to bring it about. The only way she could do it was by taking over Donna lock, stock, and barrel. This kind of possession, even when there is a definite and presumably beneficial end result, is hard to terminate unless the possessor is willing to do so and has such strong character that he or she is able to break it off when the time comes. This Gaye Spiegelman has been able to do, for I have heard no more from Donna Lake and assume she is happy with her new life.

Gaye Spiegelman, Topless Mother of Eight, is not yet in the Hollywood Wax Museum, but she has paid all her debts in this life, in one way or another, and may do better in another incarnation, hopefully longer than this one has been.

The Hollywood Psychic Scene

California has frequently been called the most eccentric state in the union, the breeding ground of unusual cults and sects, and in general the kind of climate in which oddballs are said to flourish. California is also considered the most psychic state in America, at least by a few writers. One would expect such a state to harbor a large number of psychics, mediums, clairvoyants and astrologers of all types and denominations. As a matter of fact, California is no more psychic than any other state, but it has a good climate and a leisurely pace; thus people have the opportunity perhaps to spend a little more time on occult pursuits than they have in busy industrial places like Illinois or Pennsylvania. But the number of psychic experiences in any state, or for that matter any country in the world, is commensurate with the size of the population, and California has a very large population. The *acceptance* of the reality of psychic phenomena may vary greatly from country to country. In Germany ESP is still in its infancy. In Great Britain and Ireland it has been considered part of the national character for centuries. Thus, more cases reach the public ear in the more liberal countries than in the more conservative countries. But that in no way indicates the incidence rate in the respective countries.

The fact is that I don't know a single truly gifted deep-trance medium in all of California. I have witnessed demonstrations by a few who claim they are in deep trance, but I remain unconvinced that they are truly trance mediums in the sense that Sybil Leek and Ethel Johnson Meyers are deep-trance mediums. There are, of course, religious personalities on the fringes of mediumship, such as the Reverend Richard Zenor of the Agasha Temple of Wisdom in Hollywood. But Reverend Zenor does not claim to be a clairvoyant or trance medium. He speaks with the voice of his guide and master, Agasha, and his pronouncements are mainly pastoral or at best individually tailored life counsel. It is difficult to assess the genuineness of such phenomena since we have no objective means of proving the reality or nonexistence of these master entities. The genuineness of the phenomena, scientifically speaking, should not be confused with the sincerity of the mediums. Unquestionably, Reverend Zenor performs a useful function in the community. His sermons are positive and inspiring. Nevertheless, as far as proof of survival of human personality or communication with the dead is concerned, his kind of mediumship doesn't lend itself to that purpose.

Grace Emerson, who lives in a typical old-fashioned house on Burton Way in Beverly Hills, practices a kind of life counsel that relies heavily on numerology. How much psychic insight is contained in her advice is difficult to assess. But, again, she counts among her clients some of the best names in Hollywood and Beverly Hills and approaches the occult with a wholesome, constructive point of view. Those seeking hard-core evidence will not obtain it here either. Jacqueline Easton has a reputation as a fine medium, but I have never worked with her, so I can't pass judgment on her talents.

Professional psychics and amateurs predicting the downfall of California at intervals have grabbed space in the local press and even the national wire services from time to time. Not that there is anything particularly phoney about California's danger points. The San Andreas fault is very real. I myself spent a harrowing night on the thirteenth floor of the Continental Hotel in Hollywood during the last earthquake. Only the sound construction of the hotel, with its built-in sway foundations, prevented the building from cracking. But the fear of earthquakes and natural catastrophes comes with the scenery in California. Any psychic individual predicting earthquakes is merely tuning in on the prevailing climate. When these predictions take on specific dates and circumstances, they are worthy of greater consideration. Unfortunately, very few of the predictions on record with me are that specific. When they are, I always publish them in one of my books.

Mrs. Estelle Barnes, British-born professional medium, has a good following in the movie colony. She also trains professional mediums at her spiritualist church called The First Church of Psychic Science in Los Angeles. Although her specialties are murder cases, finding lost people, and spirit photography, she gives regular sittings to anyone who requests them and is willing to pay her professional fee. "My timely warning saved the lives of two presidents, Truman and Eisenhower," Mrs. Barnes explained in her clipped British accent. "I contacted the Washington, D.C. authorities months ahead of the time the assassinations were to be carried out. I have also helped Scotland Yard in missing-persons and murder cases."

But the person to whom I am most likely to refer individuals who ask me for a truly first-rate medium in the Los Angeles and Hollywood area is that "grand old lady" of parapsychology, Lotte von Strahl. About the only thing she will not tell me about herself is her age, at least not for publication. For the record, she looks to be in her middle sixties. Tall and erect, aristocratically imperious in both gesture and phrase. Mrs. von Strahl sees some of the Hollywood greats at regular intervals. What she gives them is perhaps a mixture of clairvoyance and motherly counsel, but it seems to work, for they come back for more. Her antique-filled apartment in Westwood bears witness to an illustrious past and to the friendship of many interesting people, whose photographs, with personal dedications to her, are in evidence about the apartment.

Mrs. von Strahl has been married twice, first to a Dutch industrialist and then to a German diplomat. She discovered her psychic talents quite by accident. At the time she was living in Holland with the industrialist, she met a woman whose husband was a doctor. Apparently the woman was a psychometrist, so everyone in the group gave her something to hold in her hand in order to give them a reading. When Lotte's turn came for a private sitting with this lady, the doctor's wife looked at her in astonishment and said, "My dear, you can do the same as I can." Lotte, thinking the notion ricidulous, shook her head firmly, and refused to even consider such an idea. But the doctor's wife insisted. She handed Lotte a pencil and told her to say whatever came into her mind. Suddenly Lotte heard herself talking about a man whom she did not know. She described him in great detail and the sort of things that had happened in his life. Her description proved entirely correct. After this occurrence she tested her psychometric ability a few more times. Eventually she met the great Dutch parapsychologist Dr. Ten Hoff and began to work with him. After Lotte divorced her first husband she went to live in London. There she met the late Eileen Garrett and became even more interested in psychic research. She and Eileen Garret became close friends, and through Eileen she met such researchers as the late Harry Price, an early ghost hunter along my own lines. Despite Harry Price's preoccupation with haunted houses, however, Lotte never went to a haunted house with him. Instead she allowed the researcher to test her through psychometric experiments.

Married to a German Foreign Office member, she traveled to Guatemala, Norway and eventually to South Africa, where her husband represented Germany. When the Nazis took over the German government, all foreign officers were called home for briefing. Reluctantly Lotte and her husband returned to Germany. Her husband was about to turn over their diplomatic passports when Lotte stopped him. She told him that they would need those passports. At first her husband was reluctant, but he followed his wife's advice and went to see the South African Minister, whom they both knew very well. Out of friendship he stamped their passports. When the couple passed through the Gestapo control, her husband said he intended to go back to his post in South Africa, hoping that the Gestapo would not check this statement. For in fact he was not going back to South Africa as a diplomat.

In those days people didn't travel by air as much as they do today, so they had to take a ship to South Africa. All during the trip, two Gestapo agents sat at their table, so they had to watch every word they said to each other. Three weeks after their arrival in South Africa, World War II broke out. With the help of General Smuts, the Prime Minister, they were permitted to stay on. He found a position in the Department of Interior for her husband and made Lotte a lieutenant in the defense force.

When her superiors discovered her clairvoyant gifts, she was put to work on intelligance matters. She would take letters given to her and read the sender's character by merely touching or looking at the writing. Frequently she discovered secret messages in those letters, many of them in code. Since South Africa has a large German population, the question of espionage was always an important one. Toward the end of the war the couple left South Africa once again and went back to England. There they did not fare too well, so they decided to sell all their belongings and go to America. They arrived in the United States with a great deal of hope and little else. Lotte's aging husband couldn't find a job; neither could Lotte.

Eventually Lotte's husband became ill and passed away. For a long time Lotte had known that her husband was going to die, but she couldn't bring herself to tell him. Lotte then decided to use her psychic talents professionally. She started out by giving lectures to the public, then readings. Evenutally she graduated to private sittings only. Among those who are her close friends is actor Glenn Ford. One day she visited him at his house and found herself compelled to tell him, "You are reading a script and you will go to Mexico to make a movie." He shook his head in denial. He didn't want to go anyplace because Christmas was near and he wanted to be in Los Angeles at that time. Lotte assured him that he would be, even though he would make that movie in Mexico. A few days before Christmas Lotte received a telephone call from him. She had been entirely correct; he was making a movie in Mexico, but something had happened that interrupted the work, and the director had sent the actors home for Christmas.

Lotte von Strahl is also friendly with actress Goldie Hawn. When the actress was still an unknown, Lotte read for her, telling her that a very short time afterward she would be a big star, and that she would someday act with a very well-known actress. It seemed so preposterous to Goldie at the time that she couldn't help but laugh. In fact, Lotte liked to refer to Goldie Hawn as her little giggler. Eventually Miss Hawn telephoned Lotte and asked her to come down to Columbia Pictures to see her. She had just started work on *Cactus Flower* with movie great Ingrid Bergman.

One day at a party, Lotte met Clint Eastwood. At the time his name meant nothing. She went over to him and in her charmingly aggressive way said, "You know something? One day not so far away you will be a big name in the movie industry."

But Miss von Strahl feels less enthusiastic about Elke Sommer and her husband Joe Hyams. Her visit to their haunted house in Hollywood had been mentioned in the publicity about it. So many psychics of all shades and denominations had been called in by Elke and Joe to look into their haunted house that Lotte initially did not feel like participating. But a friend of hers, Lady Carrol, introduced her to them, and Joe Hyams was very persuasive on the telephone, and Lowe agreed to visit. "We were all upstairs when we heard a trampling," Lotte explained. "Then I went downstairs, and I saw a man leaning against the bar. He was definitely not a native American."

After the fire in the house she was called in again, but Lotte does not think the fire was caused by a ghost. She thinks two flesh-and-blood perpetrators were behind it and even described them. According to Lotte, Elke Sommer recognized one of the men and described him as someone who had worked at the house at one time. When the police showed Elke some pictures, she pointed at the culprits. It turned out that these two men had a record of setting fires elsewhere. Other psychics who have been to the house have different views on the mysterious fire, however.

Later Lotte was sought out by the department of parapsychology at the University of Southern California and taken to a house in Sunnydale, California that was allegedly haunted. Without telling Lotte anything about it, the researchers left her to walk about the house. While Lotte was doing so, the lady who had brought her left her for a moment to busy herself in the kitchen. Lotte walked into one of the rooms and found a man there whom she later described as a German national. She also spoke of all sorts of wires, later covered over by wallpaper by the new owners. "This man has a transmitter down there," she exclaimed. "It connects with a café called Little Vienna. Behind it is a house where they pickup what is being transmitted from here."

The owner of the house nodded assent. She then showed Lotte a number of photographs. Among the six pictures, Lotte easily picked out the one of the ghostly figure she had seen earlier. The man who had owned the house had been a Nazi leader during the war. He had since died.

Today, Lotte von Strahl uses mainly her clairvoyant and clairaudiant abilities. She does not like to go into trance, although she has the ability to do so, but prefers to deal with people who come to her for help, either because of personal problems or to locate a missing person. She is also very much interested in psychic healing.

"Do you have a spirit guide?" I asked her.

Lotte shook her head firmly. "No, I don't want that."

"Did you ever have one?"

"In the very beginning, but I dropped it."

She can see a person's aura and tell him what is wrong with him physically. She also gets glimpses of a person's future but hesitates to tell people everything she knows out of fear that she might influence them. "I tell them when I see bad things around them, and very often I tell them to watch out for certain things. Or someone might worry about getting married, and I tell them exactly when they *will* marry."

"Have you ever had communications with your late husbands?"

"Yes, but I sent them away because I don't believe in letting entities stay on this earth and cling to it. I've also heard from my late son. He was tortured to death by the Japanese in Java. Whenever I am not well or in physical danger, then I see my son. He usually tells me that I am going to be all right, and then he goes away."

I talked for another hour about Mrs. von Strahl's work in the healing field and eventually let her give me a personal reading. Both sessions were highly fascinating.

Probably the most interesting of California mediums is Bill Corrado. He received a great deal of publicity by being mentioned in the books of Jess Stearn, and subsequently because of his association with a well-known industrial company, which took him away a great deal. I was finally able to corner Mr. Corrado at the home of astrologer Betty Collins, and on December 15, 1973, I sat face to face with the slight, dark-haired young man of whom I'd heard so much.

"I was born in Cleveland, Ohio," Mr. Corrado explained. "Both my mother and my grandmother were psychic, although not professionals. I grew up in that environment, and when I was six years old, my own talent came out. For five days in succession, I had a vision of an auto accident in which my father figured, and I told my mother but was advised not to think about it. On the sixth day, my father was killed in an auto accident. From then on, these visions came more frequently, but I did not use my gift professionally until I came to California in 1962. I studied for the priesthood for two-and-a-half years in a Benedictine seminary, and then I left and worked as an auditor for the real estate tax department. And at one time I was also a probation officer for the police in Cleveland. When I came out to California, I first became a medic, taking care of people on welfare in their own homes, but I had some surgery which paralyzed me for a while so I could no longer work. It was then that I started to give professional readings, first to friends of mine, and they in turn started sending people to me. And before I knew what had happened, that was all I was doing, giving professional readings."

I asked Mr. Corrado whether he was advising some important business people, as I had been told.

"Yes," he nodded, "I specialize in advising corporations concerning different investments and marketing systems. I also advise on who is to be promoted, who is to be fired, who is to be hired."

"Do you get impressions about events in the future visually, or do you hear them, or do you get them from spirits?"

"Sometimes I've heard the sound of a voice, but most of my impressions are visual. I feel it is part of my mind which is more developed, so to speak, and able to tune in to what I call the universal mind."

"Have you ever seen a spirit communicator?"

"No."

I asked Bill Corrado to give me some specific examples of his being able to call the shots in people's lives. He explained that in addition to his financial wizardry he has done much work in the field of medical diagnosis and works with various medical doctors.

"I don't heal anyone, but I've been able to tell people what their illnesses are, where they are, and then I send them to a medical doctor to have it verified and let them be treated. I've been able to prescribe certain types of vitamins which have proved to be successful and have cured people. As you know, I also advise a lot of companies, some of them drilling for oil, others I help organize marketing plans in the cosmetic and vitamin field. I advise a lot of people in the entertainment world, when they come to me with a script and ask me whether or not the film will be good or not and whether they should do it. So far, I've not made many mistakes. For instance, for the last two years I've helped a man at the head of a large cosmetic company called Hollywood Magic, William Penn Patrick, who has recently passed away. I've also worked with politicians and assisted the police and sherrif's department of Los Angeles in different cases. For instance, when the Tate murder occurred, the police came to me and asked if I had any feelings about it. That was in May of that year, and I told them I saw three people involved in the murder, and they would all be apprehended in October of the same year. It turned out that they were apprehended in October. I've also been able to help people with emotional problems, for I consider a psychic to be part psychiatrist, part medical doctor, part teacher, and part businessman. Psychiatrists come to me with their files of people they handle, when they are unable to succeed with them, and many times I was able to pinpoint the real problem for them. This was especially true with people who had tried to commit suicide more than once."

"Do you compare your work in diagnosis to the work of the late Edgar Cayce?"

"Yes, I do."

Bill Corrado is hard to reach because he travels a great deal. But when he is in Los Angeles, he gives three to four readings a day, four days a week. Corrado is thirty-five years old, and has numerous calls from people who want to see him, even from abroad. "Most know about me from word of mouth," he explained. "I've been on many television shows, and some people have written about me."

"What percentage of your predictions have actually come true as made?" I asked.

"My average of accuracy has been about eighty-three percent," Bill Corrado replied without batting an eye. He insists that his clients tape-record the readings and that they report to him the accuracy of his predictions so that he may keep up with the results of his work.

Since Corrado hadn't met me before, I asked him whether on first contact he received any impressions about me. Corrado proceeded to give an extremely accurate reading of my personal life at the time, of which he could not have had any knowledge; he also predicted that I would be doing writing outside the psychic field, and that is coming true as I write these lines.

He stressed the need for some sort of test for psychics, to differentiate between reputable practitioners and those masquerading as mediums when in fact they have no talent or training. He himself has opened a school. "I will teach people how to use the amount of psychic ability they have so that they will be able to tune in to certain events in other people's lives as well as their own, teach them how to handle their emotional problems in a way where they can see a cure. It will be a five-day course and will be held here in Los Angeles. Later I expect to open schools in other cities around the United States, Canada, and even Europe." Mr. Corrado sees Los Angeles as a spiritual center, he's not worried about earthquakes, but has doubts about the safety of the San Francisco area.

Hello There, Harry Houdini

The late magician Harry Houdini continues to exercise a fascination on people long after his death. It wasn't so much that he was one of the great, skillful representatives of his art—for he was that, to be sure—but Houdini's death somehow started a rash of rumors that he would try to communicate with the living. This is particularly ironic since Harry Houdini, whose real name was Eric Weiss, firmly disallowed any possibility of spirit survival during his years on earth. If anything, Harry Houdini was interested in exposing what he thought were fraudulent mediums and spent considerable time and effort in showing the public that he, Houdini, could imitate anything a medium could possibly do. This isn't unusual for magicians. With rare exceptions people working the trade of delusion are professionally unable to accept the possibility that there are things they cannot imitate. Anything a professional magician writes about extrasensory perception or psychic phenomena should be taken with a grain of salt, since a magician is, by training, incapable of open-mindedly viewing the phenomena. There is also the tendency among such practitioners to equate the possibility of fraud with the actual occurrence of fraud. Many of the phenomena generally classified as psychic phenomena can indeed be artificially produced, but that does not mean they are always false. We can produce artificial lighting in the laboratory and yet do not disbelieve in natural lighting. We are able to produce rain through various chemical processes, yet no one doubts that rain also exists in its natural form. In fact there are a number of psychic phenomena attested to by reliable witnesses which no magician could ever duplicate—for instance, materialization phenomena when they're genuine, and the so-called process of teleportation, which calls for a rapid disassembly of solid objects, or even people, and reassembly of same at a distant location.

Actually Harry Houdini had been very much interested in mediumship and psychic communication in his early years. But after his mother passed away he attempted unsuccessfully to communicate with her. He had been extremely attached to her, and his failure to receive word from his deceased mother, together with some instances of fraud, had embittered him toward psychic communication. Toward the very end of his life, however, Houdini was no longer so sure that communication between the living and the dead was impossible. Despite the clamor in the headlines exposing fraudulent mediums, he had also met some genuine psychics and been impressed by them.

Shortly before he died in 1926, Houdini decided to prepare for the supreme test. He arranged with his wife Beatrice that whoever died first should communicate with the survivor if possible. They thought up a complicated code based on a system they had used during their early days in vaudeville—a set of signals using an old popular song as the key. Of course it was known only to themselves.

About that time the late Arthur Ford was getting somewhat of a reputation as an honest medium. Ford was also a Methodist minister, and he considered his psychic work as only a sideline to his career. According to Ford, most of the communications coming through him came from a deceased Canadian named Fletcher. To the end of his life, Ford wondered whether Fletcher was a real person or only part of his own unconscious mind. Even though he had found evidence that Fletcher had lived in Canada as claimed, Ford, ever the doubter, lacked that final proof which he was to obtain only after his own death.

In February of 1928 Fletcher began to give messages purporting to come from the late Harry Houdini. This occurred during a series of sittings in which Ford, in deep trance, spoke with the voice of Fletcher. After the first session in which Harry Houdini had identified himself, contact was made with the editor of Scientific American. From that moment on, every session was attended by a representative of Scientific American, and every word was taken down by an official stenographer. The entire case was ultimately published by that magazine. Beatrice Houdini testified, when it was all over, that the message was indeed the one that she and her late husband had agreed upon and that it had been transmitted in their own private code, which had been locked away in a bank vault. Arthur Ford found sudden fame because Harry Houdini was still making headlines and still a puzzle to his contemporaries three years after his death. At the same time, skeptics assailed Ford and accused him of fraud.

In 1959 the magician Joseph Dunninger got a great deal of publicity mileage out of his offer of ten thousand dollars to anyone who could "break the secret Houdini code." This offer was made as if the code had not yet been broken. Not only Dunninger but others who had not been in on the original sittings with Ford claimed that the code had in fact not been broken and that Houdini had not as yet given any proof of his survival after physical death.

This offer gave Mr. Dunninger a valuable opportunity to call in the press and hold a séance. For added publicity value, the séance was held on October 31—Halloween—the date of Houdini's death. Whether or not there were any results did not matter. As a matter of fact, even if there had been results, there was no certainty that the reward would have been paid out. Since the conditions were entirely in the hands of Mr. Dunninger, any psychic submitting to this test was actually only shadow-boxing.

In my first book on the psychic, Ghost Hunter, I reported how I was a somewhat reluctant witness to this séance. At the time I was not aware that the code had indeed been broken. Florence Sternfels, the great psychometrist of New Jersey, was the medium. Mr. Dunninger had brought along to a New York hotel room the alleged code message, as well as two pairs of handcuffs used by the late Harry Houdini in his act. He asked Florence to touch them and get impressions. Immediately Florence said, "How much longer will I go on with this work?" Since such a remark could hardly refer to her own work, as she was then at the height of her fame, the remark made no sense to me. However, Dunninger stated that this had been one of Houdini's favorite expressions. Joseph Dunninger had known Houdini well for many years. He had had opportunity to observe him in his work and admired him greatly. Apparently Harry Houdini had been disillusioned with his work, despite his great fame, and especially toward the end of his life had hoped for something bigger, something different.

I asked Florence if she felt Houdini's presence in the room. She nodded in reply, and touched the handcuffs again. "I get a man's name around him," she said, "a name like Burke." For a moment Joseph Dunninger could not place the name; then his face lit up and he acknowledged that Burke had been one of Houdini's teachers in magic. Dunninger then requested that Florence describe some incident concerning Houdini, something that would prove that her information came indeed from the great master. After a moment's hesitation, Florence started to speak of "two balls breaking in half." This made absolutely no sense to any of us except to Mr. Dunninger. It appears that some years before his death Houdini had sat in on a séance during which a departed medium who had known Houdini in life was asked to give some proof of her presence. The medium had then materialized what appeared to be two spheres plainly visible against a dark background. Try as he might, Houdini could not explain the appearance of those spheres by so-called natural means. Whenever the matter was discussed with Houdini in later years, he would shake his head and frankly admit that the incident had left him wondering. Dunninger felt that Florence was referring to this experience, since it had been of major importance in Houdini's attitude toward the unknown. But he continued to maintain that the secret code had not yet been broken, and that he "hoped" it would be—by some terribly clever medium.

Harry Houdini still seems very much alive in many minds. Frequently people ask me whether he has ever "come back" to communicate with the living. In 1965 a lady in New Jersey contacted me with information concerning a curious dream she had had. According to her testimony, Houdini had appeared to her in a dream, identified himself and asked that she communicate with me. He seemed troubled by the continued rejection of his coded message and wanted the world to know that he was indeed well and alive in the world beyond.

In November of 1969 Paula Davidson called my attention to the so-called Houdini mansion in the Hollywood Hills. At the time it belonged to a lady named Fania Pearson, who also owned a fabulous villa across the way into which she had moved with some dogs and one or two servants. Mrs. Pearson was interested in my psychic work and suggested that we visit the former Houdini mansion. Reportedly, this mansion was his retreat on those rare occasions when he could go to California for a rest. "Mansion" is perhaps the wrong term. The house had been in disrepair for many years and was partially in ruins. As a result trespassers had broken in time and again, and a fire had been started the summer before that destroyed even more of the once beautiful mansion. Large sums of money would have been required to restore it to its former splendor.

In April of 1970 I revisited what was left of the mansion with Paula Davison, Mrs. Pearson, and my mediumistic friend Jill Taggart. We walked up the still magnificent driveway to the mansion itself. The villa was built in the manner of an Italian country house, with terraces on all sides looking out toward the city of Los Angeles below. The house must have held some twenty rooms in its heyday. Now, however, only portions were intact. The north wing, containing the kitchen and some servants' quarters, was best preserved. What must have once been a very large living room with a fireplace was in total ruin, even to the point of the floor being partially gone, disclosing the cellar through the open portions. Careful to avoid hidden holes, we tiptoed about the ruins. Jill was walking about on her own trying to get some impressions from the place. After a while she returned, and I questioned her.

"There is something about a play being written here," she said somewhat uncertainly. "I also get the feeling of a séance being held." Jill had no idea of where she was or that the house had any connection with Harry Houdini. Mrs. Pearson nodded emphatically. According to her information, Houdini had held séances in the large living room, inviting only his closest friends and still trying to make contact with the world beyond.

I realized that only a deep-trance medium could delve into the long-forgotten mysteries of the place. This was not the best time, so I suggested that I return at some future date to hold an actual séance in the place. Mrs. Pearson was not averse to such a suggestion; however, since she was at that time trying to get public funds to restore the mansion to its former condition, she felt that any publicity that might result would be detrimental to her efforts. I readily agreed, for I know only too well how city fathers can react when psychic phenomena are involved.

The restoration never took place. The fire had given the city of Los Angeles a chance to step in, and declaring the ruins a hazard to passing traffic below, they ordered the place demolished. Shortly afterward it was leveled to the ground.

A lady named Jeanne Morris contacted me a few months later, having somehow heard of my visit to the place. Miss Morris turned out to be a twenty-two-year-old young woman who was devoting her entire time and energies to being spokeswoman for Houdini and other distinguished personalities beyond the veil. According to her, she had written a manuscript at the rate of twelve to sixteen thousand words a day, beginning March 1 and finishing by the end of the same month. None other than Harry Houdini was guiding her hand, she claimed. She had written the book during a period when she spent considerable time in the ruins of the Houdini mansion, having been permitted by the owner to do so.

Her ability as an automatic writer first manifested itself in 1967, when she was writing a letter to her grandmother Ethel. Instead of writing what she had originally intended, her hands seemed to be guided by an unseen force. Someone with the strange name of Lepos Haicanis introduced himself to her and explained that she was not to fear what was going to happen to her. She had been selected to do some automatic writing, and her life would change because of it. Her job henceforth was to serve him and others who needed her hand. Her first communicator came back the following day for about fifteen minutes and explained that it was his desire to live again through her. However, he was not the one who was going to write her first book—that was to be the late movie actor Wallace Beery. I expressed surprise at this information, since I hadn't known Mr. Beery was a writer. Somewhat flustered, Miss Morris explained that it was his spirit that wanted to express itself. However, she had not completed Mr. Beery's book. She and her mother, who had joined her in the enterprise by typing everything the daughter brought forth in longhand, were in the middle of the manuscript when they were told by a spirit guide to go to the Houdini mansion. Without questioning the order, they went directly. They were told that the house was about to be destroyed by fire and that they should hurry.

The guide, whose name was Armos, then introduced the spirit of Houdini. "Did Houdini manifest?" I asked.

"Yes,"

"What is his real name?"

"Eric White."

"What did he tell you about himself?"

"Quite a bit. He told me about his brothers and his wife. He said that there really wasn't a code, that she would know when he returned, and that the code couldn't be put across."

"Did he mention anything about any code being broken by anyone?" I asked.

"No. He said that this was added after his death, that it wasn't really established that there had been such a code before his death."

"What was his wife's name?"

"Betsy."

Apparently Mr. Houdini then dictated a book to Miss Morris, about eight hours at a time, while she was sitting in the ruined mansion in what Mr. Houdini allegedly called his "black room." Sometimes she would stay late into the night to take down what she heard or was told to write. After the manuscript was finished he wanted to add a great deal, but Miss Morris explained to Mr. Houdini that she was going to be busy with other writers and that this was all she could do. Her next book, it appears, was to be dictated by P. T. Barnum.

Jeanne Morris, who had attended ballet college for two years, aiming for an education major, was at the time of our meeting doing nothing but this automatic writing. She had no further interest in a career or making a living for herself.

"Who are some of the other people you have 'talked' to through your automatic writing?" I asked.

"Well, Jayne Mansfield described her death; then my great-grandfather came, and lots of people I don't know."

I asked Miss Morris if she could demonstrate some of her work then and there. She closed her eyes for a moment, then her hand flew over the piece of paper she had put on her lap.

"If you are the spirit control of this young lady," I said pleasantly, "would you please identify yourself by your earthly name?"

"I have not chosen a common name, but I have used the name by which the hand knows me, which is Armos."

"Can you give me a name by which you could be traced?"

"I desire not to."

"Then can you give me some communication of your own choosing that would be evidential to me?"

"I do not feel that it is my duty to make my hand prove my existence."

"Is the spirit of one Harry Houdini present with you, and if so, let him speak directly, please."

"This one is present; he shall speak. Greetings. What is it one desires to ask of me?"

"Tell me, do you have a friend with the initial B on the earth plane?"

"Initial B—I have had many friends who have had that initial."

"Have you ever known anyone by the name of Dunninger?"

"I cannot recall."

I realized that the communicator, whoever or whatever it was, was not about to give me any reasonable answers. I politely thanked it and Miss Morris and her mother for taking the trouble of visiting me. I then leafed through the so-called Houdini manuscript. There was nothing in it that could in any way be traced to the personality of the late Eric Weiss. In fact, there was no evidence that it had been dictated by anyone beyond the world of flesh.

In due time the valuable land on which the Houdini mansion used to stand will undoubtedly be the location of another building, whether a private home or an apartment building. I am wondering whether Harry Houdini will reclaim his former hideout and, if so, what tricks he will use to make his presence known.

The Latest Adventures of the Late Clifton Webb

Clifton Webb was once one of the funniest men on the screen. To me, at least, he represented the epitome of Anglo-Saxon coolness and wit. Only later did I learn that Mr. Webb came from the Midwest and that his English accent and manner were strictly stage-induced. Many remember his capers as Mr. Belvedere, the deadpan babysitter, or his many other roles in which he portrayed the reserved yet at times explosive character that contained so much of Clifton Webb himself. I saw him on the New York stage in one of Noel Coward's plays, and in the flesh he acted exactly as he had on the screen: cool, deadpan, with a biting, satirical sense of humor.

With the success of his Mr. Belvedere and several motion pictures based upon it, Webb moved into a new-found financial security and consequently went casting about for a home corresponding to his status in the movie industry. His eyes fell upon a white stucco building in one of the quieter parts of Beverly Hills. The house, set back somewhat from a side street not far from busy Sunset Boulevard, had a vaguely Spanish-style wing paralleling the street, to which a shorter wing toward the rear of the house was attached, creating an enclosed court-yard—again in the Spanish tradition. The house was and still is sur-rounded by similar buildings, all of them belonging to the well-to-do of Beverly Hills. It has had a number of distinguished owners. Grace Moore, the singer, spent some of her happiest years in it. Later, actor

Gene Lockhart lived there, and his daughter June, who is quite psychic, had a number of uncanny experiences in it at that time. Clifton Webb himself was on friendly footing with the world of the unseen. He befriended Kenny Kingsley, the professional psychic, and on more than one occasion confided that he had seen Grace Moore's spirit in his house. Evidently the restless spirit of the late singer stayed on in the house throughout its occupation by Clifton Webb and his mother, Maybelle. For it appears to me that the "dancing figure of a woman," which the current lady of the house has reportedly seen, goes back to the Grace Moore period rather than to the time of Clifton Webb.

Clifton Webb was inordinately happy in this house. At the height of his motion picture career, surrounded by friends, he made up for the arid years of his youth when he had had to struggle for survival. In 1959 his mother passed away, bringing an end to a close and sometimes overpowering relationship. Webb had never married, nor would he have wanted to. His leanings had never been hidden from the world, and he was quite content to let matters be as they were. When his mother died, Webb became more and more of a recluse. In semi-retirement, he kept to his house most of the time, seeing fewer friends as the years went on. In mid-October of 1966 he himself died, almost eight years after his mother. During those eight years, he probably continued his relationship with Maybelle, for Clifton Webb was psychic and believed in life after death. Her clothes and belongings remained in a locked room in the house right up to the time of Clifton's death.

During his twenty years of residence in this house, Webb had remodeled it somewhat and added a room that he dubbed the Greek room, which he had furnished and decorated to his particular taste, taking great care that everything should be exactly as he wanted it to be. By mid-January of 1967 the house was on the market. Word of the availability of this house came to the attention of a producer at one of the major motion picture studios in Hollywood. He and his writer-wife had been looking for precisely such a house. Within a matter of days they purchased it and prepared to move in. With the need for redecorating and making certain alterations on the house, the C.'s were not able to move in until sometime in May. Two days before their actual move, they were showing the house to a friend. While they were busy in another part of the house, the gentleman found himself alone in the Greek room. He was wearing contact lenses and felt the need to clean his lenses at that point. There is a bathroom, decorated in gray, off the Greek room. He entered the bathroom, put the contact lenses on the shelf and turned on the water faucet. When he raised his head from the sink the lenses were no longer there. He searched everywhere but couldn't locate them, and they were never found.

The new owners of the house thought nothing of the matter, but shortly afterwards another event took place that shook their confidence. On the first night of their stay in the house Mr. C.'s mother happened to be staying in the Greek room. Unfamiliar with the bathroom, she found herself unable to locate either a toothbrush receptacle or a glass. She therefore left her toothbrush on the sink. The next morning when she entered the bathroom she found the wall receptacle open and exposed and her toothbrush firmly placed into it. Since there had been no one in the room during the night but herself, she became frightened and tried to run from the room. To her amazement the door was locked and resisted opening. In panic, she fled through the window. Later, calmed down, she returned to the room.

The following morning she awoke in bed and found her cigarettes broken in half, tobacco scattered all over the bed and the package crushed. It then occurred to Mr. and Mrs. C. that the late Clifton Webb had been vehemently against smoking in his final years.

Earlier that night Mr. and Mrs. C. and Mr. C.'s mother had been standing near the pool in the courtyard. All three were looking toward the house through the master bedroom into what was then Mrs. C.'s bathroom. Suddenly they saw a ghostly swaying figure looking somewhat like the legendary ectoplasmic ghost. They rubbed their eyes and looked again, but the figure had disappeared.

Over the next few weeks several more apparitions were observed by the C.'s. In the courtyard in front of the house they always saw the same tall gray forms, shadowy, yet with some substance. There was no doubt in their minds that they were seeing human figures.

Late in July Mrs. C. was coming home one night around midnight. Stepping into the courtyard, she saw a form like an hourglass (this time completely stationary) in the living room to the left of the couch. Finally she got up enough courage to move closer; when she did so, the form remained still until it gradually dissolved.

All during those first few weeks the animals in the house behaved in a strange way. The C.'s had several cats and dogs, and whenever they would go to certain spots in the house they would screech in terror and bolt from the area. One of the dogs would not go into the Greek room no matter how much he was coaxed. Instead he would howl at it, and his hackles would rise.

Even the master bedroom was not free from phenomena. Frequently the C.'s would awaken in the middle of the night to the sound of curtains rustling and perceive a form of sorts standing in the corner of the room, observing them.

At first the producer and his wife wondered whether their own imagination and their knowledge of the background of the house were creating fantasies in them. Their doubts were dispelled, however, when they gave a dinner party and were showing a number of guests through the house. One friend, a producer who was staying with the C.'s, suddenly stopped dead while walking from the master bedroom into the hallway, which was then being used as Mr. C.'s study. He claimed he felt something cold enveloping him. Since he is a man not given to hallucinations and has no interest in the occult, his statement carried weight with the C.'s. At the time, the producer employed two servants, a Mexican maid and a butler who slept in a cottage to the rear of the house. On several occasions the maid claimed that a cold presence had attacked her and that lights had gone on and off without explanation. It terrified her and she wanted to know what was going on. The producer could only shake his head, saying he wished he knew himself.

The Greek room seemed to be the center of the activities. Women, especially, staying in the Greek room often had personal articles moved. Mr. C.'s sister, a great skeptic, visited them and was put up in that room. On the third night of her stay she awoke toward dawn feeling a warm, enveloping embrace from behind her. She screamed, jumped out of bed, and turned on the lights. There was no one in the room. The bathroom adjoining that room was also the scene of many experiences. The toilet paper in it unrolled itself on numerous occasions. Even more fantastic, the toilet had several times been used by parties unknown during the night and left unflushed, even though no human being had been in the bathroom.

In September Mrs. C. took on additional duties as a writer and hired a secretary and assistant who worked in the house with her. But it appeared as if "someone" weren't too pleased with the arrangements. All during the winter, things kept disappearing from her office or getting moved about. Her engagement calendar would turn up in the Greek room, and certain files that were kept in cabinets in her office would disappear and turn up in other parts of the house, although no one had placed them there. It appeared that someone was creating havoc in her professional life, perhaps to discourage her or perhaps only to play a prank and put the new owners of the house on notice that a previous resident hadn't quite left.

The worst was yet to come. In October there was an occurrence the C.'s will never forget. All that evening the dog had been howling and running about the house wildly as if anticipating something dreadful.

Sounds were heard for which there seemed to be no natural explanation. Then, in the middle of the night, Mr. and Mrs. C. woke up because of noises both of them heard. Someone was moaning in their bedroom, and as they looked up they saw a gray figure forming in the corner of the room.

The next morning they realized they had been through the night on which Clifton Webb had died, exactly one year to the day. What they had heard was a reenactment of that terrible moment. From then on the moaning seemed to abate.

Although neither Mr. nor Mrs. C. were exactly believers in the occult, they were open-minded enough to realize that something was terribly wrong in their house. By now they knew that the previous owner, most likely Clifton Webb, was dissatisfied with their presence in the house. They did not understand why, however. True, they had made certain changes in the house; they had rearranged the furniture, and they had used the Greek room as a guest room. They had also made some changes in the garden and courtyard, especially around the rose bushes, which had been Mr. Webb's favorites. But was that enough of a reason for Mr. Webb to want them out of the house?

In January of 1968 they were approached by a real estate agent, out of the blue, on behalf of a couple who had passed the house once and immediately become interested in acquiring it. The C.'s had no intention of selling, so they named a fantastically high price, thinking this would end the matter. They discovered to their surprise that the couple wanted to buy the house anyway. The C's then reconsidered and decided to look for another house. But they discovered that prices for similar houses had risen so much that they might as well stay where they were, and after some discussion they decided to turn down the offer.

That very night Mrs. C. was awakened at three-thirty a.m. by a rustling sound among the curtains in the master bedroom. She looked toward the disturbance and noticed an ectoplasmic form moving across the room and back. As she stared at it in disbelief, she heard a voice saying, "Well, well," over and over. It had the sound of a fading echo and gradually disappeared along with the apparition. Several days in a row Mrs. C. saw the same figure and heard the voice exclaim, as if in amusement, "Well, well, well, well." At the same time, she received the telepathic impression that the ghost was not feeling unfriendly toward her anymore and that he wanted her and her husband to know that he didn't mind their staying on in the house.

By now Mrs. C. was convinced that the ghost was none other than Clifton Webb, and she approached F. M., another producer, who had been a close personal friend of the actor's, with a view toward asking some personal questions about him. When she reported the voice's saying, "Well, well, well, well" over and over, Mr. M. remarked that Webb had been in the habit of saying "well, well" frequently, sometimes for no apparent reason. With that Mrs. C. felt that the identity of the ghostly visitor was firmly established.

That night she was awakened again by a feeling that she was not alone. She looked up and saw the silhouette of a man. This time it was clearly Clifton Webb. He was standing just outside the bedroom window in the courtyard. As she looked at the apparition, it occurred to her that he seemed taller than he had been in his movie roles. For what seemed to her several minutes, but may have been only a few seconds, she was able to observe the shadowy apparition of the actor looking into the house directly at her. Shortly afterward it dissolved into thin air. The tall appearance of the figure puzzled her somewhat, so she checked into it. To her amazement she discovered that Webb had actually been six feet tall in life.

A few days later she encountered Mr. Webb again. Her attention was drawn by the strange behavior of her cats, which ran into her office from the courtyard. She was in the habit of taking a shortcut from her office to the kitchen by walking diagonally across the courtyard. As she did so this time, she noticed the tall, erect figure of Mr. Webb in the living room. He seemed to be walking slowly across the living room as if in search of something.

It had become clear to Mr. and Mrs. C. that Webb was not altogether satisfied with the way things were, even though he seemed to be somewhat more friendly toward them. So they invited me to the house to investigate the situation with the help of a reputable psychic. I in turn asked Sybil Leek to come along with me.

On a Thursday night in October 1968 a group of us met at the house. Besides Sybil and me there were my wife Catherine, Sybil's son Julian, and several people who had known Clifton Webb intimately. They had been asked not out of curiosity but to help identify any material of an evidential nature that might come through Sybil in trance. There was the distinguished playwright Garson Kanin, his actress wife Ruth Gordon, Rupert Allen, a public relations man who had worked for Webb for many years, and two or three others who had known him.

Sybil, of course, knew nothing about the circumstances of the case, nor why she had been brought to this house. During dinner I was careful to steer the conversation away from the occult, and Sybil and I stayed out of the Greek room. But on her way to the house Sybil had already had her first clairvoyant impression. She described a tall, slender and "sexless" individual who had not been born in California. She also mentioned that she felt the initial V or something sounding like it connected with a personality in the house.

After we had grouped ourselves around Sybil in the Greek room, I began the proceedings, as is my custom, by asking the medium for clairvoyant impressions. My hope was that Mr. Webb might pay us a visit, or at any rate tell Sybil what it was that he wanted or what had kept him tied to his former home in so forceful and physical a manner.

"Sybil," I said, "do you get any impressions about the room?"

"I don't like this room," Sybil said sternly. "I wouldn't choose to be in it. I have a strange feeling on my right-hand side toward the window. I feel somebody died here very suddenly. Also I've had for some time now the initial V and the word Meadows on my mind. I would say this is the least likable room in the house. The strange thing is, I don't feel a male or a female presence; I feel something sexless."

"What sort of person is this?"

"I feel an atmosphere of frustration, an inability to do anything."

"Why is this personality frustrated?"

"Bad relationships."

I decided it was time to begin trance. After brief suggestions Sybil went under quickly and completely. I addressed myself now to the unseen presences in the atmosphere. "Whoever might be present in this room, come forward, please, peacefully and as a friend, so that we may speak to you. We have assembled here as friends. We have come to help you find peace and happiness in this house. Use this instrument, the medium; come peacefully and speak to us so that we may be of help to you in whatever may trouble you."

After a moment Sybil started to toss, eyes closed, breathing heavily. "Can't do it, won't do it. No, I won't do it," she mumbled.

I asked that whoever was speaking through her speak somewhat louder since I had difficulty making out the words. A sardonic smile stole across Sybil's face now, very unlike her own expression. "I'm thirsty, I want a drink, get me a drink."

I promised the entity a drink a little later, but first I wanted to know who it was who had come to speak to us. Instead, Sybil sighed, "It's so cold here, chill, chill. I want to sing and sing. Sing, sing, sing, la, la, la, jolly good time."

"What kind of a song do you want to sing?" I asked, going along with the gag.

"Dead men tell no tales."

"Wouldn't you like to talk to us and tell us about yourself?"

"I want to sing."

"What are you doing here?"

"Writing, writing a song."

"Are you a writer?"

"I do a lot of things."

"What else can you do?"

"Anything, anything."

"Come on, tell me about it."

"No."

"How do I know you can do those things?" I said, using the teasing method now. "You haven't even told me your name."

A snort came from Sybil's lips. "Webb of intrigue."

"What did you say? Would you mind repeating it?"

"Webb, Webb, W-E-B-B."

"Is that your name?"

"Webb, Webb, Webb."

"Why are you here?"

"I need friends."

"Well, you've got them."

"Need friends. I'm lonely. I need to sing."

"Are you a singer?"

"I sing music; music is good."

"Why are you in this particular house?"

"I have a right to be here."

"Tell us why. What does it mean to you?"

"Money, friendship."

"Whose friendship?"

"Where is Wade? Wade, to drink with. People drive me mad."

"What is it that troubles you?" I asked, as softly as I could.

"I won't tell anyone. No help from anyone. There is no help."

"Trust me."

"I'll drink another glass."

"I've come all the way from New York to help you."

"New York—I'll go to New York and watch the people, shows, singing."

"Are you alone?"

"Yes. Nobody wants people like me."

"That isn't true, for I wouldn't be here if we didn't have the feeling of friendship toward you. Why do you think we've come here?"

"Curiosity. There is a reason behind everything. Who are you?"

I explained who I was and that I'd come to try and understand him and if possible set him free from his earthly ties. He had difficulty understanding what I was talking about.

"I want to help you."

"Late."

"Please let me help you."

"Webb."

"Yes, I heard the name," I acknowledged.

"It means nothing."

"I believe there was an actor by that name."

Sybil started to sob now. "Acting, acting all my life."

"What about this house: why are you here?"

"I like it."

"What does it mean to you?"

"What does it mean to me? Lots of money here. Friends. Friends who look after me."

"Do I know them?"

"A newspaperman; I hate newspapermen. Nosey bastards. Let's have a drink. Why don't we have some music?"

"What do you do here all day long?"

"I'm here to drink, look around for a friend or two. I'd like to know a few people. Get some work."

"What kind of work?"

"Contracts. Contracts must be somehow fulfilled."

"Contracts with whom?"

"There's a man called Meadows. Harry Meadows."

"Do you have a contract with him?"

"No good."

"What were you supposed to do?"

"Sign away the house."

"What sort of business is he in?"

"Don't know what to tell you."

"Where did you meet him?"

"He came here. Sixty-four."

"I'd like to help you find peace, Mr. Webb," I said seriously.

The entity laughed somewhat bitterly. "Mr. Webb."

"How else would you want me to call you?"

"Mr. Webb—it's finished."

"Perhaps I can help you."

"Who cares, Cathy."

"Who's Cathy?"

"Where am I, I am lost."

I assured the entity that he was not lost but merely speaking through the medium of another person. Webb obviously had no idea that such things as trance mediumship were possible. He was, of course, quite shocked to find himself in the body of Sybil Leek, even temporarity. I calmed him down and again offered to help. What was it that troubled him most?

"I can't do anything now. I am drunk, I want to sing."

Patiently I explained what his true status was. What he was experiencing were memories from his past; the future was quite different.

"I want to say a lot, but nobody listens."

"I am listening."

"I'm in trouble. Money, drink, Helen."

"What about Helen?"

"I'm peculiar."

"That's your own private affair, and nobody's criticizing you for being peculiar. Also you are very talented."

"Yes." One could tell that he liked the idea of being acclaimed even after his death.

"Now tell me about Helen. Is she in one of your wills?"

"She's dead, you idiot. I wouldn't leave anything to a dead woman. She was after my money."

"What was Helen's full name?"

"Helen T. Meadows."

"How old were you on your last birthday?"

"We don't have birthdays here."

"Ahah," I said, "but then you know where you are and what you are."

"I do," the entity said, stretching the oo sound with an inimitable comic effect. Anyone who has ever heard Clifton Webb speak on screen or stage would have recognized the sound.

"You know then that you're over there. Good. Then at least we don't have to pretend with each other that I don't know and you don't know."

"I'm tired."

"Was there any other person who knew you and Helen?"

"Cathy, Cathy was a little thing that came around."

"Was there a male friend you might remember by name?"

There was distrust in Sybil's voice when the entity answered. "You're a newspaperman."

"I'm not here as a journalist but primarily to help you. Does the name Conrad mean anything to you?" I'd been told by friends of the late Clifton Webb to ask this. I myself had no idea who this Conrad was or is.

"Hmmm," the entity replied, acknowledging the question. "Initial

V, V for Victory." At the same time, Sybil took hold of a chain she used as a belt and made an unmistakable gesture as if she were about to strangle someone with it.

"Who was Conrad? Are you trying to show me something?"

Unexpectedly Sybil broke into sobbing again. "Damn you, leave me alone."

The sobbing got heavier and heavier. I decided it was time to release the entity. "Go in peace then; go in peace and never be drawn back to this house where you've had such unhappy experiences. Go and join the loved ones awaiting you on the other side of life. Good-bye, Mr. Webb. Go in peace. Leave this instrument now and let her return to her own body without any memory of what has come through her entranced lips."

A few moments later Sybil awoke, startled, rubbing her eyes and trying to figure out where she was for a moment. "I do feel a bit peculiar," Sybil said, slightly shaken. "Maybe I will have a glass of wine."

After everyone had recovered from the tense attention given to Sybil's trance performance, I invited discussion of what had just transpired. Those who had known Clifton Webb in life volunteered the information that at times Sybil's face had looked somewhat like Webb's, at least to the extent that a woman's face can look like a man's. Her voice, too, had reminded them of the actor's voice—especially in the middle of the session when the trance seemed to have been deepest. As for the names mentioned, Rupert Allen explained that the "Cathy" Sybil had named was a secretary whom Webb had employed for only a week. Also, the Helen Meadows mentioned was probably Helen Mathews, a long-time secretary and assistant of the late actor. There had been a great deal of discussion about a will in which the assistant figured. Quite possibly, Webb and Miss Mathews had been at odds toward the end of his life. As for his wanting to sing, Rupert Allen reminded us that long before Clifton Webb had become a famous actor he had been one of the top song-and-dance men on Broadway, had appeared in many musicals and musical revues and had awlays loved the musical theater. The mannerisms and some of the phrases, Mr. Allen confirmed, were very much in the style of Clifton Webb, as was his negative reaction to the idea of having a newspaperman present.

There had been no near relatives living at the time of Webb's death. Under the circumstances the estate, including the house, would go to whomever he had chosen in his will. Was there a second will that had never been found? Was it this need to show the world that a second will existed that kept Clifton Webb tied to his former home?

After the memorable séance with Sybil Leek, I inquired of the owners from time to time whether all was quiet. For a while it was. But then reports of Mr. Webb's reappearance reached me. I realized, of course, that the producer's wife herself, being psychic to a great extent, was supplying some of the energies necessary for Webb to manifest himself in this manner. But I was equally sure that she did not do so consciously. If anything, she wanted a quiet house. But the apparition of Webb and perhaps of Grace Moore, if indeed it was she in the garden, managed to convince Mrs. C. of the reality of psychic phenomena. She no longer feared to discuss her experiences in public. At first her friends looked at her askance, but gradually they came to accept the sincerity and objectivity of her testimony. Others who had never previously mentioned any unusual experiences admitted they had felt chills and uncanny feelings in various parts of the house while visiting the place.

Clifton Webb continues to maintain a foothold in the house, for better or for worse. Perhaps he likes the attention, or perhaps he's merely looking for that other will. At any rate, he no longer seems to delight in surprising the current owners of the house. After all, they know who he is and what he's up to. Mr. Webb always knew the value of a good entrance. In time, I am sure, he will also know how to make his exit.